SEEDS OF ADVENTURE
In Search of Plants

Peter Cox and
Peter Hutchison

SEEDS OF ADVENTURE
In Search of Plants

Peter Cox and
Peter Hutchison

GARDEN • ART • PRESS

TO PATRICIA AND VIRGINIA

British Library Cataloguing-in-Publication Data:
A catalogue record for this book is available from the British Library

Title page: Primula calliantha *on Cangshan.*

Frontispiece: Rhododendron yunnanense *with Mei Li in the background.*

Endpapers front: The top of the Rudong La.
back: The Subansiri river.

Printed in China for Garden Art Press, an imprint of The Antique Collectors' Club Ltd.,
Woodbridge, Suffolk IP12 4SD

CONTENTS

FOREWORD

Roy Lancaster

The idea was to climb as quickly as possible with the intention of reaching the higher regions and a more exciting flora. In the event the plan was compromised by the richness of the flora. We stopped and started as first one then another discovery attracted our attention, a rhododendron here, a peony there, and then there were the views across the valley to the mountains beyond. Someone commented that time was passing, which initiated another spurt up what had become a seriously steep, scrub-clad hillside into an area of spruce and fir. At one point we stopped to catch our breath and suddenly I suffered a bout of nausea. I sat down on a rock to recover and then stretched myself out on the ground as the world spun round. Closing my eyes, I just lay there quietly, aware of nothing but the muffled sound of voices which gradually became clearer until I recognised them as those of two of my colleagues, Peter Cox and Peter Hutchison. They were discussing rhododendrons and one in particular that was foxing them.

A few minutes later I was on my feet and feeling better. Whether my companions were aware of the incident and chose politely to let me be I did not ask but it confirmed for me, not that I had any doubt, their intense interest in the world of plants and their ability to focus on detail, especially, in Peter Cox's case, the genus *Rhododendron* on which he is an acknowledged authority. The above incident happened in September 1986 on the eastern slopes of the Yulong Shan or Jade Dragon Mountain above Lijiang in China's Yunnan province. I had been engaged by a specialist travel company to lead a group of plant enthusiasts on a tour to western China visiting both north-west Sichuan and north-west Yunnan. We were a mixed bag of men and women comprising professional horticulturists like Peter Cox, amateur enthusiasts and others that were simply seeking an adventure. An adventure it certainly was as readers will find faithfully and often entertainingly described by the two Peters in Chapter 5 of this book.

It was not the first time we had travelled together in the wild. Four years earlier I had been with the two Peters, also in Yunnan, as a member of the Sino British Expedition to the Cangshan. This was a pioneering joint effort by invitation of the Chinese that resulted in a significant number of plant collections for scientific institutions and for cultivation. The two Peters had been given responsibility for the seeds and live plant material we collected and it is thanks to their dedication and skills that so many of these plants became successfully established in British cultivation where they can be seen, studied and enjoyed today. They included a good number of new species and others introduced for the first time, such as the striking *Paris polyphylla* var. *yunnanensis* f. *alba*, *Craibiodendron*

yunnanense, Gentiana ternifolia, Anemone trullifolia and the true *Pleione forrestii*. This expedition brought important benefits both scientific and horticultural to the British and Chinese alike, but as in all such ventures, there was more to it than that. It was an experience we looked forward to, enjoyed and shall remember for the rest of our days as much for the camaraderie with our Chinese companions as for the plants seen.

One of the keys to a successful expedition, in my experience, is a sense of humour and the two Peters have that in abundance. Whether it is competing to see who can pick up the most peanuts with chopsticks or extricating themselves from tricky situations, they have the impish knack of making others laugh. Their adventures have been many and spread over a very long period. Indeed, their appetite for travel and exploration, which began with a trip to Turkey in 1962, shows no signs of waning. Sixteen of these tours, treks and expeditions are the subject of this book whilst others, to Chile for instance, must await a future publication.

Those who have travelled with the two Peters will have marvelled at their physical reserves and endurance, especially when the going gets tough and the chance of a good night's sleep seems doubtful. I have also witnessed their powers of revival when, with heads down and the pace slowing, they have spied a new plant ahead or else a promising new habitat. No bloodhound was ever so dogged on the trail of a wanted man as Peter Cox in his search for a new rhododendron. Indeed, Peter once told me of his ambition to see more *Rhododendron* species in the wild than any other individual and I have a feeling he must be very close to realising it, if he hasn't already. Peter Hutchison, meanwhile, has a penchant for primulas and gentians although, like his friend, his plant tastes are catholic and once seen he never forgets a plant.

In terms of plants discovered or rediscovered in the wild, principally in China and the Himalaya, they have few living rivals. Not since that formidable partnership of Frank Ludlow and George Sherriff in the 1930s and '40s have two plantsmen together achieved such success. In the tradition of their predecessors in the early part of the last century, they have introduced seeds of a huge number of plants, especially rhododendrons. to western cultivation. Many of these I have seen as plants established and flourishing in a number of gardens including Glendoick, the Cox's home near Perth, where over the years I have spent many happy hours in the famous woodland garden admiring and photographing plants introduced by Peter and his father Euan and more recently by Peter's son Kenneth. Three generations of plant explorers must be unusual.

Yulong Shan or Jade Dragon Mountain near Lijiang.

Although I have known Peter Cox for almost forty years and Peter Hutchison for a little less, it wasn't until recently that I at last visited Baravalla, the garden shared and planted by the two Peters on the coast of Argyll. It was a bright warm June day and the approach road to the garden and the entrance itself held no clues to the treat in store. This in part is because Baravalla is not a garden in the usual sense but a collection of plants in natural woodland. This is not to say that there is no order, no theme to it; on the contrary. All their experience in the wild has given the two Peters a sort of sixth sense as to where a plant might best grow if not flourish. Given the moist, cool, maritime climate and a deep, loamy, acidic soil sheltered by oak and beech and a scattered holly understorey, plants from more exotic places have found it a home from home. Mossy boulders and rock faces are clothed with carpeting shrublets including *Rhododendron dendrocharis* and *R. forrestii*, while glades and dells are attended by magnolias, *Pinus bhutanica*, species of *Clethra*, *Schefflera* and *Schima* and bold-foliaged rhododendrons such as *R. sinogrande*, *R. griffithianum* and *R. falconeri*.

There are shrubs and trees too from the temperate rain forests of Chile and Argentina and from the southern ocean isles of New Zealand and Tasmania. But the overwhelming theme is of Asia, principally the Himalaya and China. All plants are clearly tagged, numbered and recorded with their origin, whether wild or cultivated, together with their planting date. While I wandered, gaping in awe, the two Peters set too, tending their flock like mother hens, pulling bracken here, a light pruning there, all the while talking to each other exchanging comments and opinions and noting down things to be done on their next visit. To my eyes almost everything was growing well, some very well given they have been here for thirty years. It was a mild, moist day, ideal conditions for the midges that followed us around, covering my hands as I attempted to write a note or take a photograph and generally making a nuisance of themselves. It reminded me of similar days in China and the Himalaya and if I had happened to fall asleep and then awake again of a sudden, I might well have imagined I was indeed back there, in some high place.

Baravalla is a microcosm of the world's temperate woody flora and it perfectly demonstrated to me the necessity and benefits of *ex situ* sites in man's fight to save endangered floras. More than this, it served to remind me of what two special individuals can do given the desire, the time and the opportunity and what more could be done by others given the encouragement and the imagination.

It has been for me a great privilege and pleasure providing this foreword and now I urge readers to join the two Peters as they start back on the trail to relive their adventures.

Roy Lancaster, 2008

MAPS

Between 1962 and 2002 we two Peters, either together or Peter Cox only, made eighteen trips to Asia: 1962 Turkey; 1965 India; 1981 Yunnan; 1985 Nepal; 1986 Sichuan and Yunnan; 1988 Bhutan; 1989 Sichuan; 1990 Sichuan; spring 1992 Yunnan; autumn 1992 Yunnan; 1994 Yunnan; 1995 Sichuan and Yunnan; 1996 Tibet; 1997 Yunnan; 1998 Tibet; 1999 Sichuan and Guizhou; 2000 Yunnan; 2002 Arunachal Pradesh, India.

The coloured lines and arrows on the maps here and overleaf indicate the routes we took and in what year. The chief places we visited are marked, as are the main rivers, lakes, mountain ranges and peaks. The names used are either current ones found on most modern maps or in a few cases, very recent names. All can be looked up on the list of Place Names on pages 303 to 405 if we know of alternative names.

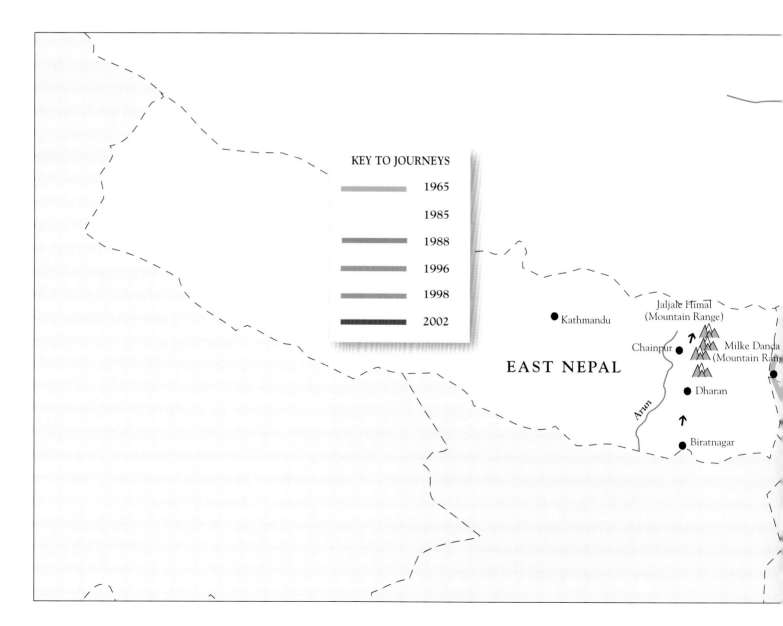

KEY TO JOURNEYS

	1965
	1985
	1988
	1996
	1998
	2002

• Kathmandu

Jaljale Himal
(Mountain Range)

Chainpur •

Milke Danda
(Mountain Ran...

EAST NEPAL

Arun

• Dharan

• Biratnagar

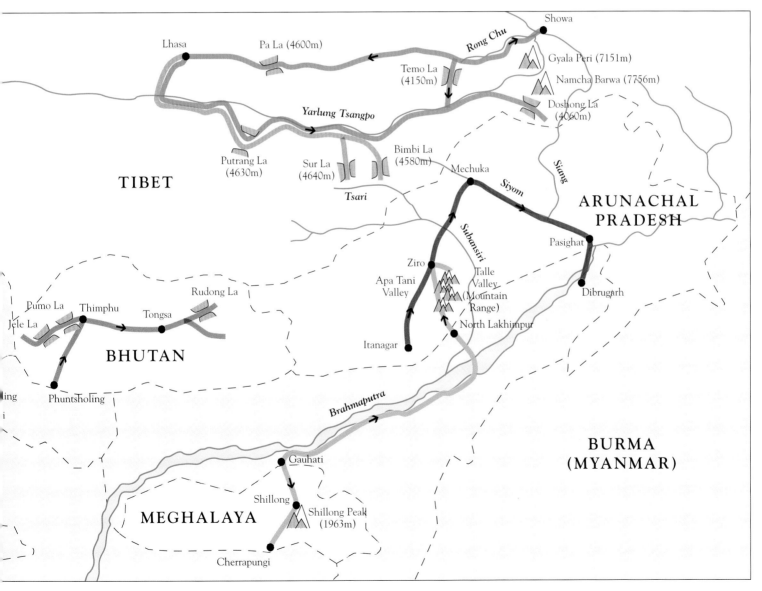

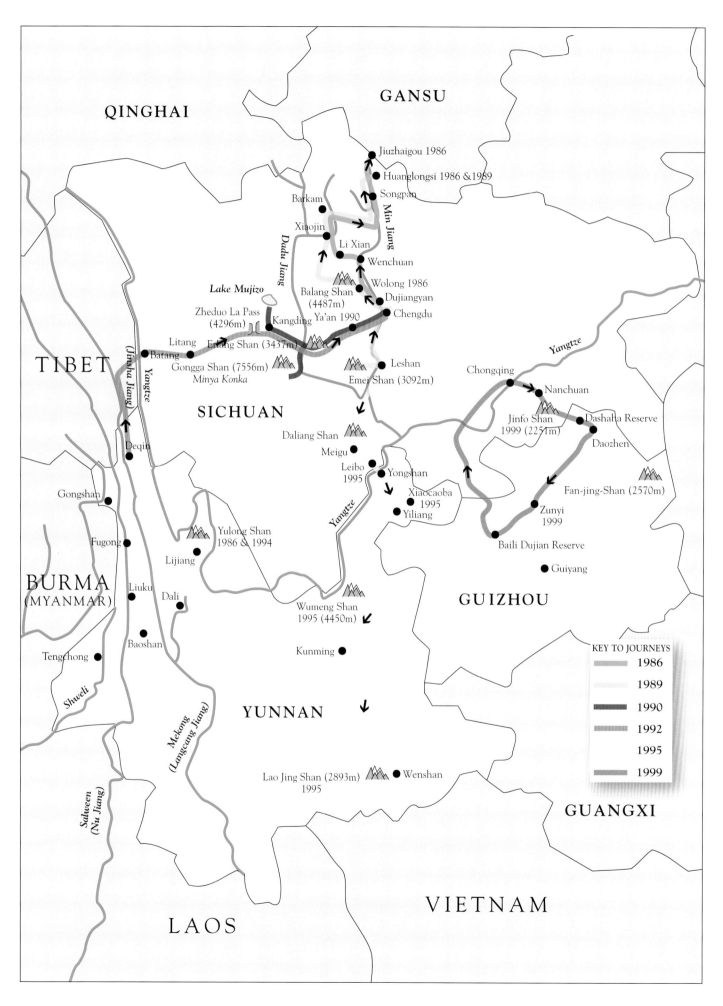

QINGHAI

GANSU

Jiuzhaigou 1986

Huanglongsi 1986 &1989

Barkam

Songpan

Xiaojin

Li Xian

Min Jiang

Wenchuan

Dadu Jiang

Wolong 1986

Lake Mujizo

Balang Shan
(4487m)

Dujiangyan

Zheduo La Pass
(4296m)

Kangding

Ya'an 1990

Chengdu

Litang

Yangtze

Erlang Shan (3437m)

Batang

(Jinsha Jiang)

Yangtze

Gongga Shan (7556m)
Minya Konka

Leshan

Chongqing

Nanchuan

Emei Shan (3092m)

TIBET

Jinfo Shan
1999 (2251m)

Dashaha Reserve

Daozhen

SICHUAN

Daliang Shan

Deqin

Meigu

Fan-jing-Shan (2570m)

Leibo
1995

Yongshan

Gongshan

Xiaocaoba
1995

Yangtze

Yiliang

Zunyi
1999

Fugong

Yulong Shan
1986 & 1994

Baili Dujian Reserve

Lijiang

Guiyang

GUIZHOU

Liuku

Dali

BURMA
(MYANMAR)

Baoshan

Wumeng Shan
1995 (4450m)

Tengchong

Shweli

Kunming

YUNNAN

KEY TO JOURNEYS

1986

1989

1990

*Mekong
(Langcang Jiang)*

*Salween
(Nu Jiang)*

1992

1995

Lao Jing Shan (2893m)
1995

Wenshan

1999

GUANGXI

VIETNAM

LAOS

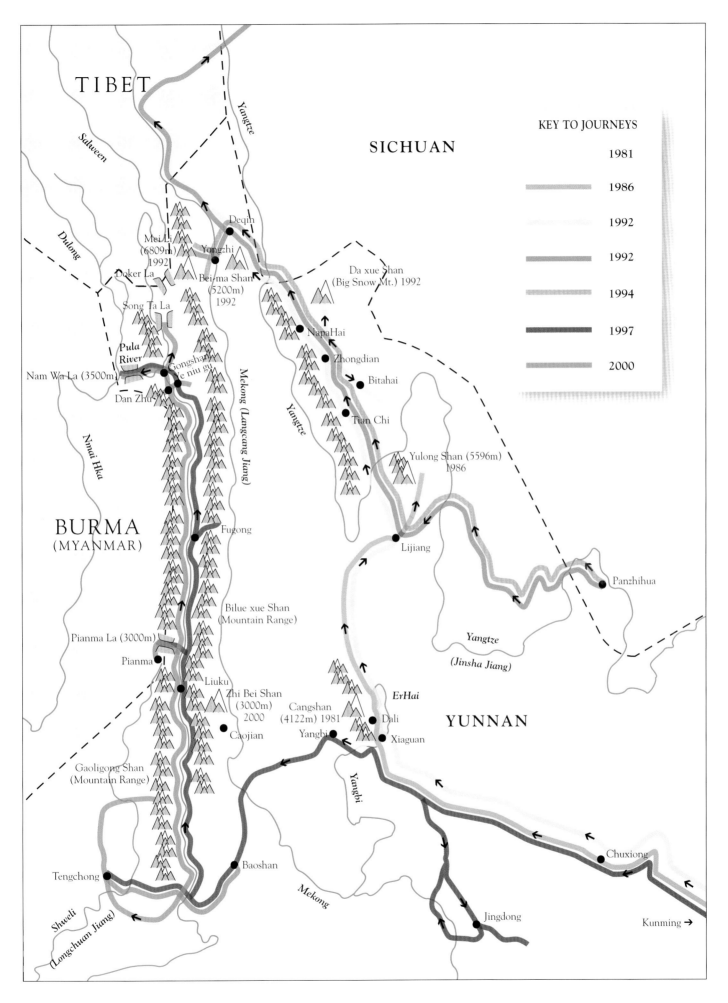

TIBET

Salween

Yangtze

SICHUAN

KEY TO JOURNEYS

1981

1986

1992

1992

1994

1997

2000

Dulong

Deqin

Mei Li
(6809m)
1992

Yongzhi

Doker La

Bei-ma Shan
(5200m)
1992

Da xue Shan
(Big Snow Mt.) 1992

Song Ta La

NapaHai

*Pula
River*

Gongshan
te niu gu

Zhongdian

Nam Wa La (3500m)

Bitahai

Dan Zhu

Tian Chi

Nmai Hka

Mekong (Langcang Jiang)

Yangtze

Yulong Shan (5596m)
1986

BURMA
(MYANMAR)

Fugong

Bilue xue Shan
(Mountain Range)

Lijiang

Yangtze

(Jinsha Jiang)

Panzhihua

Pianma La (3000m)

Pianma

Liuku

Zhi Bei Shan
(3000m)
2000

Cangshan
(4122m) 1981

ErHai

YUNNAN

Caojian

Dali

Yangbi

Xiaguan

Gaoligong Shan
(Mountain Range)

Yangbi

Tengchong

Baoshan

Chuxiong

Shweli

(Longchuan Jiang)

Mekong

Jingdong

Kunming →

11

INTRODUCTION

Peter Cox

I was brought up at Glendoick near Perth with interests connected with plant hunting in south-east Asia all around me. The house was full of books by Frank Kingdon Ward, Robert Fortune, Ernest Wilson and Reginald Farrer, plus my father's own works, including *Farrer's Last Journey* and *Plant Hunting in China*. The garden at Glendoick had many plants grown from seed collected in the wild. Furthermore, I had been fortunate to meet, alas briefly, Joseph Rock and Frank Kingdon Ward. I had met Frank Ludlow several times and George and Betty Sherriff were amongst my very special friends. The Sherriffs at Ascreavie, plus the other famous local gardeners, George and Mary Knox Finlay of Keillour Castle and John and Dorothy Renton of Branklyn, all lived close to Glendoick and frequently visited each other and endlessly compared notes on rare and difficult gems in our gardens.

In the late 1950s and early 1960s, south-east Asia was rather different politically from what it is today. India had recently gained its independence, as had Burma. China had been taken over (liberated as they call it) by the Communists and was virtually closed to foreigners, as was the recently invaded Tibet. Vietnam was still a French colony. Japan was gradually gaining its post-war prosperity. Taiwan (then usually known as Formosa) had become the Chinese Nationalists' last stronghold. Nepal had newly opened up and neighbouring Sikkim (then semi-independent) and Bhutan were very hard to get into.

My father, Euan H. M. Cox, had been to Burma with Reginald Farrer in 1919. At the age of 26, full of energy and rather at a loss as to what to do with himself after the 1914-18 war, he jumped at the idea of going plant hunting in Burma when Farrer said he was looking for a young companion. North-east Burma is very rich in rhododendrons and many species, some new, were collected. Euan had no previous interest in plants but the Burmese expedition got him hooked and, shortly after, in the early 1920s, he started planning and planting his own woodland garden at Glendoick. The plants included several of his own collecting and a few of these still grow at Glendoick at over 80 years old.

After leaving school in 1950, I spent a year's practical gardening at Glendoick before going to horticultural college in Edinburgh. While at college, I came to know intimately the rhododendron collection at the Royal Botanic Garden and made friends with H. H. Davidian, the Cypriot who was the rhododendron guru in those days, and Dr John Cowan, the assistant Regius Keeper, another rhododendron expert. I was determined to learn the names of all the rhododendron species then growing at Glendoick within the year (then probably around 60 to 70 species), which I succeeded in doing. At that time there was a sort of market garden, supplying young tomato, vegetable and annual plants to a shop in the nearest town, Perth.

There was also a fruit farm with raspberries, strawberries, blackcurrants and apples. To begin with I was supposed to go into these but somehow the idea of a rhododendron nursery arose and father and son started it together in a very small way in 1954.

Connections with plant hunting instilled in me a longing to travel to distant parts and to achieve at least a little of what my hero Frank Kingdon Ward had accomplished, often on his own and frequently under extreme adversity. Then one day in 1960 my father shouted that there was a young man with his mother at the front door who was also keen to go plant collecting. This was my first meeting with Peter Hutchison and it was not long before we really got together and planned the first trip. The first question of course was where do we go? We were young, we were keen but we were too inexperienced to do anything too ambitious. Even then, rhododendrons were my first love, and the nursery was just getting beyond the embryonic stage. So where were the nearest wild rhododendrons? Europe has only the alpenrose *R. ferrugineum* and its limestone loving neighbour *R. hirsutum* plus close relative *R. myrtifolium* (then *R. kotschyi*) further east in Yugoslavia and Romania. To see these was hardly going to lead to what we would like to term an expedition, so a little further afield would not only be desirable but a necessity. Planning for a plant hunting expedition raises lots of questions and where better to answer those relating to plants than a well known botanic garden? The famous Royal Botanic Garden, Edinburgh (RBGE), was a mere 72km/45 miles from both our homes. After consulting members of the herbarium staff, we chose north-east Turkey for our first trip in 1962.

After Turkey in 1962 and before our next adventure, I married Patricia Sherrard who is called Trish, Tish, Tricia but *never* Pat. We two Peters and Patricia started planning a much more ambitious expedition than Turkey and in 1965 headed for Arunachal Pradesh, north-east India, then the Northeast Frontier Agency (NEFA for short). There was a long gap until our next plant hunting trip in 1981. This was by no means because we did not try our hardest to go somewhere worthwhile. In 1967 we tried to get back to NEFA. Much correspondence took place with various influential people, such as Sir George Taylor, then director of the Royal Botanic Gardens, Kew (RBGK), Dr Geoffrey Herklots, Dr Father Santapau of the Botanical Survey of India (BSI), Frank Ludlow, Betty Sherriff, Simon Bowes Lyon and once we even wrote direct to the King of Bhutan via a teacher who was going out to educate the then crown prince.

Our first objective was to get to either the 4,000m/13,000ft peak called Vorjing in the Siang Division of NEFA or to Dapha Bum, the 4,600m/15,000ft peak in the eastern Lohit Division of NEFA. Between 1967 and 1973 we kept trying to get to either NEFA or Bhutan, latterly in conjunction with Bob (Robert J.)

The best form of Rhododendron sinogrande *(SBEC 0104) at Baravalla, our shared Argyll garden.*

Mitchell, then curator of the St Andrews Botanic Garden. By this time we had altered our efforts to get to NEFA to the 3,700m/12,000ft ridge between the Kameng and Subansiri divisions of NEFA, which we thought we were going to in 1965, and Vorjing. Between 1965 and 1968 we had carried on corresponding with Mr E. P. Gee, the Indian wildlife authority and former tea planter with whom we stayed in 1965 in Shillong, India. Mr Gee was a friend of Dr George Schaller, the American expert on African wildlife, with whom he had a joint project of carrying out a zoological survey of the Laya region in N.W. Bhutan with a view to establishing a national park. This was to be the culmination of Mr Gee's work on conservation. When in 1968 he heard that Dr Schaller had been refused permission to go to Bhutan, Mr Gee wrote to us and said at the end of his letter, 'I hope that the next time I write I will be less gloomy about B. [Bhutan]. At the moment I feel that all is lost and my dreams shattered.' He died shortly after, a most unhappy man.

By 1974 we had added Roy Lancaster, then of the Hillier Arboretum, and Dr David Chamberlain of the RBGE to our team. In 1976 we were told that no expeditions were being allowed into NEFA, so we again turned our attentions to Bhutan, with no success.

At one time we even thought of South Korea, Mexico and Chile. A Scandinavian party had just beaten us to it over Korea and Sir George Taylor turned that down, in addition to Mexico and Chile, which he said had been well explored botanically. He told us that we would not be eligible for a grant from the Stanley Smith Trust which he ran. We even had a shot at Burma (Myanmar) in conjunction with Jimmy Keenan of the RBGE but, needless to say, that came to nothing as well.

From 1976 on, and really starting seriously in 1978, it was all go for China, although we had tried and failed earlier, and we eventually made it in 1981. After 1981, it might have been thought that China had opened up sufficiently for us to get back quite easily, but this was far from being the case. For one thing, our friends at the Kunming Institute of Botany in Yunnan had found the logistics of organizing our Sino British Expedition to China (SBEC) so exhausting that they would never do so again. Shortly after the fulfilment of SBEC, Sir John Keswick of Jardine Matheson, who was mainly responsible for getting us into China, died suddenly while being operated on for a routine hip replacement and this proved to be a great loss to us. His widow, Lady Keswick, and his brother, Sir William (Tony) Keswick, tried their hardest on our behalf to get us back into China, but to no avail.

So in spring 1985, with Donald Maxwell MacDonald, we did a three-week trek in east Nepal to an area that had already been well explored. In the autumn of 1985, I planned to go to Fan-jing-shan in north-east Guizhou with Jim Russell, Tony Schilling of Wakehurst Place in West Sussex and John Simmons, curator of the RBGK. At the last moment, the Chinese authorities put the date forward by a month and both Tony and I were unable to go.

By 1986, travel companies were organizing tours, botanically orientated or otherwise, into China. So we decided if one cannot beat them, join them and we went on a tour to both Sichuan and Yunnan. By 1989, more of China was opening up and we two Peters and David Chamberlain were able to go under the auspices of the Sichuan University.

From 1981 onwards, it became our policy to get into parts of China where, since 1949, no other western plant hunters had been before. We managed to do this as part of every trip and in my case thirteen times: in 1981, 1986, 1989, 1990, 1992 (twice), 1994, 1995, 1996, 1997, 1998, 1999 and 2000.

We also went to Bhutan in the autumn of 1988 and in 1996 and 1998 I went to Tibet on a trip led by my son Kenneth (Ken), who led trips to Yunnan and Tibet between 1993 and 1999 and to Arunachal Pradesh from 2001 to the present, latterly with American explorer Ken Storm Jr. Our opportunity to return to Arunachal Pradesh with the two Kens came in 2002 after an interval of thirty-seven years.

INTRODUCTION

Peter Hutchison

While my early life was less connected with the famous plant collectors than that of Peter Cox, it did not lack the influence of plants and gardens. There can be few places more intriguing for a child to grow up than a Victorian walled garden as we had at my family home of Rossie, near Perth. A row of Mackenzie and Moncur glasshouses, sagging a bit but still intact, filled the back wall. In sequence there were two Tomato Houses, a Stove (nearest the boiler where the moist heat grew the most tender things like orchids), a Carnation House, two large Vineries with Black Hamburg and Muscatel grapes cordon-trained front and back, a tiny Rose House for early cutting and finally a Peach House fully 50 yards (46 metres) long with an array of nectarines, apricots and that most delectable of fruits, the greenhouse white peach. The Carnation House, which was more ornate, gave out to a double herbaceous border backed with espalier apples.

Behind the high wall was a range of potting sheds, stores, fruit room and a subterranean boiler house, reached by descending an iron ladder as if into a ship's engine room. The smells of these places were evocative: steaming loam, Mortegg Tar Wash and the fragrance of newly picked apples and pears in the fruit room. The greenhouses were heated by a battery of large cast-iron pipes that gave a gentle warmth; 'damping down' meant dousing them with water which released all sorts of earthy smells. In summer wheels were cranked to open the ventilators far above.

Presiding over this was a head gardener called Irvine. He was a kindly person more inclined to doing things than talking about them and he wore with his rolled up sleeves a tweed waistcoat. Looped across the front was a gold watch chain, a badge of office, but nobody could ever remember seeing the watch. What I do remember with the sharp eyes of a child were his enormous cracked thumbs pricking out seedlings with the delicate precision of a surgeon. Standing on a box 'helping' at the potting bench was an education in itself.

Staff were hard to find in the war and Land Girls, Italian prisoners of war and a retired butler called Tulloch all played their part in what became a market garden. Tulloch was a rather aloof man who clearly felt that gardening was a comedown in life. I remember watching him weeding, a task that was done with a dismissive plucking movement that managed to convey total disdain while leaving most of the roots in the ground.

Both my parents grew things but my mother was the real gardener. She had a wide knowledge of good plants and an instinctive eye for putting them together. She loved profusion and colour, and bare earth was just wasted space for weeds. My father grew cape gooseberries in the greenhouses and sold them to the grandest restaurants in London where chefs in white hats would pull back the papery lanterns and dip the fruits in icing sugar to serve as *petits fours*. A treat was taking the neat brown parcels, labelled Le Caprice, Mirabelle and the Berkeley Hotel, to the Forgandenny Post Office, where the door went 'pling' when it opened.

The event that took my interest in growing plants on to seeing them in the wild and collecting them was, of all things, a trip across the desert. In 1957, by this time an archaeology student at Cambridge, I was asked by Major Brian Booth, soldier, explorer and ornithologist, to join an expedition driving from north to south across the Libyan Desert in three long-wheelbase Landrovers. We were then to spend about a month on the borders of French Equatorial Africa, now Chad, doing various scientific investigations. I had known Brian Booth during my National Service with the Royal Scots Greys in Libya, where his exploits raised a few regimental eyebrows. He was liable to disappear into the desert with a small posse for weeks on end and, although these excursions were tolerated because the War had shown the value of fast travel and good navigation behind enemy lines, Brian's movements seemed to be inspired more by bird migration routes than military intelligence.

I was invited to be assistant archaeologist to Professor A. J. Arkell, a former District Commissioner in the Sudan and a distinguished expert on the predynastic cultures of the Upper Nile. It was then decided that the expedition needed a botanist and I was told I was that as well. I knew little botany, nothing about desert plants and had no idea how you collected them, so I spent some weeks in the British Museum (Natural History) learning the rudiments. By the time we returned after three months' travelling in the desert, I was hooked, secured as firmly as if caught in the branches of the Acacia with curved thorns known as the Wait-a-Minute tree. I was also in danger of being sent down from Cambridge as it was only one week from the end of term.

It had been an adventurous trip. We explored and mapped the outcrops of blue-green Amazon stone that had been quarried for the earliest beads in the Nile valley. We discovered a previously unrecorded gallery of petroglyphs on the rocks of a wadi, depicting hundreds of animals from elephants to the extinct *Megaceroides,* a relative of the giant Irish elk. We camped at the strange Wanyanga lakes where Tony Arkell, who spoke the Tebbu dialect, was welcomed by the local tribesmen who disliked the French and wanted the British to take over. They indicated the French garrison could be disposed of in one night. We left in a hurry. And we took camels into the Ennedi massif where the red sandstone gorge of Archei contained a few crocodiles that had been separated from their relatives in the Nile for a thousand years or more. Above all for me there was the revelation of the plants that defied the desert.

It was a wonderful experience but there was one flaw.

Schefflera impressa at Baravalla.

Unless you are going to work on them yourself, it is a little unfulfilling to collect all these dried specimens knowing they will disappear into the miles of herbarium cupboard, each a fragment of one dead plant and one dead moment, possibly of use to some researcher sometime, or very possibly not. How much more rewarding at the same time to be collecting plants of horticultural value that one could grow, and have the anticipation, the buzz, of seeing a plant come to flower you had last seen on a distant hillside, perhaps only as a dried seed head.

When discussing this one day with Eddie Strutt, a family friend and owner of a wonderful garden in Wigtownshire, he was astonished to find that I did not know Peter Cox, who also lived in Perthshire, and offered to make the introduction. With such a coming together of ambitions, something was surely going to happen. This book is about what did.

There is another outcome of that meeting that should be mentioned. Plant collecting leads to burgeoning seed pans, to offspring that need a home if they are to carry the hope of meeting again a flower last seen on a mountain in Asia. Rossie and Glendoick on the east coast of Scotland were getting full. So in 1969 Baravalla, a 12-hectare or 30-acre garden in the milder climate of coastal Argyll, became our secret storehouse of plants. Peter Cox and I share it with the Mackie Campbell family. Sharing a tent is one thing and sharing a garden for nearly forty years is another, but writing a book together – well, that is yet another experience.

ACKNOWLEDGEMENTS

The long series of journeys described in this book could not have been accomplished without the support, kindness and encouragement of many people; too many, in fact, for all to be mentioned and for the most part we have to acknowledge our debt collectively rather than individually.

Our starting point for any trip was usually research in the Royal Botanic Garden Edinburgh and over the years the RBGE has given us outstanding support under a succession of Regius Keepers. The herbarium, the library and the garden have all come into play and taxonomists and horticulturists alike have given generously of their time and expertise. A special mention must be made, however, of Dr David Chamberlain, the foremost authority on rhododendron taxonomy. He came with us on six of our trips and we were fortunate to have his scientific expertise as well as his companionship.

For our first Himalayan expedition we had much help from Leonard Allinson of the British High Commission in Delhi, and in Assam Mr E.P.Gee gave us kind hospitality and valuable local help. Mr Mittra organised us very efficiently in Arunachal Pradesh and from the Botanical Survey of India our colleagues A.K.Sastry and S.K.Katachi were excellent companions. Our return to that area in 2002 was led by Kenneth Cox, with Oken Tayeng and Katu Bage providing local support.

In Yunnan we would never have achieved our aims without the support of the Kunming Institute of Botany (Academia Sinica), and Professor Feng Guo-mei was a wise and knowledgeable leader, jointly with Bob Mitchell, of the seminal trip to the Cangshan in 1981. Subsequent successful trips to Yunnan involved Professor Cheng Xiao and Sun Weibang as leaders. But particular thanks are due to our friend Guan Kaiyun, the interpreter for our first trip who later became the Director of the Kunming Botanic garden. He led the 1992 expedition, was involved in almost every Yunnan trip and was advisor on other areas of China. We should also record our

thanks to Sir Murray and Lady Maclehose who were most helpful and hospitable during our stay in Hong Kong and to Charles and Carolin Clapperton who acted as our agents there.

Our first venture to Sichuan (with Yunnan) was led by Roy Lancaster who, with the help of San Choo, marshalled his flock with extraordinary good humour and shared his encyclopaedic knowledge of plants. The next visit was under the aegis of Professor Fang Mingyuan and we owe a special debt to Yuan Jiang who steered us through a difficult political period in 1989. Later trips were organised by the Sichuan Mountaineering Association and the Institute of Mountain Hazards and Disasters. Mention should be made of Rosie (Huang Yong), the interpreter in 1992 and 1994, who eased our path greatly. Two trips to Tibet were ably led by Kenneth Cox on behalf of Exodus and David Burlinson, with David's right hand man, He Hai.

Our thanks are due to all those mentioned above but also to their colleagues, to the guides, the sirdars, the porters, the drivers and the cooks who made the trips possible and to our own travelling companions who added so much value and enjoyment to the ventures.

Special thanks to our editor Erica Hunningher for all her hard work on the manuscript, to Diana Steel of Antique Collectors' Club for taking on such a mammoth task and to her staff, especially our designer Sandra Pond for all her great effort in designing such a complicated book.

Finally we must record our gratitude to those who supported us at home. Ken Cox kept his father still talking to his computer and latterly looked after the family business. The Hutchison garden would have collapsed without the skilled support of Stephen McArthur, who tended these strange plants from abroad and brought them to safe maturity. And thanks go above all to our wives, Patricia and Virginia, who waited and wondered and sometimes worried; without them there would have been no home to return to.

Opposite: Taktsang or Tiger's Nest Monastery, west Bhutan.

Chapter 1

LAND OF THE MUDUR:
Turkey 1962

Peter Hutchison

If one is going from Scotland to the north-east corner of Turkey then driving a middle-aged Landrover all the way is not the most obvious option. But this, the first of our trips together, was not going to be a quick fly-in-fly-out affair of a week or two – we had serious business with plants. We had been told that hiring a suitable vehicle out there to cope with the rough roads would be next to impossible and, beyond Ankara, hotels would be a rare luxury, or perhaps just rare. So we would have to camp.

With provisions and equipment for a month's camping, the Landrover was soon packed tighter than a suitcase. As well as all the paraphernalia of plant collecting, we took two hefty cylinders of gas for cooking which, in the event, did not see us out and, with a vision of dining decently among the sheep and goats, a table and chairs. The problem was going to be finding a matchbox among all this to light the stove.

Peter and I also reckoned that we would need a third member to share the driving and camping chores and an old friend of mine, John Apold, was keen to come. Johnnie was a delightful companion with a great ability to get on with people, from grim frontier officials to Turkish foresters.

In 1962 there were many fewer options among the classic mountain areas for those who wanted to go and look for plants. In the Himalaya, Nepal was beginning to open up but was far from the trekkers' free-for-all it was to become. Sikkim, Bhutan and Assam were difficult or impossible and China at the height of the Mao regime was out of the question. However, Turkey was the subject of a major floristic study in Edinburgh and, encouraged by Peter Davis and with much help from Ian Hedge of the Botanic Garden, we decided on the Pontus mountains, an outlying spur of the Caucasus that extends along the shores of the Black Sea with a moist and warm microclimate. It gives its name to *Rhododendron ponticum* and there are four other species of rhododendron, along with a variety of lilies and other fine horticultural plants.

The plan was to take the ferry from Grangemouth on the Forth to Amsterdam which would take over 30 hours, drive

through Holland, West Germany, Austria, the then communist countries of Yugoslavia and Bulgaria, and finally into Turkey in Europe before crossing the Bosporus to the Turkish mainland. We tried to organise part of the journey on a car train but our Landrover would not fit. In the end, the ferry and the drive to Ankara took us eight days.

Johnnie and Peter organised loading the Landrover on to the boat, a small and very ugly tub called the M.V. *Heriot* of the Gibson Rankin line, while I went to a wedding in London under suspicion of dodging the hard work. They had a bit of a panic that the vehicle with its considerable load would be too heavy for the crane hoisting cargo aboard, but all went well and we all eventually met up in Amsterdam somewhat later than anticipated. We drove 555 km/345 miles to Heidelberg for the night. The get-away the next morning was rather late as we bought some photographic equipment. Peter bought a telephoto lens which could be used as a monocular but, like many so-called dual purpose instruments, it never proved

satisfactory for either use. The second night was spent at Kitzbühel in the Austrian Tirol, where we wined and dined well, followed by a local performance of dancing and singing. The next day we were lucky to get over the Gross Glockner pass over 2,400m/8,000ft, as deep snow covered the top 100m/330ft on both sides of the road. As compensation, a bottle of white wine cooled in the snow was delicious.

There was no tunnel under the Loibl pass into Yugoslavia (now Slovenia) in those days and the road was incredibly steep in places with a 1 in 4 gradient and sharp, short hairpin bends. Our clumsy vehicle had a poor lock and a tricky gear change which Peter never really mastered. He provided some entertainment for John and me, shunting back and forth on

Above left. Samples of Rhododendron ponticum, *above Giresun, showing variations in colour.*

Above. Forested slopes of the Pontus mountains.

19

Dry rolling hills in central Turkey.

the sharpest corners with crunching gears, and we were happy to reach the customs post without incident.

We stayed the night in Ljubljana (now the capital of Slovenia) in a flat, sharing a double bed and a camp bed as, due to a jazz festival, the hotels were full. In the morning a rather edgy conversation with out hostess about changing currency (which was illegal) ended amicably with toasts of slivovitz, the local liqueur, and, having had no breakfast, we set off rather unsteadily for Belgrade. We had much difficulty in finding our hotel there, but the modern Hotel Metropol was a great contrast to the previous night and we dined in style on Russian caviar and vodka. In those days the Soviet Union and Yugoslavia were still on friendly terms. Belgrade was quite impressive with fine modern buildings and plenty of goods in the shops and, while the people were poorly dressed, they did appear to have a certain degree of freedom.

Roads tend to deteriorate the nearer one gets to the frontier and the Bulgarian one was a prime example. It was a great wide dirt road with the most terrible corrugations on which we tried all speeds to lessen the vibration, but without success. By the time we arrived, a three-inch gap had opened between our shaken luggage and the roof of the van. The Bulgarians at the customs were a nice cheerful crowd. An English girl called one official 'comrade lieutenant' which greatly amused us. The roads improved as we left the frontier and were lined with trees

with their bases painted white in French style. There were police posts all along the road but, to our surprise, we were never halted. Once we stopped to photograph a huge gang of women hoeing in the fields who immediately chased us, forcing us to make a hurried exit. The crops of maize, sunflowers, wheat and some vines were well tended with simple implements, and tractors were rarely seen.

In the capital Sofia we stayed in the Hotel Balkan, a relic of the pre-Communist era which had obviously received no maintenance since 1945. In the rococo entrance hall, all marble and melancholy, a cleaner in a knotted headscarf sloshed a mop around and in the restaurant we were presented with an enormously long menu which was immediately whisked away and the only thing they had to offer was brought. The food proved to be appalling, the local vodka rotten and the staff surly. The next morning the town was equally depressing; the people watched us with wary eyes and the shops were almost entirely empty of food or clothes, with just one or two trophy items in the windows.

We left Sofia as quickly as we could and headed for the Turkish frontier where an impenetrable fence was bordered by a cleared zone to stop Bulgarians escaping into Turkey. Unfortunately, at the border post Johnnie found that he had lost his notebook containing the return documentation and the atmosphere turned altogether less friendly. We were made to

*Above left. Our first camp in
the middle of nowhere. As soon
as we had arrived, curious locals
appeared out of thin air and this
happened every time we
camped.*

Above right. John Apold.

*Right. Fat-tailed sheep between
Sivas and Susehri. The shepherd
gave us yoghurt for breakfast.*

unpack virtually everything from the Landrover while frontier guards loitered, guns drooping from their hands and cigarettes from their mouths. Eventually we were allowed through into Turkey in Europe, where even the Coca Cola signs were welcome after the oppressive atmosphere of Bulgaria, and we bowled along through dusty, rolling country towards Istanbul.

After the Bulgarian experience, we decided that a change was needed from Communist austerity and, in spite of Peter's reservations, made for the Istanbul Hilton. The road had been

as dusty as any on our travels and when we drew up at the imposing entrance, avalanches of dust fell as we opened the back door. A bell boy with shiny buttons and white gloves carried our rucksacks at arm's length into the hall, small puffs of dust trailing on to the marble floor. The bill for the night was over £10 each, which seemed extortionate in those days, and the dinner, which was nothing exceptional, was on top of that. However, a democratic majority decided that lying full length in a bath with a cold drink at hand made it all worthwhile.

21

The village of Sebinkarahisar which lies just to the south of the Black Sea coastal mountains.

At 3 p.m., we reluctantly left the enticing and beautiful Istanbul for the ferry across the Bosporus.

We had been warned about driving in Turkey. Traffic drove on either side of the road, with or without lights, at tremendous speed and coming in from left and right without stopping. Many roads just had a metalled strip down the middle and oncoming trucks and buses drove right down this strip, forcing one to take to the dirt sides which sloped alarmingly. Driving in the dark was particularly hazardous and tiring. Johnnie and I had a self-imposed embargo on discussing rhododendrons with Peter while he was driving after a panic-stricken moment of indecision at a fork with Turkish trucks thundering in from both sides. We nearly took the middle course (which didn't exist) while Peter finished his discourse on big-leafed indumentum.

Readers will notice that plants have not been mentioned so far. Due to our intention of getting to Turkey as rapidly as possible, we rarely stopped, but we did see some fine *Gentiana verna* on the Gross Glockner and *Lilium pyrenaicum* subsp. *carniolicum* and *L. bulbiferum* in Yugoslavia.

On the way to Ankara we passed through an area of beech forest with plentiful *Rhododendron ponticum* underneath, in early June nearly past flowering at around 1,000m/3,300ft. Rather to our surprise, there was less flower than there would have been at home on this species in a similar amount of shade. We stayed three nights in Ankara, calling at the British

Embassy who were very helpful, and the Turkish Ministry of Tourism who told us that all the country east of the Euphrates was a military zone except a narrow Black Sea coastal strip. We would find out in Trabzon whether permission would be granted to enter this strip. They gave us a map showing the area we must keep to before reaching Trabzon and on 14 June we left Ankara heading for the town of Kayseri.

Central Turkey is fairly arid with a scattering of salt lakes. Birds of prey wheeled overhead and iridescent blue rollers sitting on roadside telegraph poles were a common sight. It was too dry

Rhododendron luteum *above Giresun. This species is the very popular yellow azalea with fine scented flowers and splendid autumn colour.*

and too late for many plants to be still in flower, but we did stop at a moist meadow where a large colony of *Iris lutescens* had white standards and white falls with greenish yellow markings. Near Kayseri is a 3,700m/12,000ft peak with some snow on the top, but even this had little woody vegetation.

After Kayseri on the road to Giresun the climate began to get a little moister and we started to meet genera such as *Campanula*, *Ranunculus* and *Helleborus*, with trees and shrubs like *Berberis*, *Sorbus* and *Viburnum*. But it is only when you reach the north-facing slopes of the Pontus mountains along the Black Sea that you find really wet conditions with a rainfall of up to 250cm/100in a year.

We soon discovered that the British, with their peculiar habit of camping in the countryside, were a source of interest and amusement to the local inhabitants. It did not seem to matter how remote our campsite appeared to be, a circle of onlookers would quickly appear with all the time in the world. We discovered later that one way of showing that their welcome presence has been exhausted was to shake their hands. We had been told of another ploy – to start undressing in front of them – but never dared try this. Most annoying was when they followed one into the bushes or behind a rock when

Lilium ciliatum *(ACH 50), very plentiful on a steep hillside above* Giresun.

Lilium ciliatum *at Sandyhall, Glendoick, about 1970. Alas, we no longer have this species.*

one wanted to have a crap. But all our evening and morning visitors were exceedingly friendly and often gave us milk or yoghurt. The lack of a common language was a problem, although Johnnie had great success in making them laugh without it. We found that the better educated people were more likely to speak German or French than English.

Like all too many parts of the world, the flora of Turkey suffers from overgrazing with vast herds of cattle, sheep and particularly goats which move with the season and will eat almost anything, even on the steepest of slopes. The result is that many plants can only grow and mature their seed within the thorniest of thickets. Taller bulbous plants are especially vulnerable. Forests with animals have little chance of regenerating and even the tops of the mountains are grazed to the bone.

We passed the village of Sebinkarahisar, with white storks nesting on the roofs and an impressive castle on the hill behind, and drove on through a rocky gorge with some fine campanulas, including *C. betulifolia*. The slopes above were out of reach of even the goats and there was some forest containing beech, hornbeam, hazel, maple and our first common azalea, *R. luteum*, a familiar sight in the older parks and gardens in Britain with its lovely scented yellow flowers. Further into the forest were the first lilies, *L. ponticum*, which has small turks-cap flowers of pale yellow with light to heavy streaks, closely related to the Balkan *L. carniolicum*. Then 32km/20 miles short of Giresun at 1,200m/4,000ft we came into open forest full of *R. ponticum* in varying shades from pale mauve to deep rosy-magenta, a colour rarely seen in cultivation.[1] Among the rhododendrons was a *Vaccinium*, *V. arctostaphylos* as tall as 3m/10ft with pretty white, pink or red pendulous flowers.

It was good to be among interesting plants at last and, in the mist that had gathered, we ate a celebratory evening meal of tinned vichyssoise, spaghetti and fruit salad. Darkness brought a dramatic change as the moon lit the surrounding mountain tops while the mist lingered in the valley below.

Peter woke feeling very off colour and lay under the Landrover in the shade for a while before we struggled on to the Black Sea coast. It really does have black sand and we made the mistake of driving on to it and nearly got completely bogged down. There were quantities of house-fly-like flies which went straight into our hair and bit our scalps. Eventually we extricated ourselves and drove to Trabzon where, in spite of Rose Macaulay's novel,[2] there were few romantic towers and the town had little charm and a lot of odour. We stayed at the 'best' hotel in town, the Benli Palas, where the smell from the footprint loos permeated the whole building. At least it was cheap. But we had important business here and we met the Directors General of Forestry and Agriculture who appeared to give us permission to go to the places we wanted, including Artvin and the road over the hills from Of to Bayburt.

It was suggested that we visit the ancient monastery of Mer Yemana, some 48km/30 miles south of Trabzon. We followed two forestry officials up a dreadful road, ending with a walk in exhausting heat and humidity. The monastery proved to be in a terrible state of disrepair with most of the frescos defaced or removed. We were told that the monks who had fled to Greece had made a request to come back and worship in their old church. This was granted but, when they left by boat as they had come, a hole was discovered behind the altar. It had hidden the altar silver those many years.

A reluctant Peter at the Black Sea.

Boat repairing on the Black Sea.

Lilium monadelphum *on the Zigana pass south of Trabzon. This population was previously known as* L. szovitsianum. *This makes an excellent garden plant but takes many years to flower from seed.*

The steep, forested slopes were covered with a fascinating variety of trees, shrubs and herbs. These included hornbeam *Carpinus betulus*, bladder nut *Staphylea colchica*, *Euonymus europeus*, *Juglans*, *Ulmus*, *Alnus*, *Castanea* and *Mespilus*, with the lovely yellow *Lilium monadelphum* of which we were to see more on the well known Zigana pass. We collected some corms of *Cyclamen coum* whose offspring are still growing happily at Glendoick. I hasten to add that there was no taboo on the collecting of cyclamen in those days. After returning to Trabzon for the night, we spent a day in flowery meadows on the Zigana pass where we found a splendid stand of *Lilium monadelphum* with stems up to 1.2m/4ft carrying up to nine flowers per stem. The pendulous flowers varied from cream to deep lemon yellow, with or without small spots, and they grew on a west-facing ungrazed bank below a spruce forest with a profusion of purple orchids – a lovely combination.

It was now time to move on to Artvin, which lies east of Trabzon near the Georgian frontier, some 40km/25 miles from the Black Sea coast. The road followed the coast and proved to be very slow, crossed by numerous inlets where streams tumbled down the steep slopes into the sea. Much of this area had recently been planted with tea bushes and at that time Turkey had nearly reached the stage of becoming self-sufficient. Another crop was pecan nuts. Uncultivated parts

were covered in dense, mostly deciduous forest or scrub with some *Serapias* orchids among the shrubs. We observed *Rhododendron ponticum* and *R. luteum* growing right down to sea level and noted that seed collected from here should produce heat-resistant genotypes.

We camped near the town of Borçka, which was memorable for the most remarkable frog chorus we had ever heard, starting with a barking noise, followed by quacking like ducks and finishing with bleating like sheep. The night was hot and uncomfortable and, after rising at six o'clock, we inspected our herbarium specimens and were distressed to find that some had already gone mouldy or black. The high temperatures and humidity had speeded up the decaying process and we should have been changing papers more regularly. At least there was sun to dry off the wet paper.

1. *Rhododendron ponticum* in the Pontus mountains is very variable in truss shape and colour and in the leaves. As seen near Giresun and later around Artvin, it is not all that similar to what we know growing semi-wild in the UK; the leaves are less shiny and it usually lacks the reddish stems of our plants. It has now been shown that almost all the British stock originates from the Iberian Peninsula and some of it has crossed with the North American *R. catawbiense*, particularly in Scotland where DNA indicates that up to 25 per cent may be so affected.

2. *The Towers of Trebizond* (1956).

The Mudur holds sway

We had lunch in Artvin before meeting the Mudur, the head of forestry and an important figure locally given the extent of the forested area. He was an expansive gentleman, fully aware of his importance but helpful to us, nevertheless, with our plans to visit areas with rhododendrons and other plants. However, we soon discovered that he had two hangers-on – a personal assistant/bodyguard with permanent dark glasses, a flat cap and a suspicious bulge under the left armpit of his leather jacket, and his son Tunç, a plump and spoiled youth who was attached to us periodically, ostensibly to help his English but also, we suspected, to keep an eye on what we were up to. We called him the Chunky Chick and Johnnie was adept at managing Tunç's appetite for cigarettes and sweets while keeping the relationship friendly.

After what seemed a long time, we set off up the hill above the town on a forest track. We had picked up a small forestry man in uniform named Suliman and, as the Landrover was now getting rather crowded, Johnnie rode on the mudguard, bucking about as we climbed over 1,200m/4,000ft to our campsite in a delightful forest clearing known as Mercivan, surrounded by *Rhododendron smirnowii* and *R. ungernii*. However, it was also a campsite for the forestry workers and one had to tread with care in the surrounding bushes.

Our first outing was to an open grassland area called Genya at 1,900m/6,300ft, where cattle grazed among clumps of rhododendrons and *Picea orientalis*. Two adjacent rhododendron plants proved to be of considerable interest. One had white flowers with yellowy-green spots (ACH 102), while the other had pink flowers with orangey-brown spots (ACH 103). Above these were a few *R. caucasicum* with thin brown matted indumentum and some inferior *R. ponticum* with poor trusses of a bad colour. These two plants we took to be forms of *R. ponticum* but, on checking the description at home, they were obviously *R. caucasicum* x *R. ponticum* hybrids on account of their pubescent ovaries, and some years later we found that this hybrid had been named *R.* x *sochadzeae* in 1967. A few of the seedlings from these two plants had foliage closer to *R. caucasicum*, but unfortunately none had pure white flowers.

The Mudur (the local forestry chief, seated) and his son Tunç with our bodyguard Suliman and the truck driver near Yalnızçan, south-east of Artvin. We were warned that there were brigands, wolves and bears in this area.

The track carried on some way beyond Mercivan to a hill above the tree-line called Kuru Kurun near Melo. This rocky-topped hill was heavily grazed on the south side but covered with rhododendrons and scrub facing north. Above the meadow on the south side was a large expanse of *R. caucasicum* (ACH 114) with the last few creamy yellow flowers going over. Each plant formed an extensive mat, probably of great age, some 45–90cm/1½–3ft tall and many times wider, with the branches always pointing down the slope, pressed down by the snow, of which there were patches still lying around. In contrast, the north slope was mostly covered with *R. smirnowii* (ACH 129), a more attractive plant with deep to paler mauve-pink flowers, lightly spotted with brown, and greyish foliage with a dense indumentum, cream to fawn, on the underside.

The meadow land on Kuru Kurun had some choice plants including the very fine *Campanula tridentata* var. *stenophylla* with blue flowers and a white eye but occasionally pale blue or even white. *Gentiana pyrenaica* was also there with *Stachys macrantha*

and a dark-red-flowered *Vaccinium*. Particularly desirable was *Daphne glomerata*, an almost prostrate shrub with creamy white deliciously scented flowers but a reputation for being difficult in cultivation. We were to see finer forms of this later on. Once, while I was taking photographs of the forest to the south, I dropped my exposure meter which went bounding down the steep slope. I shouted to Peter who if he had been a good cricketer might just have caught it as it flew overhead. But it had gone, deep into the valley and from then on I had to guess shutter speeds.

Below Kuru Kurun and just above the tree-line was an open area covered with large mats of rhododendrons. These were of a dirty pink and equally dirty creamy colour and appeared to be the same cross of *R. caucasicum* x *R. ponticum* (*R.* x *sochadzeae*).

The *R. smirnowii* around the camp at Mercivan was a fine form with bright pinky-mauve flowers (ACH 118), while in the shadier edges of the clearing were good plants of its cousin *R. ungernii* (ACH 119), which has larger leaves with paler

Our camp at Mercivan above Artvin in extreme north-east Turkey. The conifers are Picea orientalis. *We have heard a report that much of this forest has been felled in recent years.*

indumentum and usually white flowers. These come later in the season, are smaller and more numerous in a somewhat upright truss. With its rather distinguished foliage and late flowering habit, it is surprising that *R. ungernii* has not been used more for hybridising. I find it quite easy to grow and drought tolerant, provided its gets a certain amount of shade. In the wild it seems to need shade too, those in the open seeming unhappy, but flourishing in the forest, each little clearing having its own plant which sprawled over the whole area, layering itself as it went. Some were natural hybrids with *R. smirnowii* (ACH 120), with intermediate foliage and one was particularly attractive with a pale pink corolla and flushed with deeper pink.

Below Mercivan we collected seed off a fine form of *R.* *ponticum* with larger than usual foliage (ACH 205) and it has proved to be a superior plant in cultivation. We searched the forest in vain for the rare endemic dwarf ericaceous shrub *Epigaea (Orphanidesia) gaultherioides*, which we grow very successfully at Baravalla, but we did find some lilies with small orange, spotted flowers which excited us as we thought they might be a new species. In 1997 we heard the distressing news that all the fine forest and rhododendrons around Mercivan had been felled and cleared.

Plans were afoot to visit Yalnızçam, a mountain village to the south-east, so a final dinner was arranged at the Mercivan camp. Trees were cut by the foresters to make a table and benches and we could hear the Mudur's Jeep winding out of the

Opposite above: A beautiful white form of Rhododendron x sochadzeae, *with the Georgian frontier behind.*

Opposite below: Rhododendron caucasicum *(ACH 114) in cultivation. A difficult species to cultivate successfully but it is a parent of several very useful hardy hybrids.*

Below: Peter with a natural hybrid, probably Rhododendron x sochadzeae *of a decidedly muddy colour. This appeared to be all one plant that must have layered itself over many years.*

Rhododendron smirnowii, *Kuru Kurun above Artvin. This very hardy species mostly grows around the tree line at 2,000m/6,400ft with* R. caucasicum *above and* R. ungernii *in the forest below.*

Campanula *species, Pontus mountains. These campanulas are amongst the most showy alpines of this area.*

Stachys macrantha, *Kuru Kurun.*

Rhododendron smirnowii, *Kuru Kurun.*

valley below, horn blaring at every bend. A splendid Turkish meal had been prepared, with cucumber salad and kebabs washed down with the local raki, so when the Mudur and Tunç arrived, we were a little worried about our contribution of a tin of Dundee cake and a bottle of whisky. But as the evening progressed the raki ran out quite quickly and the Mudur gracefully accepted our whisky. The foresters came to dance, a long rhythmic line with their arms on the next man's shoulder and the end one flourishing a handkerchief. The inevitable question 'Do the English not have dances?' had to be answered: 'Not really but we are Scots and the Scots do.' So we ended the night with a sort of hybrid between a three-man Foursome and the Highland Fling to my accompaniment of the hedrum-hidrum, a nasal version of the bagpipes. The foresters clapped politely as we cavorted on the Turkish turf.

In the morning, it was very uncertain whether Yalnizçam was on or off but eventually we set out. Peter was seconded to the Fiat truck with the Mudur, who produced a box of bone hard peaches and proceeded to munch his way through eighteen. Peter had one! Johnnie and I were joined in the Landrover by the Mudur's assistant and the suspicious bulge in his jacket did indeed turn out to be a pistol with which he took pot-shots out of the window at assorted small animals, real or imagined. The noise was deafening and Johnnie, who was driving, had a hard time avoiding cavernous potholes with a background of periodic explosions.

For a while we travelled along the dry valley bottom with a big river of a horrible brown colour, a great contrast to the rain-soaked rhododendron slopes high above. Here grew the Syrian juniper *Juniperus drupacea*, wild pomegranate *Punica granatum* and wild figs. The road sometimes rose to 600m/2,000ft above the river, often with quite hair-raising drops which almost equalled some of those experienced in China and the Himalaya in recent years. We camped short of Yalnizçam in a deserted valley just above forest. An extremely tough looking guard was posted outside our tents to protect us from brigands and wood smugglers, bears and wolves.

The party was again separated, with Peter carted off to another alpine meadow near Yalnizçam. It was not his best day. They left in such a hurry that there was no time to collect a knife or polythene bags. There were masses of bulbs which he attempted to dig up with a pencil. Later he was taken to Yalnizçam where he was fed on creamy milk and doughy bread which made him feel sick, then taken off to see the beauties of the village and, still feeling ill, placed in full view of the whole gawping population for an hour of agony. In the meantime Johnnie and I had found masses of *R. caucasicum* in flower, two species of gentian (probably *G. verna* and *G. pyrenaica*) and other exciting plants. We met up for a feast that was provided on carpets laid out on the meadow with the Mudur sitting on a throne in the middle. But Peter just sat looking miserable and unable to eat a thing.

We returned to Artvin for the night and said goodbye to the Mudur and the Chunky Chick. The forestry chief had

A fine form of Daphne glomerata, *a rare species endemic to north-east Turkey and the Caucasus.*

Picnic at Yalnizçam with the Mudur on his throne.

Campanula tridentata *var.* stenophylla *at Kuru Kurun.*

Rhododendron ungernii (ACH 119) at Glendoick. *Useful for its very late flowers and handsome foliage.*

consumed all our remaining supply of Scotch whisky and his son all our sweets, but Tunç gave us each a photograph of himself inscribed to his 'darling friends'!

We set off for the road which leaves the coast at the village of Of, then crosses the mountains to Bayburt. It was so slow that we had to camp short of Of on the black sandy shore where the locals, as usual, appeared in prodigious numbers with a horde of flies which bit us all over, especially through our socks. We were forced to an early morning start by the heat and flies and drove hurriedly up to the pass. Lilies were abundant from 900m/3,000ft up to the top of the pass at 2,100m/6,900ft and were obviously the same species (*Lilium ponticum*) as we found at Artvin, which shattered our illusions of having found a new species there. The flowers varied from yellow to orange with a few spots to a large blotch. There was also *L. ciliatum*, which we had seen near Giresun. Here the species was common but appeared to be unhealthy, with the lower leaves dying off before the flowers were over, and higher up the stem many leaves were spotted. The road travelled up a long wooded valley followed by a series of sharp hairpin bends up to the pass above the tree-line. Mist and drizzle ruined any views and chances of collecting, so we drove on to just over the crest where there was an abrupt change to a much drier flora and better weather. We made camp there and watched the clouds drifting up from the Black Sea and disappearing into thin air as soon as they crossed the pass.

The next morning was lovely and clear so we put paper out to dry, changed it on our specimens and placed those that were dry in flimsies (thin non-absorbent paper), where they were to stay until we reached home. This took most of the day, apart from collecting a few specimens around camp. We had fared quite well out of the larder in the back of the Landrover and my diary notes that the evening meal consisted of onion soup, yoghurt, pâté, steak-and-kidney pudding and apple dumpling but, alas, we had run out of Kavalkaderi, the very pleasant local wine.

Another fine day was partly spoilt by an oil leak which meant a late start. We drove back over the pass and found some fine pale blue *Scilla siberica* at the edge of the snow banks with some flowers peeping through the snow, *Primula elatior* subsp. *meyeri* past flowering, a corydalis with mauve flowers and a quantity of very small *Rhododendron caucasicum* with no evidence of large flowering-size parents. Evidently these seedlings get cut off in hay or are grazed off every year so never reach any size. There were two new (to us) *Crocus* species and masses of a tiny alpine cyclamen with unmarked leaves which turned out to be *C. parviflorum*. We found some *Daphne glomerata* without red or purple colouring which, to our eyes, was the more attractive form.

33

The road we had just driven up, Of to Bayburt. The mist rolled up this valley from Of by the sea each afternoon and then cleared again in the morning.

The Way Back

It was time to set off towards home. The camp we chose near Bayburt was next to a sluggish smelly river, and crowds of local people milled around who eventually dispersed after vigorous shaking of hands. As soon as we retired into our tents, mosquitoes appeared and attacked us in ever-increasing numbers as the night progressed. Eventually we could stand this no longer and got up at 3.20 and left at 5.15. It was a fairly gruelling return drive to Ankara, the section to Sivas was dreadfully slow and we were thirteen hours driving in extreme heat. On the way we passed periodic police posts and we could see them telephoning ahead as they checked us through.

The next day the road proved to be much better and we made Ankara by the evening, where Peter made some unkind comments on the joy with which John and I fell on our gins and tonics. However, having fallen asleep during dinner, Peter

was considered to be too exhausted for a night on the town and the two of us set off to find some proper belly dancing on the theory that Ankara was the navel of Turkey. It was a cultural experience. The taxi driver was a keen Anglophile with a luxuriant moustache. As we drove he raised one finger in the air and roared, 'Winston Churchill very fine man,' then the other index finger and 'Kemal Atatürk very fine man,' and finally as we careered down the boulevard took both hands off the steering wheel, turned round and bellowed, 'Winston Churchill, Kemal Atatürk verrry good friends!'

The destination was not the underground night club we expected but a large shed-like attic over the main Ankara railway station with a stage and lots of formica-topped tables. It looked ready for a whist drive. They started clearing the table tops and we understood why when the dancers swept on stage with swords

A village just over the divide on the dry south-facing slopes of the Pontus Mountains.

clenched between their teeth and, bellies gyrating, proceeded to swipe the heads off the potted chrysanthemums,. When they moved on to the individual table tops we dived below and held on to the table legs while the human legs writhed above us apparently disconnected from the bits of anatomy further up. It was a bravura performance and the audience roared their approval.

We took a different taxi on the way home.

After an early start, we made Istanbul by 2.30 p.m. Peter and I bought nine boxes of Turkish delight, no doubt made out of the proper ingredient of camel's hoof, and we prepared to set off home. The party, and the plant material, divided at this stage with Peter flying home with the vulnerable part while Johnnie and I set off in the Landrover with the rest of the collections. Little trouble was expected from the UK Customs as we had a Plant Importation permit.

We were driving over familiar territory now and the return journey was uneventful, if a little Spartan in places. We had seriously run out of money and had just enough to pay for the petrol, a tiny reserve for emergencies but nothing for accommodation. However, I had a Diner's Club Card, which meant that it was a case of feast or famine since plastic credit had nothing like the ubiquitous cover in 1962 that it has today. We camped or slept in the Landrover across much of Communist Europe but made up for it in any watering hole that would take our card. As well as eating everything on offer in the hotels, we would stock up on sugar lumps and biscuits to take us through the next stage.

Retribution would come later, of course, in the shape of a bill but by that time we would be home with our personal bit of Turkey to show for it.

Chapter 2

INTO THE NORTH-EAST FRONTIER AGENCY:

India 1965

Peter Cox

In the days of the British Raj, most of what was then known as the Northeast Frontier Agency or NEFA, and now known as Arunachal Pradesh, was virtually out of bounds for outsiders. There were no roads and many of the tribal peoples inhabiting this wild countryside were extremely hostile to strangers. Some efforts were made towards subduing the population but this invariably ended in failure. One famous occasion was when a detachment of Assam Rifles was sent to deal with the Tagins, and the whole detachment was massacred. The tribes varied considerably in their ferocity, the Abors, Miris, Tagins and the Mishmis were reckoned to be the worst. These wild people are referred to as Lobas by the Tibetans.

Another difficulty over Arunachal Pradesh which remains to this day is its sensitivity due to China and India both claiming it. In 1914 Sir Henry McMahon drew up a convention to settle the frontier, subsequently known as the McMahon Line, which was initialled by delegates of China and Tibet, but this convention was never ratified. While Tibet did not attempt to implement or to repudiate the convention, China has never renounced its claim. Although India has long had the area under its rather loose control, Chinese maps show it included within China (Tibet). In 1962, only three years before we were there, the Chinese temporarily invaded Arunachal Pradesh and we were informed by reliable sources that the small Indian garrisons had all fled in terror. If the Chinese had opted to remain, it is very doubtful if the Indians or international pressure would have had any effect in removing them.[1]

After Indian independence the NEFA administration was appointed to govern the area on enlightened lines suggested by the distinguished anthropologists Professor von Fürer-Haimendorf and Verrier Elwin. These two underlined the advisability of maintaining the long-established ways of life of the tribal peoples and shielding them from as much outside influence as possible.

In early 1964 we put in our application to the Indian authorities to visit NEFA, after having failed to get permission to go to Bhutan. To have any hope of obtaining permission, every possible string had to be pulled. Peter's father Sir James Hutchison had been a junior

government minister and had met some people high up in Indian government circles including Mrs Pandit, Prime Minister Nehru's sister. Among various other people contacted were some members of the Indian aristocracy who still had influence. We had aimed to travel out in early spring 1965. By mid November 1964 time was running out as we had to send our heavy baggage by sea well in advance, but on the 23rd a vanishing dream turned into a possibility. A letter arrived from the British High Commission in New Delhi stating that the Indian Government had no objection to our trip in principle, provided that we were accompanied by some officials of the Botanical Survey of India (BSI) with whom we had already been in contact. We had always hoped that this could

be made a joint collecting expedition. We were also told that we would have to be self-sufficient within NEFA as the inhabitants had only just enough food to cater for their own needs.

Being the last possible moment at which the expedition could have been organised, an enormous amount of work had to be done in a very short time. Firstly, we had to gather all our kit and provisions and acquire packing cases in which to carry everything by ship to Calcutta. For food, we were generously helped by W.A. Baxter & Sons Ltd, Ross's Dairies Ltd and Erin Foods Ltd. The last provided us with freeze-dried food including excellent mince. Adam (John) Stainton sold us two unused tents and our magnificent packing cases were especially made at a small ship-

Above left. Rhododendron subansiriense (CH 418) at Baravalla

Above. The Apa Tani Valley is surrounded by mountains rising to nearly 3,000m/10.000ft to the south-east.

1. When I was in Tibet in June 1998, the Indians had just let off their A-bomb trials, much to the annoyance of the Chinese who sent troops up to the frontier at the lower end of the Tsari valley, just to the north of the Subansiri Division. This was most likely one of the places through which they entered Arunachal Pradesh in 1962.

Basket market, Shillong. The boat-shaped 'baskets' are ideal for keeping off the rain while bending down working in the fields.

building yard in which the Hutchisons had an interest. The Hutchison family had an annex to their house near Perth known as the 'bolt hole', with a large room capable of holding all our assembled kit. Everything was listed and numbered and divided into piles suitable to fill each case, of which there were eleven, ten wooden and one tin. Case No 1, for instance, contained 875 sheets of botanical drying paper weighing 112lb (50 kilos). In six weeks we had everything ready to ship to Calcutta and the shippers, Arbuckle Smith in Glasgow, handled its journey out east.

The second major task was to sell shares for seeds and plants to cover at least a good part of our expenses. Shares were £50. We were lucky in having many contacts in the horticultural world, not only in Britain but also in Europe and North America. We received a tremendous response and some societies took multiple shares. In all we sold thirty-five shares plus two extra for photographs. Our estimated expenses for the three of us were £2,899 for about three months.[2]

My wife Patricia and I set off for New Delhi on 10 March 1965, leaving our small son Kenneth aged 11 months with my cousin Averil Valentine. Without Averil's wonderful kindness, we could never have gone together. We stayed three nights at the Hotel Janpath, visiting the Ministry of External Affairs in the superb government complex designed by Sir Edwin Lutyens. We had been warned that we should not show Indian officials any of our maps. While we were waiting to be ushered into the official's office, we had a grand chance to study an excellent map on the wall, covering the area we wanted to visit. Later during our interview we were asked how we knew where we wanted to go and we quickly said that we had examined the map on the wall outside. As we had been warned, progress was slow and, even after staying another two days in a different hotel, our permits were not forthcoming, so we left it to Peter to finalize everything. In the meantime we left for Calcutta to see our heavy baggage through customs and arrange for it to be forwarded to Assam.

The one excursion out of New Delhi had to be to Agra to see the Taj Mahal. We had a hair-raising drive and kept wondering whether we might any at moment be added to the various roadside corpses of cattle, dogs etc. Something revered in one's imagination as too wondrous to contemplate somehow falls as a damp squib. I think it was the comparatively small size of the main mausoleum that disappointed me. On the way home we

followed an apparently never-ending flight of house crows flying parallel to our straight road on their way to roost and, when we eventually turned a corner away from the birds, we could see the thin straggling line disappearing into the distance.

We stayed at the old colonial Great Eastern Hotel in Calcutta where the staff were dressed in the most amazing old uniform. Living in such a hotel made us feel guilty when just outside in the streets was such poverty. At night and partly during the day hundreds of the local inhabitants were lying out on the pavements. We had various calls to make, including to the Indian Tea Association,[3] the Metal Box Company and a few Indian dignitaries to whom we had letters of introduction.[4] The Metal Box Company's official doctor inspected the medical chest we had made up on the advice of the British department of tropical medicine. The doctor scoffed and made out a completely new list. This was just as well as we two Peters were very ill in Shillong.

Clearing our heavy crates through customs proved surprisingly easy, thanks to the James Warren representative who warned us to be careful at the godown (warehouse). He told us that he had once lost his temper with a docker and had given him a push. At once he was surrounded and only just escaped being lynched. Assam Travels handled the onward transportation to Gauhati in Assam.

We were very fortunate to be able to meet Dr Father Santapau, then director of the BSI, who was a Portuguese priest in addition to being a botanist. He was the most delightful and intelligent man and we were only sorry that we could not have spent longer with him. We were able to honour him by naming one of our new species of *Rhododendron* after him, *R. santapaui*.

Some final shopping had to be done, including basic food such as rice and dhal, plus eating and cooking utensils. We were told that we could get everything at the Hog Market. This was an amazing place full of hundreds of permanent stalls. Before entering, we picked up a very essential guide who found everything we were looking for. The whole place, like most of India, was not exactly clean and here we found the most dreadful beggars, many of whom had been deliberately malformed at birth. One we particularly remember moved on all fours crabwise along the filthy gutters which edged every pathway.

2. Meanwhile Peter was doing the rounds of various societies to raise funds and was given an interview with the redoubtable head of Kew, Sir George Taylor. After an interminable discussion about trout fishing in Scotland, Taylor said, 'And how did you lot get allowed into NEFA? I've been trying to get my boys in there for ages'. But he arranged a grant.

3. The air-conditioned Indian Tea Association waiting room must have been set about 20°F (7°C) lower than the temperature outside and we had to wait over an hour with our teeth almost chattering with cold. Soon afterwards Patricia developed a nasty cough which bothered her off and on for years afterwards.

4. Other visits took us to a maharanee and a baronet, the maharaja's private box at the Calcutta racecourse, the Calcutta zoo and to a botanist, Dr Kalipada Biswas, author of *Plants of Darjeeling and the Sikkim Himalayas* (Government of West Bengal, 1967), who was obsessed with trying to find an antidote to aconite poisoning.

Shillong Peak showing the preserved forest in the catchment area for the Shillong water supply. The rest of this area had long since been cleared of trees. The chief tree here is Pinus kesiya, *the Khasi pine.*

Around Shillong

After collecting our permit for Shillong, on 25 March we were able to fly to Gauhati which lies on the south bank of the Brahmaputra river in the Assam plain. This enormous river, in places two miles or more across and much more where there are islands, originates as the Yarlung Tsangpo in Tibet, then descends nearly 3,000m/10,000ft through the famous Tsangpo Gorge, becoming the Siang (Dihang) at the frontier, before reaching the Assam plain as the Brahmaputra.

In 1965 Shillong had no airport so we had to take a taxi for the 97km/60 mile ride up the hill. The city lies in the Khasia Hills between the Assam plain and what was then East Pakistan and is now Bangladesh, on the north-facing slopes, between 1,200m/4,000ft and 1,700m/5,500ft, and somewhat in the rain shadow of the 2,000m/6,400ft Shillong Peak. It was the hill station for the tea planters of Assam, so at one time there were quite a few British there. In 1965 just a few retired tea planters were left.

Our first visit was to the BSI Eastern Circle where we met Dr A.S. Rao, who was in charge, and A.R.K. Sastry and Mr S.K. Katachi, who were to accompany us to the Subansiri. Dr Rao rang Mr E.P. Gee, a retired tea planter, with whom we had been corresponding, and told him that we had arrived. Mr Gee was in the forefront of wildlife preservation in India and wrote

the book *Wildlife of India*. In a letter he had mentioned that he would be willing to have us to stay, so there was a very awkward moment when he asked us where we planned to stay. Somewhat reluctantly he agreed to have us, but we soon got on fine and he was a tower of wisdom in knowing how to handle local officials. Mr Gee's house, Evergreen Cottage, was in Upper Shillong at 1,700m/5,500ft where he grew many species of orchid, especially *Dendrobium*, most of which he had collected himself and tied on to small trees with string.

We spent several days walking from Evergreen Cottage, both up to the peak and down into the gorge. On 28 March Peter arrived and our little party of three was complete again. He had spent several days in Delhi being passed from one official to another, but he now had assurance that the permit would be forwarded to the NEFA administration in Shillong in the next few days.

We had been told that *Rhododendron inaequale* (now *R. formosum* var. *inaequale*) grew down in the gorge. After walking a mile up the gorge and failing to find it, we sat down to eat bananas. Suddenly we spotted it straight above our heads but not yet in flower. There were about ten plants, either on rocks or epiphytic. The capsules still contained plentiful seed (CH 301). This has large, white, gorgeously scented flowers but it is only

Mr E.P. Gee with whom we stayed in Shillong. He was a retired tea planter and an expert on Indian wildlife.

Mr Derrington, Mr E.P. Gee's general factotum, here with a stick for pulling orchids off trees, an openly accepted practice in 1965.

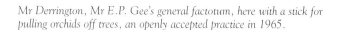

hardy in the mildest of western British gardens. A seedling 'Elizabeth Bennet' received a First Class Certificate in 1981. The 270m/900ft climb to Shillong Peak was through open forest of *Pinus kesiya*, the Khasi pine, with plentiful yellow-flowered *Dendrobium heterocarpum* on the pine trunks. Nearer the top of the peak *R. arboreum* subsp. *delavayi* (CH 305) grew in quantity, to 10.6m/35ft, covered in blood-red flowers. This has proved to be tender, slow growing and surprisingly shy flowering at Baravalla. From the top of the peak, the view looking east was a great surprise, a large plateau more or less bare of trees. On Shillong Peak itself and the ridge running north, tree cutting was forbidden as it was the catchment area for the town's water supply. Alas, recent visitors tell of the destruction of most of the forest and all that is left of the rhododendrons is sprouting stumps.

Mr Gee's general factotum, Derrington, took us to the little town of Pynursla which is situated opposite the famous Cherrapunji, one of the wettest places in the world. The road traversed some amazing country, part of it being along the top of a knife-edge ridge with drops of about 600m/2,000ft on both sides. On the journey Derrington told us many local stories including one about the Snake Goddess to which the local inhabitants were still said to make child sacrifices. We found a superb jasmine with sweetly scented white flowers, deep pink in

the bud. The Indians named it *J. subtriplinerve*. The RBGK never produced a name for it and there was no specimen in the RBGE anything like it. An amazing plant was *Agapetes odontocera*, a small evergreen tree with flowers all up the even-quite-old branches. These flowers were dull waxy red with red lines, cream towards the ends of the lobes. Alas, there was no seed on either of these two plants. On the way back we spotted a rhododendron in flower. This proved to be half way between *R. formosum* var. *formosum* and *R. formosum* var. *inaequale* (CH 320). A selection received an Award of Merit in 1988 which we named 'Khasia'. It has strongly fragrant white flowers with a yellow throat.

We had been asked to collect orchids for Kew and managed to get several species around Shillong with Mr Gee's help, both with regards to assistance and naming. A boy was found who could literally run up trees and this made their collection very easy. These are very easily transported in a dry state. Now, of course, this collecting of orchids would be totally forbidden.

We had been delayed due to having to wait for the return to Shillong of the BSI jeep from Bhutan and also because the permit for NEFA had not arrived from New Delhi. When the latter came, we received the dreadful shock that we were to be confined to the ridge south-east of the Apa Tani valley which only rises to just under 3,000m/10,000ft. The main part of the

Rhododendron formosum *var.* inaequale *(CH 301), collected in the gorge below Upper Shillong and growing at Glendoick. This variety is much more tender than var.* formosum *but has larger, more strongly scented flowers.*

Orchids in Mr Gee's garden, Evergreen Cottage, Upper Shillong. Mr Gee was keen on his orchids and tied epiphytic species on to trees with string.

A fine pink-tinged R. formosum *var.* formosum *growing in Mr Gee's garden.*

expedition was to be to the ridge between the Kameng and Subansiri divisions and this was refused, despite repeated requests that we had to get to higher than 3,000m/10,000ft for hardy plants. Furthermore our photography was to be restricted to flora only and films had to be developed in India and be inspected by the NEFA authorities for their approval. Also, Peter was not to use his cine camera. None of these restrictions had been mentioned by the Ministry of External Affairs in any interviews or correspondence. So with a heavy heart we set off.

Mr Gee found a Nepali bearer for us called Thapa who accompanied us to the Subansiri. He was quite good, considering that he had three of us to look after, but in the end he proved to be unreliable and had been hiding the fact that he had a wife and child back home. Compared to the Indian botanists who had four underlings and the Indian official who had five, we were greatly understaffed. This, in the eyes of the Indians, downgraded us as it meant that we had to do manual chores, such as erecting our own tents and pressing botanical specimens, which they would

Dendrobium heterocarpum, *the only orchid on pine trees, here on Shillong Peak.*

Rhododendron arboreum *subsp.* delavayi *on Shillong Peak in March with Patricia Cox.*

not dream of doing, all such tasks being done by their juniors.

Our heavy gear was sent ahead to North Lakhimpur, a small town situated near the confluence of the Subansiri and Brahmaputra rivers and where our road left the plain and wound into the foothills of the Himalaya. We travelled by road, first along the south bank of the Brahmaputra and then into the Kasiranga National Park where most of the remaining Indian rhinoceros live. This is a rich flood plain where the rhinos are flooded out and have to go up into the Mikir Hills where they are vulnerable to poachers, as happened in the heavy monsoons of 1998. We got up at 4.45 and were taken around the park on an elephant trained not to give way if a rhino should charge. The rhinoceros skin is divided into sections by prominent wrinkles which make them look as if

they are wearing armour plating. We were lucky to see eleven, plus one wild buffalo, two otters, samba deer and masses of birds, including pelicans. I did not enjoy the elephant ride.

We then crossed the river on three ferries, the first taking us on to Majali Island, said to be the largest inland island in the world, then two ferries over lower branches of the Subansiri. Both rivers were dotted with floating rafts of the beautiful but rampageous water hyacinth (*Eichhornia crassipes*), which also covers many of the pools and lakes of the plain.

North Lakhimpur was a hot and smelly little town where we had to eat a particularly fiery curry in the only restaurant and stay the night in the bug-ridden circuit house. We battled with the largest cockroaches we have seen anywhere.

Pynursla, Meghalaya. This village lies on the top of the escarpment east of the better known town of Cherrapungi.

A fine Jasminum *species in elfin forest near Pynursla, Meghalaya, with a really good scent.*

Forested hills, south of the Apa Tani valley. It was this photograph that our Indian official became paranoid about as we were prohibited from photographing views.

Our ferry to Majuli Island, on the Brahmaputra.

The view of paddy fields from our circuit house, Ziro, Apa Tani Valley, Subansiri Division, Arunachal Pradesh.

Arunachal Pradesh (NEFA)

Along the foothills of the Himalaya, on the north side of the Assam plain, runs the Inner Line, the boundary separating two entirely different worlds. To the north lies the intricate, folded country of the Himalaya, where everything seems to live on the near perpendicular. To the south are the immaculate tea gardens, the thatched villages with their betel nut palms and banana trees and the huge grey Brahmaputra, flanked by ever-changing mud flats.

The forest was still inhabited by wild elephants in 1965 and we were told that a herd of seven had recently gone on the rampage and flattened a school near North Lakhimpur. The silly planners had built the school right in the path that the elephants normally used. As less and less forest is left, the poor elephants become increasingly tempted to eat crops on what was once all their own territory.

We were met at Kimin on the Inner Line by officials of the NEFA administration and our onward travel was arranged with unaccustomed efficiency. We were to learn that the administrative staff of the NEFA service were something of an elite and used to making on-the-spot decisions that elsewhere in India would have been referred to superiors. On the way we were taken to an agricultural experimental station and, in a creaky bamboo hut on stilts, were fed delicious omelets, raw onions and carrots, all washed down with local rum. It was very welcome as, apart from a banana for breakfast, this was the first food we had had that day.

The then-new road threaded along the near-vertical slopes of the Panior gorge and carved its way through dense subtropical jungle. We were now in the country of the Dafla people (now Nishi) and we saw parties of them making their way to and from the plain. By now it was dark and groups were huddled around their fire under the shelter of a tree trunk. A ring-tailed civet (cat) was briefly lit up in the headlights and occasionally a giant mithun (semi-wild cattle) loomed out of the darkness.

It was a pity that we had only seen the first hour of the journey in daylight but we made up for this on the way out. We travelled up with the very nice Mr Shukla, a sociological officer who was a friend of von Fürer-Haimendorf's and had worked under Verrier Elwin. He told us about natural remedies for human complaints, including hot fern leaves for rheumatics, resin for eye troubles and human stools to force vomiting after eating the extremely poisonous aconitum. Our abode in Ziro (Hapoli), the official headquarters of the Apa Tani valley, was a brand new circuit house, perched on the top of a mound covered with *Primula denticulata*. The morning revealed a fascinating panorama. Below us the rice paddies spread in a scaly pattern across the valley, which is some 16km/10 miles long by 8km/5 miles across and lies at 1,500m/5,000ft above sea-level. This is the largest level patch of ground in the eastern Himalaya and every available corner is used for rice and vegetable crops. In 1965, some 10,000 Apa Tanis lived here and managed to grow a small food surplus which they sold to the Daflas who inhabit the hills all around the valley.

The climate of the valley is surprisingly dry with only 127–152cm/50–60in of rain compared with 254–508cm/100–200in on the slopes facing the Assam plain. We were informed that the temperature the previous November had dropped to the surprising -12°C/10°F and that in November-December it quite often drops to -5 or -6°C/23 or 21°F. There was evidence of scorching on some of the eucalyptus planted for firewood. Little snow falls, partly because the winters are mostly dry.

Low rounded hills encircled the valley. Some were scarred by the *jhum* or slash and burn cultivation of the Daflas while others were still clad in fine virgin forest. Skirting the valley were plantations of *Pinus wallichiana*, the Bhutan pine, which tradition says was brought in by the forebears of the Apa Tanis when they moved into this valley, probably from Bhutan. These grew into very substantial trees and were the main source of timber for building their houses. There were signs of it naturalising.

We were the first guests and had the luxury of new sheets and blankets. One assistant political officer and his wife, Mr & Mrs Deori, were our first callers and proved to be delightful and very helpful, inviting us to their house the following night. They were immediately followed by Mr Mittra, another assistant PO, who accompanied us on our trek to what we came to call the south-east ridge, which I only discovered in 2006 goes by the peculiar name of Talle Valley. At the dinner with the Deoris, we drank the local rum and whisky, both low on alcohol which was just as well, and the latter bore no resemblance to the real thing.

Our first outing brought us face to face with a row of Apa Tani chiefs who surveyed us up and down; visitors with pale skins must have been quite a novelty. We were greeted with cheerful grins and cries of 'Jai hind'. They were dressed in short red cloaks issued by the government as a sort of uniform. Otherwise they wore only their traditional cane belts, dyed red and brought into a tail behind. Like some of the surrounding tribes, they had their hair gathered into a topknot on their forehead, with what looked like a knitting needle stuck through it. They also had a distinguishing blue tribal mark on their chins. They were short and stocky people, somewhat Tibetan in appearance, and we could not help noticing the tremendous development of their calf muscles. They were never without their *dao*, a short chopping sword which they carry slung across their chests and under their arms.

We spent a few days collecting around the valley and making preparations for our camping trip. We had hoped to see Kingdon Ward's carmine cherry, *Prunus cerasoides*, and sure enough we found a 24m/80ft tree which stood out from the forest in a blaze of colour. Other trees were the white-flowered *Docynia indica*, *Photinia notoniana*, and *Pyrus pashia*, all members of *Rosaceae*, and we found a scented clematis. Orchids become scarcer at this altitude but the white-flowered *Coelogyne nitida* was in full bloom and we found the terrestrial *Calanthe plantaginea* with lovely scented pink flowers. *Primula denticulata* was everywhere. There were many other interesting plants in and around the forest margins, but on old cut-over areas, nothing other than bracken and species of *Rubus*.

The south-east ridge known as Talle Valley

Our south-east ridge was in full view of the circuit house and when clear of cloud we could see through our binoculars a haze of red near the top and longed to get there before all the flowers were over. Eventually on 15 April we were all set to go and we ourselves were ready by 8.30. By 10.30 quite a few porters turned up but it was another hour before the loads (we had put everything into tin trunks) were lifted. The trunks were tied to head bands with which everything was carried by the flimsiest looking strips of bamboo. 20kg/44lb was the official government load and there was much testing before everyone was satisfied. Due to a shortage of porters, Mr Katachi had to stay behind to collect more porters for the rest of their loads. Mr Mittra had Nepali porters to carry his enormous tent and some must have had 30kg/66lb or more to carry. No government restrictions for him! Eventually we left at almost 1 o'clock.

The afternoon's trek was just 8.8km/5½ miles through pines and then dense subtropical forest. We climbed a low ridge and descended to a flat marshy area to camp, having gained only 61m/200ft. Across the bog we saw two shrubs with large white flowers and there was great excitement when we found that they were *Rhododendron nuttallii* in full flower. This species has about the largest flowers in the genus but is sadly too tender for cultivating outside in Britain. Some of our porters noticed our interest in these plants, took out their *daos* and hacked both off near the ground before we could stop them. What a shame! Some fat unopened capsules proved to be bug-ridden with no seed left so we failed to introduce this form. The one seedling we found was too big for us to handle so we presented it to the BSI in Shillong.

Apa Tani porters near a stream. I am in the background in the middle.

An Apa Tani with traditional hairstyle. The younger men were giving up this tradition in 1965 and by our second visit in 2002, it had virtually disappeared.

R. maddenii in tight bud also grew at the edge of the bog, as did a scraggy *Michelia*. We set up our tents in the darkness.

The next day's trek took us on two ups and downs, crossing two rivers and camping at 2,200m/7,200ft. We soon started to find new rhododendrons. First was a small immature Ciliicalyx Alliance of subsection Maddenia growing on a log (CH 396) with almost round hairy leaves, which most of the Ciliicalyx Alliance have when young. On the way back a determined search around the bog revealed a few upright mature specimens with narrow leaves. This was subsequently named *R. coxianum* after my father E. H. M. Cox by H. H. Davidian. It is related to *R. formosum* with the same strong sweet scent as *R. formosum* var. *inaequale*. Soon we saw white flowers all along the path and eventually managed to locate some plants way up in the trees, one of which was low enough for a porter to climb up to hack a branch off. Luckily most of the flowers stayed on, as did

Rhododendron nuttallii *growing at the edge of a bog. In endeavouring to please us, one of the Apa Tanis rushed across the bog and, with one slash of his* dao, *cut off the* R. nuttallii *and presented it to us.*

Rhododendron coxianum (CH 475) *was found growing terrestrially and epiphytically around the same bog where* R. nuttallii *was growing.* R. coxianum *is closely related to* R. formosum var. inaequale *with an equally good scent.*

Rhododendron walongense *aff. (CH 373) at Glendoick. This species was always an epiphyte away up in the trees. One of our porters ran up a tree and cut off one of the lowest plants and dropped it down to us.*

plenty of seed. Davidian named this *R. parryae* (CH 373), but later it was found to be closest to *R. walongense*. In cultivation it has early flowering creamy white spicy scented flowers and a splendid deep mahogany peeling bark. We may have collected Kingdon Ward's original *R. walongense* in 2002.

What we reckoned was a poor form of *Rhododendron arboreum* turned out to be *R. arboreum* subsp. *delavayi* var. *peramoenum*. It had narrow leaves and the truss was very small. This was probably the first time this variety had been found in Arunachal Pradesh. We made no effort to collect any seed of this plant. Much superior were small 4.5m/15ft trees of *R. griffithianum* (CH 389) at 2,000m/6,500ft, alas not nearly into flower. Not surprisingly, this introduction proved to be very tender from such a low elevation. A few miserable plants of *R. edgeworthii* (CH 421) were found growing epiphytically on logs and trees. This proved to be a very unusual form with only one

very large flower per inflorescence. The *R. lindleyi* (CH 399), which was only sometimes epiphytic, is similar to the plant sometimes referred to as *R. grothausii*, with smaller more bullate leaves than the type. Yet another species was what we first called *R. ramsdenianum* but it was later identified as the closely related *R. kendrickii* (CH 416). This had tight trusses of blood red flowers with a deep nectar pouch. It grew in a narrow altitudinal band between 2,300 and 2,400m/7,500 and 8,000ft. A plant of this number in a shady position at Baravalla has not flowered yet after forty years.

Many plants other than rhododendrons grew in this dank forest. It was indeed unfortunate that only one species of *Agapetes* was in flower at the time of our visit as that was the only species of which we collected a plant. The abundance of moss on the trees favoured a large epiphytic community and this rhododendron-related genus (both are in *Ericaceae*) takes

Apa Tani porters cooking their rice by a stream as water would be very scarce further up the mountain.

full advantage of such a habitat. Most of our herbarium specimens were determined by taxonomists at the RBGK and amongst these was H. K. Airy Shaw who examined this genus. Out of our collection he named two new species: *A. similis* which had been found previously by Kingdon Ward but not named; and *A. muscorum*. In all we found six species of *Agapetes* including *A. odonticera*, found in the Khasia Hills. The one plant we did collect Airy Shaw identified as *A. smithiana* var. *major* (CH 413), the variety having been described by Airy Shaw himself in 1959 from Bhutan. This species has freely produced bright lemon yellow flowers and is now quite well established in cultivation under glass. There is an extraordinary coincidental sequel on this plant. I was attending the 1998 Hortax (horticultural taxonomy) Conference in Edinburgh and looked in on an exhibition of items for sale including botanical paintings. I pounced on a very nice painting of this plant but what was so amazing was

that it had been painted by a Patricia A. Cox with the same Christian name as my wife and the same initials as mine. Needless to say I bought the painting.

Before reaching our second camp, we all stopped at the river just below our final climb of the day. Here the porters boiled their rice for their evening meal. It was most picturesque with the smoke rising above the river boulders and the jungle crowding in above us from the steep slopes. How wise the porters had been to cook their rice by the river as the next camp proved to be completely lacking in water. We then had a long steep climb to the campsite, perched on a spur of the ridge at 2,200m/7,200ft. There we were joined by Katachi of the BSI with extra porters and supplies, having done some hard marching. They arrived after dark carrying torches of pinewood.

The next morning we were woken early with a high-pitched argument going on among the porters. It appeared that there was some sort of strike on – they wanted more money and they wanted to go home but basically the trouble was that this was the season for cultivating their rice fields and their absence would be unpopular. Mr Mittra had been plagued with deputations of porters all night but by the morning had reached the end of his tether. We heard shouting from his tent and he came rushing out brandishing his revolver in all directions and releasing torrents of abuse at the porters. This touch of drama appeared to do the trick and we were soon on the move again.

The forest above the camp was in full and spectacular flower. *Michelia* (now *Magnolia*) *doltsopa* and other magnolias were hung with fragrant and fragile flowers; in all there appeared to be three species. The stark branches of M. *rostrata* were not yet in leaf and far from flowering but the litter of cones on the forest floor were proof of last year's abundance.

Agapetes smithiana *var.* major *(CH 415) in cultivation.*

Opposite: Warm temperate rain forest with everything covered in climbers and moss. Although it did not actually rain while we were on the ridge, the humidity must have been almost 100% with constant drips off the trees.

Rhododendron grande *in the rain forest. We were very lucky to see these giants in all their glory.*

Soon *Rhododendron grande* (CH 431) began to appear, magnificent trees in full flower varying from cream to pale yellow, sometimes with a strong pink tinge, in fine, full trusses. The trees were as much as 15m/50ft high with trunks 61cm/2ft in diameter; they were a glorious sight wherever a view could be had, although standing under them we could scarcely see anything except the leaves and trusses silhouetted against the sky and well out of reach. The seed capsules were away above our heads, so it was lucky that there was an abundance of seedlings. This appeared to be a splendid form, well worthy of introduction but, alas, it comes into growth very early, resulting in frosted growth virtually every year. We have yet to see a decent plant of this introduction in cultivation and we brought back over 200 seedlings. These seedlings occurred in enormous quantities, usually in moss on fallen tree trunks. Only when the canopy is broken is there any hope of one of these reaching maturity and as many as 999 out of 1,000 must fail, so we thought we were rescuing them from a near certain and slow death. The tiny-leaved and flowered vireya rhododendron *R. vaccinioides* (CH 419) was common on the trunks and branches of *R. grande* and other trees from 2,100–2,700m/7,000–9,000ft. What an amazing contrast in size these two rhododendron species made.

We made our camp in a small damp hollow just below the peak where, again, in spite of the continual drips off the trees,

we were short of water and had to rely on a tiny trickle on the hillside. This was to be our base for exploring the ridge. It was hard even to cook a meal with the sodden wood around and before long the ground was everywhere churned to mud, as our party was in all nearly seventy strong.

The temperate rain-forest which covered the ridge was a remarkable plant community. The dominant plants were rhododendrons, particularly *R. grande*, with other evergreen trees and these formed a nearly continuous canopy 12–15m/40–50ft above the ground. Here and there we could see the sky where a deciduous tree had not broken into leaf or a tree had blown over. Below this canopy the ground was relatively clear except where brakes of bamboo occurred. Underneath there was a springy layer of organic matter often feet thick and covering the ground so completely that we scarcely saw a stone or bare rock. And everywhere, covering almost everything, was moss – thick wads of it on the upper sides of branches, drapes of it on the lower, long wisps of it hanging from twigs. A whole plant community existed in this moss wrapping of the forest. These epiphytes were species of *Agapetes*, *Vaccinium* and *Smilax* and the little *Pleione maculata*, whose white flowers occasionally studded the dark green moss.

The only plant which escaped this covering was one *Rhododendron* species, (CH 418). We called it 'Old Baldy' on account of its great trunk of pinky-brown bark, which gave the moss no foothold and left it looking rather naked in the forest. At first we thought it was a relative of *R. neriiflorum* although a tree up to 14m/45ft in height. The waxy red flowers were nearly over, in trusses of 10-15, and the growth buds were already well advanced. On showing the herbarium specimen to Davidian, he said we were way out in our identification and called it *R. hylaeum* aff. in the Thomsonii series. Later Dr David Chamberlain described it as a new species, *R. subansiriense*, related to *R. hylaeum*, *R. hookeri* and his newly described *R. faucium*. We soon realised that the plentiful *R. subansiriense*, which occurred from 2,450–2,800m/8,000–9,500ft, was the red haze we had seen from the circuit house in Ziro. This species has grown well in milder gardens in Britain but, like *R. grande*, its early growth has made it very vulnerable to spring frosts and hence not very free-flowering. Another rhododendron here we named *R. arizelum* was later changed to the related *R. falconeri* subsp. *eximium* (C&H 427). This plant has the typical persistent russet-brown indumentum on the leaf upper surface and fine rose-pink flowers that unfortunately fade out. It is a grand foliage plant.

There were a number of other interesting trees and shrubs deep within the forest. *Daphne bholua* made a small evergreen tree to 7.5m/25ft with white sweetly scented flowers stained reddish-purple. A smaller evergreen daphne was *D. sureil* with pure white flowers. *Mahonia calamicaulis* was a small species growing to 90cm/3ft with typical yellow flowers. *Clethra delavayi* (CH 453) was just coming into leaf. This collection has survived at Glendoick all these years, though it has been cut to the ground once or twice. But by far the most surreal figure in the whole community of the rainforest was a tiny-leaved holly, *Ilex nothofagifolia* (CH 424). This scarcely reached the canopy above so had to live its life in the gloom. To catch the light, its branches were spread out in horizontal fans and from these layers of foliage the moss hung as always in drapes. The tiny red berries proved to be rare. This species was first discovered by Reginald Farrer and my father Euan Cox in upper Burma in 1919 and we were the first to introduce it as two seedlings forty-six years later. We were lucky in that these two proved to be a male and a female and the fruit is quite freely produced at Baravalla, where this most attractive plant flourishes. It has proved to be too tender for Glendoick. We also found this species again in Yunnan near the Burmese frontier in 1997, and again east of the Salween in 2000, both times in small quantities, and yet again in Arunachal in 2002 at a higher elevation, so seedlings from there might turn out to be hardier.

As might be expected, herbaceous plants were scarce in the dark rainforest. We did, however, see two species of primula, one the charming little pink-flowered *P. listeri* of section Obconicolisteri, the other the well-known *P. gracilipes* of section Petiolares.

From this camp we made several excursions along the ridge and down into the rainforest that clothed its flanks. The crest itself was about 10km/6 miles long and shaped something like a tent with two small peaks at either end, the one just above our camp being 2,800m/9,500ft and the other at the far end 2,950m/9,750ft. It was cold and dismally wet up on the ridge and, although the rain was not continuous, the mist was – indeed the shrouding broke only twice for intervals of a few minutes during all the time we were up there. The spine of the ridge was often only about 90cm/3ft wide but the combination of the mist and the forest canopy prevented any feeling of vertigo from our precarious little gangway perched up in the clouds. The curious feeling of being in a private world was broken only when the mist suddenly parted, revealing a breathtaking panorama. To the north were the seemingly endless folds of the Himalaya, looking as if they had been cut from varying shades of blue cardboard. To the south the mountain ran away in an almost unbroken slope to the plains of Assam, sunlit 2,400m/8,000ft below us. We could see the twisted ribbon of the Brahmaputra and even the Subansiri running out to join it. It was only minutes before the mist hemmed us in again.

The very tips of the two peaks had been deliberately cleared of forest, presumably for some strategic purpose. On the first peak we found two more rhododendrons, *R. leptocarpum* (CH 420), which has small yellow flowers on long pedicels. Here this commonly

Rhododendron falconeri *subsp.* eximium *(C&H 427). This was growing right on the top of the ridge and grew into huge flat-topped specimens.*

Rhododendron santapaui (CH 459) at Glendoick. This most attractive
member of subsection Pseudovireya was one of the three new
rhododendron species that we discovered in 1965. It hung from the trunks
of huge broad-leaved trees.

epiphytic species was forced to grow terrestrially. The second
species was R. neriiflorum subsp. phaedropum (CH 422), which has
grown vigorously at Baravalla, where it produces abundant red
flowers in loose trusses. In contrast to R. subansiriense, this plant
grows late in the season. In between the two peaks R. maddenii
subsp. maddenii (CH 438) was fairly common but, of course, far
from being in flower. Only a few were epiphytic and most of those
growing terrestrially sprawled along the ground with erect young
shoots and a tremendous variety of leaf forms. This introduction
did not prove to be hardy at Glendoick or even Baravalla.

Other interesting plants on the peaks were Leucothoe
griffithiana, an evergreen ericaceous shrub with arching
branches, Osmanthus suavis with sweetly scented small white
flowers, Buddleja limitanea, 30cm to 1.8m/1 to 6ft with arching
growth, Vaccinium retusum with attractive rich pink flower
buds and Hypericum hookerianum (CH 439), which has proved
quite hardy. Looming out of the clouds were trees of Magnolia
campbellii, with its typical great white flowers looking like
white birds perched on the branches.

During our trek on the south-east ridge we had collected 116
herbarium specimens, all in duplicate for the RBGK and the
RBGE, plus those of woody plants for the National Arboretum,
Washington DC, USA. The continual extreme dampness made
the drying of some 250 or more specimens extremely difficult,
with no means other than hanging the paper on strings near a
fire, with drips and rain often making the paper wetter than
when first hung up. The resultant dried specimens often left
much to be desired and, in extreme cases, like those of
Rhododendron falconeri subsp. eximium, they often completely fell
to bits, covered in mould. Making, noting and looking after
herbarium specimens is a lot of work and we were often still busy
on them long after everyone else had gone to bed.

Another hazard of damp, subtropical conditions was various
crawling or flying nasties. The most obvious were leeches, which are
always at their worst after rain. These occurred in various sorts.

Water leeches attack anyone who has to enter static water, such as
the Apa Tanis planting their rice. Another kind waits on the ends
of blades of grass and other herbs for some animal to brush past,
while a third, the large striped tiger leech, waggles back and forth
on the leaf tips of shrubs and small trees, ready to attach itself to
larger animals like cattle and humans. Leeches can squeeze through
tiny apertures like the lace holes on boots. Fire or salt are death to
them – the way they shrivel up after putting salt or a cigarette on
them is amazing. We soaked our socks in salt which went some way
towards keeping off the grass type of leech. Filled with blood, they
blow up to several times their original size and the anticoagulant
they inject into the incision induces extra blood to flow around the
wound. Being careful, like constantly watching all of one's body and
not being a leader on a leech-infested path, can keep attacks to a
minimum. We all had some, mostly on our legs. A second, perhaps
worse, pest was the blood blister, dim-dam or dam-dim fly. As with
leeches, one does not feel the bite and the actual fly is small and
innocent-looking. We all had several bites which form little blisters
and itch for weeks. A third nasty, and perhaps the worst, were ticks,
here the size of a new penny. Patricia had her vest pinned to her
back by one and I had one on my big toe. These big ones are painful,
devils to extract, can carry diseases and also itch for a long time
afterwards. Lastly, the case of one man's bread being another man's
poison. At the top camp there were quantities of tiny frogs hopping
about, often in and out of our tents. Patricia and I not only tolerated
them but enjoyed having them around; not so Peter, who almost
had hysterics when one ventured into his tent!

Another visitor to Peter's tent was Mr Mittra, who crawled
in one evening and asked to see his camera. 'Very powerful
camera,' he said, turning it over in his hands. Peter protested,
saying it was a fairly ordinary 35mm model. 'Very powerful lens,'
said Mr Mittra and again Peter protested, but Mr Mittra fixed
him with a beady glare. 'Does it focus to infinity?' he asked
triumphantly. There was no answer to this and Peter's film was
confiscated and developed locally.

The whole of the south-east ridge is uninhabited and covered
in virgin forest apart from the tops of the two peaks. The paths are
used for hunting deer, which we heard barking, and other animals.
By the time we had made thorough collections on and below the
ridge it was getting on in April. The porters were getting restive
and they had little protection against the cold and wet. Patricia
had a regular flow of requests for aspirins and 'something to take
the cold away'. We had assembled quite a nursery of seedling
plants, bedded down in the hollow of an old tree and 21 April was
spent packing them into baskets. We left the next morning,
shedding layers of clothes while it grew appreciably warmer as we
dropped altitude. When we reached the boggy area of our first
camp, some time was spent exploring the surrounding forest.

In addition to finding three mature plants of what was later
named R. coxianum (CH 475), Peter spotted a curious epiphytic

shrub, dangling from the trunk of a forest tree. It had small leathery leaves and capsules that dehisced right back. At first we did not recognise the genus but, after examining the capsules exuding seeds with long tails at each end, we realised that it must be a member of the then Vaccinioides series of Rhododendron, now subgenus Vireya, section Pseudovireya. One of two small collected plants flowered before long and we were delighted to find that it was a new species. After consulting with our BSI colleagues, we decided to name it after the director of the BSI, Dr Father Santapau as *R. santapaui* (CH 459). This has become quite widely distributed in cultivation, having reached Australia from the first seed set in cultivation. It has little waxy white, freely-produced flowers in trusses of one to four, often flowering in the autumn as well as spring. The red-brown stamens make a pretty centre.

It would be an omission not to mention the many lush broad-leaved evergreens that made up much of the forest just above the level of the Apa Tani valley. To the uninitiated, many of these trees and shrubs look similar but not only do they mostly belong to different genera but also different plant families. On fallen tree-trunks covered in moss were seedlings *en masse* showing us how natural regeneration of the forest takes place.

Shortly after arriving back at Ziro our worst fears were confirmed. We received a telegram informing us that we were to be restricted to the area we had just visited. As a great concession, they said that we could stay and collect on the south-east ridge for an extra period to 15 June. Mr Gee had told us that failing the west ridge, we should be able to get permission to go to the Se La, which is a high pass with a road crossing it in the north-west of the Kameng division, not far from the Bhutanese and Tibetan frontiers. Although there is no doubt that another trip up the south-east ridge by a different path might have been rewarding, we decided to cut our losses and leave for Shillong as soon as possible. We were now left with far too much food, which we divided up for Mr Gee and the BSI, who were reluctant to accept it. It would have been fruitless to attempt to give any to the Apa Tanis as it would have been completely unfamiliar to them.

We had much packing up to do but there were frequent interruptions as new (to us) people kept turning up. The plants were packed into a wooden box in two layers with polythene between each layer. Two boards were nailed to the top edges with sacking in between. There was a tall weedy-looking forest officer who was in charge of all the planting around the valley. He had little of interest to say and had no intention of taking any advice from us. In contrast, there was a charming and interesting fisheries expert, Mr Malik, who claimed to have been responsible for the very successful introductions of trout to the rivers of Kashmir and Bhutan. He said that there were trout of up to 6.8kg/15lb in Bhutan with no one to catch them. The NEFA authorities called him in here to advise on stocking the Subansiri. We visited Mr Shukla's museum where we saw beautifully made cane baskets and hats and some good weaving, the most colourful coming from the Lohit and Manipur.

Mr Mittra took us to see Dutta village and into two houses which were firmly built with bamboo on stilts with platforms front and back. Several families live in one house. A fire for cooking is in the middle of the bamboo floor and we could not understand why the whole house did not go up in flames. It was a fair way in the dark to the far end where we could just see the light coming in the other door. We groped our way while fleas attacked us in droves as we went.

We had our first meeting with the PO, a large dignified Sikh full of airs and graces but impossible to talk to. He did appear to be sorry and apologetic about our refused permission but we came to the conclusion that he had no say in the matter anyway. One evening we asked Sastry and Katachi to eat with us and persuaded the former to eat a little chicken for the first time. We played the card game O-Hell which we had taught our friends, and Sastry had quickly become a dab hand at, but I just managed to beat him.

On our last night we had an invitation from the PO for 'Pot Luck' as he called it. We frantically attempted to clean our clothes, which proved to be pointless as we got dust through everything on our journey up to the valley. All the local dignitaries plus their wives turned up, the women dressed in beautiful saris lining one end of the room while the men congregated at the other. Our entertainment started with a charming Hill Miri dance with young girls in a half circle and one in the middle singing, with the others joining in the chorus. After a while we were asked to join in. This was followed by two films showing various ceremonies in the major centres of NEFA. The masks and scarves of the Kameng division were extremely colourful and they fairly threw themselves around. A few local chiefs came in, including one with eight wives. One Miri had a hat with a hornbill bill and feathers pointing backwards and a hairy front to his topknot. We were the guests of honour so had the embarrassing task of helping ourselves first at what proved to be a good meal.

Return to Shillong

The only vehicles we could get were two rickety old weapon carriers for ourselves and the BSI. Progress was slow due to half an hour's wait to get through the first gate, and delays from road works, plus our vehicle being hard to start when overheated and having a wheel wobble. Ten Apa Tanis attached themselves to various parts of the exterior for a lift down to Kimin. The result was a very slow journey which would almost have been quicker to walk. We noticed many new plants including bauhinias in flower and could have made a hundred more herbarium specimens if time had permitted. Near to Kimin we noticed memorial stones to the road builders inscribed 'Killed by wild tusker', 'Pushed over precipice' and so on.

Mawsmai Falls, near Cherrapungi. I was lucky to get this shot as within seconds the view was blotted out by clouds.

We noticed that our Apa Tani driver and the vehicle owner wore European-type clothes as did most of our passengers. There is no doubt that contact with the outside world is inevitable and will eventually lead to all, except possibly the most remote villagers, dropping their tribal dress. Female Apa Tanis traditionally wear nose plugs (very ugly to our eyes) and these get enlarged as children get older. This custom is likely to disappear gradually.

We missed the train from North Lakhimpur to Gauhati, so had to fly in a Dakota with stops at Jorhat and Tezpur. We arrived at Evergreen Cottage by taxi to find Mr Gee still away in Bhutan and Darjeeling, so had to stay in the Pinewood Hotel. On our return to Shillong there was no news of our permit to visit the Se La. The following day we took our plants up to Evergreen Cottage to bed them out under a tree and found Mr Gee back and busy planting his newly collected plants. We had an embarrassing time wondering whether he was going to ask us to stay again or not, but eventually he said that he had visitors for the next four days but we could stay after that.

We had a meal in the hotel, including some fish that Peter and I ate. Soon after getting to bed, I started to shiver violently and all hell let loose at both ends. My temperature was 40°C/104°F. The morning revealed that Peter had the same problem, but not as severely. A Dr Deb diagnosed a form of enteritis and put us onto Chlorostrep, a powerful new drug acquired in Calcutta. In the meantime, Patricia and Thapa went off to buy baskets to contain our plants for the journey home. Thapa wrapped the plants in little balls of moss tied around with darning wool. Peter recovered rapidly but I tried to get up and had to rush back to bed with my head swimming. Much of the time was spent playing O-Hell.

Feeling that the locals did not have the authority to issue a permit for the Se La, on 6 May Peter flew to New Delhi. Leonard Allinson of the British High Commission who had been so helpful before arranged for him to meet Mr Rasgotra, one of the three departmental heads at the Ministry of Interior. After going over the whole story Rasgotra said, pointing to the map, 'This is where you have been and this where you would like to go?' There was a pause, then 'Quite impossible, Mr Hutchison, and I am afraid that the answer to the Se La is also no.' Peter played his last card and on a letter of introduction to Mrs Vidayalakshmi Pandit (Prime Minister Nehru's sister) had arranged an appointment the next day. Sipping lime juice in her garden after pouring out the story again he could hear the rattle of Hindi as she telephoned Rasgotra. When she emerged her face told the story before she said quietly, 'I'm afraid not'. The next day we received a telegram from Peter 'Permission for Se La flatly refused. Am leaving India Thursday 13th. Nuts to everyone.'

On the 8th Patricia and I moved back to Evergreen Cottage with all our luggage. The mostly healthy-looking plants were rebedded in a shady place by some big bamboos in half-rotted pine needles. It was a glorious sunny day so all our pressing

We had forgotten to photograph Baxter's soup to advertise their product when camping earlier, so Patricia and I did a mockup camp near Mr Gee's house, Upper Shillong. Baxters of Fochabers had given us a fine supply of their soups.

From the right, our bearer, driver and a young friend near Phalut. Our bearer was very helpful and nice.

paper was put out to dry, as were some mouldy specimens that were left too long and some of the leaves crinkled. My film would not rewind and came out of its cassette in a not totally dark cupboard so was partly ruined. We also spent some time cleaning seed, especially those still within berries.

We went back to the *Rhododendron formosum* var. *inaequale* site and found a branch still in full flower. On 12 May we woke after the wettest night either of us could remember and great gusts of wind nearly blew the tin roof off the house. All buildings in Shillong had corrugated iron roofs owing to the area being earthquake prone and the noise of the rain on our roof was almost deafening. Several fruit trees in the garden had branches broken. The electricity went off and many trees came down in Shillong with four people killed. Mr Gee said it was the worst storm in the six years he had been there. At first it was reported that over 70 people were killed in what was then East Pakistan;

three days later the death toll had risen to 6,000-8,000.

On receiving Peter's telegram and after some debating, we decided to go to Sandak Phu, which is on the Singalila ridge near the Sikkim frontier north of Darjeeling. In the meantime we took a trip to Cherrapungi. On reaching the town the mist came down and the rain really did its stuff for a while, then we went off waterfall viewing, not easy as the mist kept coming and going. While Mr Gee was still getting his Leica out, I was lucky in getting two shots of the tremendous Mawsmai falls before the mist blotted everything out. We were lucky again in getting the Momloh falls with five other falls plunging down the escarpment. We had brief views of the plains below and achieved better views of the falls by walking down some steps well-made under the British Raj. These steps apparently go all the way down to the plain. The record rainfall here is due to the escarpment that drops straight down into Bangladesh (East Pakistan), which was

Our party near the Apa Tani valley. Back row left to right: Patricia Cox, Peter, Mr Mittra, myself, Mr S.K. Kataki and members of the Botanical Survey of India team and Apa Tani porters. Photo Mr A.R.K. Sastry.

only 13km/8 miles from where we stood. The monsoon blows the cloud up from the Bay of Bengal, hits the escarpment, rises, and then drops its load with a vengeance. Mr Gee told us that it is actually the nearby village of Mousanram that has the heaviest rainfall. We were told a story that when the army of the Raj were garrisoned at Cherrapungi, they got so fed up with the rain that they all queued up at the rain-gauge before going to bed at night. The rainfall that year increased from 1,000 to 1,500cm/400 to 600in and thereafter they were moved to Shillong! We collected some herbarium specimens and noticed a great variety of trees on the escarpment where the slope was not too steep. Above the escarpment there are only remnants of elfin forest and grass, the rainfall being too heavy (resulting in severe soil leaching) for large trees to grow.

We suffered the usual trouble of no one being in when we attempted to get a permit for Sandak Phu. Eventually we decided to go back to Calcutta for a permit. We did a last collection of orchids, now easy as we could pick them off fallen trees. I had my hair cut and could not stop them taking too much off. The barbers had an extraordinary way of massaging the back of the head by slapping it hard. We went across the road with Thapa to do a mock-up scene for Baxters for advertising their soup, something we had forgotten to do earlier. While packing everything up, we watched a hatching of winged termites and birds gobbling them up as soon as they emerged. We looked at our now processed photographs. Mr Gee said that

most were overexposed, but did say that one was quite good! As it was our last night with Mr Gee, we were given whisky, then another, and the poor local cherry brandy after dinner.

Thapa was given careful instructions how to meet us in Darjeeling before we left Shillong. The day we left we were up at 4.50 and arrived at Gauhati at 9 a.m. Our heavy boxes were left at James Warren's godown until our return. Our forward arrangements in Calcutta were amazingly easy, permit for Sandak Phu and all, plus the journey home for us and our plants. The flight to Siliguri was on another Dakota with no lining, folding seats and no pressurisation. Tea was served from an urn on the floor. We had a shared taxi to Darjeeling. The road crossed and re-crossed the railway umpteen times and we passed no less than ten trains on the way. We had drizzle and mist most of the way and the windscreen wiper was operated by the driver putting his hand out and round on to the windscreen! We were lucky to get into Mrs Oakly's New Elgin Hotel as our fellow passengers were refused. There was no sign of Thapa.

Mrs Oakly, who still spoke with a broad Yorkshire accent, was most helpful in getting us organised and before long we had a Landrover and driver, a new bearer (an excellent fellow called Larma), food, etc. and we were off just after 11 a.m. We were warned that if a government official or minister wanted the dak bungalow at Sandak Phu, we would have to vacate it, but the district commissioner said with a twinkle in his eye that no official would dream of going there.

Kanchenjunga from Sandak Phu, West Bengal, early morning after a stormy night.

Sandak Phu

The first part of the road was good and we soon passed *Rhododendron dalhousiae*, its large creamy yellow flowers hanging over the road just on the outskirts of the town. There were very fine white-flowered coelogynes on the trees and rocks all around Darjeeling up to 2,700m/9,000ft. We passed some of the famous Darjeeling tea gardens on steep slopes, some terraced. Much of the country had been partially cleared of trees, giving many of those remaining a battered weather-beaten appearance. *R. grande* (long past flowering) occurred at about 2,600m/8,500ft, followed by *R. falconeri* (CH 584) at 2,700m/9,000ft. The form there was what we would call the old introduction with somewhat pendulous flowers. A seedling from here planted at Baravalla, started to flower only in 1998. *R. arboreum*, not surprisingly, was mostly over and largely pink-flowered, also nearly over was *R. cinnabarinum* Roylei Group (CH 579). Two outstanding plants from seed collected here have been flowering for many years at Baravalla. A few *R. lindleyi*, out of reach along

the roadside, were also mostly past flowering. We stopped at a fine *Enkianthus deflexus* (CH 578) from which we got only one seedling, which is also growing at Baravalla.

We were enveloped in chilling mist nearly all the way up so views were non-existent. The road became rougher and rougher and went up and down for a while before eventually climbing up to Sandak Phu at 3,600m/11,800ft. By the time we got back, the almost-new Landrover had broken springs. We had to stop at two check posts to show our permits but, having given two policemen a lift, they helped us on our way. Through the mist we made out some inferior *R. wallichii* and on the meadow surrounding the bungalow were masses of the blue and white flowered *Anemone obtusiloba*. We had a large meal and probably went to bed too quickly, resulting in little sleep. An open fire was prepared for us by Larma, while the useless chokadar in charge of the bungalow did nothing. A great storm arose in the night with howling wind, thunder and battering

Rhododendron falconeri *below Sandak Phu. We collected seedlings growing in the subsoil at the edge of the road.*

rain on the corrugated iron roof. At times the lightning dazzled us. I had great hopes that this would clear for a fine morning.

Shouts of 'Everest in view' from Larma had us up at 4.30. The panorama of the Himalaya was breathtaking. We gasped at the pure white snow with blue light reflecting on it. We could see the mountains all the way from the Chomlang (7,450m/24,500ft) in the north-west, then Mt Everest to the north-east to Pandim, east of Kanchenjunga. From this distance (322km/200 miles), Mt Everest did not look much of a peak but the nearer Kanchenjunga was most impressive. The snow line could have been drawn with a ruler. The sun started shining on the Everest end and then moved to Kanchenjunga while Everest became hazy. I took nearly a roll of film.

After a large breakfast, we drove off to the north in the direction of Phalut. There was an occasional white-flowered *Rhododendron wallichii* amongst the mauve. We found a wonderful bed of primulas in full flower, a few of which we attempted to dig up for Mr Gee and were surprised by the horrible smell off the roots. This is a diagnostic feature for *P. calderiana*. This Petiolares species had a reddish-violet flower with a yellowish-green eye. The calyx, pedicel and scapes were partially covered in farina. A grove of rhododendrons contained *R. arboreum*, here pink and red, *R. wallichii*, *R. cinnabarinum* (these turned out to be Blandfordiiflorum Group) and our first *R. hodgsonii* (CH 581), followed by *R. barbatum* (CH 580). We now have substantial plants of the last from this collection both at Glendoick and Baravalla, but they are not equal in merit to some previous introductions. After a drop in elevation, we found *R. falconeri* once more, often mixed with *R. hodgsonii*, with a whole group of natural hybrids between them, ranging all the way from one species to the other. The flowers were often decidedly muddy in colour. The flower colour of *R. hodgsonii*

varied from deep cherry red to a good pink.

The landscape gradually became bleaker with dying *Abies spectabilis* and rhododendrons. The whole area was heavily grazed, mostly by numerous horses and their foals. When the mist started to roll in, everything became gaunt and depressing, so 10km/6 miles short of Phalut we turned back to Sandak Phu, which disappointed our police passengers who were hoping for a lift the whole way. When it was getting dark, we attempted to photograph the mountains but mist blotted most of them out.

Neither of us felt good in the morning. I had a headache, probably due to altitude sickness. We met some European hikers and one said that the day before he had been able to see, with binoculars, Indian climbers on Mt Everest; very unlikely, we thought. Various stops on the way back to Darjeeling included collecting some *Rhododendron falconeri* seedlings growing in bare roadside soil which no doubt would have been

Rhododendron wallichii at Sandak Phu. This species takes the place of R. campanulatum *from extreme east Nepal to Arunachal Pradesh.*

removed during road maintenance. One plant of the yellow-flowered *R. triflorum* was our last rhododendron.

We drove through thick and thin mist, the thickest at Ghoom. At Siliguri railway station, an Indian of slight build carried all our luggage, which included a tin trunk, suitcase and rucksack all on his head and the plants in one hand; heaven knows how he managed it all. The heat, smelly bodies lying all over the platform plus quantities of flies made waiting for the late train most unpleasant. In the end, we nearly got on the wrong train. We had a most luxurious air-conditioned sleeping compartment with a private bathroom attached. Just as we were attempting to settle in, a succession of staff came in: a floor cleaner, a lavatory cleaner, an insecticide dispeller, a ticket collector, a man asking about meals and finally, as we were settling down for the night, a man with lumpy pillows and another to turn off the tap we had left on when nothing was coming out! Before it got dark, I took some photographs of the Bhutanese mountains rising straight out of the plain to around 3,000m/10,000ft. They looked most inviting.

We waited ages for someone else to share a taxi for our return to Shillong. Mr Gee had heard nothing about his proposed trips to the Se La and to Manipur. Thapa had turned up and made excuses about the train being late, the taxi being too expensive. Mr Gee had thought of taking him on but sent him away with a flea in his ear. On packing up the plants, we found that Thapa had tied some of them in bunches of twos and threes so we had to retie them. However, they had made their first growth flush and were looking good.

As usual, we had great problems with officials, this time in getting a transit permit for the plants; the head man was away, his underling would not sign and eventually we had to go to the Forestry department and then back to the NEFA department. Oh, the joys of Indian bureaucracy! Another permit had to be had from the District Council but they were amazingly efficient. Dr Father Santapau, Dr Rao and Katachi all turned up for tea and we ate Marmite sandwiches. We discussed the possibility of them sending us seeds but nothing ever came of it. They virtually never answered any letters.

Before leaving Shillong in the morning, the plants had their final packing. All the little baskets had polythene tied round the outside around the root areas and the baskets were wired together. With hindsight, the one mistake that we made was not tying every plant to the baskets but, of course, this would have taken ages. After an uncomfortable and expensive night in Gauhati we were off, but I nearly missed the bus when photographing some flowering trees.

Primula calderiana near Sandak Phu.

Pleione hookeriana, *epiphytic in* Abies spectabilis, *Sandak Phu.*

We found Calcutta extremely hot and sticky, with 38°C/100°F temperature and 100% humidity. Sweat poured off us and filled our shoes! At the airport the plants were stored in air-conditioning but they had obviously been taken apart and searched. They were now tied up in sacking and sealed so we had no chance of looking at them again.

Engine trouble bothered us all the way to Rome. We circled Istanbul for over half an hour, then the pilot announced that it was too cloudy to land and it would take one hour to clear, adding that we did not have enough fuel to circle for that long so we would carry on to Athens which would take 55 minutes! Most passengers must either have been asleep or were too dense to work out the significance of the pilot's statement as no obvious panic ensued. Needless to say we made Athens all right, although the landing was the roughest we have ever experienced! We arrived in London 5½ hours late, the journey from Calcutta having taken 19 hours. We decided that we would avoid Qantas in future.

The RBGK had arranged to take all the plants and inspect them to avoid any difficulties with customs and quarantine. Eventually I had to stay in London over the weekend and until Monday evening as there was no mycologist available until Monday. After all the trouble and care we had taken with the plants, I was foolish enough to trust a London taxi driver to have the baskets in the open luggage space in the front. Going round a corner too fast in Hyde Park, the baskets shot out and burst open, resulting in most of the plants being scattered over the road. By pure luck, no vehicle came past on the left at that moment, so I was able to rescue all the plants.

The plants, in fact, travelled surprisingly well with very few eventual casualties. But, as we had feared, many proved to be too tender and/or too early into growth to make good garden plants in Britain. Soon after arriving home, we took the herbarium specimens to Davidian in the RBGE. He soon picked out two new species, subsequently named *R. coxianum* and *R. santapaui* but he would not commit himself on 'Old Baldy'.

On arriving home my father was in quite a state. He said that he had sent a telegram to us to come straight home when the conflict between India and Pakistan had blown up in early May. It was just as well that we never received that telegram as there was nothing in it to say why we should go home and it would have placed us in a terrible dilemma. Obviously Cox senior got into a panic when he heard about the war on the news and sent the telegram without really thinking.

As we had failed to collect anything like the number of seeds we had originally anticipated and there was no question of attempting or being given permission to go back in the autumn, we reckoned that we had let our subscribers down. So after some deliberation, we decided that we had to return all the moneys subscribed. Almost without exception, they all returned our cheques, which was extremely kind.

Despite our great disappointments, it had been a marvellous adventure and we had been very fortunate to be allowed into a part of the world where very few non-Indians had been. We had discovered and introduced three new Rhododendron species and *Agapetes smithiana* var. *major* from botanically virgin territory

Chapter 3

CHINA SAYS YES AFTER ELEVEN YEARS:

SBEC 1981

Peter Hutchison

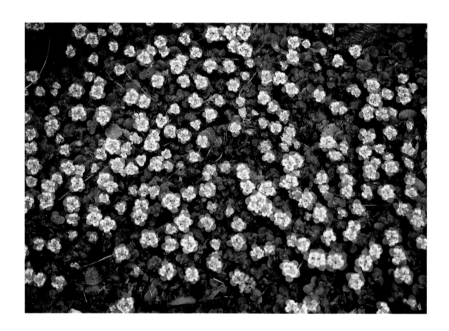

In the late 1970s the mounting of a collecting trip to western China, that storehouse of wonderful plants, was an enticing prospect but a very remote one. China was still in the iron grip of the Maoist regime and the Red Guards rampaged across the country. For a number of years approaches were made to the authorities, sometimes with a negative reply, often with none at all. Then in 1980 curious things started to happen, which led to the first Sino British Expedition to China (SBEC). A Swiss individual approached us saying that he heard we were going to be allowed a collecting trip and could he come too. We had still heard nothing direct. Then the Royal Society, that august body charged with scientific interchange, wrote to us saying they understood we were going to be allowed a joint field trip, which was something of a first, and asking (politely) who we were.

We started to gather a team of knowledgeable plant people. Apart from Peter and me, it included Dr David Chamberlain, rhododendron taxonomist of the RBGE, Roy Lancaster, formerly curator of Hillier's Arboretum and now a freelance plantsman, Bob Mitchell, formerly curator of St Andrews Botanic Garden, and Tony Schilling, then assistant curator at Kew's Wakehurst Place.[1]

Since 1981 much of China has gradually opened up to visitors but we were the first field expedition allowed into Yunnan since the Communists took over, although there had been an excursion by Americans in Hubei in autumn 1980. The Chinese had been starved of outside contact and the memory of the Cultural Revolution was all too recent for them, although the full horrors of it were not yet understood by the outside world. Our future colleagues tended to react with a nervous laugh when asked about it. By the time of our 1997 visit, sixteen years later, the whole of Yunnan had been opened, modern hotels had sprung up in every major city and much of the novelty of visiting China had worn off. But in 1981 it was all new and the trip attracted much interest, not just from the plant world.

On the whole we found the Chinese easier to deal with than the Indians and more prepared to take decisions. If they

Above: The ridge above Camp Two at Shangchang on the west flank of the Cangshan: the hillside on the dry sunny side of the ridge is bare, while the moister north-facing slope is covered in vegetation.

Above left: One of our most valuable introductions and now well established in cultivation is this super golden saxifrage Chrysosplenium davidianum which flourishes in a damp shady site. It makes our native species look exceedingly dull.

Right: SBEC Expedition group. Back row left to right: Peter, Gaby Lock, David Chamberlain, unknown; centre: myself, He Qungan (driver), Tien-lu Ming, Tao Deding, Guan Kaiyun (interpreter); front row: Lu Zhenwei, Roy Lancaster, Guo-mei Feng (Chinese leader), Bob Mitchell, Mrs Fang Rhizen.

1. Bob Mitchell took over the role of leader of the British party and the rest of us owe Bob a great deal of gratitude for the enormous amount of work he put into getting the expedition off the ground at a time of difficult personal circumstances. Being the first joint Sino-British expedition of this kind made the organisation on both sides all the more onerous. We also have to thank the trusts, societies and individuals who helped us for their financial and other support. They were too numerous to list but particular mention must be made of Sir John Keswick, whose contacts and knowledge of China were invaluable.

encouraged you to think things were possible, they usually came off in the end, though there were exceptions. Thus when we started to get the go ahead in January 1980, they did not let us down. Much work went on behind the scenes with the Royal Society and Academia Sinica (the Chinese Academy of Sciences). Professor Wu Cheng-yih of the Kunming Institute of Botany was in charge of organising everything from the Chinese side. We gave the Chinese ideas of what areas we were interested in and the importance of getting to high elevations for hardy plants. The Chinese suggested the Cangshan mountains (formerly Tali range or Tsangshan mountains) as our objective. While we might have preferred somewhere less well explored in the past, we knew this to be very rich in good plants, especially rhododendrons which were the chief interest of David Chamberlain and Peter. Anyway, they gave us no choice.

Hong Kong: Rhododendrons in favour at Government House

At last, after over four years of negotiation, we left Britain for Hong Kong on 20 April 1981. Sadly, Tony Schilling had to call off as he had just been operated on for peritonitis. Tired after a long although comfortable journey with Cathay Pacific, we piled into two taxis and headed for the YMCA but on our arrival found it was the wrong one. So off we went in two more taxis, having bundled each others kit into the boots. At our right destination, we sorted our luggage and to his horror Peter found that his small rucksack was missing. Among lesser items, he lost two cameras, lenses, all his notes, some travellers' cheques and two books which were to be gifts for the Kunming Botanical Institute. After visits to the police, the first YMCA and an advertisement in the paper, nothing more was heard of it. Shopping for replacements

was none too easy and he had to make do with a school haversack instead of the lost small rucksack, while one new camera had to suffice for the two lost. But he was determined to forget about this mishap and enjoy the expedition.

I went with Peter on this unhappy tour around Hong Kong but had to intervene between him and a grizzled police sergeant. Peter was now rather sensitive about losing things and insisted that a well-chewed Biro he had been given for form-filling was his property while the policeman, all too familiar with people who nicked small things, got angry and seemed close to laying a charge of felony. A couple of virginal Biros from my own supply restored international relations.

We were fortunate in having several valuable contacts in Hong Kong. On the following day embossed invitations arrived from Government House and shortly after two enormous black limousines with gold crowns back and front drew up outside our modest YM. Even the seats had starched white covers to match the drivers' uniforms and we put on our best anoraks and headed for lunch with the Governor, Sir Murray Maclehose, and his wife. Lady Maclehose, rather improbably known as Squeak, was a keen plant enthusiast with a wide knowledge of the Hong Kong flora and took most of our party on a tour of Victoria Peak. When we mentioned that we would like to see the six species of *Rhododendron* native to Hong Kong in their wild habitats, she introduced us to the government botanist, Mr Lau, and this was very kindly laid on for us. The rarest species, *R. championae*, is on Victoria Peak on Hong Kong Island and we had been warned that there was only a single plant left. Sure enough, there it was, alongside one of the main tracks near the summit. This species belongs to subsection Choniastrum and is easily identified as the only species in the subsection covered in bristles. The pale pink

Terraced and flooded paddy fields being prepared for the hand-planting of rice seedlings.

Myself on Ma on Shan or the Hunchbacks, New Territories, Hong Kong. There are plants of Rhododendron simiarum *both in front and behind me. This heat-resistant species is exceptionally slow-growing in Scotland and is not surprisingly unsuitable for our climate.*

to white flowers are slightly fragrant. It has just succeeded out of doors in a few Cornish gardens. Growing with *R. championae* were *R. farreri*, a rather dull azalea of section Brachycalyx which flowers around mid-winter, and the ubiquitous azalea, *R. simsii*.

Our second visit was to Ma on Shan, known as the Hunchbacks, in the New Territories, where *R. farreri* and *R. simsii* also grew, here on burnt, rocky hillsides. Plants of the former species showed juvenile foliage with leaves up the stems, although the adult semi-evergreen leaves are terminal and in threes. The latter species was covered in typical large red flowers. The main object of this excursion was to see *R. simiarum*, which grew near the top of a lush gully facing north-east at 500m/1,500ft in surprisingly cold, misty conditions where it made compact bushes of 90 to 180cm/3 to 6ft. This member of subsection Argyrophylla is widely distributed in southern China and surprisingly it has turned out to be reasonably hardy at Glendoick, although incredibly slow-growing and hard to please. It has proved to be a good parent for producing heat-resistant hybrids for places like California and Australia. The thick, rigid, broad leaves are covered with a compacted indumentum on the underside and the flowers are white to a light rose, usually spotted. A fifth rhododendron grew nearby, *R. hongkongense*, a close relative of *R. ovatum* in section Azaleastrum. The masses of white flowers spotted violet may be seen in March/April in the

RBGE Vireya House where the young shoots are often an attractive purple colour. At the time of our visit, the leaves had turned a normal green and the flowers were long since over.

To see the last Hong Kong rhododendron, we had to travel some distance to Wu Kan Tang in the north-eastern part of the New Territories. At a little over 100m/338ft in very lush forest grew *R. westlandii* (now a synonym of *R. moulmainense*). This had brilliant pinkish red young growth which made brightly coloured patches in the lush undergrowth not far from the sea.

Our five-day stay in Hong Kong was not all plant hunting, however, and we were well entertained at both Government houses on Hong Kong Island and the New Territories. Charles Clapperton, who had acted as our agent in the area, was fortunately in charge of Jardine's hospitality junk and took us on a tour of the harbour with its spectacular skyline, followed by a seafood dinner on one of the islands.

At the station where we caught the train to Guangzhou (Canton) there was a seething scrum through which we followed what looked like a towering parcel on the point of disintegrating. It was David Chamberlain, an old China hand, invisible below a rucksack topped by tent, boots, mugs, bedroll and assorted kit. It was a relief when the train trundled into the countryside with our first sight of the timeless pattern of paddy fields and scattered knolls with mop-topped *Pinus massoniana*, stripped of its lower branches.

A very fine form of Lyonia ovalifolia *at* Hua hong dong. *This species is extremely widespread and variable, most forms being too tender for much of the UK.*

Kunming: Temples and Excursions

We flew to Kunming, Yunnan, where we had a tremendous welcome from our Chinese hosts, including Professor Wu, a distinguished member of the Academia Sinica, and Professor Feng Guomei, who had been sent to the fields for re-education during the Cultural Revolution but now carried an air of authority. He was to come with us as joint leader with Bob.[2] Guan Kaiyun, then known to us as Clyde, was our interpreter and the taxonomists who were to accompany us were Mr Ming Tianlu, the expert on *Rhododendron* subgenus *Hymenanthes*, and Mrs Fang Rizhen, the expert on subgenus *Rhododendron* and *Ericaceae* in general. We were given an enormous feast of about thirty courses, consumed over several hours, and we probably ate more than we have ever eaten in our lives, before or since. Titbits out of each dish were put in our bowls and had to be eaten or surreptitiously dropped on the floor! Some were delicious but others, like a helping of deer tendons, were difficult. Our lack of expertise with chopsticks forced us to eat more slowly than we might have done later on in the trip, which was probably just as well.

We spent four days in Kunming, staying in a government guesthouse, then one of the few places permitted to foreigners. One day was spent among the dusty shelves of the herbarium but on the other three our colleagues took us on excursions. A temple was often the destination; there are many round Kunming, but at least on one occasion it was never reached due to our enthusiasm for stopping for plants. On a hillside just behind Kunming we found our first rhododendron in the diminutive and widespread evergreen azalea, *R. microphyton*, very variable in flower colour from pale pink to deep magenta-purple.

It was our first taste of the western Chinese flora which, in many places, is regularly hacked down for firewood and fodder, and often grazed as well. But the flora was strikingly rich in spite of this drastic regime and many woody species managed to flower and fruit. One does not know, of course, how many casualties there have been on the way. Perversely, it made our task easier – a mature canopy above our heads would have been much less easy to observe and collect – and on our first afternoon at Dao Shao around 2,300m/7,500ft we scrambled among the scrub, delighted to find friends we had known only in cultivation and others we did not know at all. So this was the famous flora of western China, battered but full of promise.

The *Ericaceae* were numerous. *Pieris formosa* was too stunted to fruit or flower but we met for the first time *Craibiodendron yunnanense*, which has young foliage to rival it in shades of bronzy-pink to red. Unfortunately, it is of borderline hardiness. *Lyonia ovalifolia* was to be a regular companion at these altitudes and something of a chameleon plant, so variable according to aspect and degree of hacking. Peter found *Rhododendron*

Clematis chrysocoma comes from the foothills of the Cangshan and, as would be expected, is rather tender.

spinuliferum (SBEC K058)[3] and it and its relative *R. scabrifolium* var. *spiciferum* were common, the latter with some good deep pinks. We also found a pinkish-flowered plant which appeared to be a hybrid between these two taxa which Professor Feng immediately identified as *R.* x *duclouxii*; later we found another plant, quite different but obviously the same cross. The herbaria in both the Kunming Botanical Institute and the RBGE have many specimens of this hybrid. Our collection of *R. spinuliferum* from only 2,400m/8,000ft has proved hardy enough to survive at Glendoick on a sheltered wall but grows and flowers freely at Baravalla. The curious upright tubular flowers with protruding styles vary from deep pink to brick red. Other rhododendrons here were *R. decorum* (K063) and *R. siderophyllum* (K064). The latter is a close relative of *R. yunnanense* but usually comes from lower elevations and this number has proved to be tender.

There were many other interesting plants here. Plump and already fragrant buds were showing on *Michelia yunnanensis*, a neat small-leaved relative of the magnolias. Unlike many plants from this area, it is proving unexpectedly hardy in many British gardens. *Camellia saluenensis* had finished flowering and was into new growth. This is a parent of all the *C.* x *williamsii* hybrids. A pink leguminous shrub, *Campylotropis polygantha*, made a pretty combination with the white *Rosa longicuspis* and, scrambling

among *Rhododendron scabrifolium*, Roy found what he said was the true *Clematis chrysocoma*, those labelled so in cultivation being impostors. In a damp ravine I found two Gesneriads, a species of *Petrocosmea* with violet-blue flowers just appearing, and a plant with crinkled leaves pressed against the cliff face, probably a *Didissandra* species. But perhaps the two most striking plants were a rose, *Rosa gigantea*, a great sprawling bush of creamy flowers reminiscent of 'Frühlingsgold' and the other a dock. Billowing masses of the docken relative *Rumex hastatus* stained acres of the countryside with its rose-red fruiting stems.

We spent a day in Kunming looking at herbarium specimens and discussing itineraries, transport and supplies, which we later learned were causing problems in the aftermath of the Cultural Revolution. We asked whether they could provide botanical pressing paper. 'Toilet paper,' said the Professor firmly, then seeing our faces, 'Chinese toilet paper', adding with a grin, 'British toilet paper no good.'

2. We soon established good relations with out Chinese colleagues and Professor Feng took a genial tutorial role. Holding up a scrap of plant, he would say, 'What? What, what is . . . ?' and from the depths of a thicket would come a cry of 'Professor Lancaster [we had all become honorary professors for the trip], Professor Lancaster, new species!'

3. K numbers refer to those collected in the vicinity of Kunming to distinguish them from those collected later on Cangshan.

Bob Mitchell measuring a huge Cupressus duclouxiana *at Caoxi Temple, An Ning.*

On 29 April we went out to the Western Hills where the Dragon Gate Temple has one of the most dramatic locations of any in China, perched on the cliff side and cut out of the rock hundreds of feet above Dainchi, the great lake of Kunming. An extraordinary sight was people lying in hammocks slung out over the abyss. A little nearer Kunming is the Tai Hua temple and, as so often, it was surrounded by veteran trees, some possibly planted, others remnants of the original virgin forest which has disappeared throughout much of China. There were huge trees of *Ginkgo biloba*, reckoned to be almost 600 years old, and *Albizia mollis*, which has feathery pinnate foliage and a fluffy cream inflorescence.

The following day at the temple of Caoxi near the settlement of An Ning we saw an even better example of how a temple gives protection to a cluster of ancient trees. *Sapindus delavayi* was some 20m/65ft high and had handsome walnut-like foliage and spiky heads of dense greenish yellow flowers. But the grandfather was undoubtedly *Pistacia chinensis*, which must have been 30m/100ft in height and required a joint effort to measure its girth at 463cm/182in. It is occasionally cultivated in Britain but is undoubtedly happier in warmer climates such as California. A smaller relative, *P. weinmanniana*, had fine red foliage on the younger shoots and, among the smaller trees, *Catalpa fargesii* f. *duclouxii* and *Populus yunnanensis* were impressive. A single tree of *Firmiana major*, with bold foliage similar to the commoner *F. simplex*, stood at the back of the temple where *Olea yunnanensis*, with large and variable leaves, looked quite unlike the European olive. The

fruit is not edible. In the temple grounds *Pittosporum brevicalyx* was very attractive, a glossy leaved shrub of 1.8m/6ft or so with domed clusters of scented yellow flowers.

Apart from the ubiquitous *Pinus yunnanensis*, there were two interesting conifers. *Cupressus duclouxiana* made exclamation marks scattered across the dry hillsides as do Italian cypresses in the Mediterranean, but only at the temple did it reach great size and one specimen must have been close to 30m/100ft in height with a girth of 1.8m/6ft at chest height. *Keteleeria evelyniana* bears large erect cones like an *Abies* but they do not break up like the latter. Keteleerias are a speciality of the area and the Professor remarked that they must be lime-haters as they are found only on acid soils in the south and west. Roy Lancaster proved to have excellent climbing abilities and shinned up both the *Keteleeria* and a black-fruited holly, *Ilex macrocarpa*, for the seed. We spent the evening cleaning the seeds but there were more bugs than seeds and we had many live ones crawling around our room. In the temple courtyard stood a veteran apricot, *Prunus mume*, said to be 700 years old, all wrinkled stem and almost devoid of leaves, while on the other side stood a fine *Magnolia delavayi* reputed to be one hundred years of age. It was covered in plump ovoid buds but, alas, none were open.

Opposite: Dragon Gate, Western Hills, overlooking Dianchi Lake which lies to the west of Kunming, is cut out of a sheer cliff.

The pretty little Vaccinium fragile *growing on a very dry, eroded roadside bank. Generally coming from low elevations, this species was at one time introduced, but is evidently no longer in cultivation.*

Rhododendron ciliicalyx *or* R. pachypodum *on a bank above the road between Kunming and Dali. These members of subsection Maddenia are very closely related.*

To Xiaguan and the Cangshan

The long road from Kunming to Xiaguan (Hsia Kuan) of 400km/250 miles is now well surfaced and familiar to travellers, but in 1981 it was potholed, rutted and winding and we lurched along in our minibus for twelve and a half hours before arriving in the shadow of the Cangshan mountain range. However, it was all new and exciting to us and there was enough, in addition to the potholes, to keep us awake. Apart from a fine gorge and wooded valley, where the Kunming-Chengdu railway crossed and re-crossed, there was little forest left and the fields looked too dry to grow a crop. The professor showed a steely determination to avoid stopping for roadside enticements, rightly in view of the journey, but after about 240km/150 miles, dollops of white appearing on the scrubby hillside brought a crescendo of cries and he gave way to avoid a riot. It was a rhododendron of the *ciliicalyx* group, *R. pachypodum* with large white scented flowers, sometimes flushed pink and with a varying amount of yellow flare in the throat. We were later to find it common at lower altitudes around the Cangshan. Another plant of dryish scrub is *R. scabrifolium* var. *scabrifolium* (K.145). This has softer leaves than the related *R. spinuliferum* with smaller hairs. The white flowers are rather insignificant for the size of the leaves. A plant has survived at Glendoick all these years from this collection, despite coming from only 2,100m/7,000ft. *R. arboreum* subsp. *delavayi* and *R. decorum* were also seen on astonishingly dry, bare hillsides. Before crossing a pass into Xiaguan, the road skirted the side of the fertile valley full of golden wheat which glowed in the evening light and Bob ventured endless photographs out of the shuggling minibus.

It was getting dark as we approached Xiaguan, which lies at the south-west corner of Er Hai or Ear Lake. We could just make out the water, the fertile plain and, above it, the silhouette of the Cangshan away up to the left. Before retiring to the basic but reasonably comfortable 'hotel' in Xiaguan, we had our first meeting with a local dignitary, this time the vice-chairman of Dali prefecture, with interpreted speeches and tea. These meetings proved to be a regular feature of our trip, both before and after our journeys in the wild, with lots of platitudes from both sides. The tea, usually flavoured with jasmine, was always made in individual mugs, often with a lid to keep it hot. The leaves floated to the top, so some invariably ended in one's mouth.

The beautiful Er Hai lies at 1,950m/6,300ft with a shelving plain between the lake and the mountains. The Cangshan range, some 48km/30 miles long, acts as a continuous backdrop rising to 4,100m/13,600ft, with several peaks over 3,960m/13,000ft. Between the road and the mountains is an area of rough grazed herbage full of holes where boulders of marble and granite have been dug out. Below this it is all cultivation with countless scattered villages. The chief crops are wheat over the winter and rice during the summer. The historic town of Dali lies in the middle of the plain and in George Forrest's day was surrounded by a fortified wall; by 1981 this had largely disappeared, apart from sections by the main gates which had been stripped of all ornamentation and painted red during the Cultural Revolution. The town had changed very little except for the inevitable overhead lines and

The Cangshan range over a field of maize.

Different methods of fishing on Er Hai, including using cormorants on the left and right.

Forrest's photograph of the main gate into Dali from the south, taken in the early 20th century. The town was completely walled in Forrest's day.

The gate into Dali in 1981, by which time most of the town walls had disappeared and the gate's superstructure had been destroyed.

The gate in 1992, with its superstructure restored.

Few modern tourists would be interested in buying these old bottles on sale in the main street in Dali.

bicycles instead of mules, but subsequent visits in 1992 and 1997 showed remarkable changes from the quiet village-like atmosphere to a bustling tourist centre, and large sections of the old buildings had gone forever.

It was the May Day holiday and people were flocking everywhere with transistors at full blast as we visited the new Er Hai Park at the south end of the lake, where a new public garden was being made. There was an extraordinary collection of pot plants with hollyhocks mixed up with Trachycarpus palms and antirrhinums. Quite a few rhododendrons were being grown on in pots and a whole collection of *Magnolia delavayi* carried egg-shaped flower buds. Here and in the courtyards of the many temples we visited, plants in containers were usually poorly grown using just the local soil with no extra organic matter. *R. arboreum* subsp. *delavayi* and *R. decorum* being fairly tolerant of poor conditions were not doing too badly, but poor *R. sinogrande* was miserable, with leaves a fraction of the normal huge size on young seedlings. Some disease was evident and the widely cultivated *Camellia reticulata* nearly always suffered from viruses.

Mules carrying some of our gear on the way to Camp One on the west side of the Cangshan.

Yangbi and the First Camp

After a visit to the hot springs for a bath, we left for Yangbi, situated on the west flank of Cangshan, on which we were to have two camps. The first part of the drive was down the gorge that contains the river from Er Hai, which eventually reaches the Mekong. When we went back in 1997 the whole gorge was in a terrible mess as they were completely rebuilding the road and on both occasions the river was full of pollutant-ridden foam. This is part of the Burma Road which carries a huge number of trucks.

Our lodgings in Yangbi were of a decidedly lower standard than we had in Xiaguan, with powerful odours wafting up from the loo outside. We were given a generous feast in a large barn with ten different dishes on our table. Huge tureens of dough balls and rice stood by and chickens pecked in the straw around our feet. A peanut picking competition was won by Peter getting three into his mouth on his chopsticks at one time and we all weighed ourselves on the grain sack scales, a competition that I won with a not very flattering 88 kilos (194lb). It was followed by an extraordinary procession down the village street to see a film about the local Bai Minority people. We were warned we might be looked at but nothing prepared us for the hundreds of people who lined the street with the children running alongside. Roy was chucking them under the chin and playing pranks and by the time we reached the 'cinema', a large hall with wooden benches, we had to carve our way through the crowds with bells ringing as we mounted the steps. Inside a quick head count revealed about 1,000 people and from our seats of honour in the middle we saw all the rows in front turn their backs on the screen to look at us – the first time any of us had competed with a film as the main attraction! We were told that the last European to visit Yangbi was in 1949 and he was also looking for plants, so it is very likely that this was Joseph Rock.

In Forrest's day, the west flank of Cangshan was heavily wooded and wetter than the east side, as it catches the south-west monsoon. By the time we got there in 1981, much of the forest had been or was in the process of being destroyed. There was no virgin forest left up to our first camp and beyond as far as we could see; where cultivation ceased the open areas were heavily grazed by flocks of cattle, sheep, goats and pigs, with little chance for regeneration. Many of the lower slopes were covered with the famous Yangbi walnut trees, all of which were numbered, to check if any of them should be chopped down. The nuts are exported all over the world and the locals kindly allowed us to sample them, and excellent they were too. Toiling up among the walnuts we found the attractive climber *Pueraria peduncularis*, like a white wisteria but with a lovely scent, then a fine colony of *Iris tectorum* (SBEC 0031) with large, frilly, pale violet-blue flowers. We had been looking for an excuse to catch our breath so it became known as the 'Rest Iris'. It has proved to be hardy and easy in cultivation, surviving many years in central Scotland despite coming from a relatively low elevation around 2,000m/6,500ft.

Iris tectorum above Yangbi in a clearing amongst cultivated walnuts. This iris is often associated with graveyards in China.

Our first camp at Dapingdi on the east flank of the Cangshan at 2,700m/9,000ft, set in a cleared part of the forest.

The first rhododendrons occurred not far above the upper limit of cultivation and consisted of three species, *R. arboreum* subsp. *delavayi* (SBEC 0120), *R. decorum* and *R. irroratum* (SBEC 0064), and apparent hybrids between all three, all past flowering. Later, at Camp Two we found a pink-flowered plant with seven lobed corollas which indicates *R. decorum* parentage, the other obviously being *R. arboreum* subsp.

Rhododendron irroratum (SBEC 0064) cultivated at Glendoick. This was among the first rhododendron species that we saw just above the end of cultivation. It requires a protected site in most parts of the UK.

delavayi. David was delighted to find this as it matched herbarium specimens of *R. agastum* which he had suspected to be a natural hybrid with this parentage; so it is now written *R. x agastum*. The *R. arboreum* subsp. *delavayi* from 2,900m/9,500ft struggles on at Baravalla, while the *R. irroratum* has produced its very pale pink to white, lightly spotted flowers freely at Glendoick and Baravalla, but both flowers and growth are very prone to spring frost damage. The latter species on Cangshan tends to be pale flowered, sometimes with a hint of light yellow, and is superior to some other introductions which are rather dirty spotted pinks.

After the hot, dusty climb the path swung across the hillside to the welcome sight of smoke from fires. Our first camp, known as Dapingdi, was set at 2,700m/9,000ft at the edge of a bracken-covered clearing, overlooking a steep drop into forest to the east. Plants of *R. arboreum* subsp. *delavayi* were scattered across the clearing beyond the camp, the only survivors of what must have been fine forest before the destructive hand of man came along. Edging the clearing, the remnants of this once rich forest included *Juniperus recurva*, probably in its form *coxii*, named after Peter's father who, with Reginald Farrer, first found it in Upper Burma. *Myrsine semiserrata* (SBEC 0048) was an evergreen shrub of around 3m/10ft with conspicuous fruit which turns from pink through mauve to blue. Two evergreen trees standing near our tents were *Keteleeria evelyniana* (18m/60ft in height) and *Quercus*

Bob Mitchell was thrilled by the number of different Paris that we found in 1981. This one, P. polyphylla *var.* yunnanensis *forma* alba *(SBEC 0510) was new to science and is now well established in cultivation.*

Professor Feng Guomi, our China leader, with a branch of Rhododendron sinogrande, *which has the largest leaves of all rhododendrons.*

gilliana. On a private excursion I found *Primula denticulata* subsp. *alta* and *Daphne papyracea*, a large evergreen species with a heavy musky scent. Bob was particularly delighted with *Paris polyphylla*, a speciality of his.

Just above camp was a dying plant of *Rhododendron pachypodum* (SBEC 0115), the only time we found it with seed. We had previously seen it in the Yangbi gorge and at the end of the expedition we found masses of it on the open lower slopes of the east flank above the Qingbixu gorge in full sun with no shade or shelter. Where there was surviving forest at a similar elevation, this species grew to 3m/10ft, occasionally more. Seedlings of this collection have good large flowers, white flushed pink, produced later than most of its close relatives in subsection Maddenia, but it is only suitable for growing indoors except in very mild localities.

The following day, 3 May, we found *Rhododendron rubiginosum* common above camp but it was having an off season for flower. Peter selected a plant with wide leaves from which to collect seed (SBEC 0121), as this will often produce better flowers than those with narrow leaves. Plants raised from this number in cultivation do have good quality flowers and

grow vigorously in eastern Scotland, sometimes being used as an interior windbreak. Just at the edge of the forest, we were most surprised to find magnificent specimens of *R. sinogrande* (SBEC 0104), a species that had not apparently been recorded on Cangshan before, yet we subsequently found it at both Camps Two and Four. Some had grown to 14m/45ft but, as we found with other larger species, this was an off year for flower and only the occasional plant was flowering. The previous year had obviously been prolific with masses of old seed capsules on nearly every plant. Its altitude range was 2,950 to 3,000m/9,800 to 10,000ft and similar in the other two sites. We had great hopes that, being the most easterly known population, this introduction would prove to be hardier than previous collections and, indeed, it has flourished and flowered at Baravalla. However the winter of 1995–6 damaged it both in my garden and at Glendoick to the extent that a winter similar to 1981–2 would surely have killed them all.

The final surprises for the day were left to our return. As we came back down our driver (known to us as 'Old Blackteeth') appeared over the ridge giving us a cavernous grin and bearing splodges of yellow. He had found not only *R. sulfureum* but also

The true Pleione forrestii *being photographed near Camp One.*

Pleione forrestii – what a right and left! After much photography and photographs of photographers, our only regret was we had not seen them *in situ* ourselves, but this was to be put right later.

On the 4th we climbed quickly over previously covered ground until we found *R. anthosphaerum* (SBEC 0163) growing at Duanqing in dense forest at 3,000m/10,000ft. Like its relation *R. irroratum*, this species comes into growth very early so suffers badly in seasons with late frosts. The flowers are often hot shades of mauve, rose to magenta and they open very early. Higher up *R. neriiflorum* (SBEC 0172) was numerous with plentiful red flowers. With this collecting and two other numbers of this species collected later, we found around 50 per cent turned out to be natural hybrids, mostly with *R. rex* subsp. *fictolacteum* and *R. dichroanthum*. These natural hybrids never seem to occur in the same percentages in the wild as they do with seedlings cultivated from wild seed. No doubt nature has a way of eliminating the vast majority of these hybrids, probably by diseases, and it is apparent in cultivation that these are often the first to succumb to honey fungus and other root pathogens.

After lunch among the sinogrande woods and with our first rain drifting in, we found *Rhododendron facetum*. This late flowerer has brilliant scarlet trusses and just survives at Glendoick in a favourable site, though it is liable to get cut back. It grows very late in the season leading to frosted growth that cannot be replaced before winter, which often results in

die-back. It grew in forest at Duanqing and in bamboo at Camp Two and we found it just coming into flower at Camp Four.

There have been some arguments about the naming of the daphne (SBEC 0158) I had found earlier above this camp at a little under 3,000m/10,000ft. The Chinese taxonomists wanted to call it *D. feddei* but the plant we managed to get home has been called *D. papyracea* by daphne experts in Britain. It has creamy white sweetly scented flowers of considerable merit and so far has been amenable to cultivation and reasonably hardy. In the forest we found a large colony of *Cardiocrinum giganteum* var. *yunnanense* (SBEC 0187) with the typical dark stems of this variety, still some weeks off flowering. This has proved to be a fine and vigorous introduction but coming into growth unusually early sometimes results in it being ruined by frost.

On our last day at Camp One we split into two parties: David and Peter went high to Dashichang accompanied by Mr Ming while I explored with the others the valley up from the camp to Xieniupingdi. The first group with their guide climbed 500m/1,500ft without a stop to reach the previous day's lunch place. At 3,200m/10,500ft *Rhododendron heliolepis* took over from the related *R. rubiginosum*. It flowers late in the season and does not grow as tall or as vigorously as *R. rubiginosum*. Plants grown from seed collected there have purplish-pink flowers of doubtful merit. A much more refined plant, the endemic *R. cyanocarpum*, covered the whole hillside between 3,400 and 3,700m/11,000

The true Pleione forrestii *which we introduced in 1981. The original introduction, presumably by George Forrest who discovered it in 1906, proved to be a hybrid.*

This fine form of the lovely Rhododendron edgeworthii *was growing on the same mossy rock as* Pleione bulbocodioides. *One of our favourite rhododendron species, this requires perfect drainage in cultivation.*

and 12,000ft and may be the most plentiful rhododendron species on Cangshan. I have not found this relative of the well-known *R. thomsonii* difficult in cultivation, although it has a reputation for dying suddenly. It is a very pretty plant at its best, especially in the pure white and rose-pink forms.

At around 3,400m/11,000ft Peter and David found *R. sulfureum* in flower on a rocky crag. This species has flowers which are a little small in comparison with the leaf size but of a fine deep yellow. Collected here and at Camp Three, this introduction has proved to be hardier than most previous collections, and most of Peter's plants at Glendoick have survived since being planted in sheltered positions in 1984. I have also found it a useful pot plant. At 3,600m/11,700ft they came across a barren zone with a rock scree and only a few scattered rhododendrons and junipers. All was silent and the mist hung around with an eerie effect; no wind stirred and no bird sang. There was a call to start the descent and Peter hurriedly had a look at the edge of the scree. There at last was the rhododendron we most wanted to see, *R. lacteum*. There were several plants with old twisted and leaning trunks, 3–4.6m/10–15ft high with branches swathed in a 76mm/3in layer of spongy moss. They scrambled to collect as many capsules as possible in case it was not found again, but it was plentiful at Camps Two and Three.

Meanwhile our party – Bob, Roy and I – set off with Professor Feng towards a valley called Xieniupingdi which even the professor had never visited before so it was completely new territory. After a dull start we reached the previous day's lunch spot where there were some interesting herbs including a *Disporopsis* species and a tiny pink Solomon's seal, *Polygonatum delavayi*. We then cut north-west up a valley and quickly found ourselves in marvellous virgin forest. In places *Rhododendron sinogrande* dominated and it was an extraordinary experience to

walk under the canopy of great propellers 12 to 14m/40 to 45ft above; the girth of one was measured at 50in (126cm). Fine trees surrounded us with large specimens of *Acer campbellii* subsp. *flabellatum*, the Chinese yew *Taxus yunnanensis*, and a host of other genera, *Sorbus, Meliosma, Viburnum, Neolitsea, Lindera, Euonymus, Lithocarpus* – the list seemed endless.

There were many herbs and bulbs on the forest floor and one, *Chrysosplenium davidianum* (SBEC 0231), has proved a great success in cultivation and now drapes itself over the waterfall in the Rock Garden in the RBGE. It is much more showy than its British counterpart and makes a carpet of yellow with a profusion of flattened yellow flower heads, providing perfect ground cover for a damp shady place. The elegant genus *Paris* was present and Bob Mitchell, who has made a major contribution to our knowledge of them in China, busied himself with them. There are two species on the Cangshan: *P. violacea* with silvery markings on its whorl of dark green leaves and *P. polyphylla* which has three well defined varieties in *appendiculata, yunnanensis* and *thibetica*. A most striking new form was found near Camp Three with yellow leaf-like sepals, yellow anthers and a white ovary which has been named *forma alba* (SBEC 0510) and is now doing well in cultivation.

The professor had some difficulties with heights so Roy and I left him with Bob and his *Paris* and pressed on. We passed young magnolias, probably the form of *Magnolia wilsonii* that is sometimes called *M. taliensis*, and passing into some dead bamboo thicket found ourselves surrounded with the most wonderful scent. A cry from Roy ahead and suddenly we were standing in a magic clearing in the forest where a moss-covered rump of rock was scattered with a splendid form of *Rhododendron edgeworthii* (SBEC 0207). Abundant flowers with pink tipped corollas gave off the fragrance that had taken our breath away among the bamboos.

Pleione bulbocodioides *was growing in the same magic clearing in the forest as* Rhododendron edgeworthii.

Euphorbia griffithii *is a striking perennial which was common near Huadianba and is not touched by livestock owing to its poisonous nature.*

With it on the rock were the butter-yellow flowers of *Rhododendron sulfureum* and an outstanding *Pleione* (SBEC 0205). The flowers were carried on unusually tall stems of 10-24cm/4-6in with outer segments of carmine-pink and the fringed lip was mottled with rich red markings. This handsome plant used to be called *Pleione delavayi* and we found it at several locations on the Cangshan but it has recently been combined under *P. bulbocodioides*, usually a much more modest affair, of which it must be a distinct and desirable variant. Then to complete this posse of aristocratic flowers, we spotted a splash of bright yellow. It was a generous group of *Pleione forrestii*, our hoped for golden pleione, and we fell on our knees to admire the gorgeous yellow flowers set off by the red markings on the fringed lip, oblivious of the cliff edge and the river rushing below.

It took a moment to recover from our slightly dazed state and

then the cameras rattled, Roy talked breathlessly to his little recording machine, we fell on seed capsules and carefully selected a few pseudobulbs from the two pleiones, just enough we felt to introduce them to cultivation. It turned out in fact that this was the first introduction of the true *P. forrestii*. George Forrest had found it in 1910 on the east flank of the Cangshan but the first supposed introduction was from further west on the Shweli-Salween divide in 1924. It reached the RBGE via Caerhays but only a single pseudobulb was left after the 1939-45 war. It was successfully multiplied and distributed as *P. forrestii*, but experts began to doubt if it was the true species and it was identified as a natural hybrid with *P. albiflora* and given the appropriate name of *P.* x *confusa*. Such are the vagaries of plant introduction but our yellow orchid from the rock ledge on the Cangshan received an Award of Merit from the RHS in 1985.

Acer forrestii is a most attractive and graceful maple that is common in south-west China.

The Chinese ivy Hedera nepalensis var. sinensis *has very striking fruit.*

Camp Two, Shangchang

It was now time to move to our next camp further north on the same west flank of Cangshan and we were to make the move on foot. Our party of seventeen set out into a hot day with blazing sun and, at the fairly low elevation of 2,100m/7,000ft, the many ups and downs crossing ridge after ridge with little shade proved to be very tiring. Cultivation was being attempted on the steepest of slopes but much wanton destruction of the remaining natural trees was seen even on slopes too steep to use for anything, with trees sometimes cut and just left to rot. One remaining plant of note was a fine specimen of *Decaisnea fargesii* with its large compound leaves and peculiar but attractive greenish-yellow flowers which are followed by amazing blue bean-like pods in which the seeds are embedded in a glutinous jelly that sticks to everything. The cutting of vegetation and cultivation of steep slopes leads to loss of precious soil and the local Lisu people must have to work extremely hard for tiny crops which may fail in a dry season or be washed away in a wet one.

The afternoon was particularly gruelling. We sometimes dropped 300m/1,000ft to a sweltering bottom from which we could see the train of mules outlined on the ridge above, reminding us of the climb to come. Heat and dehydration gave a dreamlike feel and the sight of Peter, who had acquired a half-grown beard, flourishing his ice-axe at a dog which had tried to attack him made one wonder if we had strayed into the Mexican Badlands. Eventually we were invited into a farmhouse with four generations of the family and gallons of tea were provided by these generous and undemanding people. Fortified by this, Peter developed a third or fourth wind for the final climb but along with Bob and Clyde I had acquired a nasty virus and a cough and eventually the three of us staggered into the new campsite exhausted. Our plants looked equally

tired but they were to be taken down to Xiaguan the next day to be kept in a shed with just one small window.

Our campsite, which was named Shangchang, faced north-west some 180m/600ft higher than the last one and needed much levelling to pitch tents. Behind was some fine, mostly deciduous forest with two species of *Styrax* including a fine 10.6m/35ft tree of *S. limprichtii* just coming into flower, also an ash, a nice bird cherry, *Prunus brachypoda*, and no less than six species of maple. *Corylus ferox* was masquerading as a castanopsis with prickly clustered fruits but the parallel-veined leaves with pronounced midrib gave it away. One surprise was an ivy, *Hedera nepalensis* var. *sinensis*, with orange-yellow berries instead of the usual red.

Near the camp were numerous *Rhododendron sinogrande*, similar to those at Camp One, and some juvenile plants carried enormous leaves. Roy climbed into one of the largest specimens and borrowed Peter's ice-axe to hack off a branch with seed on it. In his enthusiasm, he hacked just a little too hard and cracked the wooden shaft in addition to the branch. Fortunately my ice-axe survived the trip and indeed all my subsequent ones so that most useful weapon for plant collectors is now a rather battered veteran. Just below the ridge were many more plants dwarfed by the poor conditions and a tiny one even had an opening flower bud. Unfortunately we failed to find any seed at this higher altitude. We also found our first plants of *R. maddenii* subsp. *crassum* with dark leathery leaves but we were, of course, too early for the flowers.

A little above camp was a semi-deciduous viburnum that none of us had seen before which layered itself into a thicket. It was in full flower with masses of small, slightly scented white to pale pink flowers that nevertheless made quite a show en

We were the first to introduce Viburnum chingii *in 1981. This hardy species eventually grows to 3m/10ft and produces masses of slightly fragrant white, tinged pink flowers in spring.*

masse. Nobody else seemed to be going to do anything about collecting it, so as we were descending one evening, Peter hurriedly dug up a bit, which survived the journey home. It has done well in cultivation, proving to be hardy in our bit of Scotland and it sometimes produces its blue-black fruit with fertile seeds. It was only named *V. chingii* in 1966 and was new to cultivation. A vigorous buddleja with large leaves which Roy thought was *B. monostachya* (SBEC 0360) and probably also new to cultivation has unfortunately not proved very hardy but the small drooping heads of lilac flowers with an orange eye are of little merit anyway.

Our first effort to reach the ridge above the camp was a dreadful scramble through a large thicket of thorny scrub and climbers. We were all scratched and exhausted by the time we reached the ridge and I was struck in the eye by a branch whipping back, causing double vision for a few days but I recovered. A path ran in both directions along the top of the knife-edged ridge fringed with a fine colony of *Rhododendron yunnanense* in full flower with the usual variation of white to pink and differing amounts and colours of spots. *Pieris formosa* var. *forrestii*, which had been with us since the camp, was here reduced to a tight bush with smallish leaves, although the young growth was a fine rich red. Alas, there was no seed up there, but we did collect it under SBEC 0332 from the woods around the camp 300m/1,000ft lower down, where it made a large shrub up to 6m/20ft. There were signs of the bronzy foliage having been frosted, but it has proved reasonably hardy in cultivation and is a useful windbreak under trees where it is fairly tolerant of dry conditions.

Opposite. Pieris formosa *(SBEC 0332A) in full flower on the exposed ridge above Camp Two. This forms quite a compact plant in cultivation, with crimson-brown young growth.*

Rhododendron yunnanense *is a very common species throughout much of Yunnan and adjacent areas. It varies from white to pink, on scrubby banks, and is extremely free-flowering in cultivation.*

Although said to have been found elsewhere, typical Rhododendron haematodes subsp. haematodes appears to be confined to Cangshan where it grows from around the tree-line to the tops of the ridge. It is undoubtedly one of the finest and hardiest of the smaller red-flowered species, both for foliage and flower. In cultivation at Glendoick.

Rhododendron selense subsp. jucundum is the commonest rhododendron species in the belt of Abies delavayi. It is proving to be the best subspecies of R. selense in cultivation, here at Glendoick.

The path eventually led up to the top of the main Cangshan crest ridge and one day we made full use of this. On the way we found one small rhododendron clump containing five species, *R. trichocladum, R. rubiginosum, R. cyanocarpum, R. rex* subsp. *fictolacteum* and our first *R. haematodes* just opening its waxy scarlet flowers. *R. cyanocarpum* was common on this south-east aspect but as soon as the slope turned to the north-west one of the most exciting finds of the trip revealed itself. Before us was a whole forest of *Rhododendron lacteum* growing in a thick spongy carpet of sphagnum moss with only a few *R. haematodes* to keep it company as an understorey.

By 1981, *R. lacteum*, which some would regard as the finest hardy yellow, had become extremely scarce in cultivation. The few mature plants had become known by the garden name – the Blackhills lacteum, the Corsock lacteums and so on – and they regularly swept the board when they appeared at shows. But they were tricky in cultivation and difficult to propagate so

a substantial reintroduction was badly needed. Peter and I immediately got busy collecting seed capsules and ended up with quite a haul (SBEC 0345), enough we reckoned to satisfy the demand for this species for years to come and so it proved. In addition, a large quantity of *R. lacteum* seedlings grew in the moss and we lifted a few for our store in Xiaguan. Alas, there were no flowers out but we opened several of the swelling buds and these revealed a mixture from good yellow to a pale form, both with and without blotches.

Professor Feng had warned us that we would not find seedlings of *Rhododendron haematodes* in the moss and he proved to be right. The seed turned out to be quite fertile and there was no apparent reason for this phenomenon as most other species seed themselves in quantity. We also collected seed of *R. trichocladum* (SBEC 0351), *R. cyanocarpum, R. heliolepis* and *R. selense* var. *jucundum*.

All this collecting took a long time while the rest of the

Viburnum nervosum *was common on the forested hillsides and quite conspicuous from a distance away. This species was previously known as V.* cordifolium.

party (minus poor Bob who had to stay in camp with a bad cold) had gone on to the ridge where they were rewarded with a magnificent view of Er Hai lake. Along the ridge were fine large specimens of a viburnum in full flower. We called this *V. veitchii* but this was later changed to *V. nervosum*, because at the time the leaves had not expanded but later become bullate, hence the name *nervosum*. David came back to where the two of us were still collecting seed full of excitement to say he had found a

population of *Rhododendron roxieanum* var. *cucullatum* (SBEC 0350) with thick woolly indumentum and persistent bud scales.[4]

In the meantime Bob had been busy in camp drying seeds and binding Peter's ice-axe shaft. He made an excellent job of it for not only did it last out this expedition but the next as well.

We were all quite tired after several days of climbing so we had earned an easy one around our camp, which could fairly be called maple and deutzia day. The maples occurred in great variety. These were *Acer tetramerum* (now *A. stachyophyllum*), *A. campbellii* subsp. *flabellatum*, *A. sterculaceum* subsp. *franchetii* with large handsome leaves, *A. cappadocicum* var. *sinicum*, *A. davidii* and *A. forrestii*, the last two being so-called snake-

4. Ever since collecting this, there has been uncertainty about whether it should be called *R. roxieanum* var. *cucullatum* or just be regarded as a form of *R. taliense*. However, it has now flowered in cultivation and would appear to fit into *R. taliense* with a thicker than usual indumentum.

barked species. Being spring, there was little seed to be had but we did get some of *A. campbellii* subsp. *flabellatum* (SBEC 0383) which has handsome shiny seven-lobed leaves, reddish in spring, and it has made a nice small tree at Baravalla. One plant of *A. davidii* (SBEC 0466) did give us a good haul. This species has a wide altitudinal range and as a result varies much in hardiness but, unfortunately, this collection came from only 2,400m/8,000ft and has proved to be both winter tender and unable to ripen its shoots in autumn.

The two days had produced a good harvest which kept us busy until late in the evening, often with the aid of torches and candles. Peter and I were in charge of the living material so seeds and fruits had to be cleaned, dried, packeted and labelled while the small plants were bundled in moss held by rubber bands and installed in a small nursery under a shady tree. We were very sparing in collecting small plants but it should be remembered that it was May when seed was often unobtainable; the Chinese fully accepted what we were doing and this was the first time in decades that anyone had been allowed to collect this rich flora – but how much longer would it last?

Meanwhile, the pressing of herbarium specimens was in full swing with our Chinese colleagues and the other three from our party crouched round the lamp chattering in several languages, squeezing and squashing and taking notes. Eight specimens of each number were taken for various institutions and we were already up to 400 numbers.

On the long walk back to Yangbi, we passed *Cornus capitata* in full flower and snacked on orange-fruited brambles growing beside the path. At the evening symposium with local government chiefs, we discussed agriculture and alternative fruit crops, and Bob gave a stern lecture on the need to protect the forest environment. Strongly backed by our Professor, his words were received with nods and verbal reassurances. But I could not help thinking of the dots of red seen glowing in the dusk on distant hills, the patches of burnt forest and the herds of goats, sheep and ponies driven up each day to the mountain pastures around our camp.

On our way back to Xiaguan we stopped at the baths where hot springs from the hillside fed into family-sized tanks of marble and we took ourselves and our underwear in for a badly needed wash. Due to a misunderstanding with a football sized bung in the floor, my smalls were swept off into the outside world and, although I rushed to the door, the prospect of pursuing my underpants down the village street, still steaming in the nude, seemed unattractive. By the time the Chinese joined the commotion, they were gone forever, or were possibly being recycled somewhere downstream.

The splendid evergreen Cornus capitata *is one of the most showy small trees native to south-west China. Unfortunately, it is only hardy in the mildest of UK gardens.*

Cornus *in captivity, on its way to the evening pressing.*

Rhododendron virgatum *subsp.* oleifolium *below Camp Three. This species is invariably found on hot, dry banks, often away from all other rhododendrons; all forms appear to be tender in cultivation, despite our attempts to collect it at as high an elevation as possible, around 3,000m/10,000ft.*

The east side of the Cangshan; Camp Three

An early start for our first camp on the east flank was interrupted by the usual tea and compliments with the dignitaries of Dali. We also acquired an armed guard, 'in case of the bears', who handled his sub-machine gun with relaxed incompetence and turned out to be something of a fall-guy. If there was a log to trip over, he would find it and he spent much of the time scooping mud from the barrel of this alarming weapon. After a short bus drive we were on our feet again and soon found three rhododendrons, *R. microphyton*, tiny *R. pachypodum*, only 15cm/6in high but with flowers, and *R. virgatum* subsp. *oleifolium*. We found scattered plants of the last species in various places on Cangshan, but always in a similar habitat – dry sunny banks with little organic matter. Two collections around the 3,000m/10,000ft mark, which was the highest we found it, proved to be too tender to grow in eastern Scotland. Its pretty pale pink flowers usually occur singly up the young growth. A

short distance on there were three more rhododendron species, the ubiquitous *R. racemosum*, *R. simsii* and *R. decorum*, all hard grazed down to 60cm/2ft or less. Around 2,400m/8,000ft were five more species, *R. trichocladum*, *R. neriiflorum*, *R. maddenii* subsp. *crassum*, *R. edgeworthii* and more *R. pachypodum*, the last three all growing within a few feet of each other on a little cliff.

We were beginning to get a peculiar feeling that something was wrong and soon we realised that our guide had taken us up the wrong track. I was exasperated and exhausted. After climbing the best part of 800m/2,500ft, there was a yawning gap opening between us and where we ought to be. This was not unknown territory, the marble quarries and the radio station were somewhere

Cangshan is famous for its marble which is quarried up the mountain and here are a few samples of what was for sale to tourists. Various other artefacts are made and now sold on numerous stalls around the pagodas.

View along the ridge of Cangshan from Longquan Peak northwards. The highest peaks are all in the region of 4,000m/13,000ft.

above us. Peter said he felt like taking his ice axe to the guide and David went off to investigate if there was any way to our correct ridge, but he came back to announce that there was a deep gorge between. So back to the foot of the mountain we had to go.

The minibus picked us up, drove almost back into Dali, then up the roughest of roads imaginable. Eventually, having got us three-quarters of the way to our campsite, the bus ground to a halt against a large boulder. After some heaving of rocks, the bus was able to turn and we set off to walk the last few miles up the road, reaching our third camp at the end of the track, tired and hungry at 6 p.m.

Once up on our ledge, however, we were among the gods. Below us the ground dropped precipitously some 1,200m/4,000ft to the plain where the Chong Sheng temples looked like toys. Beyond, the Er Hai lake shimmered in the evening light. On one side was the deep ravine that had foiled us earlier in the day and above us the crags rose with a dark fringe of *Abies delavayi* among patches of snow to the final crest of *Longquan Peak*.

An oddity was a hut by the road containing a generator, which meant that we could have lights in our tents – quite a luxury. We were able to do our specimens and write notes in half of the hut while those not involved watched television in the

Abies delavayi on cliffs above Camp Three. This slow-growing fir has brilliant blue cones from quite a young age in cultivation.

From Xiaguan, below the southern most end of Cangshan, we could see a mass of yellow flowers up on the ridge. This was Piptanthus nepalensis, a colourful member of the pea family, common at around 3,000m/ 10,000ft on sun-facing hillsides.

Deutzia compacta (D. hookeriana?) SBEC 0529 in cultivation. One of our best introductions, this was collected above Camp Three amongst Rhododendron trichocladum. It has a neat habit and flowers very freely every year.

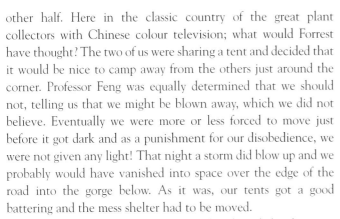

other half. Here in the classic country of the great plant collectors with Chinese colour television; what would Forrest have thought? The two of us were sharing a tent and decided that it would be nice to camp away from the others just around the corner. Professor Feng was equally determined that we should not, telling us that we might be blown away, which we did not believe. Eventually we were more or less forced to move just before it got dark and as a punishment for our disobedience, we were not given any light! That night a storm did blow up and we probably would have vanished into space over the edge of the road into the gorge below. As it was, our tents got a good battering and the mess shelter had to be moved.

The next morning revealed that the slope behind us was mostly composed of *Rhododendron trichocladum*, which sported pale yellow flowers and bronzy young foliage, an attractive combination. A rather poor form of *R. racemosum* was scattered through it, along with a *Piptanthus species* and *Syringa yunnanensis*. As we worked our way up we were glad to see our first nomocharis, *N. pardanthina*, and Bob was particularly pleased with a form of *Paris polyphylla* with chrome yellow bracts.

Abies delavayi (SBEC 0505) became the dominant tree above 3,400m/11,000ft. It was scattered among the crags and often appeared part of them, weathered, bent and clinging to improbable situations. Later in the year it carries barrel-shaped cones of brilliant blue-purple. Under it, *R. neriiflorum* (SBEC 0507) was just shedding its red flowers. We have found that the Cangshan collections of this species have not produced particularly good forms but selected ones are definitely worth growing on account of their hardiness, something lacking in some of the superior forms from further west. *R. sulfureum* was also perched on nearby rocks and that altitude made us optimistic for its hardiness, correctly as it turned out.

We stopped for a bite of lunch on a rickety platform of logs that formed part of the path strung along a rock-face. Our guide, who had led us astray yesterday, lit a fire on it and when we pointed out that this might be unwise on this structure he started leaping about and stamping to put it out. Smoke billowed, a gust came, the flames roared and we were all nearly asphyxiated; I was almost set alight and had to dive for cover.

Higher still the canopy of *Abies* was shared with *Rhododendron selense* var. *jucundum*, and under it we found the best display of primulas we were to see. We had found occasional plants of *Primula sonchifolia* before but here it was in profusion and in flower, both the ice-blue and occasional white forms. With it were growing clumps of the very fine Nivalid

Rhododendron sulfureum (SBEC 0249) was always found growing on rocks and pinnacles around the 3,400m/11,000ft level and has proved to be reasonably hardy at Glendoick in a well-drained sheltered situation.

The beautiful Primula calliantha *is very common on Cangshan from the rhododendron forest up to the top of the ridge. Alas, no one has succeeded in growing it really successfully in cultivation.*

A fine form of Enkianthus chinensis *near Camp Three.*

Typical Primula sonchifolia *and a rare white plant. Very widespread in south-west China, this splendid species enjoys very moist conditions in cultivation, the best situation being in shade along the sides of a stream.*

Primula calliantha. The flowers are deep violet and fragrant with a yellow eye and a pronounced annulus while typically for the section the leaves have a dense coating of yellowish green farina beneath. Unfortunately, it is difficult to cultivate successfully. A mountain stream running under this canopy, its banks studded with *P. calliantha* and *P. sonchifolia*, made an unforgettable sight for us all.

At about the tree line a strip for pylons had been cut in the vegetation, where the richness of the rhododendron flora was demonstrated. In this small area jostled thirteen species, ranging from the tiny *R. impeditum* to the big-leafed *R. rex* subsp. *fictolacteum*, with many of the intermediate species.[5]

A little further up a diapensia with yellow tubular flowers was hugging the rock faces, neatly paired with mossy mats of a primula, *P. bella*, unfortunately not in flower. In spite of its colour the diapensia has been sunk under *D. purpurea*. We were now not far from the crest ridge in an almost solid mass, about 90cm/3ft high, of what David thought was *Rhododendron balfourianum*, interspersed with a few *R. taliense*. However the seed collected produced no *R. balfourianum* and when we returned in spring 1992 we saw little sign of the latter and a mass of *R. taliense* in flower. Beneath it *R. campylogynum* grew as ground cover, a form with dark shiny leaves and fine, large claret-coloured flowers with a bloom on the outside. Some very good selections have been made from the seedlings of this collection.

We were not alone on our craggy hillside. A group of photographers from the local Government press came puffing up the hillside to record the novelty of foreign botanists among their bushes. Peter was much put out by their flashes going off while he was busy up a rhododendron collecting seed capsules. Then from the communications hut right at the top of the hill a party emerged, armed to the teeth with a cage, rat-sized mouse traps, machine guns, revolvers and a shotgun. They said

Diapensia purpurea (D. bulleyana) *in a rocky forest clearing near the tree-line above Camp Three. Normally found above the tree-line on exposed slopes, this exquisite species can also be white or shades of pink. Alas, it is nearly impossible to cultivate successfully.*

5. *Rhododendron impeditum, R. campylogynum, R. taliense, R. cyanocarpum, R. rex* subsp. *fictolacteum, R. haematodes, R. heliolepis, R. lacteum, R. trichocladum, R. rubiginosum, R. neriiflorum, R. selense* subsp. *jucundum,* and *R. balfourianum.*

Incarvillea arguta on the hillside above Dali. This species invariably grows on hot, dry banks, often in river valleys at fairly low elevations.

they were setting off to kill mice for scientific purposes.

As the mist rolled over the summit we drifted downhill through this classic Cangshan flora, wondering how often George Forrest or Père Delavay must have hurried here too before the weather closed in on them. Just before we reached our camp there came a last treat in a rich little gully with a rushing stream where, among other plants, grew *Meconopsis wilsonii, Trillium tschonoskii* and a fine bush of *Rhododendron edgeworthii* with scented white flowers flushed with pink. An interesting find was the orange *R. dichroanthum* subsp. *dichroanthum*, which is endemic to the Cangshan but this was one of only two clumps we saw. From the camp we dropped steeply towards Dali, passing *Dipelta yunnanensis* (not as showy as *D. floribunda*), another endemic in *R. brachyanthum* subsp. *brachyanthum* and then one of the most extraordinary plants of the Cangshan, *Cypripedium margaritaceum* with its purple pouch of a flower nestling in the broad pleated and spotted leaves.

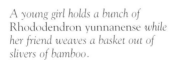

A young girl holds a bunch of Rhododendron yunnanense *while her friend weaves a basket out of slivers of bamboo.*

Above and opposite: Autumn colour on the Cangshan.

Below: Looking down on Lake Er Hai from the Cangshan.
Opposite: Gentiana melandrifolia growing under rhododendrons on Cangshan. We cultivated this in Scotland for several years by covering it in winter.

A later look at the Cangshan

In 1997 we broke the drive back to Kunming at Dali, which some of us had visited before but neither Peter nor I had seen in the autumn. It had become something of a backpackers' stopover since last seen in 1992 and David Chamberlain and I found ourselves swapping memories like ancient travellers. But the one-day excursion above Dali revealed the mountainside in a rich tapestry of autumn colour mingled with the dark greens of conifers and rhododendrons. *Gentiana melandrifolia* was a star of the occasion; plants from our 1981 trip had proved difficult in cultivation but here it was in profusion, spreading mats with a splendid range of blues from Oxford to Cambridge. It was our first chance to collect *Abies delavayi* from its classic location, its cones, the colour of purple-blue plums, dribbling resin. Seed was generally plentiful, including the primulas, although whether we will be able to keep *P. calliantha* in cultivation is a matter of doubt. I was glad to find *Iris delavayi* with its bold foliage and a small 'ilex' with red berries, which turned out to be squishy and therefore not a holly at all, but an *Ardisia* species.

Then the long drive back to Kunming, which was in the usual frenzy of development. Accommodation was not a problem as there were now 527 establishments whereas on our first visit in 1981, Clyde told us, there had been only five hotels of which three were classified as suitable for foreigners.

This amazing orchid was found on our way down to Dali from Camp Three. Cypripedium margaritaceum seems to be quite rare as we have never seen it anywhere else and these were the only two of flowering size.

Magnolia wilsonii on the way to our fourth camp at Huadianba. This plant on Cangshan was formerly called M. taliensis. This is one of the best magnolia species for Scotland.

Cypripedium flavum, *one of the gorgeous slipper orchids, was growing happily in open scrub, near to* Magnolia wilsonii.

Paeonia delavayi *Lutea Group, an unusual form with characters of both P. lutea and P. delavayi, and showing why these two previous species have been amalgamated.*

Camp Four: Huadianba

Our fourth camp was to be in very different territory further north on the east flank of the Cangshan, just before the top end of the lake and after a bus drive of 48km/30 miles. The first part of our walk was along desperately eroded paths, sometimes cut so deep that we could not even see over the sides. The pouring rain just added to the mud and erosion and our difficulties in clambering up this path. The surrounding countryside was devoid of trees and had few shrubs and herbs. A sign of poor, dry soil was the presence of *Incarvillea arguta* which usually inhabits dry river valleys and *Rumex hastatus*, a relative of sheep's sorrel. On the way, Peter saw three cuckoos together and announced this was more than he had ever seen before. We had an early lunch in a house with masses of flies, the first time on this trip that we had been bothered by them in quantity.

We soon entered an area of scrub, all about the same height of 1.8-2.4m/6-8ft. It became evident that the local population cut this scrub to the ground, an area at a time, in rotation every five to ten years. We heard numerous pheasants calling and later we saw the feathers of a Reeve's pheasant with a

magnificent long black-and-white tail. It had been shot but unfortunately the cook had eaten the rest. With its impenetrable, often spiny, vegetation, this type of scrub makes an ideal habitat for pheasants.

One part of this scrub proved to be most exciting for the plants it contained. White blobs scattered through the scrub invited further investigation and we were delighted when these turned out to be the flowers of a magnolia. At first we called it M. *taliensis* but this is generally treated as a synonym of the well known M. *wilsonii* with its pendulous white flowers and a strong lily of the valley scent. Growing by the magnolia was a lovely yellow-flowered orchid, *Cypripedium flavum*, formerly known as C. *luteum*. A third meritorious plant was a good form of *Paeonia delavayi* Lutea Group. Most of this population had varying amounts of red in the base of the flower. We also collected red fruit from *Lonicera setifera* (SBEC 0656), the name referring to the bristly stems and leaves. This shrubby honeysuckle produces white tubular flowers in winter and is

not often seen but well worth growing. Roy claims that it is scented but I have never managed to locate any scent. Plants from this collection are now well established in cultivation. Lastly, we collected *Roscoea tibetica* with delightful purple flowers with a white tube. A member of the ginger family, it looks more like an orchid. It grew plentifully on a mound and seedlings from a collected plant have been widely distributed.

We were on our way to a medicinal farm known as Huadianba. Several years before, the Chinese had attempted to establish quite a large community up here as the ground is comparatively level by Yunnan standards, but the elevation proved to be too high to grow many of the crops they were trying to produce. In the end, most of the population left and only a few Bai people remained, growing a limited number of medicinal plants that were suited to the conditions at nearly 3,000m/10,000ft. A road had been built but, as there was now little being transported, it fell into disrepair and stretches of it became impassable, hence our long walk. However, the last section was largely intact, flat and straight and fearfully tedious to walk along with our goal seemingly not getting any nearer. A little relief came from a boggy stream with masses of *Primula poissonii* growing in the water, with its magenta flowers in whorls, typical of the candelabras.

When we eventually made it, we found that we were to be housed in wooden shed-like buildings and not tents. Electric light soon came on and then went out for the evening, so all our work had to be done by candle light, including a haul of 62 specimens for the day with anything up to eight sheets of each.

The surrounding country was very different from the previous three camps, with low rounded hills rising only 300 to 600m/1,000 to 2,000ft above the wide valley. We soon discovered that those to the north were of limestone and those

Bai women hoeing on the medicinal farm at Huadianba.

to the south granite, with very dissimilar plants. Our first day, 18 May, was spent in the north, starting with a walk through scrub with *Quercus* and *Lithocarpus*, interspersed with *Rhododendron yunnanense*, *R. racemosum*, both very variable in flower colour, and very fine *R. decorum* with flushed pink and pure white forms (SBEC 1059 and 1060), both producing some excellent plants in cultivation. Most of these plants had been hacked about and one little *R. decorum* about 30cm/1ft high had capsules bigger than the leaves. One hollow was full of big arisaemas and overhung with large plants of *Syringa*

Our cook with the tail feathers of a Reeve's pheasant which had recently been shot.

Members of the Bai Minority, whose numbers are around one million, most of whom live on the Dali plain between Cangshan and Er Hai.

A fine form of Rhododendron yunnanense *behind Huadianba.*

yunnanensis (SBEC 0758). Seedlings of this lilac have grown with enormous vigour and one at Glendoick reached 6m/20ft with pale pink scented flowers. They were painfully slow to collect, however, and I averaged one seed for every thirty pods. Two other plants collected on this hillside were an asparagus, A. *pseudofilasimum* (SBEC 0765), which has grown well in the RBGE, and *Cotoneaster microphyllus* (SBEC 0782). The latter is very strong growing in cultivation and is useful for stopping erosion on steep banks. Lovely *Incarvillea mairei* occurred intermittently up to the top of the ridge and *Schisandra rubriflora* was climbing over many bushes with its striking crimson flowers.

Near the top of the ridge we began to see *Rhododendron fastigiatum*, giving us a foretaste of what was to come. Rounding the corner, a glorious sight unfolded. We were on the edge of a big bowl with herds of yak grazing the alpine pastures in the distance and the whole immediate hillside was covered from top to bottom with dwarf rhododendrons in full flower. There was a wonderful mixture of the near-blue *R. fastigiatum* (SBEC 0804), and creamy white *R. cephalanthum* (SBEC 0751). Beyond,

R. cephalanthum disappeared and a belt of *R. fastigiatum* was accompanied by yellow *R. trichocladum*. The *R. fastigiatum* here was typical of the species with glaucous leaves, in contrast to the green-leaved *R. impeditum* above Camp Three. Seedlings of SBEC 0804 have flourished at Glendoick where Peter created a big bed containing about thirty plants which show just enough variation in foliage and flower colour to give added interest. Bob shouted that he had found a pink-flowered variation of *R. fastigiatum*. The colour was really quite a reasonable pink and Peter was able to remove two little bits off the side of the plant with some roots. They were successfully taken back to the RBGE but the quarantine house proved too hot for them and they died. To our surprise two seedlings from seed collected from the original pink plant are the same colour. In contrast, seed of the *R. cephalanthum* did not germinate, but a small plant survived and has been propagated and distributed. Like many of the section Pogonanthum, it has proved fussy to grow. *R. racemosum* (SBEC 0806) also grew in some quantity, including some nice rich pinks, and Peter found an obvious hybrid with *R. trichocladum*. One seedling from the *R. racemosum* turned out to be the same hybrid

To the north of the low hill behind Huadianba medicinal farm was our first real sight of a hillside covered with dwarf rhododendrons in full flower. Here Peter was mesmerized by being surrounded by a sea of Rhododendron cephalanthum *and* R. fastigiatum.

To the north of the dwarf rhododendron hillside were plains surrounded by low knolls on which the first yaks most of us had ever seen grazed. That night we ate yak for dinner.

On the same hillside just beyond the mixture of Rhododendron cephalanthum *and* R. fastigiatum, R. trichocladum *took over from the former, most likely due to the soil being more acid.*

Rhododendron cephalanthum *growing on limestone rubble.*

with nearly deciduous leaves and creamy flowers. This hybrid has been named *R. mekongense* var. *rubrolineatum* and the flower colour varies through to pink. George Forrest found similar plants and suspected that this was a natural hybrid.

Several *R. cephalanthum* were growing straight out of lime rubble and a sample of this taken home gave a pH reading of 8.1. It is a pity that we did not collect a soil sample further along the hill, but we suspect that it would have been acid there with *R. fastigiatum* being tolerant of higher and lower pH values.

Several alpine gems grew on this hillside among the dwarf rhododendrons. A beautiful blue corydalis similar to *C.*

Anemone trullifolia (SBEC 0799), *a close relative of the better-known* A. obtusiloba, *has proved to be an excellent introduction, and is now well-established in cultivation.*

Incarvillea mairei *was particularly fine around Huadianba. The more flamboyant species in this genus are inclined to look rather out of place compared with the more subdued flowers of most other perennials in Yunnan.*

Leptodermis forrestii *was a common little shrub on dry warm banks. It is only likely to succeed in cultivation in a sunny, warm well-drained position.*

cashmeriana turned out to be C. *curviflora* var. *rosthornii* (SBEC 0727) and was established in the RBGE. A small anemone, A. *trullifolia* (SBEC 0797) related to the blue and white A. *obtusiloba*, has been a great success in cultivation and is now readily available. There were more incarvilleas and a very small-leaved prostrate willow. Just as we were due to go back to camp, I wandered a little further and found a colony of the gorgeous *Omphalogramma vinciflora*, a primula relative with deep violet flowers the size of a 50p piece. These upright soldiers in violet uniforms above a sea of ice-blue corydalis made a brilliant sight. A moment later I was brought down to earth by being confronted with the first yak I had ever met at close range. We stared for a moment and then both of us bolted, the yak with its tail up and I with mine down!

Below the rhododendron hillside was a flat grassy plain with hundreds of yaks grazing as far as the eye could see, just as

We saw only one plant of this beautiful Meconopsis lancifolia, *growing in a gully at 3,200m/10,500ft to the north of Huadianba. Herbarium specimens of this species show even finer forms with huge flowers that would be very desirable for our gardens.*

The seedlings resulting from this fine pink-flowered Rhododendron decorum *(SBEC 1059) at Huadianba have been widely distributed in cultivation from Glendoick.*

we were to see them in future years around the Tibetan plateau, and all round the margins of the plain masses of *R. fastigiatum* were flowering in a hazy purple rim, reminiscent of heather on the Scottish hills but bluer in colour. The rhododendrons and the yak meadow combined to make this one of the most idyllic places we had ever been. Back at camp with memories of my rather undignified retreat I quite enjoyed some rather tough yak meat for supper.

One day it had to rain and 19 May broke with that quiet but determined rain I knew in the west of Scotland. Fortunately, we

were not going far and the morning walk was through a lush valley which included a huge cut-back poplar, one of three species locally. A rubble bank above the path had developed into a seed bed teeming with rhododendrons, mostly *R. rubiginosum* and *R. sinogrande*. There were very few mature *R. sinogrande* to produce those seedlings which occurred in all sizes, with remarkably stiff wide leaves developing their pale plastered indumentum when very young.

A good form of *Betula utilis* with dark brown exfoliating bark was the first birch we had seen and we collected a few seedlings. A

Near the pink-flowered Rhododendron decorum *(above) was the common white form of* R. decorum *(SBEC 1060).*

Rhododendron sinogrande *and* R. rubiginosum *seedlings flourishing on a disturbed bank which had made an ideal seed bed.*

97

Acer caudatum *var.* georgei *(SBEC 0908) growing at Glendoick. In the wild near Huadianba, we had not noticed the attractive peeling bark and another interesting feature is its upright inflorescence.*

We saw only one mature tree of this striking form of Betula utilis *in a wooded area to the south of Huadianba.*

We could hardly believe our eyes when we first saw this shrub, Helwingia chinensis, *with its flowers and fruit in the middle of its leaves. They are actually on a stem that is joined on to the leaf midrib. Too tender for most UK gardens.*

small-leaved holly, *Ilex yunnanensis*, had an erect habit and attractive reddish young growth. A dwarf mahonia, quite plentiful, proved to be *M. veitchiorum* var. *kingdonwardianum* (SBEC 0884). There was a surprising lack of primulas in this forest but this was made up for by a rich variety of herbaceous and bulbous plants such as *Actaea*, *Clintonia udensis*, *Cardiocrinum*, *Paris*, *Polygonatum*, *Smilacina* and *Trillium*, plus an *Arisaema* species which could be new. Wet seeds were laid out on drying paper; it is no use attempting to collect seed into paper packets when it is wet as the gum comes unstuck or even the whole envelope goes to mush.

Most of us had kept healthy throughout the expedition but poor Bob had a return of his cold and sore throat and was confined to camp. Hens were a bit of a problem here: although they were useful for cleaning up inedible scraps that we surreptitiously dropped on the floor when eating, their foraging meant we had to protect our little nursery with a fence. Everything got rather wet but little charcoal fires helped to dry us and our clothes as well as specimens and seeds. We heard that a bear had been shot locally, which at least gave some credence to the story of our armed guard being there to protect us.

The endemic Rhododendron cyanocarpum *is perhaps the commonest rhododendron on Cangshan. The flower colour varies from pure white through pink to purplish-rose. In cultivation at Baravalla, SBEC 0361.*

Our next excursion was to a different part of the forested area to the south. In the woods we found *Acer caudatum* var. *georgei* (SBEC 0908) which grows into a 9m/30ft tree. Roy has a poor opinion of it but some trees raised from this seed have attractive peeling light fawn trunks which are often admired. This species has unusual erect clusters of flowers which become pendulous in fruit. We used the dry stream beds as paths but for some reason progress was slow and Peter was in his must-get-high mood, so he and Roy carried on at speed well ahead of the others. Professor Feng got rather agitated and was shouting 'Cox, Cox,' but Peter was well out of earshot. Eventually we all caught up with him but Peter was not entirely popular.

Rhododendron rex subsp. *fictolacteum* (SBEC 0957) proved to be more plentiful here, with grand old rugged specimens covered in moss, up to 7.6m/25ft in height and as much across, with good deep-coloured indumentum. The only flowers to be found were on two old dying plants, white with a deep blotch and spots. As elsewhere, all the others were having a year off and even *R. rubiginosum* had few flowers. Up the middle of the stream bed were numerous plants of *Primula sonchifolia* (SBEC 0913) which had finished flowering and had almost ripe seed. It was a great opportunity to reintroduce this superb species as, even if the plants failed, we might get some good seed, and so it proved. Plants raised from this collection have reddish petioles and slightly deeper coloured, earlier flowers than the old form in cultivation. Our collection has done well, especially at Baravalla and Cluny near Aberfeldy in Perthshire.

At the top of the stream bed the going got difficult and we had to push our way through a soaking bamboo thicket to reach the top at 3,300m/10,700ft. There were a few fine old warriors of *Rhododendron cyanocarpum* (SBEC 0971) there, 4.5 to 6m/15 to

20ft tall with grand pinky-brown peeling trunks, fairly smooth and free of moss but struggling to compete with the bamboo. Some had long horizontal branches while others had stouter ones a little above ground level and we ate our lunch sitting on these. These old specimens could have been 150 to 200 years old or even more and some of the seedlings have produced excellent pink flowers. The only other woody plants on the top were a few *R. rex* subsp. *fictolacteum*, *Viburnum nervosum*, *Litsea cubeba* and a cherry. Under the bamboo grew lovely yellow or red-tinged *Fritillaria cirrhosa*, a tiny arisaema and *Clintonia udensis* (SBEC 0939) with pale blue flowers.

For a while the mist cleared and we had excellent views in both directions. On the way up we had noticed a bare slope which we thought might have interesting plants and we worked our way towards it, but the Chinese obviously thought differently as they had no intention of following us. They had the laugh on us as we found absolutely nothing. Overall it had been somewhat disappointing and not nearly so rich as the previous day when we had been just two valleys away. We wondered why, for instance, was there no *Rhododendron sinogrande*?

For our last day at Huadianba we split into two parties, Roy, Peter and I to the limestone hills to the north, while the others did a circuit going up the main valley and then round into the forest to the south where they found more *R. sinogrande* and *R. facetum* in flower. It was good to get back to upland pastures again. I had been finding the dripping forests rather claustrophobic and here

One of our best introductions. Roy and I found these gentians out of flower. They were later identified as G. ternifolia, which has proved to be very accommodating in cultivation, often flowering well into October or even November.

Philadelphus delavayi, with pretty scented flowers, is a common shrub in Yunnan but it grows too large for most gardens, and with its lack of interest for most of the year, it is not a popular garden plant.

we were up with the sky on a beautiful day. We aimed for a rocky gully and were walking across green mossy turf when the same thought struck both Roy and me simultaneously – gentians! Our turf was a carpet of a gentian of the Ornata group which proved to be G. *ternifolia*, then new to cultivation but which has been a great success. It is easy to please except in a very dry summer and two clones have been named appropriately 'Cangshan' and 'Dali'. It is a late flowerer of a lighter blue than some species and forms substantial mats which appreciate being divided every two to three years. Roy found a green morina recently named *Cryptothladia chlorantha*, which we failed to introduce successfully but it was perhaps more curious than beautiful. Much more attractive was a single meconopsis flower with three little prickly buds still to come. The almost flat flower was a superb rich purple with a boss of yellow anthers. This was M. *lancifolia* which has since been introduced from elsewhere by Kew but not in such a fine form.

The black bear cub which our driver was taking home to Kunming, its mother having been killed near to Huabianba farm. Bears are often horribly treated in China.

Herbarium specimens show that good forms exist and if they are ever introduced, beware of growing them anywhere near related monocarpic species like the M. *horridula* group or they will hybridise, resulting in either sterility or inferior plants.

We circled back through two plateaus where *Rhododendron fastigiatum* hugged the bases of the surrounding low hills, more numerous on the north-facing slopes. On the plain below us some 600 yak were grazing and a stream meandered across the narrows, only to disappear underground with a roar, to re-appear heaven knows where – such underground streams are common in many limestone areas. We saw interesting birds that day including several cuckoos, choughs calling and wheeling, skylarks rose in front of us and again we heard pheasants calling.

We finally had to tear ourselves away, back over the rim and down to camp rather late to face another 2½ hour film of Chinese opera. But not before one last splendid sight of an eagle soaring over being mobbed by choughs, to which it paid, quite properly, no attention whatever. That day we reached over 1,000 collections, including all herbarium, plant and seed numbers.

The local Bai farm leaders attended our feast that night, our last out in the countryside; then came the anticipated film, about the ninth we had seen. The Bai people are the largest minority in the Dali region and the young girls are very colourfully dressed until they are married, especially their head dresses; once married, their apparel becomes more sober. Although in some tourist places minorities dress specially to please visitors, here the genuine local costume was worn as every-day garb as well as on important occasions. Dali County itself had a population in 1981 of 260,000 distributed in some 355 villages. Their main crops are rice, wheat, beans and brassicas.

The way down was fairly uneventful and seemed much shorter than on the way up. We noticed that many philadelphus, spiraeas and deutzias had come into flower. We paused at the same fly-ridden hovel as we had on the way up and then hurried down the eroded muddy paths to the road where the bus was waiting. We stopped on our way back at Butterfly Springs, where a grove of camphor trees round a natural spring brings butterflies in huge numbers and nearly as many tourists today. That day there were few butterflies but rather more sightseers and we had difficulties because in 1981 Western faces were still a novelty and the crowds showed more interest in us than the butterflies. In Dali on the way back Roy and Peter took themselves for a walk and attempted to look into a courtyard, only to be attacked by a seemingly vicious dog. Roy's only weapon was his camera box which he swung in self-defence but it did put the dog off. Chinese dogs are usually scared off by threats and the Chinese throw stones at them, but rabies is a risk there and confrontation is better avoided. When we finally reached the store room in Xiaguan we were pleased to find that most of our previous collections were looking well in spite of our absence.

That evening another 'feast' had been arranged at the

An unusual form of Rosa longicuspis that we found on our last day at Santaipo to the south of Xiaguan. Normally white-flowered, this single specimen has also been called a near relative or synonym, R. lutens.

municipality, with the local magistrate and the usual speeches, a courtesy observed when you have been working in their territory. But the surprise was a baby black bear, probably hardly weaned, which our Kunming team suddenly produced. Presumably it was the offspring of the one we heard had been shot when we were at Huadianba. It was a delightful little thing with a rough woolly coat, all black apart from a white 'V' on its chest and a smaller one under its chin. I played with it for a bit, already its forelegs were developed with out of proportion strength and quite large claws. We looked after and fed it as well as we could until we parted but, although they said it would be taken to a zoo, its future did not look good. Bears in China are often kept in tiny cages to have bile drawn off them, or fattened up for eating, the paws being a particular 'delicacy'.

Excursions on the low ground

We had two day excursions at low elevation, accompanied by Professor Wu, a distinguished botanist and head of the Kunming Botanical Institute. The first was to a gorge called Qingbixu not far from Dali. The foothills were almost bare of vegetation but from the distance we could make out little patches of white on the steepest parts. These were *Rhododendron pachypodum* again, a remarkable survivor when one considers that it grows naturally in a woodland environment. Similarly, grazed or hacked off plants of the ericaceous *Craibiodendron yunnanense* (SBEC 1147) produced attractive reddish-pink young foliage. This collection has just survived for many years at Baravalla but it has proved to be more successful in the milder climate of coastal Cornwall. A hardier plant was *Veratrum taliensis* (SBEC 1142) with typical greenish white flowers of the genus but without the bold foliage of *V. album* and *V. nigrum*. We tried to collect some cuttings of a fine form of *Deutzia calycosa* with the reverse of the petals a deep rose but, alas, the cuttings proved to be too soft and rotted. We walked up into the gorge among increasing vegetation until a waterfall halted our progress. Up on the moist cliffs by the falls were plants of *Rhododendron edgeworthii* and *R. maddenii* subsp. *crassum*. Upright plants of *R. microphyton* were still in bloom, here only with dark purple flowers. Under the overhang of a large rock I found little scraps of dried leaves with only a tiny heart of greeny yellow showing it was alive. It was in fact a primula, *P. membranifolia*, a rare endemic of the Cangshan and although it was raining at the time the moss below the overhang was quite dry. A good adaptive strategy, it would come to life in the saturated atmosphere of the monsoon, now only a week or two away. A similar dormancy was shown by *Begonia taliensis* under the same rock.

Our last day was to Santaipo, 18km/11 miles south of Xiaguan, and this proved to be very different from the previous day with some forest remnants and hillsides covered with *Gaultheria forrestii* (SBEC 1224) and *Rhododendron decorum* (SBEC 1225), both around 2,400m/7,800ft. As expected, these last two collections

Schisandra grandiflora: this genus of vigorous twining climbers has a great variation in flower colour – white, pink, yellow, orange and, most commonly, red in S. rubriflora.

A form of Rhododendron decorum (SBEC 1225), which Peter noticed at the low elevation of 2,350m/7,700ft at Santaipo. It was far from flowering there in late May and in cultivation it blooms intermittently from July to September. Tender in the East, it has survived at Baravalla.

have not turned out to be very hardy but the *R. decorum* is of considerable interest.

Obtaining rhododendron seed in spring always entails looking for every capsule that might contain the odd seed, and keeping a special lookout for those that are not entirely opened. Completely closed capsules need a careful examination to be sure that there is no tell-tale little hole indicating that it is bug-ridden and may have no good seeds in it. It is essential that grubs are rigorously eliminated before packing or one may return home to find little piles of dust.

Our last evening involved more meetings and yet another feast with local delicacies including deer tendons and Er Hai snails. In the bowls of chicken soup floated little dry sticks that looked very like Twiglets. When I asked what they were the enigmatic answer was, 'Summer grass, winter worm'; on further enquiry, 'In your language, caterpillars.' On the high pastures the larvae of the moth *Hepialus amoricanus* are infected by the fungus *Cordyceps sinensis* in late May, entering through the mouthparts, and the fungus grows, filling the body with mycelium. They are then collected by the Chinese as a great delicacy. We were watched to make sure we ate them and we crunched away with a swig of *piju* (beer) as a necessary chaser. It was very unusual to be given a pudding in China; this one was made with gelatine from a palm and was tasteless and barely sweet. Sweet red wine and mau tai, the local firewater, went round and round the table with cries of 'Ganpei' (cheers) as a small glassful was knocked back in one. The mau tai was a present to Professor Feng, wrapped in paper covered with Bob's caricatures of all the members of the party.

Kunming again: temples and talks, farewell to friends

We made Kunming in the relatively quick time of eleven hours and the plants were taken to the room shared by the two of us. We were horrified by their appearance. Many were topsy-turvy and one of the six baskets was seriously squashed. No doubt they received an awful bouncing in the back of the truck on potholed roads and many of the softer plants, primulas in particular, were in a sorry, moribund-looking state. When we later heard that all soil would have to be washed from their roots for phytosanitary inspection, we really despaired of their survival, given that it would be twelve days from the last collecting in Huadianba until their arrival in Scotland and they might have to be packed and repacked four times in between.

The next day we visited a number of temples and then a part of the Kunming Institute's botanic garden. Many familiar

The native palm, Trachycarpus fortunei, *is frequently cultivated in Yunnan where its old fronds are harvested to make an excellent rain 'coat' for use when bending in the paddy fields.*

rhododendrons from lower altitudes were there but a new plant to us was *R. excellens*, which appeared to fall somewhere between *R. nuttallii* and *R. lindleyi*. Among other interesting plants was a Douglas fir, *Pseudotsuga sinensis*, which surprisingly grows near Kunming, although its relative *P. forrestii* grows further north near Atuntze (Deqin). The garden has been greatly extended over recent years.

The whole of 29 May was given up to talks given by the British contingent to an audience of about eighty from various institutions. As each talk had to be translated by the hard-working Clyde, it took a long time and my piece using Cox slides took 1½ hours with questions. The temperature rose, the room grew stuffier and the influence of the toilets below grew stronger, so we were glad to escape into the courtyard for the dreaded phytosanitary inspection. Fortunately, the bare-root requirement was rescinded and the plants escaped quite lightly for, although the inspectors were thorough, they did little more than remove some rotting leaves. We left after about ninety minutes with considerable relief.

All that now remained to do was to pack everything up for the journey home. Our share of the herbarium specimens (four sets) had to be sent by post as air freight was not then possible from Kunming. The cost was double our estimate at a horrific £600. Peter and I spent the last afternoon packing the plants and thought we had done a reasonable job until Professor Feng arrived with six new containers and we had to start cutting up bits of basket again. Eventually we ended with five baskets, two with a double layer of plants, and it was 2 a.m. before we got to bed. Peter was soon up again chasing cockroaches around the bathroom, crash, bang, wallop, followed by two dead insects and some complaints in the morning from the others next door. I had heard these onslaughts before and just retreated under the bedclothes.

It was our turn to give a banquet for our Chinese friends who had been so generous and helpful. There were at least twelve individual dishes for each person (which avoided the host's duty being to distribute the choicest bits), each artistically prepared with all manner of delicacies: frog's legs, wings of pigeon, so called tiger's lips, elephant trunks and bear's paws – we could never be sure whether it was the real thing but the last reminded us of our poor little bear which had travelled with us. All were accompanied by cries of 'Mau Tai' and 'Ganpei' and there was much talk of future trips and exchange of plant material, although even then we were warned that future collecting on this scale would be difficult. Dinner was followed by an astonishing acrobatic display including contortionist ladies with apparently no vertebrae, one of whom managed to rest her bottom on the back of her head. There was a rather dim conjuror and Roy got loose on the stage and managed to break the key in the box in which the 'magician' was supposed to be locked so the whole act had to be done again. But it was a magic evening, just the same.

All our Chinese friends came to see us off at the airport with shouts of 'Come back to Yunnan.' The Chinese love posed photographs and we had endless group shots taken by each member of our party and as we flew away we could see our friends still waving to us from the runway.

In the cavernous Tung Fang Hotel in Guangzhou, Roy and Peter had super haircuts which took one hour each with literally each hair being cut separately, followed by head massages from a pretty girl who did soothing things to them. Both came back like bouncing schoolboys and agreed it was the best haircut they had ever had.

Messages had gone ahead to Charles and Carolin Clapperton, our agents in Hong Kong, about our anxieties for the plants and further unpacking and inspection. It was still a surprise as we came down the airport gangway to be met by the small but redoubtable figure of the Governor's wife, Lady Maclehose, arms akimbo and flanked by two equerries who whisked the plants off to Government House under her personal charge. Later she told us that while she was watering them a leech had been found looping its way up her shoulder. 'A first for Government House,' she said crisply. We had also mentioned our worries about plants going in the aeroplane hold but then a call came from Cathay Pacific, 'Government House has told us of your concern. Unfortunately the main cabin is chock-a-block so we'll have to upgrade the plants to First Class,' (there was a pause) 'and I suppose you will have to travel with them.'

So we and all our plants flew back in unexpected luxury.

Looking back - a Chinese perspective

In retrospect it had been a ground-breaking trip for the Chinese as well as for us and some twenty years later I asked Guan Kaiyun, who had become Director of the Kunming Botanic Garden, what it had been like for the Chinese to look after and live with five British plant enthusiasts, including extended bouts of camping in the hills.

Remembering this time, Guan said, 'China had been very closed for many years and few of us had much contact with foreigners. We did not know much about their culture, their likes and dislikes, even what they would eat.' He said that one problem was mealtimes. The British did not understand the controlled economy that operated at that time and all across China meals took place on a strict timetable; breakfast at 7.30

a.m., lunch at 12.00 and supper at 6.00 p.m. Cooks went home at 6.00 p.m. If you returned later and wanted a meal, you could not have it. The logistics presented enormous problems as supplies in Dali were even more limited than in Kunming and most had to be brought in on the twelve-hour journey.

'We thought a large supply of apples would be a good standby,' said Guan, 'and we brought half a truck load to put in a cold store. Unfortunately the temperature was turned too low and they were frozen solid and had to be destroyed. Beer was quite scarce then, not like now, and we were a bit worried at the first camp when nearly the whole supply was drunk on the first night. It had to be brought up by porters and you will remember the time when we went up the wrong side of the ravine and we had to go back to the bottom and start again. We all did a lot of climbing that day and by the time we reached the camp the porters had drunk most of the beer.'

In spite of the difficulties, Guan had good memories of the trip: 'We were all bound together by a common interest in plants. For us the important thing was that this was the first time not just in recent years but in our history that we had a truly joint co-operation to study our plants in the field.'

As for the British, this expedition had been a dream come true and it proved to be more successful than any of us had dared to hope. Considering how frequently Cangshan had been hunted for plants in the past, it was amazing how many new plants we managed to introduce. We were, of course, exceptionally fortunate in being permitted to collect plants in addition to seed, something that was to be clamped down on in the future. We were also blessed with excellent Chinese companions and with all the help we had, especially in Hong Kong, in getting the plants home.

Peter grew a beard for the first and last time on the SBEC Expedition, partly as it was the only expedition after India 1965 that was long enough!

Chapter 4

UP THE MILKE DANDA:

Nepal 1985

Peter Hutchison

Peter and I suffered endless frustration in attempting to get another China trip under way. Eventually we had had enough and set our caps at Nepal, which we knew we could get to without endless obstacles being put in our way. We decided that it would be good to have a third member and Donald Maxwell MacDonald was an admirable choice in every way.

We chose ExplorAsia to organise our trip as they specialized in treks for small parties who wanted to do their own thing. Advice was sought from two experts on Nepal, our friends Tony Schilling and Roy Lancaster. After much discussion, we decided upon the Milke Danda as it was in the moister east of the country, rich in our favourite rhododendrons and primulas and off the beaten track for regular organised treks.

Timing was important to see the maximum in flower and yet avoid too much trouble from the remains of the previous winter's snow or from the onset of the summer monsoon, which hits the extreme east of Nepal with a vengeance. So we set off from London on 11 May 1995. Peter and I had, of course, been

to India in 1965 so knew roughly what to expect when we arrived in New Delhi, but the chaos at the airport seemed much worse than we remembered. The Indians must have handled endless trekkers on their way to Nepal, but they seemed to be utterly confused as to how to deal with our circumstances. We were not allowed to get to our baggage for ages and were relieved to find that it was all still there when our arguing finally prevailed. We had to wheel luggage trolleys from one terminal to another on a sort of cross country steeplechase. Eventually we found the other terminal and our flight for Kathmandu.

Both of us had an image of Kathmandu which was somewhat shattered on arrival. Instead of a small town perched half way up the Himalaya with snowy peaks all round, we found a sprawling city in the foot of a subtropical valley. Visitors sometimes complain that Kathmandu is smelly and crumbling, and indeed some parts are rather unsavoury. But it is full of colour, with silks and saris, and the richly carved

woodwork everywhere gives a sense of romantic history. The streets are lined with *Grevillea robusta*, an Australian import, and the lovely blue jacarandas were in full flower when we arrived in May. Flying foxes (fruit bats) hung from many of the trees and we watched them leave their roosts at dusk. Persil-white egrets nesting in drapes of bougainvillea made startling contrast with the magenta flowers.

ExplorAsia became Mountain Travel in Nepal and we visited their office to be briefed on our programme and staff. We were to have five sherpas, including the sirdar Chombi, plus about twenty porters to start with when our provisions would be at their heaviest as nothing is available up on the Milke Danda where there are no villages.

I had just bought myself a second-hand Hasselblad camera, which was heavy and took me a long time to get ready for a photograph, often cursing in the process. From then on the camera was known as the 'bloody hassle' and I became Sir Hassle. Later on the trek a small black-and-white dog joined

our party and attached itself to me and it became known as the Hassle Hound. Little sleep was had that night in our Kathmandu hotel due to mosquitoes. Peter and I made frequent sorties after them with a damp towel with little overall effect and finished spraying the whole room with insecticide.

We flew to Biratnagar which is situated on the plain just below the foothills and near the Indian frontier. The plane was not full of chickens as expected. We were met by Chombi, Lakhpa the cook and Phuri an assistant, plus two more Lakhpas, with a long wheel-based Landrover which drove through a belt of broad-leaved forest to the village of Dharan (Phursiri). Here we met a load of kit (tents, food, etc.) and expected a second vehicle but none appeared. By the time everything was loaded on

Opposite left: Donald Maxwell MacDonald and Peter Cox practising with their cameras and tripods in Kathmandu.

Above: Makalu, one of the giants of the Himalaya, at 8,475m/27,800ft.

Proprietor of the Hile Hilton. Hile was where we set off from on foot for our nineteen-day trek.

the one with most on the roof, there was just room for us to squeeze inside. The quite short drive over a low pass to the village of Hile took over six hours, owing to having to stop every half hour to top up the radiator with water as it kept boiling, and a boy sat on the mudguard for this purpose. We had climbed from 120m/350ft to the pass at 1,400m/4,700ft, down again to the Arun river, then a long climb up to Hile, by which time we all had sore behinds! Until recently this journey had to be done on foot, often in great heat, and we heard that some would-be trekkers to the Milke Danda had to give up before ever reaching Hile due to heat exhaustion. I like to think that we would have made it, although from the very short daily stages that we were given to begin with, the sherpas obviously thought that we looked totally unfit. Admittedly, Donald and I were on the heavy side and Peter just skin and bones!

Around Hile it was all either cultivated or long since cut over without even any secondary forest in sight. The three of us slept in a curious building, part temple, part doss-house, with an exotic Tibetan proprietor. Religious paraphernalia mingled with sprouting potatoes and grain bags, while house martins roosted overhead and rats ran about in the rafters. We called it the Hile Hilton. Unlike the Chinese, the Nepalese need no encouragement to make early starts and we were up at 5.30 and off before 8 o'clock. It was a long dull walk before we saw anything of interest apart from occasional hacked plants of low elevation, *Rhododendron arboreum* subsp. *arboreum* which always has a plastered silvery indumentum and red flowers. Then a more interesting shrubby flora started to appear.[1]

We had lunch at 10.30 which would normally be far too early but our tummies were reminding us of the 5 a.m. start. A

good bit of forest started in a small gorge but it was being vigorously destroyed from the Chitare end where we stayed the night. We heard the steady hack, hack of axes going all the time it was daylight. There were many huge, evidently ancient mahonias full of moss and epiphytes including some beautiful plants of *Rhododendron dalhousiae* with its exotic lily-like flowers, yellowish green in colour flushed deeper in the throat. I had a long session with the 'Hassle' photographing these. The road was being continued to Chitare and beyond, so future access to the Milke Danda will become all too easy.

Chitare was our first camp, living in some style with a tent each, plus mess and loo tents, a table and camp chairs. The mess tent was lit by tilly lamps which helped to warm the tent in addition to lighting it. Donald and I opened our Grouse whisky and Peter his traditional Sauternes. We felt quite colonial.

Our next lunch stop was by some fine *Quercus lamellosa* of nearly 30m/100ft, covered in epiphytes. A large liana climbing into the oaks turned out to be the climbing elaeagnus, *E. infundibularis*. As we gained altitude, the mahonias died out and a forest of *Rhododendron arboreum* took over. To our surprise, these were nearly all subsp. *cinnamomeum* with pale pink to reddish-crimson flowers and the characteristic rusty coloured indumentum. The trusses were disappointing but this may have been due to them being nearly over. Surprisingly there was no sign of last year's capsules but, as this was at only

1. It included *Viburnum erubescens*, remnants of *Mahonia napaulensis*, *Prunus cerasoides*, *Castanopsis*, *Daphne bholua*, *Acer campbellii*, one *Magnolia campbellii* and underneath *Sarcococca*, *Arisaema* and *Paris* with the epiphytes *Vaccinium retusum* and *Agapetes serpens* with cream to scarlet flowers.

2,600m/8,500ft, we were not really interested in collecting seed anyway as any plants raised would be tender. They made magnificent trees, many over 15m/50ft, and one by our camp had a girth of 3m/10ft and must have been over 24m/80ft high. One clearing surrounded by these towering giants was an unforgettable sight. It was noticeable how trees which had been cut down or partly mutilated were able to sprout. We also found three plants of *R. arboreum* subsp. *arboreum*, much earlier into growth than subsp. *cinnamomeum* and with much paler leaves, making them easy to pick out. No crosses between the two subspecies were found despite a thorough search. A curious fasciated growth occurred quite widely on *R. arboreum* which usually lacked chlorophyll and was pinky-red coloured or sometimes very pale green with a little chlorophyll, but both seemed capable of growing on for a year or two.

We saw our first yellow-billed blue magpie, an amazing bird with an extraordinarily long tail. We also had a glimpse of our first pheasant, which took off as Peter and I were rummaging through the rather uninteresting forest behind the camp. Later we saw some pheasant families with small chicks and, sadly, several snares set across the paths with closely pushed in bamboo sticks to guide a bird into the noose. We also saw black eagles and jungle crows with more magpies and later that day several nutcrackers, a crow-relative we had previously seen in Yugoslavia so it is widely distributed. On the Milke Danda we were very surprised to see and hear a woodcock roding one evening.

Daphne bholua grew all around our camp with plenty of seedlings or suckers. This daphne, now more widely grown, has an upright habit and grows to 3m/10ft with evergreen or deciduous leaves, the latter usually being at the highest altitudes of up to 3,400m/11,000ft. Its abundant reddish mauve flowers appear in January-March and the superb scent fills the air all around. This fine plant used to have a reputation for being rather tender but with no hard winters in the last ten years it has survived outside without wall protection in both our gardens. At Glendoick Peter noted that in the harsh 1995/6 winter it was an evergreen plant that just survived while two deciduous forms including the clone 'Gurkha' succumbed. In our opinion, this is by far the finest of all winter-flowering shrubs and as it is quick-growing, it can be rapidly replaced. But in Nepal it had long since finished flowering with no signs of seed being set. Other plants here were a large *Magnolia campbellii* which had been hacked off at 15m/50ft and trees of the large-leaved holly, *Ilex dipyrena*, had been similarly cut well above the ground. Chombi told us that the young leaves are used for spring fodder.

This was a most attractive and comparatively peaceful camp. Our sherpas were in jolly form playing cards and it was great to be in the hills again. A herders' hut stood in the middle of the clearing with several more further up. A village we had

passed through had been totally burnt down, not surprising considering that they have their fires in the middle of the floors with no chimney, or even a hole for the smoke to escape.

The ridge carried on with ups and downs but no great gains in altitude until we reached a north-facing slope and the vegetation changed with *Rhododendron barbatum* appearing at 2,700m/9,000ft, now past flowering. However, *R. triflorum* with its typical mahogany peeling bark of the western form was showing quite good yellow flowers (CHM 2003). A bit lower in very dense shade was an apparently non-flowering colony of *Cardiocrinum giganteum*.

This camp, Chauki, faced west in a large park-like clearing with a poor looking village full of all too inquisitive inhabitants. Women were harvesting their crop of barley with scissors. While we were writing notes in the sunshine, a thunderstorm was raging away to the north, which soon reached us, with one thunderbolt about as near as it could be without actually hitting us. Hail soon covered the ground and our staff hurriedly dug trenches with our ice axes around our tents which proved to be a wise move. The storm lasted forty minutes and we took many photographs of the cloud boiling up the valley towards us.

Searching the vicinity of the clearing around our camp revealed an incredibly steep ravine into which we peered and saw a large shrub covered in huge white flowers. This could only be

Arisaema speciosum, *one of the few plants of interest on the walk to Chitare.*

Rhododendron lindleyi, *with comparatively broad corollas and partially reflexed lobes typical of the original introduction, was growing in a tree so full of other epiphytes that it was impossible to ascertain what the original tree was.*

Rhododendron griffithianum and we made plans to come back in the morning. We celebrated a good day with Grouse whisky and sauternes both before and after supper! The night was not one of our best, however, not due to alcohol but dogs barking in relays for two thirds of the night with the odd thunder and rain in between. As often happens, the morning was bright and clear with splendid views of the mountains including Kanchenjunga. Our porters set off while we went back to our ravine, but by now the light was hopeless for photography and it proved to be a desperately hazardous spot with the fine *R. griffithianum* totally out of reach without ropes. There were some seedlings in an amazingly dry position under a rock and how they could have germinated, let alone grow, was a mystery. Peter collected his first tick of the trip, as large as those of Arunachal Pradesh, but caught it before it was fully embedded in his armpit.

We kept looking out for more ravines containing *Rhododendron griffithianum*. One ravine had a tree of at least 12m/40ft with a straight smooth trunk but no capsules in reach, but the next place had numerous younger specimens of 3-6m/10-20ft and at last one containing capsules. The flowers in both these gullies were too far gone for photography. All these plants were in north- or east-facing deep gullies and were always associated with a particularly unpleasant undergrowth of a semi-creeping raspberry. Seedlings from this collection (CHM 2006) at Baravalla used to get their first growth frosted, but it has come through these last three years and Peter tells me that one at Glendoick, planted inside the old mill, is making remarkable growth, and in 2007 had been flowering for five years.

For a while *Rhododendron arboreum* and *R. barbatum* grew together and the latter actually replaced the former as the dominant species. There was no evidence of hybrids between these two species, although they must often flower over the same period. A single plant of *R. cinnabarinum* appeared at the path side covered with good orange flowers, early for this species but it must have been a straggler at only 2,700m/9,000ft. Its foliage was very blotched and appeared to

be infected by powdery mildew. This was of particular interest as, of all the different forms of the species, the orange ones are undoubtedly the most susceptible to this disease.

Drizzle came on, then thunder, followed by a multitude of hail stones, getting worse and worse all the time. Soon the paths were awash with hail soup and, despite our umbrellas, we were soaked through. What a joy it was to find our tents already erected and our fresh clothes perfectly dry. This was camping in style! We photographed some hail stones as big as marbles in a sherpa's hand and the rivers of hail slush around our tents. The storm carried on for most of the evening.

We had met a Swedish couple trekking and were rather offended when the Hassle hound, which had become a constant companion, transferred his allegiance to them. However he reappeared during the day and resumed his habit of sleeping under my flysheet at night.

I found a large specimen of *R. lindleyi* (CHM 2011) high up in a tree, which was brimming over with moss and epiphytes, but occasional branches managed to appear at all angles out of this tousled mass. This plant was typical of the early introductions of this species with only two large heavily scented flowers to the truss, and the corolla more open than in recent introductions.

The Milke Danda

The view ahead showed that we were rapidly approaching the Milke Danda ridge from the east, apparently about mid-way between its start and the beginning of the higher Jaljale Himal to the north with snow on it. It was a rather bare camp but nearby was a *pokhari* (small lake), very still with reflections of a few old *R. arboreum* at its rim. Peter and I took our cameras to it and the resulting photographs were exactly the same view as one in the 1998 Exodus brochure, although theirs showed the mountains behind. The lovely *Pleione hookerianum* was common on rocks around here, with flowers varying from white to pink.

The morning of 20th May looked dreadful but it cleared somewhat. The weather was amazingly changeable there. One moment it could be sunny with a clear sky all around, the next the clouds would be boiling up from below, to be followed shortly by a violent hailstorm. There were many ups and downs before finally reaching the Milke Danda at just over 3,400m/11,000ft. We had fun photographing yaks along the trail, each animal seeming more photogenic than the last.[2]

Rhododendrons became more plentiful and varied. A group of immature big-leaved plants with plastered white

2. The yaks varied from black, grey, to black and white and other combinations. These were proper yaks with long shaggy hair almost to the ground and a broad tail of hair. If the hair is shorter and less shaggy, they are probably *dzos*, crosses between yaks and cattle.

The Jaljale Himal from the north end of the 3,700m/12,000ft Milke Danda ridge. It took a great deal of persuasion to get our staff to let us go on to the Jaljale, where we found many plants different from those we had seen on the Milke Danda. Beyond the Jaljale is Topke Gola where several plant-hunting trips have been.

Sir Hassle and the Hassle Hound admiring the view from 3,700m/12,000ft on the Milke Danda ridge. Very often this view would be blotted out within minutes as cloud surged up from the valleys below, frequently followed by a hail storm.

Above left: We were intrigued to find different-coloured forms of Rhododendron cinnabarinum growing together on the Milke Danda ridge. Orange flowers appeared to be the commonest. Alas, they also seem to be the most susceptible to powdery mildew.

Above right: A fine form of Rhododendron cinnabarinum with red flowers, which would place it in the Roylei Group.

Left: Yellow, the third colour form of Rhododendron cinnabarinum that grew mixed together. This is rather different from the plant long grown as R. xanthocodon in cultivation, which has paler, shorter leaves and a shorter corolla.

A fine specimen of Rhododendron campylocarpum *on the Milke Danda ridge.*

Peter Cox and Donald Maxwell MacDonald having afternoon tea in the rain. The bowl contains potassium permanganate for washing.

indumentum appeared to be *R. grande* at 3,200m/10,500ft, but we soon got into plentiful *R. hodgsonii* which sometimes had a not dissimilar indumentum. *R. arboreum* became more and more stunted and *R. cinnabarinum* appeared in quantity in full flower. The different forms of the latter intrigued us; in one place three adjacent plants had orange, pale orange and yellow flowers, while others with red flowers were a short distance away which would fit into Roylei Group. Soon *R. campanulatum* and *R. campylocarpum* appeared. The former had a good continuous but pale indumentum and the flowers varied from a good bluish-mauve, heavily spotted, to a wishy-washy pale mauve. Seed taken from a good form has proved equally variable at Broich (CHM 2024). The *R. campylocarpum* were a good uniform yellow, with or without a small blotch and sometimes with orange buds. *R. hodgsonii* was mostly over but some were very deep coloured and some also had very large leaves. We also saw our first *R. thomsonii* and one plant of the epiphytic *R. camelliiflorum*.

There was more rain during supper when we ate some quite good yak and endured thunder most of the night. We had been finding seed scarce. While 1984 could have been a poor flowering season, the frequent hail storms would be bound to knock off some of last years capsules. Most places we have been to in China in the spring have been much more successful for collecting rhododendron seed but the springs there have been drier, with few, if any, hail storms.

We had started to organise our plant collecting properly and acquired some bamboo trays on which we sewed seedlings with roots wrapped in moss. These trays were then fitted in layers into a basket, which was carried on a porter's back, the whole thing surmounted by an umbrella to keep the sun off. Even if it looked a bit odd, it worked well, but some of our seedlings had already suffered from the combination of sun and being covered with polythene and the foliage had been somewhat scorched.

We found a few stragglers of *R. arboreum* subsp. *cinnamomeum* (CHM 2036) at 3,300m/10,700ft with good crimson-red flowers. There was no seed so we collected a few seedlings. One has flowered at Glendoick with excellent rufous indumentum and rose-red flowers as seen on its parent. It came through the fairly severe winter of 1995-6 unscathed.

Up to now we had found no natural hybrid rhododendrons but on 22 May this was fully rectified. We found several pink-flowered plants which were undoubtedly *R. thomsonii* x *R. campylocarpum* (formerly called *R. thomsonii* var. *candelabrum*), two creamy-spotted flowered plants being *R. campanulatum* x *R. campylocarpum*, and a horrible dirty magenta-flowered *R. campanulatum* x *R. thomsonii*.

We were now on top of the Milke Danda ridge, which went up and down to our second ridge camp. It was a good thing that we had an excellent view of what lay ahead as Chombi wanted us to stop here and just do day treks. It was obvious that there were two more Milke Danda peaks of about 3,700m/12,000ft before the Jaljale which looked formidable, and we certainly wanted to get at least on to the Jaljale and perhaps beyond. So we persuaded Chombi to move on to the second peak. The only new rhododendron for the day was *R. anthopogon* with pale yellow flowers and it turned out that all the plants on the ridge were of that colour. This was an attractive form, compact with unusual glaucous leaves but, sadly, it developed a high susceptibility to rust fungus in cultivation and Peter says that all the plants at Glendoick had to be destroyed. Chombi collected quantities of leaves of this species for incense. We selected seedlings of various plants including different forms of *R. lepidotum* that we had been seeing for some time but only one low-elevation pinkish one was in flower. In cultivation, it turned out to be an upright form with largish leaves and purple flowers but a dwarfish plant had smaller leaves with yellow flowers. In one place there was an undulating hollow on the ridge populated entirely with *R. lepidotum*. This may sound dull but it was the most beautiful natural rock garden.

Primula calderiana *subsp.* strumosa.

Primula obliqua *on the Jaljale out above the tree-line. The mound it has built up and all the old foliage indicate that it grows to a great age.*

The finest plant we saw of Primula gracilipes *on the Jaljale. This is one of the easiest Petiolarid primulas in cultivation.*

A fine rosette of the monocarpic Meconopsis paniculata *which would be likely to flower later that year and then die.*

Another gully had several ancient moss-covered *Prunus rufa*. Unfortunately the moss covered the trunks, hiding the often-beautiful peeling bark of this species.

We collected plants of three gaultherias, *G. pyroloides* (CHM 2032) with round leaves and blue fruit, the tiny *G. trichophylla* (CHM 2031) with surprisingly large blue fruit and the spreading *G. nummularioides* (CHM 2033) in a better, hardier form than we had previously seen in cultivation.

This camp at 3,500m/11,500ft was perched right on top of a hill and we became somewhat worried that we might be blown away. Indeed the tents did shake a little in the wind during the night but were quite secure. We woke to a beautiful morning with gorgeous views all round so lots of photographs were taken. We found a fine *Rhododendron campylocarpum* sheltered under a cliff; it was the only plant of this lovely species that had good seed on it and it has proved attractive in cultivation. An extremely interesting and unlikely natural hybrid with just one truss was *R. hodgsonii* x *R. thomsonii* with reddish crimson flowers. Nearby was our first *Cassiope fastigiata* just opening its little white bells.

The splendid trunks of a grove of Rhododendron thomsonii.

We reached the camp near the end of the Milke Danda much earlier than expected and the sherpas produced the usual excuse for not going on, saying that there was no water. We set off at midday to recce the situation and it took us two hours to reach near the foot of the little dip between the Milke Danda and the Jaljale. We passed places where the ridge was very narrow and the path traversed the edges of sheer precipices down into the Arun valley to the west. We had arguments as to how many hundreds or thousands of feet high these cliffs might be.

Up the Jaljale
The following morning we managed to persuade Chombi to let us set off to the Jaljale with Phuri, the three Lakhpas and three porters. We dropped 300m/1,000ft into the dip in one and a quarter hours and then went straight on, eventually finding a suitable campsite at 3,800m/12,500ft. On the way we found the tiny dwarf creeping *Ilex intricata*, *Fritillaria cirrhosa* not yet out, superb yellow *Primula calderiana* subsp. *strumosa* and lots of ancient-looking plants of *P. obliqua* with fine scented creamy-white flowers just opening. This species forms large raised clumps with skirts of many years of old leaves hanging down, but it is intractable in cultivation, which is a great pity. Peter managed to grow some large healthy-looking specimens at Glendoick from a later seed collection, only to find that they completely disappeared over winter. They obviously miss the protection of continuous winter snow cover. There were two other primulas, one with pinkish flowers on rock faces, the other was higher up, tiny with blue flowers, probably a member of section Minutissima. A species of section Petiolares had been common, often right on the path. This had pink to rose-magenta flowers with a white eye and was probably *P. gracilipes*. Among the primulas were numerous golden rosettes of *Meconopsis paniculata*.

On the way up the Jaljale, we passed through splendid rhododendron forest, mostly *R. hodgsonii* and *R. thomsonii* (CHM

Rhododendron thomsonii *with red calyces. The damage to the corolla, which often happens with early reds in cultivation, is caused by birds, presumably to get at the nectar.*

2054). There were many huge rounded specimens of up to 6m/20ft or more; most of which had dark crimson-red flowers with red calyces, while a few were paler with cream calyces. One large specimen which was definitely not a hybrid had clear pink flowers with a dark throat. We tried collecting scions to take home. Incidentally, there was no *R. campylocarpum* on the Jaljale. Above the tree-line we found the dwarf *R. setosum* (CHM 2049), easily identified by its hairy leaves; one plant was just opening its purple flowers. This species formed a wind-sheared closely knit carpet with *R. anthopogon* and *Cassiope fastigiata*.

113

The sun rising above Kanchenjunga, its massive crown above a sea of cloud.

We were woken before 5 o'clock to the most beautiful morning yet. Our camp was in a little hollow without a view but a few steps up to the surrounding rocks revealed the most breathtaking panorama. All the land below 3,500m/11,500ft was enveloped in a huge tablecloth of cloud, above it every peak was clear and we watched the sun rise right over the crown of Kanchenjunga. We took endless photographs in both directions. Lakhpa two, also known as 'Laughing or Dancing Boy' climbed up the vertical rock with ease and lit a juniper fire on top of it from which drifted a trail of aromatic smoke, a tribute to the gods.

We climbed 250m/800ft in an hour, past a boulder scree with snow above, around a rocky peak (all breaking up and about to add to the scree) and out on to a level path with rocks and cliffs on the left. The Jaljale Himal is a much wider, bigger chunk of mountain than the Milke Danda, with several minor peaks of its own. There was a new primula to us on the rocks with grey-mauve flowers and farinaceous leaves like *P. farinosa*. Searches revealed no new rhododendrons. We had hoped to see both *R. wightii* and *R. fulgens*, but we later found out that these only occur some way further on around Topke Gola. If we had not wasted so much time with short treks early on, it might have been possible to get that far in the nineteen days we had. Isolated clumps of *R. campanulatum* grew as high as 4,100m/13,500ft, but just as subsp. *campanulatum*, not the hoped for subsp. *aeruginosum* with its glaucous foliage. The

light was brilliant and with many snow patches and pools about and having no dark glasses, we became a little worried about snow blindness. It was quite obvious from the lack of tracks that no one had been up here before us that spring. Anyway, we had to hurry down as we had to get back to the top Milke Danda camp and, once again, we were lucky in just getting into camp before the rain descended in torrents. At the end I think we all felt fairly tired having during the day climbed 300m/1,000ft, then dropped 850m/2,700ft, then up again 300m/1,000ft, with various little ups and downs between.

On the way down the Milke Danda we came across an area where the ground was covered with green leaves, mostly those of *R. thomsonii*, and then when we came to some *R. hodgsonii*, its leaves were in shreds. In contrast the leaves of *R. barbatum*, more pendulous at that time of year, had hardly been damaged at all. A mile on there was no damage. It was obvious to us that a very local hailstorm, with hailstones maybe as big as golf balls, had been the cause but when we asked Chombi what he thought caused it, he answered with one word, 'Monkeys'!

That afternoon we packed plants for several hours. Lakhpa one produced some yak butter, to our surprise not rancid but it was full of yak hairs. Our evening meal was rather good tuna noodles with yet more cauliflower of which by now we were getting decidedly tired. Lakhpa had been very clever in the number of ways he thought up of cooking cauliflower; we estimated about fifteen different recipes!

Rhododendron hodgsonii, *the only big-leaved species to grow on the Milke Danda ridge.*

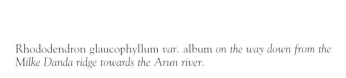

Rhododendron glaucophyllum *var.* album *on the way down from the Milke Danda ridge towards the Arun river.*

The descent

We were woken at 4.50 a.m. to a horrible day of mist and drizzle. Donald went off to photograph *R. hodgsonii* leaves being used for channelling water and when he returned he and I were chased into clearing our tents quickly while Peter for once was better organised. That night had been our last on the Milke Danda and we were now to descend towards the Arun river, on the opposite side of the ridge to the one that we came up by. Roy Lancaster's description of the area we were to walk through was mouth-watering for its richness in interesting plants, but the weather became worse and worse and we had steady heavy rain the whole day. We started at 3,500m/11,500ft and soon turned down a side ridge.

One special rhododendron recorded on this side ridge was *R. glaucophyllum* var. *album* (CHM 2069) and Donald was the first to find it while Peter was examining a pink- and green-flowered *R. lepidotum*. Luck was with us in that the *R. glaucophyllum* was in full flower, although photography was almost impossible with that weather. This white form evidently occurs only in Nepal

and, in fact, there may be no pinks. It is a pretty plant with its white bells on long stalks but it is generally more tender than the type from further east. At 200m/660ft lower we found *R. ciliatum* over a small area but with plenty of seedlings. We attempted to collect a seedling of what we thought was an attractive hornbeam, *Carpinus viminea*, but it was a case of mistaken identity as it turned out to be the hazel, *Corylus ferox*, which has similar long leaves. We also collected seedlings of *Populus* (*jacquemontiana* var.) *glauca*. This is a most striking poplar with large glaucous leaves that appear in mid-June, by which time one is giving it up for dead. Another seedling collected was a schefflera which we added to our Arunachal one at Baravalla. Both are now fine trees (2007). We believe that we were the first to introduce scheffleras hardy enough to grow outside in Britain as the majority are grown as house plants.

As we descended from higher up, between 3,400 and 3,000m/11,000 and 10,000ft, the huge silvery rosettes of a meconopsis species, probably the pale blue M. *wallichii*, were

Colourful crowds of locals in the village of Kharang, close to the Arun river where we camped.

plentiful but, surprisingly, none were showing signs of producing flowering stems. In cultivation, this species often flowers in its second season if it has been well grown. *Rhododendron cinnabarinum* continued down the slope to at least as low as 2,900m/9,500ft and at this altitude the flowers were all an amazingly uniform orange. At one point, all the local rhododendrons[3] met in a proliferation of moss and epiphytes that were almost the equal of those we saw in Arunachal Pradesh in 1965. There were trees growing on trees and shrubs on shrubs with a clotted mass of *Vaccinium*, *Agapetes* and moss with *Pleione*. We soon descended into evergreen forest where *Quercus* and *Castanopsis* made huge trees.

The day was miserable and we were very frustrated over the richness of the flora for which we had too little time, and the weather certainly did not help. A torrential shower made the path all the more treacherous and even some of the porters slipped and fell. Chombi saw a black snake on the path, probably a black mamba, and the lowish elevation and wet inevitably meant a mass of leeches, so we kept stopping to scrape them off our hands and legs. Donald removed a tick just in time from his armpit and acquired a good selection of leeches which were all carefully recorded with his macro-lens.

We walked down and down, into and through much terraced ground. Our first stop for a campsite was rejected as the

owner said that the land was too good. Anyway the porters refused to stop, a sort of walk-on strike, as they reckoned that they were within half an hour of Sita Pokhari where *chang*[4], cigarettes and more food were available. After our tents had been erected, another downpour started and soon we were

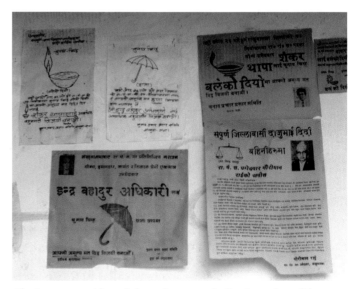

Election posters with symbols, such as an umbrella, for each candidate.

Part of the track along the Arun river which rises up in the main Himalayan range.

sitting in our mess tent with our feet in water. This rain did have the benefit of driving away our village audience and we actually washed our feet for the first time on the trek, treated our bites and rubbed our aching knees. The temperature was sweltering, which was not surprising as we had dropped 2,000m/6,500ft in the day, having been on the move for 10½ hours. We had a change of diet to a welcome but tough chicken and the Hasslehound enjoyed the bits. We wrote up our notes to the crescendo of tiny croaking frogs, coming from the pond, fields and even inside our mess tent. Mosquitoes were surprisingly scarce but as Peter was just nodding off to sleep, he felt something wet on his nose; torch and knife were soon into action and the leech was cut into many pieces outside his tent.

3. *R. ciliatum, R. glaucophyllum* var. *album, R. barbatum, R. arboreum, R. cinnabarinum, R. lepidotum*, a uniformly pale *R. triflorum* and, a little lower, two plants of *R. dalhousiae.*

4. A sort of beer made from fermenting rice and millet, out of which the drink is squeezed.

117

By the morning the frogs had quietened but a pack of jackals howled at the top of their voices just outside our tents. A gentle path passed through lopped forest and we could hear monkey noises in the trees around. We spent some time in the very attractive and photogenic village of Chainpur. We camped above the village of Kharang which, as it was market day, was full of people and flocks of children. We slept a night on the mud floor of a new school building with rickety steps up to the veranda which would hardly pass our British health and safety standards.

We left very early after a hot night to avoid the worst of the day's heat and we were all delighted to have the chance of bathing in a small river just before its confluence with the much bigger Arun. Even Peter, who is known for his aversion to outdoor bathing, splashed around in a pair of white underpants and a potting shed hat. Shortly after our bath, we tested the temperature of the Arun and found it much colder, no doubt due to its size and even more because it rises in the main snow peaks of the Himalaya. Our path now followed the Arun, starting at 400m/1,320ft; one stretch was cut out of a cliff where a concrete bridge had a horrific sag in it. We watched a ferry which was little more than a dugout holding about ten people crossing the river, back and forth, taking guests to a wedding party on the far bank. As the river was very rapid, the boat had to be hauled back up river after each trip. This stretch of the river was pretty muddy and some of the soil on the banks was an amazing shade of red. We passed a trekking party led by a Mr Mike Cheyney, which was the only party of foreigners apart from the Swedish couple that we actually saw during our nineteen days.

We spent the day trying to escape heavy showers, the first two quite successfully sheltering in houses and trying to avoid the drips, but the last one caught us out and soaked us to the skin too late in the day to dry out again. All our clothes were now wet or damp and getting smellier by the day. It was a question of selecting the least damp of our limited wardrobe and everything had been recycled more than once.

As we were walking along the narrow walls between paddy fields, we met a fierce-looking officer who managed to relate in uncertain English that another 300 police were to follow and indeed we could see the long zigzag of soldiers, sinister in their brown raincoats. I had a carefully polite conversation with him, asking where they were heading for and was told that they were investigating an air crash further up the valley. A little shocked, I asked if this had just happened; 'Oh no,' he replied, 'three months ago.'

A more likely explanation was that the police were there to control the forthcoming elections when rival parties are liable to attack each other. As much of the population was illiterate, election posters had different objects such as a cow or an aeroplane to represent each party or candidate.

The Hasslehound barked half the night and a sunny morning made it hotter than ever. We were shortly due to start the long climb back up to Hile, which was bound to be hard in the heat with little or no shade. One needs to get into the right frame of mind for such a stiff climb. We started off going fine until there was a sudden halt. And we stopped and we stopped, partly due to the slowness of the porters who had regular diversions. Every house sold *chang* and we tried some. Donald and I took little more than cautious sips but Peter made the mistake of having rather more which, for a start, made him burp all afternoon. The porters got further and further behind, exasperating Peter who decided to stride out, walking up the hill in great style. Thank heavens the porters made it in time to set up camp. We had climbed about 1,000m/3,300ft in that heat and repeated stops made it much more difficult. Our plants looked in reasonable shape considering the heat but the top two trays needed a really good soaking. As usual, thunder appeared in the late afternoon, although the rain was nothing like the deluge of the previous two days.

Peter made his usual night excursion with ice axe and stones to silence barking dogs, but suddenly the effect of the *chang* hit him with a vengeance and he had a very uncomfortable remainder of the night. Donald and I fared better, feeling just a little off colour. Peter said later that the struggle to climb the remaining 600m/2,000ft to Hile was the worst he could ever remember and he certainly looked ghastly. The chang was no doubt made with unboiled water but I also kept thinking of the woman showing us how it was made as she squeezed the millet with dirty hands.

We set up camp just below Hile and Peter lay out in the sun where he recovered remarkably quickly. Our horrible soggy clothes and mouldering boots were also laid out to dry. The Hasslehound joined us for tea but seemed very tired and would not eat our dry biscuits, which was unusual. We had a photographing session with our porters and gave our personal porter (who was supposed to be older and therefore given our mountain of personal packs) a hundred rupees. Much to our surprise, we were told that it had not rained in Hile all the time we had been trekking.

The Hasslehound guarded us all night and only barked at intruders occasionally. We got to work on the final packing of our plants and tied in each layer with string. All the ends of the bamboo supports were cut off and bound. Not surprisingly, the pink *R. thomsonii* scions looked poorly, with most of the leaves having shed. To pass the time waiting to be picked up, we photographed yet one more leech. This time we had a Willis Jeep, Indian style, and somehow we packed everything in and on, although Dancing Boy Lakhpa and Phuri came on by bus. We were not exactly comfortable. This time a boy hung on at the back to do the radiator filling routine while we were climbing. We camped at Phursiri where we were besieged by locals and

Peter was seen pursuing small children who had invaded his tent around the sports ground, waving his ice axe. I hardly think they were in any danger but they were sometimes followed into our tents by their mothers which presented a bigger problem. Before leaving for the airport, we had the ceremony of thanking our staff who had been cheerful stalwarts and good companions.

Just after we got into the plane at Biratnagar, an ambulance pulled up and a very sick man was clumsily draped over the seats directly opposite us. Despite drips, artificial respiration and a doctor massaging his chest, he was obviously dying. By the time we arrived in Kathmandu, the doctor was making only feeble efforts to pretend to the already wailing wife that he was still alive and a great lamentation set up in the plane.

There was no one to meet us from Mountain Travel so we took two taxis. Half way to our hotel, one taxi ran out of fuel so some was siphoned into a plastic can from the following taxi and then siphoned into ours. Our small ratty man from Mountain Travel met us at the hotel with excuses that the plane times had changed, which they had not. However, everyone was very helpful in putting together the numerous papers we would need to get our plants through, including a tough and efficient little lady called Manita who was promptly given the nickname 'Man Eater'!

As we had time to spare, we visited the botanic garden which had been set up by Tony Schilling in an attractive site below a peak covered with fine forest, some distance east of Kathmandu. Tony had already told us that he despaired for its future, but it was worse that we could possibly have imagined. The only things in flower were a few petunias and pelargoniums. Cattle were grazing and empty flowerbeds were used for slaughtering poultry and animals, with piles of feathers, trails of blood and several carcasses lying around. Some greenhouses were virtually empty and a few orchids and ferns were poorly maintained.

Apart from Peter's affair with *chang*, we had kept remarkably healthy but Donald ate some pâté in the Yak and Yeti Hotel and, as a result, was violently ill all the way to our stop in Dubai. Our own travel was relatively straightforward but the plants were still in the basketwork cake stand which had been fine for travelling around Nepal on a porter's back, but it was not well suited to modern air travel. At Delhi airport, we had a most objectionable Indian British Airways official who refused to accept the plants. We thought that we had eventually persuaded him to take them, helped by a back hander to the porter, but when we collected our luggage at Heathrow, there were no plants.

Everyone at Heathrow was most helpful and we were even allowed to look into the containers which had come off the plane. Delhi was telexed and the answer came back that there was no room for them, which was nonsense as several containers had been empty. Peter went home but I had to

Our collected plants, for which we had an import permit, were carried in this basket. The plants were tied to small bamboo 'trays', which were wired into the basket at three levels. The umbrella is to keep the sun off.

remain in London anyway and spent most of the next day at the airport, telexing, meeting planes and chatting up the Customs. The Customs official was a keen gardener and most sympathetic to our sad tale. When the plants eventually did arrive, looking dry and more shaken than ever, the Customs tea kettle was ready to give them a thorough dousing and, in spite of their ordeal, a number did survive and grow into decent specimens.

It had been an unusual three weeks, travelling around eastern Nepal in colonial style, with camps prepared ahead of our arrival and being woken at 5 a.m. by a cry of 'Bed Tea' as a steaming mug was thrust into the tent. It had not been outstanding for plants but then we had expected that, and we did have our first taste of the mountain flora of the Himalaya, for in India in 1965 we had little chance of getting above the subtropical zone. The scenery had been magnificent although we could have wished for fewer downpours, but watching the sun rise over Kanchenjunga from another peak in the Himalaya with a carpet of cloud shutting off the world beneath is an experience one does not forget.

Chapter 5

THE RED GRASSLANDS AND JADE DRAGON MOUNTAIN:

China 1986

Peter Hutchison

After our repeated failures to get back to China on our own, the next best thing was to go on an organised tour and who better to go with than our great friend, the ultimate plantsman Roy Lancaster? In the short time since China started opening up, Roy had been there several times, one of these being our groundbreaking trip in 1981, and had amassed an astonishing knowledge of the Chinese flora. The trouble with tours is that one has no say in who one's fellow travellers are or where one is going. It turned out to be the biggest party we had ever travelled with, eighteen in total excluding guides, cooks and porters. Raoul Moxley had earned a reputation for pioneering new areas in China and Roy's cheerful enthusiasm and profound knowledge of plants had gathered a fan club of elderly ladies known as 'Roy's Girls', although several of them had little interest in plants. On the Chinese side, San Choo combined efficient organization with an outsize sense of humour and a fund of dubious jokes.

In the Heathrow foyer we eyed our fellow travellers with

some curiosity, but this time Peter was accompanied by his wife Patricia and I had my son James with me on his first plant trip. There was Donald Maxwell Macdonald, the third member on our Nepal trip, who usually managed to find a funny side at our direst moments and the planty side was completed by Count Philippe de Spoelberch, well known in dendrologist circles, and Fritz Smit from Holland who kept disappearing but would usually be found flat on the ground photographing something very small.

In China the original plan often ends by being changed, on this occasion to a considerable extent. The direct route up the Min river had been 'broken', as the Chinese say when a road gets swept away by a landside, and it meant a long and sometimes tedious detour, adding a large amount to our mileage by bus. The second half of the tour was to go to Baoshan and on to Ruili in west Yunnan, but this was changed to Lijiang and Yulong Shan in north-west Yunnan, much to our delight as the Ruili area is semi-tropical. We were heading for Wilson country.[1]

We started by losing a day through having to spend a night and

the best part of a day in Guangzhou (Canton). Our food was good, Cantonese style, but it was thrown at us at the double so as to get in another set of clients as quickly as possible. Also it was monotonous. As often happens in China, the last two dishes were rice followed by watery soup. San was full of stories about eating dogs and cats. He assured us that one restaurant sold only 'dragon and tiger' (snake and cat) while another sold only dog. One story related how a woman in a Chinese restaurant in Germany brought in her dog and pointed to the dog then her mouth to indicate it needed feeding. Back came the dog cooked with its head and tail arranged at each end of the dish.

In Chengdu we were taken to the fine new Jin Jiang Hotel with an enormous glass chandelier like a waterfall which was all the more impressive as a burst pipe ensured it had real water pouring through it on to the polished granite floor. The next morning we crossed the big flat plain, the breadbasket of China, leading to the mountains. There is no more exhilarating sight for plant people than a range of mountains appearing as a thin blue line and bulking ever larger as you approach. A ragged cheer went up from the bus, ragged because we were bouncing along on what seemed to be a bed of small boulders where the Chinese were making a major new highway to Guan Xian (now Dujiangyan).

1. Ernest Wilson (1876-1930) was the only western plant hunter to have explored, in the early years of the 20th century, the country we were heading for. At first he collected for the great nursery firm of Veitch and then changed his allegiance to the Arnold Arboretum of Boston, eastern USA. He did a pretty thorough job as there have been surprisingly few new species found in the areas that he covered.

Above left: Aconitum volubile, *a climbing aconite, valuable for its late flowering.* Jiuzhaigou.

Above: The Hongyuan plain, the vast undulating Red Grasslands, really the beginning of the Tibetan plateau.

We passed the 2,000-year-old irrigation scheme where the Min river enters the plain and is diverted into irrigation channels to produce the enormous crops which feed the 100 million or more population of Sichuan. We turned up the Min gorge and the hills crowded around us. Plumes of bamboo and *Miscanthus sinensis* sprouted among the cement kilns and piles of coal, which shared space with *Hydrangea strigosa*. Then we branched left for the Wolong Panda Reserve where their first panda cub had just been born. We were not allowed in, but the Duke of Edinburgh was luckier a few weeks later.

We set about exploring two side valleys and James, spotting our first rhododendron, sprinted up the hill with enviable agility to collect the Triflora *R. polylepis* (CHM 2500) with its distinctive variable sized leaf scales. Peter found some seedlings of *R. augustinii* on a slide area and then spotted a larger leaved species, probably *R. calophytum*, across the river. With the narrow-leaved *R. argyrophyllum*, only four species of rhododendron were found in the first gorge.

The second gorge on the south bank was more spectacular and we stumbled through the first of four tunnels without torches, which was especially hazardous in the dark as we hurried back. Our first rhododendron here was the yellow-flowered Triflora *R. lutescens* and then we saw a fine large-leaved specimen away below us next to the cascading stream. At first we were

puzzled as to what this could be and then suddenly it dawned that it must be *R. galactinum*, a rare species endemic to this area; this was confirmed when Roy found a seedling by the path. Peter had suspicions that *R. galactinum* might be a natural hybrid but this find plus further sightings in 1989 and 1990 confirmed that it is a good and very distinct plant. Roy also found two seedlings of *R. wiltonii* with its unusual rugose leaves.

Roy was intrigued by a group of shrubs near the river at the foot of the gorge which included the unusual willow *Salix magnifica* with large handsome leaves. In all we saw at least six species of maple including *Acer davidii*, *A. laxiflorum*, *A. cappadocicum* subsp. *sinicum*, *A. stachyophyllum*, *A. sterculiaceum* subsp. *franchetii* and *A. longipes*. Roy found a cotoneaster with black fruit which proved to be new and was duly named after its finder, *C. lancasteri* (CHM 2502). It was a great shame that we did not have more time to explore this scenic area, rich in plants, but our hopes to return sometime were fulfilled in 1989. After dinner we visited the Wolong Reserve museum, with poorly stuffed birds, animals and legless insects, which nevertheless told the story quite well.

As we drove north the following morning, we were enthralled by the scenery, which was just like a Chinese picture with mist drifting around precipitous mountains. The gorge became more arid and more cultivated with terraces cut out of

From left to right: James Hutchison, unknown woman, Patricia Cox, Peter Cox and Donald Maxwell MacDonald.

Maize is the staple diet of the minorities living up in the mountains of western China. After harvest, it is put out to dry, here on the roof of a typical Tibetan stone-built, flat-roofed house, and then stored for the winter.

the less steep parts of the slopes and tiny houses like dots far away above the cliffs. Imagine having to carry everything necessary to live (apart from one's own produce) up and down these slopes and then probably having to cross the river on a rope or wire. These people have learned to live simply with only the bare necessities to keep alive. Along the foot of the valley, life must be somewhat easier and we noticed apple and pear orchards, with crops of aubergines, large ugly tomatoes, green peppers, chillies and masses of corn cobs drying on the flat roofs of square, stone, Tibetan-style houses. At our lunch stop in Wenchuan, our appetites dwindled when James pointed out a foot-long and quite transparent sea-slug sitting on a bowl of rice by our table.

Across the river was an obvious path, much of it cut out of the cliff side, and we thought of Ernest Wilson who must have travelled on this very path. It was around here that he had a nasty fall when the pony he was riding slipped and nearly landed him in the river. The path looked most frightening from our side but having since been on many similar paths ourselves, they are often not quite as bad as they look.

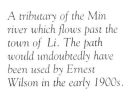

A tributary of the Min river which flows past the town of Li. The path would undoubtedly have been used by Ernest Wilson in the early 1900s.

The Red Grasslands, unlike most of the Tibetan plateau, are well-watered and home to nomads and their yak herds.

The rain cleared and we stopped to look for plants. Masses of *Incarvillea arguta* grew on the dry banks and it still had its pretty pink tubular flowers, in addition to masses of long, narrow seed pods full of fluffy seed. This plant is widespread on the banks of dry river valleys in south-west China where it is a sub-shrub. While it is easy to germinate in cultivation, it is not easy to keep alive in our damp winters. There were also species of those useful autumn-flowering shrubs, *Ceratostigma* and *Caryopteris*, both in flower as expected at this time of year.

We arrived at Li in Li County which proved to be quite a surprise. It had, by Chinese standards, decent-looking modern buildings and clean, tidy and well-stocked shops. Unfortunately the loos were hardly up to the standard of the shops and were voted the worst yet. The local Tibetan people were of the Qing minority, often beautifully dressed with dark head dresses. Up behind the town grew quantities of scrub, mostly thorny with a variety of roses (CHM 2506, 2507).

James started to have trouble from altitude sickness here; he was eighteen at the time and had grown very fast which may have contributed to the problem. But it was surprisingly low at around 2,000m/6,500ft and our lady doctor from Edinburgh gave him hot water with sugar and glucose and told him to keep warm and lie flat.

We had an extremely early start, up at 4.30 and off at 5.10, for we had 521km/324 miles to drive and we were promised a picnic breakfast on the way. After a gruelling day we finally pulled into Songpan at 8.55 p.m. One of the worst aspects of these long drives is that stops have to be short and infrequent which is very frustrating as we were passing through some

exceptionally interesting country. As we wound up to the Zhegu pass at 4,200m/14,400ft, James was showing more signs of distress from altitude sickness and altogether had a dreadful trip. We laid him out, grey faced, across a row of bus seats. By the end of the day we were all suffering a bit from the endless jolting and I had a fierce headache which shouted at every pothole. There were many, many potholes.

Just after crossing what we called Breakfast pass we came upon a splendid looking hillside of rhododendrons, but they would not stop, saying it was too dangerous. We did eventually halt for breakfast below the best area and soon found *R. przewalskii* (CHM 2509) and *R. phaeochrysum* var. *levistratum* (CHM 2517), while Roy found a third Taliensia, *R. rufum* (CHM 2516) with rather sparse and loose woolly indumentum. I found a curious *Pogonanthum* with tiny dark leaves that did not really fit into either *R. cephalanthum* or *R. sargentianum* because it did not have persistent bud scales; it may have been just a compact form of the ubiquitous *R. primuliflorum*, which we have since found in various shapes and sizes elsewhere. There was also a fine rowan with foliage just beginning to turn reddish-purple.

At this stage of our limited experience of being driven around China, we failed to make the best use of our occasional stops; the rule should be 'if the place is good, stay put until the leader is about to tear his hair out'! We dropped down to a seemingly endless plain scattered with bogs and small tarns and edged with low rolling hills. There were thousands of yaks in scattered herds as far as the eye could see. This is known as the Hongyuan, the Red Grasslands. Although the grass was still quite green in the autumn sunshine, it was a beautiful sight indeed.

There was one very special plant that Peter really wanted to find and reintroduce on this trip. He remembered many years ago seeing it in flower at Keillour Castle, near Methven, Perthshire, the famous garden of George and Mary Knox Finlay, and being astonished by its distinctiveness, colour and beauty. A few years later there was a group of this plant there and he noticed that they looked sick. That year was the end of this plant in cultivation. They all died and failed to set seed, no doubt having become too inbred to perpetuate themselves anymore and nobody else had any left. This plant was the scarlet poppywort, *Meconopsis punicea*, and we were now within the area of its recorded distribution.

We had stopped by a boggy area with a small, sluggish stream when Peter suddenly spotted something red. He knew at once that he had found his prize and rushed over to find the last flower of the season. I followed shortly after, amazed to see this last drooping flag of the red army that had invaded the marsh in high summer. But if it looked a little tired, it was surrounded by plump ripe capsules and the seed that Roy, Peter and I distributed from here and from two later locations was sufficient to re-establish it widely in cultivation. Peter was elated by this find and said it was one of the best discoveries in his years of plant hunting – and it was not even a rhododendron! Nobody else re-collected it until about 2003.

This flower of Meconopsis punicea *found on the Kangali pass is rather a different shape from the Zhegu one.*

The splendid Zhegu Meconopsis punicea, *which was one of the chief attractions of going to northern Sichuan.*

Buddhist player flags forming an elaborate pyramid at Hongyuan.

A large Cremanthodium, *possibly* C. arnicoides, *on the Hongyuan plain. Most are much dwarfer, growing at high altitudes, and difficult to cultivate.*

Soon after we added Farrer's lampshade poppy, the yellow M. *integrifolia* (CHM 2520) to our trophies of the day.

At a later stop some good gentians appeared and then a Tibetan encampment with pyramids of fluttering prayer flags and a *chongpen* broke the tedium. The interminable plain finally gave way to a view of distant snow peaks and forests of *Picea asperata* and we dropped down to the Min river and the small town of Songpan. It was a relief to us all, particularly James, and we fell into bed and slept soundly, regardless of the hard boards and the dripping ceiling above.

Daylight did not improve Songpan greatly – the streets were exceptionally mucky and, although our hostel was unusual in having plumbing, it simply served to redistribute the proceeds around other rooms. Ernest Wilson was more impressed in his day and said if he ever had to live in China this was where he would choose. It was from here in 1903 that he first discovered *Meconopsis punicea* on the Kangali pass north of the town. We took photographs to compare the place with his photograph taken in 1910 and the description written by Captain William Gill in 1880.

Not far from Songpan are two areas of great beauty and with many extraordinary natural features, mostly based on the limy nature of the rocks, rivers and pools.

Huanglongsi and Jiuzhaigou are also a major destination for the hordes of tourists, nearly all Chinese, which even then were coming from cities like Shanghai and Hong Kong.

Huanglongsi

We approached Huanglongsi over a pass with a road that appeared to be about to crumble away into the valley below. It had rained heavily overnight but luckily the driver had the sense to drive slowly. The surrounding mountains were still shrouded in low cloud. On the pass grew *Rhododendron capitatum* (CHM 2525), an early-flowering, erect member of subsection Lapponica, and more *R. przewalskii* (CHM 2531), this time the form with no indumentum and thus the subspecies *dabanshanense* with completely glabrous leaves.

To reach the extraordinary limy stream known as the Yellow Dragon, we walked through fine forest on a stone-lined path. Among the beautiful *Betula albosinensis* with its splendid peeling trunks were several rhododendron species. That aberrant member of subsection Grandia, *R. watsonii* (CHM 2528), was plentiful with its prominent yellow midrib and flattened petiole, *R. rufum* (CHM 2527), usually only retaining one year's leaves, *R. oreodoxa* and what we thought must be the rare *R. anthopogonoides*. On our spring visit of 1989 we again saw this in flower and sadly it was only *R. primuliflorum* (CHM 2530), still in a tall, straggly form. Something we thought might be *R. maculiferum* turned out to be a hybrid, probably *R. oreodoxa* x *rufum* (CHM 2526). An unusual herbaceous plant was *Triosteum pinnatifidum* (CHM 2548) with white fruit which Peter says has done well at Glendoick. We walked up the falls to an area where mineral water has built up into a kind of tufa cascade with shallow scalloped pools and startlingly clear water trickling over limy walls.

We did have time to stop on our return across the pass where our previous trophy *Meconopsis punicea* (CHM 2544) was plentiful, here on an alpine meadow so a very different habitat from the first boggy site, although there it had been growing on tussocks. There was also M. *prattii* (CHM 2543) with one plant still carrying two deep blue flowers and an abundant *Cremanthodium*, a genus of *Asteraceae* which had typically attractive pendent yellow flowers.

Jiuzhaigou

On the way to the second scenic area of Jiuzhaigou (pronounced jews-i-go), there were some splendid rugged peaks, patched with snow and partly hidden in cloud. We passed through some good native forest, at first coniferous and then mixed conifer and birch. Among it there were patches of cultivation with beans, potatoes, maize, sunflowers, oats, wheat and pretty pink-flowered buckwheat. Sometimes there were huge plants of cannabis, said to be grown for its fibre.

Jiuzhaigou had a proper park entrance at which our staff filled in forms to the sound of triumphal arias in Chinese on a tinny loudspeaker. While we were waiting, we noticed plants of the ledum-like *Rhododendron micranthum* with narrower leaves than that usually seen in cultivation. This species has a wide distribution in north and west China. We drove up a fine valley with lakes of that strange blue that often comes from the

Right: *Jiuzhaigou is an extremely popular tourist attraction, even more so now than when we were there. This limestone area is of great beauty with its lakes, mountains, forests and waterfalls. This is known as 'Mirror Lake'.*

Below: *Blue Lake, Jiuzhaigou.*

Nuorilang Falls, Jiuzhaigou. Above these falls is a porous limestone flat, largely covered in scrub.

limestone, then past the broad Nuorilang waterfall with a braided rim of shrubbery on the tufa through which the water trickles, giving a curious fringed effect.

When we arrived at Jiuzhaigou, it turned out to be a sort of Chinese Butlins-in-the-Hills with rows of huts and, although recently built, our 'hotel' was rather lacking in finesse. It did, however, have a bathroom with a real bath. Unfortunately, you almost had to swim to get to it as there was usually more water on the floor than in the bath but hot water came on every evening at 8 p.m. for which we were grateful. Dinner was in a vast hall with glass globes apparently lit by tired glow worms so eating was strictly by touch and taste on the stab-it-and-see principle. Our notes fell horribly behind.

Above the 'hotel', the valley splits into two and our first day was spent up the left-hand valley. We were driven to a large lake at 2,900m/9,500ft and trekked back some 14km/9 miles through splendid scenery and plants. Birches, as would be expected, were among the dominant trees and there appeared to be three species, *B. albosinensis*, *B. szechuanica* and *B. utilis* var. *prattii*. The first tended to occupy the highest elevations with its beautiful pinkish peeling bark and it can be identified by its prominent tufts on the leaf underside plus longer, more pointed

leaves which are a fresher green than in *B. utilis*. *B. szechuanica* had trunks largely cream to white which could be quite showy and it sometimes occurred with *B. albosinensis*. The trunks on *B. utilis* were a nice pinkish colour but became dull with age; it was found at both high and low elevations.

We found the deciduous *Daphne giraldii* (CHM 2565) and the evergreen *D. tangutica* next to each other but only the former had any fruit. It proved to be very disappointing in cultivation with its yellow flowers being so small that for a year or two we even failed to notice them. Four maples were noted, *Acer caudatum*, *A. stachyophyllum*, *A. caesium* subsp. *giraldii* and *A. davidii*. The intensely spiny *Aralia chinensis* (CHM 2566) grew to 6m/20ft. Seedlings have grown well but the suckers have proved to be a menace, appearing several metres/yards away from the parent plant.

We found only two rhododendrons here, *R. oreodoxa* (CHM 2567) and a puzzling plant (CHM 2568) that illustrates well the hazards of identifying in the field, particularly when plants are out of flower. It had the look of a small-leaved Triflora and a check with Cullen's description indicated that it was nearest to *R. davidsonianum* and *R. tatsienense*, although the leaf shape and the general appearance was nearer *R.*

concinnum. Plants grown from the seed remained upright and small leaved, but reluctant to flower. Peter once showed the plant to Jim Russell who took a sniff of it and at once pronounced it to be a *Heliolepida*. From its small leaf size Peter deduced it to be *R. bracteatum*, rare in cultivation but nice enough in its best blotched forms. And thus it remained labelled – until at last it flowered, early and a poor, pale mauve thing which ruled out the very late-flowering, blotched *R.*

bracteatum. But what was this rather miserable thing we had waited so long for? At last, with David Chamberlain's help, we came to the conclusion that it is *R. invictum* which was discovered by Reginald Farrer in Gansu, just over the Minshan mountains to the north, but never previously introduced.

There were some interesting herbaceous plants, a nice sage *Salvia przewalskii*, a fine blue-flowered climbing *Aconitum species* and *Rodgersia aesculifolia* on cliff faces. But the most

Elsholtzia stauntonii (polystachia?), *a sub-shrub, useful for its late flowers. Alas, it rarely performs in cultivation like this fine form.*

A good form of Anemone hupehensis *which makes a great show in autumn in many parts of China, varying from white to deep pink. Jiuzhaigou.*

Right: Betula albosinensis *at Jiuzhaigou. This fine species differs from the much more widespread B. utilis *in its glabrous branchlets and its narrower leaves, thinner in texture.*

Leontopodium *species Jiuzhaigou. Edelweiss are by no means confined to the Alps of Europe and numerous species are found in eastern Asia.*

remarkable was a Solomon's seal, *Polygonatum* species, no less than 3.3m/11ft tall. Among the trees was a very aromatic *Tetradium (Euodia)* species with dense clusters of dark red fruit. The fir here was the handsome *Abies recurvata* with firm upturned needles (hence its name) while the spruce was the Dragon spruce, *Picea asperata*, possibly accompanied by *Picea purpurea* with richer green foliage and leaves more closely angled to the stem. *Larix mastersiana* represented the larches.

We got back to find the bath water was finished, which was bad news after the long walk, and it was too dark to write notes, which was an excuse to broach Donald's whisky. He and I had a brief turn round on the dance floor together but knees kept getting in the way of each other and finally James and I went off to buy some sweet Chinese red wine as our contribution to the party. Poor Fritz, who did not always enjoy our odd humour, went off to get a chair, leaving his balloon of Armagnac with Donald. This was passed round the company, finally being drained by Roy and when Fritz came back, Donald protested that he had only been left in charge of the glass, not the Armagnac.

After a very wet night, we ventured up the second valley to the east which, on the whole, was not as interesting as the first. From the top of the road at 3,100m/10,200ft, we walked up a

Mother and daughter on the Kangali pass.

small dry river bed where I spotted the attractive *Lonicera prostrata* (CHM 2573) with bright red fruit. In the excitement I did not see a strategic root on the path and tumbled into the river bed but it was such a copybook forward roll that I picked myself up unbruised and set about the *Lonicera* berries in revenge. As often happens, it is disappointing in cultivation and I have yet to see a flower on my plant, admittedly growing in shade. Perhaps it needs a dose of deprivation. In the neighbouring forest we identified *Rhododendron watsonii, R. rufum, R. oreodoxa* plus a few seedlings of *R. przewalskii. R. watsonii* had particularly good foliage with green and occasionally red buds. The sides of the river were lined with masses of seedlings and these included obvious hybrids of all the above species, but the location would probably mean that few if any would reach maturity. Just below the top of the road were fine specimens of *R. oreodoxa* up to 7.6m/25ft.[2]

In the evening, Roy, Patricia and Peter walked down below the Nuorilang waterfall where they found a large-growing Lonicera species (CHM 2659) with succulent red fruit and a funny little lilac, *Syringa pinnatifolia* (CHM 2658). The latter is often used to test the knowledge of supposed experts on shrubs as it has small compound pinnate leaves, unlike all other lilac species. At Glendoick, the tiny white flowers have been produced in enough profusion to put on quite a good show.

To get back to Songpan we had to cross another pass. On the way we drove through a dry area with lots of cotoneaster and berberis and a group of daphnes with varying foliage that seemed to bridge the difference between *D. retusa* and *D. tangutica*. The pass, now called the Kangali (Kangala of Wilson), was at just about the tree-line of around 3,400m/11,000ft. Roy and Peter crossed the road and walked up through mossy forest of *Abies fargesii* var. *faxoniana* and just one rhododendron species, *R. rufum*, growing to 4.5m/15ft. This species differs from *R. bureavioides* in the absence of tomentum on the young shoots and seedlings take longer to develop indumentum.

2. A sample of the shrubs and trees recorded here: *Deutzia longifolia* (CHM 2575), *Fraxinus chinensis* (CHM 2579), which has already made a small flowering tree at Broich, *Euonymus porphyreus* (CHM 2661) with most decorative winged fruit and *Philadelphus sericanthus* (CHM 2574).

Our bus after our driver swerved to avoid a dog on our way back south across the Hongyuan plain. Philippe took charge of numerous locals and a truck. and the bus was hauled back on to the road.

The others had been searching a damp area along the top of the forest where two Nivalid primulas were found with more *Meconopsis integrifolia* and M. *punicea*. The two primulas proved to be *P. tangutica* and *P. orbicularis*, neither of which was in cultivation. The former has curious rather than beautiful narrow-petalled and reflexed flowers, maroon in colour, with what most people consider to be an unpleasant scent. This collection kept going in cultivation up to about 1997 and then was lost in that very dry summer. The prettier *P. orbicularis* with attractive yellow flowers did not last as long. It is sad that we do not seem to be able to keep these primulas going indefinitely.

We left Songpan at 5.10 a.m. on what proved to be the longest day's journey by road that any of us have ever experienced. A drizzly morning meant wet roads and the bald tyres invited trouble. On a dull part of the Hongyuan plain the driver braked to avoid a dog, we skidded and with a crunch lurched over the edge of the road, the bus leaning at an alarming angle. Others may have had higher thoughts but my only one was to get out before it toppled over. The liaison girl panicked and was blocking the exit trying to get her suitcase off the rack but Roy gave her a decisive shove and she vanished into the bog.

There was a silence outside broken only by the steam hissing from the exhaust. We were going to need a careful tow but the plain was deserted. Finally a bus arrived full

A somewhat over-dressed child at Hongyuan.

of Shanghai tourists, then a large lorry and soon a crowd of about forty was running around offering forty different solutions in Chinese. Philippe de Spoelberch took control, leaping around the bog, and soon the motley crowd was carrying stones for a causeway. A hawser was attached and, wires pinging, the bus was dragged out of the bog, none the worse apart from a missing exhaust. But we lost nearly two hours.

After lunch in Hongyuan town we took a walk down the main street which was filled with a great variety of characters and costumes from the tribal areas around. At a later comfort stop we had a chance to examine the gentians in shades of Oxbridge blue we had seen flying past the bus windows. The paler ones with very narrow leaves resembled G. *farreri* as collected by Reginald Farrer in Gansu, the darker ones were close to G. *sino-ornata*. These gentians are the glory of the Tibetan marches at this time of year, often covering large areas with a blue haze.

With the continuing rain, the bus slithered about alarmingly and we often had anxious moments when we passed loaded timber trucks. Even where there is little room to spare, the general attitude of Chinese drivers is to trust one's judgement at speed and never slow down under any circumstances. On one occasion, we remember all too vividly lurching past a timber truck when a baulk of timber was literally within one and a half inches of our window.

Gentiana farreri (*left*) *and* G. sino-ornata.

Gentiana sino-ornata, *a rich blue form, favours damp positions in the wild.*

The gentians were our last stop before arrival near midnight in Wenchuan. We are not sure which had the greatest endurance, the driver or our bladders! Not surprisingly only twelve of us had a meal this late but the owner of the restaurant produced a good spread and he stood in his white cap watching us eat every mouthful. The guesthouse was appalling, however, and my room resembled a bare cell in a third world jail – concrete floor, cement walls painted green to a yard or so and filthy round the bottom where the mop had slopped out, a bare bulb hanging from the ceiling with a switch half way down the passage outside, the usual board bed without springs, a linen drugget and two greasy pillows. I fell asleep wondering whether cockroaches could climb bed legs.

On the way back to Wenchuan, we had had to re-cross the exciting Zhegu pass where we had been promised a short stop. When we got there, it was getting dark but still light enough to look for plants which Peter and I were desperate to do. It was refused and I have rarely seen Peter so angry; he was incandescent. Admittedly it was snowing, we were hours late, and poor Mary Harrison was suffering so badly from altitude

Gentiana carinata, *an annual gentian. Small annual gentians are numerous in south-east Asia and this is one of the more showy ones.*

An annual white-flowered gentian.

A Delphinium species.

and exhaustion that we wondered if she would ever see her fourteen grandchildren again. We mused grumpily on all the plants out there as we lurched on into the darkness.

Back in Chengdu Peter and I with Roy and Philippe went off to the Sichuan University in the hope of seeing the herbarium. This was not possible but we met Professor Fang Ming Yuan, son of Professor Fang Weipei of Emei Shan fame, and we were to meet him again in 1989 when he took us to Emei Shan itself. We showed the professor some specimens we had collected but he was unwilling to commit himself on anything except the typical short-winged petiole of *Rhododendron watsonii*.

Yunnan

We took the overnight train from Chengdu to Kunming on 16 September, travelling in comparative comfort, four to a compartment. The evening was convivial. After trying the local *Actinidia chinensis* wine (like sweet white port), Philippe produced a bottle of French claret, which had travelled all over Sichuan, to remind us of the grape's potential. The journey is famous for its tunnels, more than a hundred of them, and it was rather like a slide show, a new scene appearing every time we came out of the darkness. The track keeps crossing the river with scrub-covered gorges and waterfalls followed by bare grassy hills, then patches of forest once Yunnan is entered. We found

The Fish Pond Fair, held annually at the north end of the Dali plain and Er Hai lake.

This sulky gentleman, known to us as 'Grey Suit', was sent to make sure we did not collect any plant material.

Satyrium nepalense *is easily grown in cultivation and flowers in autumn. Dali-Lijiang road.*

Habenaria limprichtii *on the Dali-Lijiang roadside.*

Kunming much spruced up since 1981, with temples being restored, hotels being built and our Queen was just due to visit.

The journey from Kunming to Xiaguan was long and tedious, due to a bloody-minded bus driver, who had been called at short notice and was grumpy about missing the Moon Festival. It took fourteen hours instead of the usual eleven to reach Xiaguan, from where our guide kept telephoning to see if we had had an accident. Even so, the journey seemed tame after the adventures up north. Our hotel in Xiaguan, now called the Er Hai Hotel, had been beautifully rebuilt in the local style. There was the luxury of soft beds, hot water for short periods, western loos that generally worked, but for some strange reason, the loo, basin and bath were all different colours.

There was a lot of argument about where we were allowed to go

Young growth of Craibiodendron yunnanense *on the lower slopes of the Cangshan. This ericaceous shrub or small tree rarely gets a chance to grow to maturity, as the young shoots are a delicacy to passing livestock.*

but eventually it transpired that we were limited to the Dali plain, which seemed ridiculous after we had travelled all over Cangshan in 1981. All we were offered was a temple near a famous old camellia (which in the end we did not see). We found the usual low elevation rhododendrons, *R. virgatum* subsp. *oleifolium*, *R. racemosum*, *R. decorum* and *R.microphyton*. We had a suspicious-looking guide in a grey suit who luckily wore a white hat which could be seen bobbing among the bushes, but Roy was spotted digging plants. He did an expert job in explaining that he was only gathering material to show the rest of the party and asked if he could pick more which was allowed. At lunch an old friend from 1981 appeared who gave us a great welcome and turned out to be grey suit's boss. From then on 'Grey Suit' was harmless and friendly.

We were told of the guiles of Japanese collectors pretending to be locals and going into prohibited areas. One girl dressed up as a Bai, spoke the language and collected for others. Another girl tried to export special large-grained Dali rice but was caught at customs. Two others had caught 2,000 butterflies including one very rare one. Many orchids were collected and exported to Japan and other countries illegally.

Dali had changed in the five years since our 1981 trip. Tourism was already on the increase and the street where the grey marble was sold now had stalls with all sorts of elaborate ornaments, goblets, pagodas and the like which threatened our luggage. But the most striking change was the main gate in the ancient walls (see page 72). Having been stripped of all ornament in the Mao period and painted dull red, it now sported a large pagoda-like confection painted bright Chinese colours with a tip-tilted roof and new gilding that shone in the sun.

Yulong Shan or Jade Dragon Mountain near Lijiang. The trees in the foreground are Pinus yunnanensis, *dwarfened by the poor limy soil.*

Jade Dragon Mountain

On our journey north to Lijiang a fair was in full swing at the north end of the Er Hai lake. The roads around were clogged with mule carts, hand tractors and ancient buses packed with swaying multitudes. The girls were done up in their best Bai costumes of blue and red, but the roadside was dull with little natural vegetation left and hillside cultivation had resulted in horrible erosion with washed out gullies below each field. Pines were cropped and mutilated and the ground below was grazed to the bone by goats.

We stopped twice and Peter shook his head over stunted and chopped *Rhododendron decorum, R. arboreum* subsp. *delavayi, R. yunnanense* and plentiful *R. racemosum* (CHM 2606) which has proved to be very variable in flower colour and early-flowering. But I was pleased with an oasis of *Primula poissonii* surrounded by ground orchids, perhaps six or seven species. We also collected seed of *Viburnum cylindricum* (CHM 2609), an evergreen species with handsome leaves, waxy above and black fruit. Although collected at only 2,700m/9,000ft, this proved quite hardy but very vulnerable to snow damage.

From our hotel balcony in Lijiang we woke to sparkling views of the splendid Yulong Shan or Jade Dragon mountain range. It was a favourite plant hunting ground of George Forrest and Joseph Rock and its beetling limestone crags and cliffs are spectacular. A Chinese journalist told us about the fate of the American-Chinese expedition that had attempted

to be the first to raft down the upper reaches of the Yangtze, including the great bend of the river as it sweeps round Yulong Shan. Five Chinese had been drowned. Some of the party were staying in our hotel.

We had two full days on the mountain but to get there had to cross a wide plain at around 2,700m/9,000ft. A party set off, Patricia and James providing family back-up together with Donald and Roy, who brought a couple of his 'girls' along. As we started to climb, the stunted and burnt pine gave way to *Picea likiangensis*, then the larch *Larix potaninii* and higher still *Abies forrestii* with stiff upright needles striped white below. A covey of young pheasants burst from the undergrowth as we reached the firs.

A similar sequence of rhododendrons produced *R. racemosum* and *R. decorum*, followed by masses of a stiff and upright *R. yunnanense* (CHM 2621), which seemed to merge with *R. rigidum* and over which Peter and I had learned disagreement. We were all puzzled by a single rhododendron of about 3.6m/12ft that Donald found and then *R. rubiginosum* (CHM 2635) became plentiful, a collection that, surprisingly, has not done well in cultivation. A rocky area gave us that large (and rather dull) Lapponica *R. cuneatum*, neat *R. primuliflorum* (CHM 2640) and a very compact *Lapponica, R. telmateium*, not at all like the erect form in cultivation but similar to what was previously known as *R. diacritum*.

Peter was determined to get higher and set a cracking pace

Peter and Roy Lancaster on Yulong Shan.

Allium beesianum *on Yulong Shan. This is one of the most desirable small alliums.*

straight up the mountain side. The rest of us took a more cautious approach, climbing diagonally; I was puffing and James and Roy were feeling the altitude a little. Besides, there was plenty to see and collect on the way, *Viburnum betulifolium*, schisandras and various maples. We had lunch under a rock covered with *Primula forrestii* in every crevice, and ate our ration of spam wrapped in loo paper but the dough balls were inedible and we used them to try and dislodge seed heads on the maples above.

Primula forrestii (CHM 2360) is endemic to the area, always growing in dry situations as we found it and often under overhanging rocks. It is a beautiful species with soft hairy leaves and bright yellow flowers, but like many primulas is not easy to satisfy in cultivation, although a few gardeners have managed to grow an occasional plant to a ripe old age when the stem becomes more or less woody.

Further up there was a surprisingly low-growing *Rhododendron adenogynum* (CHM 2638) which has kept its compact habit in cultivation, producing very pale pink flowers. By contrast *R. vernicosum* (CHM 2620) reached 6m/20ft and has since produced flowers of a good pink, though its early growth can be frosted. The seed from these two species has produced in cultivation about 10% of natural hybrids between them, although this cross was not seen among wild plants. This hybrid has been called *R.* x *detonsum* and the name has also been applied to name the cross between *R. adenogynum* and *R. decorum* as some are scented. The final species found before having to turn back at 3,750m/12,000ft was *R. traillianum* (CHM 2639), taller and more upright than its relative *R. adenogynum*, producing small neat trusses of unspotted white flowers in cultivation.

Peter was excited over an upright-growing gentian, *G. microdonta* (CHM 2690) with electric blue flowers that were closed. Unfortunately this was not due to lack of sun as we supposed but was a congenital bad habit. A better find was *Codonopsis meleagris* which has a striped interior to its flower, but unfortunately the seed did not germinate. Such are the vagaries that accompany collecting in the wild.

On the second day we again had trouble with the bus driver.

He had been seen with a bottle of Mau Tai the evening before, trying to lean on non-existent pillars and, instead of driving over the plain to the Whitewater river, he stopped several miles short of even where we had reached yesterday, pleading lack of fuel and leaving us with an enormous walk to the hills. After a sit-in strike and various threats, he eventually crawled on, grumbling, to where we had stopped the previous day. A bonus, however, was that we passed the village where Joseph Rock had lived, on and off, for twenty-six years while writing his three-volume account of the Naxi people. The original work was apparently lost at sea and has never been published in its entirety.

Roy felt that he should stay with the older part of his flock, so Peter and I, with Patricia and James, and Donald and Fritz, decided to push ahead up a low ridge where the pines had been burnt. It was a gradual climb through a lot of the plants we had seen the day before. But it was getting into moister territory and we ate lunch including '100 year eggs' in a pretty clearing with an *Impatiens* (CHM 2645) with yellow flowers all round us. The walk steepened through untouched primary forest and great trunks of *Abies* rose through an understorey of shrubs, much of it enormous plants of *Rhododendron rubiginosum*. But little new appeared until, just as we were thinking of turning back, Donald's mystery plant of yesterday appeared and was pronounced to be *R. uvarifolium*. I was unimpressed with its greyish-white ('Glasgow') indumentum but, having now flowered it in cultivation, I have to eat my words as the pink, blotched flowers are attractive. The dark forest brightened and we were out on the lip of a huge precipice. Cries of delight from Peter ahead signalled that he had found *R. beesianum* but he was upset that, as it was 3,800m/12,500ft and getting late, there was no time to look for more. If he had known that on later trips we would see quantities more of this species he would have been less concerned.

We turned back, plunging down into the vertical forest, slithering and sliding towards the river with occasional 'ouches' coming from those who clutched a stem of *Rosa moyesii* to slow them down. Eventually we came out on to a great boulder scree full of good plants delivered from the

Bai minority girls in an old village near the north end of the Dali plain.

A pretty little gorge on the White Water river, Yulong Shan, with an extensive colony of Rhododendron tatsienense *growing on the banks.*

mountain above. There was a good *Cyananthus* species, more *Rhododendron cuneatum* and embarrassingly, fine hummocks of what was first called *R. impeditum* but which turned out not even to be a rhododendron but a species of daphne, probably *D. calcicola*, closely related to the taller *R. aurantiaca* which we found plentiful above the Zhongdian plateau in 1992.

At last we came to the river and a vehicle track alongside. Such ready access did not bode well for the virgin forest above and we heard later reports that it had been cut down. All along the river bank were thickets of a rhododendron which Peter identified as *R. tatsienense* (CHM 2652). He had held a theory that it was a natural hybrid but, as there was a large uniform population stretching for about half a mile along the river bank, this seems unlikely. From this altitude there were doubts about how hardy it would be and, indeed, both Peter and I have found it tender in eastern Scotland but it does well at Baravalla in the west, one producing white flowers instead of the usual pink.

We strode on enjoying level ground and a dirt track until we met up with the senior group of our party at the Whitewater bridge. We fell on the *piju* after our stiff climb; it has rarely tasted so good. The bus had returned and there was much to talk about our day; it was the last of our precious few days on the hillside and I left my boots on a rock by the Whitewater river with the Yulong Shan towering above, crabbit crags and snow fringed with dark trees. They say you will return if you do that and, although the tread had gone, the boots were serviceable. As the bus drove away I turned to look back. The boots had already gone.

On the way back we stopped at the Butterfly Springs which had been greatly renovated since 1981. There were no butterflies, just springs with a few golden carp and a lot of litter. We also stopped in a most attractive old Bai village with girls dressed in their minority costume, the younger ones with a velvet short top, a white apron and an impractical looking head dress in every sort of riotous colour. Back in Xiaguan we found that green seed capsules which had been put into polythene bags with steriliser were beginning to deteriorate so we laid them out in the blazing sun which did them a lot of good. Despite worries to the contrary, most of the seed germinated well.

Driving back to Kunming the next day the long journey was made even longer by an enormous traffic jam in a village where the lorry drivers had parked their vehicles three abreast and gone off for lunch or a siesta. The traffic system, if that is the right word, was quite anarchic and it appeared that reversing involved loss of face and must be avoided at all costs. But the Chinese are remarkably patient with it all. Otherwise the two stops permitted produced only *Rhododendron scabrifolium* var. *scabrifolium* and *R. spinuliferum* covered in spiders. Back in Kunming the following morning, and only fifteen minutes before we left for the airport, our friend and interpreter from 1981 Guan Kaiyun (Clyde) arrived to see us on his bicycle, having ridden from the far side of Kunming. There was too much to say in too little time.

We all agreed in retrospect that the trip programme had been too ambitious. It was a mistake to try and cover North Sichuan and then, after a long journey, a very rich part of Yunnan – it resulted in too much travelling and too little time on our feet. It was also difficult to manage a very mixed group of different ages where some were interested in plants and some were not. From then on our journeys were going to be much more focused!

Nevertheless we had seen a huge variety of plants and collected a good selection of them and, as it matures, the results of this harvest are still being assessed. The scenery, from the Red Grasslands to the peaks of Yulong Shan, had been magnificent and we had had a glimpse of China as it emerged from its long and recently painful nightmare under the Maoist regime.

Chapter 6
THE LAND OF THE THUNDER DRAGON:
Bhutan 1988
Peter Cox

This small Himalayan country, known as the Land of the Thunder Dragon, is little known as it rarely makes the news and allows few visitors. Mention Bhutan and many people would be hard pressed to place it on a blank map of Asia.

In the introduction, we described our efforts to get to Bhutan in the late 1960s and early '70s. Ludlow and Sherriff and our Indian tea-planter mentor E. P. Gee had told us much about this wonderful little country, perched on the southern slopes of the Himalayan massif, so in 1988, when we heard that Bhutan was now opened to tourist groups, we jumped at the idea. We gathered a party for an autumn trip when we hoped for better weather after the monsoon and some fine views of the Himalaya. It was organised by Exodus, a fairly new travel company, and correspondence was with David Burlinson whose name will crop up again in 1992 and later. Our leader was Keith Rushforth who had already been to Bhutan. A knowledgeable plantsman, Keith was an able guide in finding the plants we most wanted to see.

Our party on this occasion was very much plant orientated. Two Americans, Warren Berg and Garratt Richardson were into rhododendrons and rarely glanced at anything else, Donald Maxwell MacDonald had been with us in Nepal three years earlier, Ted and Romy Millais, well known for their rhododendron nursery in Surrey, Peter's son James, Keith, Peter and I completed our little party.

Before leaving, my son Kenneth suggested I had far too much luggage and that I would not be able to handle it all at once. (In Thimphu, the capital of Bhutan, he was proved

Above: Our party having a badly needed rest, still being unfit. Left to right: Keith Rushforth, Peter Cox, Peter Hutchison, Donald Maxwell MacDonald, Warren Berg, James Hutchison (behind), Romy Millais, Garrett Richardson and Ted Millais.

Opposite: Our leader Keith Rushforth busy collecting on the edge of nothing.

Erythrina *species between Phuntsholing and Thimphu.*

wrong but only just!) We spent the night at Peter's mother's house in London where the portly manservant examined with some disapproval my expedition outfit, a rather crumpled khaki drill suit with shiny anchor buttons which made me look as if I had survived a revolution somewhere – but only just.

Since 1995 New Delhi boasted a new airport which was a decided improvement. It is a city of many birds, raucous house crows, shrieking green parakeets, vultures[1] and noble kites, waiting for some animal to die and acting as street cleansers much as they did in London three centuries ago. Striped ground squirrels like chipmunks scurried about the grounds of temples.

The flight on to Bagdogra was crowded and the road to the Bhutanese frontier was riddled with potholes. Our first night was spent in Phuntsholing, just into Bhutan but still on the plain so it was extremely hot. I shared a room with Donald who slept totally starkers without even a sheet on top of him and, whether this kept him awake or not, he did not sleep until 6.30 and appeared for the bus with his eyes half shut at 6.45.

The contrast between India and Bhutan was at once amazingly evident. The King of Bhutan had decreed that national dress should be worn very much as a statement of national identity.[2] For the same reason royal decree encourages local styles of building and decoration and the results are colourful and attractive.

On the way up from the plains we were allowed plenty of stops to look for plants and the first one revealed *Rhododendron dalhousiae, R. grande* and *R. griffithianum* at about 2,000m/6,500ft. From this altitude, none would be likely to be hardy in Britain. Later we saw *R. arboreum*. Conifers here included the attractive *Cupressus corneyana*, the Bhutan cypress, the tender *Pinus roxburghii, P. wallichiana* and *Cryptomeria*, the last of course introduced from Japan or

eastern China. After crossing two low passes of 2,100m/7,000ft and 2,400m/8,000ft, it became noticeably drier with the southern slopes only clad in scattered desiccated vegetation.

The Motithang Hotel, ornately decorated in Bhutanese style, was set in pine woods above Thimphu, which must be one of the smallest capitals in the world, but one of the most attractive. In the evening we went shopping in the one main street where James bought a *goh* to use as a dressing gown and was given much assistance by the local ladies on how to wear it, Peter purchased the local kilt stockings (made in Japan) and I more prosaically bought a foam mat to lie on. We also met our staff: our guide Kandu, drivers Lobsang and Tashi, and Sigi, our cheerful camp factotum, who bought our food.

Our itinerary that Keith negotiated with the tourism chief sounded promising, but it did not include the Tang Chu, which I had specially requested in order to find *Rhododendron pogonophyllum*, a tiny member of section Pogonanthum that has never been introduced into cultivation. We were to go to the Rudong La pass and just over it but would be unable to go right down the other side to be picked up, as the road had been broken by a landslide. We were to do a tough two-day trek westwards to the Paro valley but our first destination was the Dochu La, alias Dokyong La of 3,100m/10,200ft, which was one and a half hours drive to the east.

---

1. The vultures in India have since been almost totally wiped out by them feeding on the carcasses of cattle treated with a certain chemical (lethal to vultures) to improve their health.

2. I was struck by the reverse parallel with Scotland where after the 1745 Rebellion the English banned the kilt as a nationalist symbol. Indeed the *goh* – a kind of dressing gown hitched up at the waist and worn with tartan patterned stockings – has much the look of a kilt and plaid, so different from the white nightshirts worn by the Indian men and saris by the women.

The government building in Thimphu, the capital of Bhutan. Attractive traditional architecture, including new buildings, is to be seen all over Bhutan.

A modern Bhutanese house with maize drying under the eaves.

Snake charmers. Snakes are said to be deaf but can possibly feel vibrations from the music.

Bhutanese children, one (on the right) wearing Bhutanese dress.

141

A huge specimen of Rhododendron kesangiae. *This large-leaved species of subsection Grandia was described only recently and yet it is the commonest large species in Bhutan.*

The Dochu La

The west side of this pass is fairly dry with a forest mostly made up of *Pinus wallichiana*, *Picea spinulosa* and *Juniperus recurva* on the top. We soon met up with the *Rhododendron kesangiae*, then newly named after the queen mother of Bhutan. It is quite extraordinary that this was never recognised as a distinct species by either Ludlow and Sherriff or the taxonomists back home. Keith Rushforth said that he was the first to point out that it must be new. This fine species is common and widespread between 2,900 and 3,500m/9,500 and 11,500ft and appears, in fact, to be the commonest big-leaved species in Bhutan. Most herbarium specimens collected prior to the 1980s were named *R. hodgsonii* x *R. falconeri*, unlikely parents as neither have the characteristic rounded bud of *R. kesangiae*. The species is very variable with the indumentum on the leaf underside ranging from woolly to almost plastered and silvery white to brownish fawn. The flowers vary from rose to pale pink but are usually white in east Bhutan and Arunachal Pradesh (var. *album.*). It is hardy to at least –17.8C°/0°F but its chief drawback in cultivation is its intolerance of wind, with leaf stalks that invariably break in exposed sites.

Another common species on the Dochu La is *R. camelliiflorum*. This is an epiphyte with dark narrowish to quite wide leaves and small camellia-like flowers late in the season. While these are commonly white to cream in east Nepal, in west Bhutan they can vary to pink or even deep wine-red. If given very well-drained conditions, it is quite hardy in gardens as cold as Glendoick. A third common rhododendron on the Dochu La is *R. keysii*, a rather leggy

plant with curious two-tone flowers in dense clusters, usually red or reddish-orange with white or yellow lobes. It appears to take the equivalent place of *R. rubiginosum* in Yunnan as a vigorous lepidote of open woodlands. Here it was grazed by cattle that roamed the forest near to the road without apparently doing them any harm.

The east side of the Dochu La was obviously wetter, with some fine trees and shrubs. The elegant *Tetracentron sinense* var. *himalense* was there along with two magnolias, M. *campbellii* and M. *globosa*. The latter has done well in Peter's relatively cold garden in Stirlingshire along with a good form of *Buddleja colvilei* from our Bhutan trip, which flowers well on a wall. Among good foliage plants were *Sorbus vestita* with broad glaucous leaves and yellow fruits, a brownish-barked *Betula utilis* and an old friend, *Populus jacquemontiana* var. *glauca* with striking foliage, sometimes known simply as *P. glauca*. *Rhododendron falconeri* was in fine form and, at the lowest point we reached on the east side, there was a third big-leaved rhododendron *R. grande*, also *Decaisnea insignis* which Keith said had never been introduced into cultivation but may be too tender for most of us to grow.

Among this rather aristocratic collection of woody but flowerless plants I was glad to find *Primula capitata* making splashes of colour with its drumsticks of rich purple, a much more refined plant than the spring-flowering *P. denticulata*. *P. whitei* was also there but not in flower. Thus ended our first day out, filled with good plants and the promise of more to come.

Buddleja colvilei *is the largest-flowered relatively hardy buddleja and can grow into a small tree in favourable localities. Both of us now have substantial specimens from this collecting.*

Primula capitata, *a relative of the well-known* P. denticulata, *flowers regularly in the autumn in the wild. While easy to grow, it is short-lived, so needs to be grown regularly from seed.*

Thimphu to Paro

The next two days (21 and 22 September) were to be spent walking from Thimphu to Paro, a tough trek which involved crossing two ridges each over 3,400m/11,000ft, dropping to camp in the valley between. It was mostly on the ancient track that had been superseded by a tarmac road that wound in and out the hillsides.

To our surprise, we started our walk to the Pumo La directly from the back of the hotel, passing the zoo. The first part was through dry forest of pines with *Pieris* as an understorey and little else. This dull forest went on a long way until 3,400m/11,000ft when the pines gave way to spruce and the only rhododendrons we had so far seen, *R. arboreum* and *R. triflorum*. The lack of interest intensified our feeling of weariness as none of us had had a chance to get fit or acclimatized. It was probably misjudged to have tackled this so early so there was not much sympathy for Keith Rushforth who appeared to be having as much difficulty with the climb as the rest of us, frequently disappearing behind bushes. But Peter was happy to find that James did not suffer from the altitude sickness that had troubled him in China.

Suddenly all sorts of exciting things appeared with something different everywhere we looked and all feelings of fatigue vanished. Warren was away ahead and reported *Rhododendron cinnabarinum*; two plants had the odd flower, one a good yellow,

the other orange, both with short-tubed flowers. Next there was *R. campylocarpum* and a probable hybrid between this and *R. arboreum* and, in an open place, the dwarf *R. setosum*, again with an occasional purple flower. In the clearings were sheets of the blue-flowered *Cyananthus lobatus* and this became better and better as we climbed. The pass was gay with the *Cyananthus* and two gentians, the commonest of which had flowers of a light violet-blue which opened its rounded lobes in the sun, while the second with tubular flowers of a deep gentian colour was more reluctant to display. All this was complemented by a deep pink *Pedicularis* species scattered through the carpet of blue.

Further rhododendrons were *R. argipeplum* (formerly *R. smithii*), *R. wallichii* and plentiful *R. lepidotum* showing a few crimson-purple to pink flowers. Just over the pass *R. succothii* became common. It is endemic to Bhutan and adjacent west Arunachal Pradesh. It has an attractive peeling bark, dark stemless leaves pressed to the branch and tight trusses of early red flowers.

Around the pass of 3,500m/11,500ft, the Pumo La, were fine trees to 9m/30ft or more of *Juniperus recurva*, also beautiful specimens of *Larix griffithii*, an architectural tree up to 15m/50ft with long, rather sparse pendulous branches, also a fir and pine, making four conifers in all. Over the pass was splendid forest with huge spruce and grand *Tsuga dumosa* and then equally good oak, *Quercus semecarpifolia*, to 37m/120ft high. Long may this forest remain.

The most attractive campanula relative, Cyananthus lobatus, *with a deep pink-flowered* Pedicularis *species.*

To our surprise, our vehicles had been able to reach our campsite between the two passes. Warren and Garratt both went down with tummy bugs in the morning; very often Americans are the first to suffer, due to overdoing hygiene at home. Today's trek started up a steep slope and then, unfortunately, down again before climbing once more to the Jele La. The plants here were poor compared with the Pumo La, with few rhododendrons and poor cyananthus and gentians. The only 'new' plant was *R. thomsonii* in the shape of two rather miserable specimens by the path and three *R. barbatum. R. lepidotum* followed us all the way down to the Paro valley. We looked hard for *R. papillatum* (recorded here by Roland Cooper), to no avail. This member of subsection Irrorata seems a doubtful species and could well be a hybrid occurring in small quantities.

There were even better trees of *Tsuga dumosa* on the pass, some with burnt holes at their bases where chilled Bhutanese had made fires to warm themselves, but in spite of this the trees appeared to be healthy. Spruce trees were also impressive but overall the forest was inferior to that of the Pumo La. Going down, we had fine views of the wide Paro valley until we were picked up near the Paro Dzong and driven to our abode of spacious chalets.[3] In the evening we watched an archery competition with some incredibly accurate marksmanship. It is the national sport of Bhutan and they were aiming at small targets a hundred metres/yards away. A cheer went up every time the target was struck but barracking was allowed while the archer took aim to distract him.

We drove up the Paro valley for a walk to the famous Taktsang (Tiger's Nest) Monastery built on the side of a huge cliff. This is photographed by virtually every visitor to Bhutan. After crossing a river on a springy bridge, we had a fairly level

Takin, the national animal of Bhutan, in Thimphu zoo. This rare ungulate inhabits temperate forest in the Himalaya and western China and is hunted for meat.

3. Dzongs are most imposing buildings architecturally, usually set in strategic positions. They dominate the green landscape, serve as administrative centres, and often as monasteries as well. Unfortunately, they were temporarily closed to visitors at the time we were in Bhutan.

A water-powered prayer wheel which saves Buddhists from having to turn it by hand.

Magnificent virgin forest opposite Chendebje. Bhutan is notable for its extensive untouched forest.

walk through a forest of *Quercus griffithii*, a fine deciduous oak with large toothed leaves. We passed a *chorten* with a prayer wheel turned by running water and bells tinkling, followed by a stiff climb to a restaurant which looks across at the spectacularly sited monastery, still some way off.

Peter and James decided to go with Keith Rushforth to look for a single *Rhododendron edgeworthii* he had recorded there, while the others went up to the restaurant. There was some question whether the single plant might have been planted but we eventually found a further three, confirming that they were indeed of wild origin.

The walk on to an excellent viewpoint opposite the monastery took longer than expected but was well worth it as all but the best pictures fail to do it justice. We were supposed to go no further but continued against orders, although Romy and I soon fell back, suffering from vertigo. Warren and Garratt went on some way and reported that it was very scary and Peter and James had to agree.

That evening we drove all the way back to the Dochu La, where some of us slept in tents and others in a roadside cafeteria. Noisy dogs and cats and hooting horns kept us awake much of the night and we were up bleary-eyed at 6 o'clock in the dripping mist. Four of us set off into the moist woods and soon found obvious natural hybrids between *Rhododendron falconeri* and *R. kesangiae* with a distinctly darker indumentum than either parent. Keith and I were picked up by a truck which took us down to 2,400m/8,000ft, where we found ourselves in a very rich warm temperate forest. A species of *Tetradium* (*Euodia*) with large handsome compound leaves and red fruit has proved to be tender

in cultivation. We found two little plants of the tiny vireya *Rhododendron vaccinioides* plus *R. lindleyi*, *R. griffithianum* and *R. dalhousiae*. *Magnolia campbellii* had already shed its seed. Meanwhile Donald and the two Hutchisons took a short cut which brought them glissading down a chute of stones and ending in a pile of debris under a large *Rhododendron grande*.

We all then drove on to Wangdi Phodrang in a dry valley on

the concourse of the Mo and Tang Chu (rivers) where we watched a group of young boys practising archery. On the way, some of us stopped to see the only known location in west Bhutan for the rare *Pinus bhutanica* at about 1,800m/6,000ft. It was described only in 1980 as a result of the RBGE investigations for the *Flora of Bhutan* and it is remarkable that such a handsome conifer should remain undiscovered for so long. Perhaps it was confused with *P. wallichiana* to which it is related, but it is distinctive with its long pendulous and glaucous leaves. It is proving hardier than expected in cultivation. Nearby were some *Rhododendron arboreum* with exceptionally large leaves resembling those of subsp. *zeylanicum*.

We drove up the Tang Chu where seedlings were profuse. *R. maddenii* grew on roadside cliffs at 2,400m/8,000ft, and 500m/1,500ft higher we found the most amazing mixture of rhododendron seedlings on a steep rocky bank above the road. It was a kind of jostling teenage slum of eleven species and many would never see maturity.[4]

Before reaching the Pele La, we turned off the main road to go over the Noa La, a pass of some 3,200m/10,500ft. Here were excellent specimens of *R. falconeri*, mostly showing indumentum on the upper leaf surface, thus near to subsp. *eximium*. A report from here in spring indicated that plants on the lower slopes had lemon-yellow flowers while those higher were pink and therefore subsp. *eximium*.

We then dropped to our campsite for the night below the Gante Gompa, an impressive building somewhere between a monastery and a fortress that dominated the valley and was much photographed. The valley itself was quite dry and did not produce many plants of interest. On the last gentle slopes before the flat were numerous *R. arboreum* and *R. thomsonii*, together with some hybrids, a cross that has been named *R. sikkimense* by the botanists in Sikkim. We had been told that *R. thomsonii* often grows in damp ground in Bhutan and here it was doing just that, along the edges of slowly trickling water, but the plants were undoubtedly most unhappy, stunted and with miserable foliage. So why do they grow there? Peter and James made an evening excursion to the other side of the valley, finding few plants of interest apart from some large *R. keysii* in pine forest, but the views were so magnificent that they drifted slowly back to the camp to find that the rest of us were about to send out a search party.

The next day and back on the main road we ascended the Pele La, higher than the Noa La at over 3,400m/11,000ft. We split into two groups but, having struggled through bamboo brakes, emerged on to the high ground among massed

Pinus bhutanica in the Mo Chu valley. This rare pine occurs in a few isolated sites, mostly in east Bhutan, particularly at low elevations, but so far is proving hardier than expected. It is closely related to P. wallichiana, *the Bhutan pine, and is very attractive.*

Rhododendron hodgsonii, the first time we had seen it, mixed through with *R. kesangiae*. In what was virtually rhododendron forest the difference that immediately struck one lay in the trunks which were clean flaky-purple in *R. hodgsonii* but all green with a dense coat of moss in *R. kesangiae*. Closer up the first of these big-leaved species sported a smart reddish brown indumentum on the young leaves and pointed buds with stipules (tails) at the apex, while *R. kesangiae* had a more golden indumentum, either woolly or plastered, that faded to greyish white in the second year. The distinctive buds were

Opposite. Taktsang or Tiger's Nest Monastery, near Paro, west Bhutan, is the most famous landmark in Bhutan, but it was closed to visitors in 1988.

4. For the record they were *R. lindleyi, R. grande, R. thomsonii, R. falconeri, R. virgatum, R. campylocarpum, R. edgeworthii, R. arboreum, R. camelliiflorum, R. keysii* and *R. cinnabarinum.*

147

rounded, varying from almost black through reddish to light green. There were several hybrid seedlings around with an indumentum noticeably darker than either parent, but it was interesting to note that there appears to be an inhibiting factor that selects out these crosses before maturity. One adult was tracked down, however, and was seriously photographed.

We drove a long way down to spend the night at Chendebje, a picturesque site by the busy river with a *chorten* of Bhutanese construction, a more elaborate Nepalese-style one which would be known in Nepal as a *stupa* and a *mani* or prayer wall. Our tents were perched on a ledge above the river and it all looked rather idyllic apart from the leeches which were numerous and aggressive.[5]

With so much unspoilt countryside, Bhutan is a mecca for bird watchers. Amongst those birds seen so far were black eagles, large flocks of choughs on the Jele La and elsewhere, long-tailed magpies plus ordinary magpies (which appeared to be larger than ours), several rather tame hoopoes, Tibetan snowcock, Kalaji pheasants and, on the river at Chendebje, dippers. Later we saw monkeys and wild pigs.

The plan for the morning of the 26th was to go back up the Pele La but it produced one of those situations where misty

mountains, rudimentary maps and confused optimism lead to a lot of extra walking. On a recce from the pass the previous day Warren, Garratt and Peter had seen glimpses of a small peak which looked as if it could be reached from a little further on the road. What they did not know was that a deep valley lay hidden between, and that the road took a big loop round the valley, so 2½ hours were spent in an up and down exercise which just brought them back to the road they had left with a climb still ahead!

I was a little under the weather and took two of the party along the road while the rest assaulted the peak. It turned out to be an exhausting climb, which did not produce any new rhododendrons. However, there were some good shrubs in the *Abies* forest: a *Viburnum* species with broad, deeply impressed leaves and an attractive *Euonymus* species in full autumn dressing of pendent pink fruits. Meanwhile my party pottering along the road had, to the others' slight irritation, found a tally

5. One dined off Peter unnoticed while he ate his breakfast and his shirt was covered in blood – an important consideration when clean shirts are calculated to last so many days – but a little salt dispatched the offender. Some 55 years earlier Ludlow and Sherriff had suffered from the same Chendebje leeches and Sherriff wrote of one miserable evening when the river had invaded their hut: 'We all sat on the table with our feet on the chairs and ate like that. I also remember a plate of soup being brought in with a leech on the edge of it.'

Two chortens *(shrines) at Chendebje and a* mani *(prayer wall) with our camp. It is essential to walk round a* mani *clockwise. Early the next morning the whole area was cleared of brush to allow the King of Bhutan and the Indian Prime Minister Rajiv Gandhi to camp the following night.*

Looking across the Mangde Chu to Tongsa Dzong with monks in the foreground.

of nine rhododendrons with some hybrids, although none were of particular interest.

When you are living in a tent there are few sounds more unwelcome as you wake in a warm sleeping bag than the sound of rain pattering on the tent roof. But on our second night at Chendebje it was not just the rain that woke us but a great commotion and, peering out, we saw dozens of local people hacking at the bracken and scrub. Apparently the King was due to pass that way having been in discussion with Rajiv Gandhi, the Indian premier, at Bumthang (Jakar). As we were leaving, they were putting up a splendid tent with heraldic designs for their stop and we were later held up at the Tongsa hotel as the royal entourage passed.

We drove to Tongsa along a spectacular road, photographing *Pleione praecox* on the way, and rounded the corner to find a great view of what is the largest dzong in Bhutan. Three monks perched on a wall made an excellent foreground for more photographs and a crowd of people passed with their flocks wearing comical little flat hats of basketwork. Our driver said they were mostly herders from central Bhutan. He obviously did not have a very high opinion of them, saying, 'Not very civilized peoples, they not have baths, they stinks.' But our driver was a smart sort of lad with sunglasses and a red T-shirt. It was at this viewpoint that we first noticed how spectacularly bald the vehicle's tyres were.

Sorbus insignis in fruit. This species is often epiphytic, along with the closely related S. harrowiana, which is common in parts of Yunnan and generally has fewer leaflets.

Cosmos bipinnatus *from southern USA and Mexico has naturalised in the Bumthang valley.*

Our next pass was the Yutong La and this proved to be the most grazed and hacked-about pass we had seen so far, with many trees removed near the road. Keith and I stopped twice, first at 2,900m/9,500ft, the second some 200m/660ft higher. At the first there was good mossy forest a little way off the road and we found some *R. lindleyi, R. edgeworthii* and a huge *R. argipeplum* with narrow, lightly indumentumed leaves. Leeches abounded and at one time I had three on one finger. At the second stop were *R. falconeri* and *R. kesangiae*, the latter always with plastered silvery indumentum here and with seedlings around 90cm/3ft high, often being glabrous or with only partial indumentum like *R. protistum*. Of special interest to Keith was *Sorbus insignis*, found here by him before but not previously officially recorded in Bhutan. It was always epiphytic or started as an epiphyte and eventually rooted into the ground. We found the closely related *S. harrowiana* in west Yunnan behaving similarly in 1997. In the meantime the rest of the party had

gone straight to the top of the pass at 3,500m/11,500ft. Here grew similar *R. kesangiae, R. hodgsonii* with fine dark indumentum and plentiful *R. argipeplum* with one *R. succothii* and a few *R. thomsonii*, all in a rather boggy area.

At Tongsa the hotel was almost full with a party of rather superior retired diplomats who belonged to the Royal Society for Asian Affairs. They regarded our scruffy botanical group with some disdain and their relationships seemed complex to say the least, so we renamed them the Society for Having Asian Affairs. As a result we had to split and for those in the lucky half, it was to be their last bed, washbasin and the like before the trek on the Rudong La. For the rest of us it was a case of a downtown dosser with a vast population of fleas; I had two bites but the more succulent Donald, with whom I was sharing again, suffered at least fifty!

The pass at Yutong produced a dwarf *Skimmia* species with purply-blue fruits, *Meconopsis villosa*, sadly without its capsules which had been eaten by cows, and a lorry-load of singing monks. In their maroon robes with shaved heads they looked like teenagers, laughing and singing on their way back from an away-win match, but perhaps they had more religious matters in mind.

East of the Yutong La it became much drier, first with pines and a few spruce, later only pines and no rhododendrons. This dry country continued to Bumthang, which proved to be a rather hovelly place where two dejected rows of wooden huts, some containing shops, made up the Bond Street of Bumthang. But a fine *dzong* stood on a distant hill, aloof from the grubbiness, and an excursion to a Swiss factory on the town outskirts produced delicious cheese and apple juice. Meanwhile our Bhutanese staff were dealing with our minibus tyres, one of which had worn to the second layer of canvas. The roads are too precipitous to enjoy the view while driving with bald tyres.

We drove on again, at first on the main road, then up a newly constructed dirt road which had been bulldozed out of the hillside. Soon the car had to give up, then the minibus, but the 4WD Toyota truck, normally used by our staff, was waiting for us and we had a bumpy and somewhat hair-raising drive, often teetering on the edge of the bank with a drop into the river. The attractive campsite called Miserthang was by the river, full of fine fishing pools and equally fine trout. Trout which were introduced to Bhutan about 1950, soon established, have continued to do well and reach a good size. We had eaten trout caught by our staff on two previous occasions, but here they lost their artificial minnow, so could not catch any more as they had no hooks or flies. The Toyota had to go back down for our luggage so to pass the time we looked at a water mill which ground buckwheat between large millstones. Warren entertained us and our Bhutanese staff with rope tricks and James and the cook boy got theirs hopelessly entangled.

Prayer flags on the Rudong La.

The Rudong La

We left our pleasant camp at Miserthang for one of our major events, the excursion to the Rudong La. After a disappointingly late start, we made good progress (or perhaps we were just getting fitter) on the first part, involving a climb of around 850m/2,700ft. We passed through a dryish belt with dwarf bamboo and then large thickets of a *Piptanthus* species with glaucous foliage which Keith thought might be described as a new species but the *Flora of Bhutan* indicates that this form is near to the Chinese *P. tomentosus*. *Rhododendron thomsonii* appeared, as usual growing in a bog, as was *R. lepidotum* further on. The latter dwarf species is commonly found on dry banks and moorland in other parts of its wide distribution. There was also an interesting *R. triflorum* which mostly had red buds, rather wider than normal leaves and a tendency to have a non-peeling bark. Perhaps there is a gradual change over from here eastwards to the totally non-peeling-barked plants in south-east Tibet. Soon we entered fine spruce forest with trees as much as 40m/130ft high, with an understorey of *R. arboreum*.

Most of the party took it in turn to ride ponies, some with more confidence than others, and poor Warren rode into a branch, badly bruising the top of his nose and receiving two black eyes. The first sight of a fine specimen of *R. succothii* indicated the flora might be changing and, after passing through more forest, we came quite suddenly to a large boggy meadow in the area known as Phokphey. We had seen it from a distance looking like a gash in the dense forest and a ledge at the top end was to be our camp for the night.

The altitude here was 3,750m/12,200ft and beyond the clearing on higher ground was some splendid forest of *Abies densa*. But we spent the rest of the day squelching around the clearing which proved to have many exciting, and sometimes surprising, plants growing in the wetter parts. There were numerous rhododendrons and, growing on tussocks, were two dwarf ones, the strongly aromatic *R. anthopogon* and a very neat, compact form of *R. fragariflorum*, which grows extremely tight in cultivation. Other rhododendrons here were *R. campylocarpum*, *R. wallichii* with a very dark indumentum, *R. campanulatum* subsp. *aeruginosum*, *R. hodgsonii* and, best of all, a huge bush of *R. flinckii*, some 3.6m/12ft high and 6m/20ft wide. This had many enticing capsules but being on its own would most likely produce hybrids with other species nearby. This species is closely related to *R. lanatum* but has thinner leaves and a redder and less thick indumentum. It definitely seems to be easier to cultivate than *R. lanatum*. Described by Davidian and later sunk into *R. lanatum* by Chamberlain, it was then resurrected to specific status in the *Flora of Bhutan*. Apart from the rhododendrons there were other interesting plants including four species of primula and the remains of a good stand of very tall *Meconopsis*

Early morning, looking south from Phokphey camp.

paniculata, while Peter was glad to find some desiccated stems and capsules of what was probably a *Notholirion* rather than a lily. The primulas included the ubiquitous *P. sikkimensis* and also the yellow candelabra *P. smithii*. The latter is closely related to *P. helodoxa* and *P. prolifera* and, in fact, Richards sinks the former two into the last named species. *P. smithii* here grew very tall with small flowers and is in general not such a good garden plant as *P. helodoxa*. Keith Rushforth has a fascination with the genus *Sorbus* and he pointed out *S. rufopilosa*, a delightful species with finely divided leaves which gives it a ferny look. It keeps step with *S. arachnoides* at around this height on the mountainsides.

We hardly noticed the time passing until it was almost dark and we realized there were still no ponies. It would not have been a happy camp without our baggage but they duly arrived and a jolly evening ensued. But at 3,750m/12,200ft it was cold at night here and both Peter and I found ourselves piling all our clothes on top of sleeping bags to keep warm. We were up at 5 o'clock but not off until 7.30, destination the Rudong La.

After crossing a shoulder by the camp, we walked through lofty *Abies* forest with plentiful *Rhododendron hodgsonii* around and then we came upon our first plants of the true *R. wightii*. As most *Rhododendron* species enthusiasts now know, this is entirely different from the hybrid that has been masquerading under this name in cultivation. It has the same sticky buds as its relatives, *R. beesianum* and *R. dignabile*. My notes indicate that the indumentum was a little more plastered and the leaves shorter

than plants grown from recent Nepal collecting. There seems to be little doubt that the reason that there were no plants of the true species in cultivation until the BLM introduction of 1971, is the difficulty in growing on seedlings, which germinate with no problem but then start dying off.

We found more *R. flinckii* and it kept appearing until well over the pass, often fine bushes to 3m/10ft or more, less on cliffs. We opened flower buds which showed a pink tinge although a photograph that Roy Lancaster took here shows pale yellow flowers.[6] *R. campanulatum* subsp. *aeruginosum* was also common, some with decidedly bluer young foliage than others so selection is important. *R. bhutanense* was also much in evidence around the pass in two apparent forms, one with orange-brown indumentum, the other greyish-brown, the latter more common. There was no evidence that any hybridity was involved in this variation. At a distance this species could be picked out by its upright pointing leaves. *R. succothii* grew into huge specimens on both sides of the pass but with none on the top. Some had grown to 7.3m/24ft high with trunks up to 30cm/1ft in diameter.

The view from the top of the pass at over 4,000m/13,000ft was of an undulating sea of solid rhododendrons, while to the north we could just make out the main Himalayan axis without being able to see the snow peaks properly. They are said to be most visible in the winter months but we could just make out some streaks of white. On the pass itself the three dwarf rhododendrons were accompanied by *Cassiope fastigiata*. Two

Above the tree-line on the Rudong La there are solid rhododendrons as far as the eye can see.

Polygonaceae species were common, one quite neat but the other had bold leaves and still carried a few flowers of strong magenta. This must be the *Polygonum griffithii* (now *Persicaria bistorta*) that Sherriff referred to on his 1949 trip, having collected thousands of seed heads but only getting sixteen seeds. Having found one box-like capsule of *Lilium nanum*, I hunted around and found dozens more, so the pass must be a cheerful sight with their nodding heads earlier in the year.

Most of the rhododendrons carried on over the pass,[7] plus a population of *R. fulgens*, the first we had seen of this species in the wild and not recorded here by Ludlow and Sherriff. But the best of all was yet to come. Only Keith, the two Millais and I carried on for some distance down the east side from the pass. It proved to be a good path having been the main east-west route before the building of the roads.[8] The path was built up over gullies and good steps had been made on the steepest sections. In the distance appeared what looked like another group of typical *R. hodgsonii*, but when we examined these the indumentum was a super thick

dark chocolate brown. We had noticed earlier on the trip that hybrids of *R. hodgsonii* x *R. kesangiae* had darker indumentum than either parent, but this plant was infinitely more striking in the thickness and rich colour of its indumentum. All the plants seemed virtually identical and we could see no evidence of either putative parent in the vicinity. Seedlings have proved to be

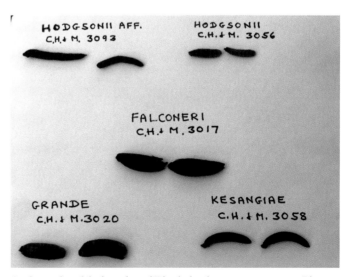

Seed capsules of the large-leaved Rhododendron *species native to Bhutan. The size and shape of* R. hodgsonii *aff. capsules appear to be half way between* R. hodgsonii *and* R. kesangiae, *which helps to confirm our thoughts on the origins of this plant.*

6. In cultivation, seedlings have been quite variable in colour, some being a dirty off-white, while others have been a very nice pale yellow. The plants look similar otherwise, with no signs of hybridisation.

7. These included *R. flinckii, R. campanulatum* subsp. *aeruginosum, R. thomsonii, R. campylocarpum* and *R. cinnabarinum.*

8. The main road inside Bhutan very roughly follows the major east-west path used by Ludlow and Sherriff, but there has been an attempt to cut out some of the passes, such as the Rudong La, and the much lower path approaching Tongsa from the west.

Splendid virgin Abies densa *forest at Phokphey on the way to the Rudong La.*

One of the most photographed signposts in Bhutan. The message was the same on both sides.

equally uniform. The bud shape and the opening flowers as seen by Roy Lancaster some years later indicated the closeness to *R. hodgsonii*, as did the similar bark and the widely cup-shaped hairs. The short capsules most closely resembled those of *R. arizelum*. At present we call this plant *R. hodgsonii* aff. and hope that sometime in the not too distant future that it will receive a varietal name.

Keith and I went on down a little further to a cliff area where we found *R. glaucophyllum* var. *tubiforme* with two interesting *Sorbus* and a *Vaccinium* species, perhaps close to or a form of *V. sikkimense*. There were many other *Ericaceae* including *Lyonia villosa* and some fine blue gentians. The guide kept on pointing ahead saying, 'No good,' so with great reluctance we had to turn back. After walking back towards the cliff area, we found two ponies brought down for us, which were much appreciated as there was still 300-400m/1,000-1,320ft to climb up. I somehow lack compatibility with horses and, having been on one only once in my life before, I kept slipping backwards on the very uncomfortable saddle. Even so, I made it to the top! It was altogether a great day, interesting and productive, with no less than eighteen rhododendron taxa. The weather had been kind with just a little mist and there had been great views.

It was now 1 October and after the brilliant skies of the night before we woke at 5 a.m. to find a sharp hoar on the grass outside our tents. Cries from the ever-cheerful Sigi at the tent flap got us going, 'Tea sah, milluk, one sugah two,' and we soon had the pack ponies loaded and were dropping fast in the long walk down to Miserthang. There the track was too bad for the minibus so we had a sporting ride in the 4WD vehicle. Our supply of eggs came off worst and Sigi wrapped those that were only cracked and not shattered in his anorak.

Looking north, two snow peaks were just visible over the nearer mountains and looking south-west we could clearly see the sharp outline of the Black Mountains. They looked formidable, much steeper than most peaks we had seen in Bhutan. What a pity it had not been as clear yesterday. Our vehicles were still missing when we reached the main road so we hitched a lift in a passing lorry.

We wanted to reach some cliffs on the Urasheltang La where

Keith had previously located some *Rhododendron pendulum*, and sure enough we found several plants. These were up to 90cm/3ft tall and across and were either pendulous or upright, depending on where they were growing, on the cliffs or on a jutting out platform of rock. Peter could not muster much enthusiasm about this rarity with fuzzy little leaves, finding it distinct rather than distinguished. Also here were good *R. flinckii*, *R. campylocarpum*, *R. kesangiae*, *R. cinnabarinum* (one seen with yellow flowers) and *R. camelliiflorum*. The rest of the pass was rather dry so we did not stop again before camping at the village of Ura.

In the morning we set off eastwards to the Thrumseng La and Sengor on a very precipitous road with some nerve-racking land slips to cross, finally reaching the major land slip where bulldozers were attempting to remake a driveable track through the mud. Hopefully the driver was paid danger money as he and his bulldozer could so easily have slid many hundreds of feet into the valley below. It was this mud-slide that prevented us from crossing the Rudong La to the next valley where we were meant to be picked up and also prevented us from driving any further east. Nearby was a fine twin waterfall near which we found two new rhododendrons for the expedition, *R. neriiflorum* subsp. *phaedropum* and *R. kendrickii*. This is evidently about as far west as the former species has been found. The latter seemed to have a limited altitudinal range of 200m/660ft at under 3,000m/10,000ft, about the same range as we saw this species in north-east India in 1965. Here it grew to 9m/30ft, usually less.[9]

On the way to Sengor we had driven through magnificent, largely uninhabited fir forest up to the Thrumseng La which, according to the notice on the top, is the highest road pass in Bhutan at nearly 3,800m/12,500ft. On the top grew *R. campanulatum* subsp. *aeruginosum* and *R. wightii*, here with rather small, short leaves, *R. succothii*, *R. campylocarpum*, variable *R. cinnabarinum*, good *R. flinckii* and masses of typical *R. hodgsonii*. On either side of the pass were apparent stable populations of *R. kesangiae* with conical instead of rounded buds but without the long tails of *R. hodgsonii*. Both the bark and indumentum were nearer *R. kesangiae* and Keith said that the flowers are pale pink fading to near white. Down the gully on the west side of the pass

Gentiana prolata *on the Rudong La at around 3,850m/12,700ft.*

were numerous Petiolares primulas, probably *P. bhutanica*, and species of *Sorbus* were turning fiery orange and red.

On the way back to Ura we had terrific views over the very deep mist-filled valley which we attempted to photograph from the moving bus. We had had plans to try climbing the 4,300m/14,000ft rounded peak on the way to the Thrumseng La, but we were down to only three tyres by the evening so our next day was limited to the area between Ura and Bumthang.

Garratt, Warren and I walked uphill straight above our camp at Ura, passing damp stream sides inhabited by the usual sick-looking *Rhododendron thomsonii*. Further on it was too dry for much of special interest but beyond was park-like grazing until reaching the north-facing slope, which was clad in thick forest. Along the forest edge were splendid rounded specimens of *R. succothii*, *R. cinnabarinum* and typical *R. hodgsonii*. We took photographs of each other sitting in a tree of this species. On the way back we saw the following natural hybrids: *R. thomsonii* x *R. wallichii*, *R. thomsonii* x *R. campylocarpum* and probable *R. arboreum* x *R. flinckii*.

We had a comfortable night in the new guesthouse in Bumthang with unfamiliar bits of civilisation, such as sprung beds and a bath, even if the water was only 5cm/2in deep, by candlelight. The generator could supply light to only one room at a time so priorities had to be set. Warren produced gin from some mysterious source for anyone that wanted it and beer at suppertime was very welcome.

On the morning of 4 October we set off on the long journey of about 260km/160 miles back to Thimphu. This may not sound far but we were able to average only 32km/20 miles an hour and it would have been tedious without the excitement of wondering which of our bald tyres would blow first. In the end it was the

front left that went with a loud report, fortunately on a straight bit of road with no precipice. The spare which replaced it had even less rubber and two layers of canvas on which bits of wire were visible. Lunch was eaten at a small stand of *Cupressus cornyana* on limestone and I kept looking out for the rare *Luculia grandiflora* which had been found by Ludlow and Sherriff between Tongsa and Chendebje. We came to the conclusion that they used a path at a much lower elevation long before the road was made. The old path crosses the river just below Tongsa. None of us would have given much chance of the tyres lasting the remaining 97km/60 miles or so but Lobsang drove carefully after the blow-out and there were no mishaps, the day's journey to Thimphu having taken ten hours in all. Very welcome baths and hair washes followed, once we had heaved our luggage up to the top floor of the Motithang Hotel; luckily we were all fit by then.

The next day none of us, not even the driver, were prepared to go a mile further on the old canvas wraps, so for the drive back to Phuntsholing we were given a 'new' minibus with only semi bald tyres. The journey was broken by lunch in fly-ridden Bunaka where to our delight there was plenty of beer, but afterwards it took many kilometres with open windows to clear the flies from the mini-bus. Despite the plan to go back up the road some way to Takhti Peak the following day, we had to get our passports stamped before entering Phuntsholing and again twice the next day. Alas, the Druk Hotel was full, so we ended up in a dreadful flea-hole with clanking fans to circulate the oppressive heat and a convention of Bengali bicycle salesmen as companions. It was called the Paradise Hotel.

9. Also growing here were *R. pendulum*, *R. maddenii*, *R. lindleyi*, *R. edgeworthii*, *R. grande* and large *R. camelliiflorum*.

A huge specimen of Rhododendron argipeplum *showing off its beautiful trunk on Takhti Peak.*

Takhti Peak

We made an excursion the next day to Takhti peak, a mountain nearby of some 3,400m/11,000ft. Most of us were glad of any excuse to get away from the heat of Phuntsholing, but Warren, Garratt and Donald were put off by the reputation of the road for landslips and obstructions and stayed in town. In the event our struggle to reach the top left us too little time to do thoroughly the bit from about 2,600m/8,500ft to the top, which was very rich and contained some fine specimens of tree-like rhododendrons.

It was indeed a rough road and our now rather bolshie driver Lobsang was not up to handling it, rushing at the steep bits in too high a gear, and finally announced he would go no further. Fortunately, we were able to hitch a ride on the back of a large orange timber lorry which heaved and jerked its way up another 300m/1,000ft or so where some huge *Rhododendron falconeri*

were being cut and loaded on to two more trucks. It was the first time we had seen much sign of anything being felled and I was shocked by what must have been some of the finest specimens of this species in existence lying on the ground. There were great heaps of russet foliage by the road and sections of trunk from trees which must have reached 15–18m/50–60ft.

There was a surprising lack of such rhododendrons as *R. maddenii*, *R. dalhousiae* and *R. griffithianum* here, but higher up *R. falconeri* changed to *R. kesangiae*. Examining plants of the last named here confirmed that western populations tend to have more woolly indumentum with a brownish tinge, in contrast to the whitish more plastered indumentum of further east. The usual *R. falconeri* x *R. kesangiae* hybrids were observed with darker indumentum than either parent. There were also splendid specimens of *R. argipeplum* with almost no cordate leaf base but darker indumentum than those seen earlier. There were scheffleras here too, an Araliad genus in which we both had developed an interest, and the one lower down with 10 to 12 leaflets looked rather similar to the *S. impressa* that we had collected in Arunachal Pradesh.

We walked briskly up the last 300m/1,000ft or so to the top at just over 3,400m/11,000ft, congratulating ourselves on our fitness, and were given unexpected tea and biscuits in fine china cups by the courteous engineer at the microwave radio repeating station there. It is Bhutan's main link with Calcutta and the outside world but the tea took ages to appear and it left us little time to botanise much on our way down. Before we left, we had glimpses of the peak of Chomholari away to the north-west in Tibet and we were told that in the morning we would have had the rare sight of it clear of cloud. But mist was boiling up round our own mountain and it was time to leave.

The path down from the top revealed a good population of *Rhododendron glaucophyllum* with comparatively large, dark foliage and other plants of interest included *Sorbus insignis* aff. and *S. rufopilosa*, with an Aria type of *Sorbus* further down.

On our last drive down from the Bhutanese hills we passed a party of wild pigs rootling in the undergrowth, much more lithe and active than their domestic counterparts, and then some villages. But, alas, we missed Ted Millais' woman with a padlock in her nose. He told us about it afterwards, in his kind and concerned way, but we instructed him that next time he saw a woman with a padlock in any part of her anatomy, he should tell us immediately.

We had a terrifyingly reckless drive back to Phuntsholing in the fog, which often forms here in the evenings, tearing round corners with thick mist in front of us and a precipice beside. Lobsang had become thoroughly bolshie with our criticism of his driving and was going to take it out on us, regardless of the outcome. This time we got into the Druk Hotel, which was all but empty, but we did not get to bed until 11.20 through having to sort out our luggage. Kandu, our sirdar, had warned us that we would be searched for plant material and sure enough in the morning this took place. It was an extremely thorough process with well worn socks being unrolled and inspected, but they found nothing, apart from a *Notholirion* capsule in Peter's bag which was confiscated and a souvenir piece of rock which James had been given.

Our drive by Lobsang to Bagdogra became more and more reckless, looping between the potholes, and how he avoided hitting anything we will never know. The nearest was a cyclist who was shoved off the road and his overtaking on bends was horrific. Shaken by the drive, we found our plane had not even come in so we had a delay of some hours. It turned out to be very crowded with fidgety Indians, many of whom were on the move throughout the flight.

Trunks of Rhododendron falconeri *being loaded on to a truck on Takhti Peak. We were so horror struck at this sight that we failed to ask what the timber was for.*

As it was James's 21st birthday, we had planned a celebration in Delhi, but it was the seventh day of the month on which the Government had decreed abstinence there, so no alcoholic drink was allowed. Finally we were put in a partitioned off bit of a huge empty ballroom while waiters furtively brought champagne through the screens. Once dinner was over and midnight passed, an amazing collection of liqueurs suddenly appeared. It was an odd way to celebrate his coming of age.

The flight to London was due out at 3 a.m. but was postponed until 2.30 the following afternoon, so we were moved to a superior hotel with even more marble and were able to get some sleep. Soon after takeoff we heard a thump and the pilot announced in that reassuring voice which pilots acquire that we had struck a bird but that the plane was perfectly all right. 'Can't say the same for the vulture,' he added with a comforting chuckle. Apparently Delhi was prone to such events because the municipal rubbish dump where the vultures used to circle was near the end of the runway.

In spite of the reassurance, in Dubai we were told that the bird-mince engine would have to be replaced, with the inevitable delay. Everything in Dubai looked new and covered in even more marble but we were only offered free orange juice by BA which did not suit certain members of the party who ordered excessively expensive gins that they were lucky to get in an Arab country. Only one and a quarter hours' sleep was possible before we had to catch a Singapore Airlines plane which was nothing special considering it had won the 'best airlines' prize for the last two years. In all, we estimated that our journey from Phuntsholing had taken 57 hours. Most of us were very weary and I took almost a week to get over jet lag.

Overall it had been a good trip through a very lovely and unspoiled country. We had not been able to cross the Rudong La to the east side but we had found most of the rhododendrons native to Bhutan and we were able to spend adequate time in the field studying different populations of several species, *R. arboreum* being the most widespread occurring in no less than seventeen different places. We had hopes to go back in the spring sometime to see what must be an astonishing display of flowers.

Chapter 7

STIRRINGS IN CHINA:
1989

Peter Hutchison

The arrivals hall was obviously not used to tumbles of rhododendron flowers on the airport seats and the grey suits hurrying for their taxis peered curiously at the three grown-up men clucking over their quarry. We were on our way to Sichuan, a select party of only three, and I had gone to Heathrow to meet Peter and David Chamberlain off their flight from Edinburgh. David had been our companion on the Cangshan in 1981 and the next day, 12 May, we were all leaving for Hong Kong and Chengdu.

The rhododendrons which Peter brought in a bin bag were from our 1981 expedition to the Cangshan and this was our first journey together since that pioneering trip. Many of the plants we had collected then were now flowering, among them a splendid pink-flushed *Rhododendron decorum*, the deep red *R. haematodes* and a natural hybrid between it and *R. rex* subsp. *fictolacteum*, best described as curious rather than beautiful. There was a rather better hybrid of salmon colour between *R. neriiflorum* and *R. dichroanthum* and we were pleased with *R.*

selense subsp. *jucundum*, exclusive to the Cangshan, which we had not seen in flower at the time but which now showed great promise. A collection of *R. yunnanense* tumbled out in varying shades of pink but unfortunately without labels or numbers as these had been scattered when one of Peter's shooting guests had dropped a pheasant through the roof of his greenhouse! It was a good aperitif to our journey.

We were met at Chengdu airport by our interpreter, Yuan Jiang, who taught English at the University of Chengdu. A slight, bespectacled figure with a mop of black hair, he was to prove an intelligent and likeable companion on our travels. Also meeting us was Yang Man Yeh who was to be our general factotum, whom we nicknamed Alphonso. The usual Toyota minibus took us to

Above: Caltha scaposa *at Huanglongsi enjoying damp soil.*

Opposite: Mountains, river and forest just before the Huanglongsi National Park.

A collection of bamboos near Sichuan University, Chengdu.

the Jin Jiang Hotel where we had stayed in 1986; the same high brown rooms and cavernous dining hall, but the waterfall which had been pouring through the chandelier had dried up.

We were to learn over the years that plans made with faxes and letters rarely look the same when you finally arrive. Professor Fang Mingyuan (son of the famous Professor Fang Weng Pei) soon arrived to tell us the bad news that a landslide had blocked the road from Wenchuan to Li and that he had only arranged for Emei Shan and Guan Xian (now Dujiangyan). He also claimed that we had not asked for Wolong (which was not true) and informed us that we had come too soon and that he could not come with us to Emei Shan for another four days.

So we were stuck in Chendgu for three days on a mixed fare of culture and herbarium visits, interspersed with huge meals where course followed course. The food was good, if rather spicy in the Sichuan style, but David Chamberlain kept asking details of the ingredients when it was often better to be ignorant. There was the usual temple to visit along with Du Fu's Cottage which had nothing cottagey about it. Du Fu was a Tang Dynasty poet and the museum walls were hung with his poems inscribed on tablets by famous calligraphers which got me, as something of an amateur calligrapher, going with Yuan Jiang on the nuances of Chinese and European scripts.

The herbarium was all dusty shelves and a strong smell of camphor. The rhododendron specimens were apparently chaotic

but I found the primulas quite orderly as Professor Hu Chi Minh, who was writing up the genus for the *Flora Sinica*, had been sorting them out. It was in the airless hush of the herbarium that we first heard the chanting of the students, faint at first then getting louder. We had heard some noises the previous evening that sounded like a demonstration, but now the chorus was unmistakable and our mentors told us we had to 'rest' in the sofa room. It was puzzling rather than alarming; student demonstrations were nothing new in the west, but was China moving so fast? Little did we realize that we were witnessing the start of one of the most important events in modern Chinese history.

We spent some time going over our itinerary, which looked satisfactory if it could be achieved. But further bad news on roads indicated that the Balang pass north of Wolong might be impossible due to snow and the landslide reported between Wenchuan and Li was, in fact, between Wenchuan and Songpan, the same as in 1986. Also each destination had to be confirmed by the local authority of that county.

On 17 May we drove through the smoky suburbs of Chengdu and out on to the plains, heading for Emei Shan. Here the wheat was being harvested and occasional patches of brilliant green showed the young rice being raised for later planting. Spirits rose apart from the driver's who was stopped for speeding. He cannot have been very observant as the policeman was standing in the middle of the road waving a

Fast food, Chinese style, on a Chengdu street. We have always avoided buying food in the streets, but freshly cooked, it is probably just as safe as in a restaurant.

We have never seen so many bicycles anywhere in the world as at Chengdu, the provincial capital of Sichuan. It is quite an art to dodge cyclists when crossing a street.

battered radar gun and gesticulating. At a lunchtime café further diversion was provided when a roadside fight broke out over a lorry which had parked where the café owner hoped that tourist buses might stop, but eventually the police were called and everyone settled down to a good afternoon's arguing. Tourist turf wars and speed traps – China was indeed changing.

At the town of Emei, an undistinguished collection of concrete blocks, we dropped our bags at the hotel that oddly belonged to the University of Traffic and were then taken on a tour of the foothills. There was a mêlée of tourists, mostly

Chinese, among the subtropical forest and assorted temples and we wandered around unhappily, fending off the monkeys that jumped on our shoulders and feeling we were probably wasting valuable time. On our return we found the demonstrations had spread, with processions straggling through the streets, but the students from the modern campus nearby seemed relaxed, almost half-hearted, and Professor Fang said dismissively that they were just copying their counterparts in Beijing. We also learned, however, that the Chengdu students had gone on strike, a more serious matter.

Ducks on a river in Chengdu. Duck is one of the favourite meals in China.

The inaccessible cliffs on Emei Shan are covered with vegetation owing to the heavy rainfall. Rhododendron williamsianum *grows on one of these cliffs but nobody has located it since Wilson introduced it in 1908.*

Emei Shan

A long discussion was held about our plans for the next two days. Other people who had been to Emei Shan had warned us that it is all too easy to make a bad job of it. We were now told that we had to fit what normally takes three days into one and a half. We regretted even more that they had not taken us up to the top after our arrival instead of on our fruitless evening excursion.

Emei Shan, or Mount Omei, is a sacred mountain fabled for the richness of its flora. Home of the dove tree, *Davidia involucrata,* and innumerable rhododendrons, some of which had yet to reach cultivation, it was a goal for several of the early plant hunters but it did not give up its secrets easily. It had a legendary, rich and remote air.

A few illusions were shattered on that first full day. There was a steady stream of tourists, again mostly Chinese, going to and from its 3,092m/10,167ft crown, with a large bus park near the top and a cable car for the last 550m/1,700ft. For those who take their pleasures the hard way, there are two sets of stone steps paid for by devout pilgrims from bottom to summit and those who have walked up the steeper one say this is extremely hard going, partly because the steps were made for little Chinese feet and not ours! Over the whole length of these trails there is a skitter of discarded coke cans and paper junk, stalls selling souvenirs and dreadful bits of dried animal that are supposed to have medicinal properties.[1] If you step a few feet from the track you will find a linear lavatory.

At the top the Golden Temple, rebuilt and re-gilded after a fire, had a certain gaudy magnificence, but in 1989 it was surrounded by shacks, piles of rubbish, building materials and smells from rotting garbage and worse. In spite of all the muck, the flora is magnificent and the tourists make a very thin scar on a steep and bulky mountain, contained on one side by breathtaking precipices and on the other by dense thickets that defeat even a determined botanist.

We drove to the car park in two hours with a couple of stops for photographs of paulownias and the view. The cable car ride then took only three minutes and, stepping out on the summit, we went to the edge of the cliffs. The neat little Lapponica rhododendron *R. nitidulum* var. *omeiense,* not yet in flower, formed cushions among the rocks and the Taliensia *R. faberi* was hanging from every ledge. Unfortunately, 'nature's neat abandon' was somewhat spoiled by a pair of discarded trousers

Monkey skeletons for use in alternative medicines.

Rhododendron calophytum *is the commonest species around the summit of Emei Shan.*

Dicentra macrantha *on Emei Shan.*

draped over the bushes. Keith Rushforth had also collected the yellow Triflora *Rhododendron ambiguum*; some seedlings were tinged pink, which Peter thought were hybrids with *R. concinnum*, but his revisit in spring 2007 proved them to be all variations of *R. ambiguum*, as *R. triflorum* does in Tibet.[2]

We worked our way down the famous steps until, on the edge of the big cliff, we found a thicket of *R. wiltonii* (CCH 3906), a population with rather thin indumentum, quite unlike those Peter was to find on Erlang Shan to the north-west in 1990. I clambered out to an enormous bush hanging by the cliff but obviously it had little flower the previous year and capsules were scarce. Perhaps it is competition that drives *R. wiltonii* to frequent these rocky locations? It was about here on the cliff that Wilson found *R. williamsianum* but, as far as we know, none of the many plant enthusiasts visiting Emei in recent years have re-located it.

On our drive up we had seen explosions of pink and white in the shrubbery from the flowers of *R. calophytum*, one of the commonest large rhododendrons here, which we saw again on our walk down forming tree-like umbrella-shaped specimens. It varied from white to a good pale pink, always with a blotch, and there did seem to be some correlation between green buds and white flowers and pink buds and pink flowers, which has also been observed in cultivation. Alas, all trusses were out of reach for taking a close up photograph. *R. pingianum/argyrophyllum* (CCH 3905) had been covered in clear pink flowers on the way up but at the higher altitude where we were walking it was not yet out. This was sad as we wanted to examine the ovaries to ascertain whether any followed Fang Weng Pei's description of *R. pingianum* having rufous tomentose instead of the pale tomentose ovaries of *R. argyrophyllum*.

One of the very special rhododendrons known to inhabit

Emei Shan is the epiphytic *R. dendrocharis* (CCH 3915), a dwarfer, smaller relative of the better known *R. moupinense*, and we were determined to find it. I spotted a neat-leafed cushion high on a mossy rock in a cleft filled with broken bottles, cans and debris and later David and Peter found another group. All were on rocks or cliffs but mature ones were out of reach. A few of the deep pink flower buds were beginning to open a little paler. As it occurred quite high up the mountain, we reckoned there should be no problem with hardiness and this has proved correct.

We have described the rhododendron populations, which were often confusing, in some detail but there was of course a wide variety of other trees and shrubs, frequently inaccessible from the path. A *Michelia* species was showing some flower, there was a yellow-flowered *Dicentra macrantha* and two very different dogwoods, one of the *Cornus mas* persuasion and the other with showy bracts. Under the dense woody canopy there were not many herbs but *Chrysosplenium davidianum*, last seen on the Cangshan, made a ground cover and *Berneuxia thibetica* perched on mossy stumps with its leathery leaves and lopsided tufts of pinky-white flowers.

Berneuxia thibetica, *a creeping woodlander related to* Shortia, *has shiny evergreen foliage and pretty pink buds opening to white flowers. Widespread in western China, it was recently introduced to cultivation.*

1. Some animals, such as tiger and rhinoceros, used in alternative medicine are in grave danger of extinction; others, such as monkey skeletons, are decidedly grisly to us.

2. A little lower was a mixed population of *Rhododendron oreodoxa* in flower and *R. pachytrichum* with hybrids between them. Keith Rushforth collected seed from these in 1980, calling it *R. davidii*, which obviously it is not. Among the *R. pachytrichum* with typical pale to clear pink flowers were some nearer to red and David suggested that these were hybrids with *R. strigillosum*. However the lack of any obvious population of *R. strigillosum* (which is recorded on the mountain) made the situation doubtful, although we did find a single plant of darker red lower down.

David Chamberlain, the pied piper of Tsing Chien temple.

The head of the giant Buddha at Leshan, overlooking the Min River.

The garden around Wan-Nian temple on Emei Shan, one of the most sacred mountains in China, is exceptional in that it is well kept. In the background is what we would class as a poor form of Cardiocrinum giganteum *var.* yunnanensis.

Our second day was entirely unproductive, though not uninteresting. The start from the hotel had been delayed by a large Chinese party attacking their breakfast noodles, but finally we started the stiff climb to the famous Wan-Nian temple, much of which had been burned down in 1945 and now rebuilt. Fortunately the great dome housing the solid copper elephant,

all 66 tons of him, cast in the Sung Dynasty (980 AD) was still intact. His back legs had been rubbed shiny by countless devotees wishing to bring themselves the blessing of Buddha whose enormous figure sat on a lotus leaf on top of the elephant. Plump looking monks with faces as un-seamed and inscrutable as Buddha himself occasionally rang gongs, while little bent

There were massive demonstrations in Chengdu on 21 May 1989, mostly of chanting students of the pro-democracy movement. At this stage everyone was cheerful and friendly.

female monks with faces very seamed indeed crept around lighting incense sticks. The temple gardens were a delight, with traditional Chinese flowers, including *Viburnum plicatum* in flower, peonies, roses and even cardiocrinums prodding through the herbage. Many of the temples have lost their horticultural skills although they may retain their ancient trees.

To our dismay we then had to descend, on yet more steps and harassed by sedan chairs, right down to the river, which we followed through slit-like gorges full of superb sub-tropical forest. Many of the plants we could not identify, although there were several handsome and different *Araliaceae* and I was glad to see our first primula, *P. obconica*, studding the shadiest cliffs with deepest pink.

The sedan chairs were a menace. The name has images of a relaxed imperial past but these came from the new China of raw enterprise. All that was needed was a couple of bamboo poles with some bamboo strapping to make a seat and, coupled with two pairs of strong shoulders, you had a business. They went at a sharp trot ferrying the new tourist money, army officers and bouncing giggling girlfriends up and down the mountain by stages and, in the Chinese fashion, they did it noisily, plastic sandals slapping on steps, using grunts, oaths and shouts to clear people off the path. As Peter and I dived yet again into the bushes, he muttered, 'What these folk need is a good dose of old fashioned Communism.'

Peter was bitterly disappointed when it became clear that we were not going to reach his main objective, which as far as we know is the one group in the world of *Rhododendron hemsleyanum* in the wild. It is a fine Fortunea that, in addition to bold foliage, has scented flowers almost as late as *R. auriculatum*. The combination of a late start, the elephant temple that took most of the morning and looking at things up the gorge had destroyed our chances. The professor said that it would have taken at least two hours there with a further two hours back from the highest point we reached. He also told us that sadly many of the accessible *R. hemsleyanum* and *R. hanceanum* that grow

underneath it have been destroyed by clearing for building.

It would take a full week to do anything like justice to Emei Shan and the value of our all too short visit was curtailed by a series of diversions. Whether we would have survived those steps for much longer is another matter, for we were stiff and sore with calf muscles registering serious protests. As so often, going down is worse than up. The crown is scarred but it is still a beautiful mountain with many of the steeper parts inaccessible and it has a superb flora. The steep south side is decidedly wetter than the gentler north slopes where the road climbs and where there is some scattered cultivation, but the middle and lower reaches, particularly where the mountain verges on precipice, are virtually untouched.

The final evening our Chinese colleagues deserted us as soon as they decently could and were seen huddled round television sets watching events unfold in Tienanmen Square. The next day we headed back to Chengdu in rain that hardly let up all day so would have been miserable on the mountain anyway. We made a deviation to see the giant Buddha in the sheer cliff overlooking the Min river at Leshan. It is 71m/234ft high and was carved out of solid rock around 719AD by someone with a wish to impress. It certainly impressed us. There is a platform where you can see it eye to eye, but its stone eye is about the height of a man, staring out over the river Min as it has done for over a thousand years.

Back in Chengdu we had a rest day with an opportunity for legs to recover from the 1,001 steps of Emei Shan. We went on a supposed shopping expedition but our interpreter, Yuan Jiang, was as keen as us to see what was happening on the streets. The main focus was on the city steps surrounding a massive statue of Chairman Mao, which had now been draped with banners and slogans; columns of chanting marchers from the various Chengdu Universities were everywhere on the move, there was haranguing at every corner and all over the city little knots of people were reading the posters pasted up by students, which were the main means of spreading the news – and the protest.

The marchers seemed good-natured and cheerful, there was

A butterfly on Cardamine macrophylla *in the garden at Masanping.*

almost a holiday atmosphere about and they waved to us and beckoned onlookers to join in. But like most people, we were too anxious about repercussions to go marching. We were told they were demanding freedom of expression, particularly in the press, 'democracy' and less corruption, better pay and more jobs. My diary note reads, 'It all seems fairly spontaneous and so long as it is confined to the students (only 1% of the population goes to university) the Government can probably contain the situation. But they must be deeply worried and we understand that martial law has been declared in Beijing, although the troops have not yet moved in.' By the time they did move in we had left for the hills.

Our shopping proved to be difficult as even Jiang found it hard to locate ballpoint pens, water bottles or even tea! Peter and David later went to see a garden situated on a low hill just north of Chengdu. This proved to be a trial garden for testing trees suitable for the streets of Chengdu and it proved to be extremely interesting and indeed surprising. They were lucky in meeting up with a senior member of staff who told them that the garden area was some 100 acres (40 hectares) with a staff of over 100 and it had been established for 10 years. Seven hundred different trees were on trial and what struck them most was the number of different species and quantities of magnolias. These included a whole avenue along a concrete path of M. *grandiflora*, several evergreen tropical species as well as deciduous ones such as M. *denudata* and M. *officinalis*. They were planted closely but we were told that thinning would be done. The garden also supplies plants for flower shows. The majority were growing well in very sticky soil which proved to be hard for Peter and David to get off their boots.[3]

On 22 May we left Chengdu for Guan Xian. The road was now completed and it was an astonishing change from 1986

with an immaculate surface all the way, and it took barely an hour and a quarter to drive. But the local farmers still treated this runway-sized expanse of tarmac as a harvesting aid: they scattered straw about for the traffic to thresh and the verges were a hive of milling and winnowing; six lanes were reduced to four or even two, and ducks pottered to and fro.

In the afternoon we were taken to Mt Tsing Chien with a Daoist Temple of Tien Shi Tung on the top which we rated quite highly (we were getting quite choosy about our temples). Our legs had recovered sufficiently to take us up the inevitable steps to the 1,200m/4,000ft summit. I went hunting for *Primula chienii*, a Petiolarid found only once in 1937 on grassy slopes, but 'grassy slopes' were in short supply and the forest was a fairly lush evergreen with many Araliads. One wonders whether the species still exists.

While we were driving around we learnt a little about Jiang's background. He had to do two years 'education' in the country prior to university. This consisted of getting up at 3 a.m. and continuing work until 10 p.m. For six months the job was carrying soil washed down in the rainy season back up the hill. He was fed on nothing but sweet potatoes which he still cannot face and he suffers stomach and heart problems. He never ceased to amaze us with his knowledge of all sorts of worldly things and he had an all-consuming interest in Britain and the British way of life.

Masanping

We were due to visit Masanping, a rather remarkable venture, part nature reserve, part display garden and part propagation centre for Chinese mountain flowers, particularly rhododendrons and primulas.

The road went up the right bank of the Min river opposite the road to Wolong and Wenchuan, past an awful polluting factory, then up a gorge where limestone was being quarried by hand. The road gradually deteriorated until we could get no further. We walked the rest of the way, passing cryptomeria and cunninghamia plantations. We were shown the nursery where rhododendron seed was sown outside on raised beds of sandy soil with some covering of moss and liverwort at one end, but in too open a position. A few seedlings could be located here and there. Nearby were beds of primulas including some *P. sonchifolia* with their leaves cut, said to have come from Emei Shan, mostly doing quite well. Beyond was a nursery with hundreds of quite healthy *Rhododendron davidii* about 30cm/1ft high.

The display garden was an entirely different story and consisted of plants scattered about on an open hillside in the nature reserve. Far too big plants had been lifted in the wild,

---

3. Other genera noted were: *Prunus, Osmanthus, Photinia, Chaenomeles, Nyssa, Liquidamber, Pterostyrax, Bauhinia* and *Catalpa*, plus conifers such as *Taxodium mucronatum, T. ascendens, Taiwania* and *Fokienia*.

Rhododendron augustinii *in the Wolong Panda Reserve where it is quite plentiful along the river banks. As it grows at a rather low elevation, much of its habitat has been destroyed elsewhere, so it is a threatened species in many areas. These Wolong plants were good blues. In other areas they can be pale blue or even white or pink.*

with a totally inadequate root system for their size, and they had been planted on mounds in a good brackeny mixture but some of this was mounded up the trunk with what little roots they had buried up to 30cm/1ft. It was obvious which plants had come some distance as they had fared the worst and had probably been dragged and dried out up the last stretch where there was no road. Some local species, notably *R. davidii*, were doing better. Other species attempted were *R. longesquamatum, R. hunnewellianum, R. oreodoxa, R. calophytum* and a curious *R. argyrophyllum* with short leaves with a fawn indumentum which we later saw in the wild. It had pretty white flowers with a glabrous ovary and, surprisingly, about sixteen stamens. There were also *R. ambiguum, R. polylepis, R. augustinii,* all of which we were to see wild later, plus *R. lutescens, R. pachytrichum* and even three little *R. stamineum* from Emei Shan.

Beyond the shoulder which held the display garden, we came to the wide hanging valley that held the reserve proper. The base was around 1,800m/6,000ft, fringed by a rim of high hills with what appeared to be virgin forest on the slopes. We were told that access to the top was extremely difficult and that some twenty species of rhododendron were native to the reserve; also there were reputed to be seven pandas, although poaching as usual was a problem. We followed a dry stream bed with some *Rhododendron calophytum* on the banks and more interestingly a population of *R. davidii.* From a horticultural viewpoint, the flowers of the latter are usually purplish to lilac which is valuable among the pinks or whites of this early group. Unfortunately they had been shed, but the distinguishing

feature of the elongated rachis was still very evident. There was a misunderstanding over seed collection which the diplomatic Jiang managed to sort out and this rarely grown species was heavily photographed. The same treatment was given to a single specimen of *Davidia involucrata*, hanging with the handkerchief-like bracts, and some trees of *Cercidiphyllum.* Both are protected species.

We had to be back in the evening for a full banquet with the Vice Mayor of Guan Xian, which had just been elevated to the status of a city and celebrated by changing its name to Dujiangyan. Endless toasts and platitudinous speeches are the norm for these occasions, but at this event the food was outstandingly lavish and the whole dinner drifted into drowsing time. As we returned, well fed and drunk, to Chengdu we were shunted off the road where the minibus was given a compulsory wash with us in it! We realized later that this was a regular occurrence for those entering the city and presumably keeps the users of their new motorway suitably clean and tidy.

Wolong and Balang

On 25 May we set off on the main leg of our trip in a new minibus with better clearance and a young driver with better reactions. We were going to need both. We stopped in Guankou again and, as we lunched on quails' eggs and ginkgo seeds, were told that the city had a reputation as a gastronomic centre and people often came there from Chengdu for dinner. The ginkgo seeds were about the size of butter beans or very small potatoes and were rather tasteless, but our Chinese colleagues tucked in

167

Calanthe tricarinata, *a very fine terrestrial orchid, widespread in western China.*

Yang Man Yeh at the entrance to one of the tunnels in Heroes' Gorge.

well, saying the food would not be so good from now on.

We handed in a note advising the Masanping Authorities how to plant and look after their rhododendrons better and then headed north. Our destination was the Wolong Panda Reserve which both Peter and I had been to briefly in 1986 but was new to David. We turned off the main road on to a dirt track with timber lorries lurching by; looking up we could see clumps of *Coelogyne* in flower and a dash of pink from a *Dendrobium* on the cliff above. There was the shrubby *Polygala arillata* with yellow flowers and a *Deutzia*, probably *D. longifolia*, with dense panicles of white. Cries of 'Primula!' brought us to a halt. Studding the mossy cliffs was *P. kialensis*, a dainty thing from Section Yunnanensis with pink or often white flowers on an inch or so of scape. There were three species of corydalis including a blue one near to *C. flexuosa*, now common in cultivation, although Peter says it is a bit of a thug!

Then, just before the panda station, was the most stirring sight. High on the cliffs above us were dabs of that wonderful violet blue that only *Rhododendron augustinii* in full bloom can make. Before dinner we took a walk up a side valley where clouds of it could be seen on the cliff faces that it seemed to favour, generally of a good even blue. It was a privilege to be there at a time when one of the finest of all flowering shrubs was in full cry, in the wild and among wonderful scenery. Other good things in the side valley were a lovely calanthe orchid with greenish-yellow flowers and a viburnum, new to us, which filled the air with its scent. There was

a whole bank of the blue corydalis, two species of berberis and two of daphne, one probably *D. tangutica* and one with unscented lilac flowers. On the cliff a magnolia was in full and inaccessible flower, probably *M. sinensis*, and *Rhododendron hunnewellianum* was shedding its flowers equally beyond reach. It was indeed a rich area.

To let the habitat recover for pandas and other wildlife the Chinese authorities had forbidden farming in parts of the Wolong area and moved villagers away. Looking down we could see how the natural vegetation was rapidly taking over and the abandoned terraces looked like green ribs on the hillside. Peter was very pessimistic about these efforts, pointing to the settlements and cultivation still visible, which he thought would be havens for poachers. I was less sure, the problems of poaching lying less with impoverished villagers than with the wildlife traders who bribed them and, given the problems of bamboo flowering and dying, it was important to restore the quality and range of the habitat. We agreed, however, that the Chinese had the authority if they wished to use it to save this symbol of the conservation movement.

After a wet night Peter was somewhat under the weather with a cold and was given Chinese pills by Jiang, sometimes a risky option. But they seemed to work and we set off up the

Opposite: Heroes' Gorge (Yin Xiong Guo) near the Wolong Panda Reserve headquarters.

Primula kialensis *without a scape and* P. polyneura *with a scape and geranium-shaped leaves growing on a moist north-facing bank. The former is hard to keep going in cultivation, the latter is easier.*

Heroes' Gorge or Valley of Heroes (Yin Xiong Guo). Above and behind the panda station lies a tumbled landscape of cliffs, screes and boulders with drifts of mist threaded among dark hills. There are four tunnels, hacked out of the hillside at the cost of a number of the Heroes' lives, the first short, the second fairly long and dark, the third very long and very dark and the fourth shorter but cascading with drips.

At the foot we saw one of the most cheerful sights, damp rock

A good form of Rhododendron pachytrichum. *This species is associated with* R. oreodoxa *and they hybridise readily.*

faces covered in a mixed mass of *Primula kialensis* and *P. polyneura*, both of a similar magenta colour but the first small and pert with a white eye, and *P. polyneura* taller and softer. In between the tunnels we were again struck by the richness of the area but it was often very frustrating with plants out of reach. The big *Rhododendron galactinum* across the gorge had only one truss but was obviously full of capsules, alas unobtainable. Further up we spotted some twenty plants across the river of a very good pink form but tantalizingly out of reach. The same applied to *R. wiltonii*, but white and pink forms of *R. pachytrichum* grew on the path side. There was a great diversity of willows, from the bold *Salix fargesii* to dwarf carpeting species, and we spent much time photographing tiny things on dripping rocks, such as a white-flowered pinguicula and a deep pink pleione.

As we emerged from the tunnels I spotted a flash of pink in the branches high above us, then more in different shades. It was a great find of *Rhododendron dendrocharis* (CCH 4012) in full flower and varying from a good rich pink with blotch to nearly white. Related to the well-known early-flowering *R. moupinense*, this fine species is dwarfer, hardier and flowers later. Sometimes on cliffs but more usually growing on trees, it was a true epiphyte which is a much less common feature in colder areas. We assembled and while David and Peter searched along the foot of a cliff, I worked my way up, passing masses of *Primula moupinensis* on the way until I was able to edge out, legs dangling on each side,

A fine pink form of the newly introduced Rhododendron dendrocharis. *This species was epiphytic on broad-leaved trees and on cliffs.*

along the tree that hung out from the cliff. Fortunately the nearest plant was a good form and was heavily photographed from my perch; the next one along the trunk was almost white.

After the tunnels the valley and path levelled out and the flora became less rich. We went up a steep side path through birch, fir, larch and hemlock. Some of these conifers had been felled but how did they get the timber out? Rhododendrons here were *R. pachytrichum* (CCH 3919), a small-flowered *R. lutescens*, along with *R. polylepis*, and *R. concinnum* which can both produce rather harsh shades of mauvy-purple, although the last species with broader leaves has some good garden forms. *R. asterochnoum/calophytum* seemed to vary from the scattering of hairs on the leaf underside of *R. asterochnoum* to the hairs being confined to the veins and, therefore, nearer *R. calophytum*. They

are undoubtedly very closely related. On the way down, David shinned up a very steep bank looking for *R. wiltonii* which could not be reached but, to our surprise, found *R. longesquamatum* (CCH 3920) in a good form. The final touch was a fallen log covered in rhododendron seedlings among which Peter spotted an obvious little *R. orbiculare* among a jostle of species we had already seen. But where was the parent?

So ended a very exciting day for plants with *R. dendrocharis* as the highlight and on the veranda of the guesthouse that evening it seemed appropriate to broach the gin and tonic, that Great British invention, which I had acquired from the Jin Jiang Hotel. Peter celebrated with a small glass from his usual bottle of Sauternes that he miraculously manages to make last a whole trip.

Peter Cox and David Chamberlain photographing Rhododendron dendrocharis. *Back to back they faced each other, drew their swords and shot.*

A white form of the well-known indoor pot plant Primula malacoides *at Wolong.*

171

A crumbling crag with twenty or so plants of R. orbiculare *just coming out, and a good form, too.*

The second full day at Wolong was Orbiculare day. Our guide, the janitor of the local museum with a bad cough and a face that looked as if it had collided with something large, took us to a panda observation post further down the valley. We dropped some 4km/2½ miles below the guesthouse, crossed a bouncy wire bridge and climbed a steep path which zigzagged through scrub containing some fine *R. augustinii* until we reached our objective.

The observation post consisted of a large hut surrounded by rotting tents and contained a very relaxed American from Toledo Zoo, Ohio, reading a book beside the fire and occasionally fiddling with the tracking gear for pandas with radio collars. He had been there a week, intended to stay another week and reckoned that he had been lucky to hear a panda grunt on one occasion. He said there were about fourteen pandas in this part of Wolong but mostly they just disappear silently through the bamboo. At that point only one panda had been bred at the panda station and much more recently it was on the news that they have so far not managed to breed enough pandas to make up for the ones that die in captivity.

We attempted to describe *Rhododendron orbiculare* to the janitor through Jiang and were told that some grew further up the path, but the janitor had been bitten by our first leech or perhaps was bored – anyhow he was not willing to take us there. After a fairly long and dull walk, we came to a crag with

a crumbling cliff and a loose scree at the foot. A quick search at the base revealed nothing so we took the path on to the top, which to our great delight was covered with *R. orbiculare* (CCH 4016) either in flower or coming out. This proved to be an excellent form with bigger leaves than any seen previously in cultivation and the large flowers were fine shades of rose with deeper lines and no hint of a bluish tinge. The large leaves have been confirmed on resulting plants in cultivation but the flowers are rather pale. We saw only this one group, a rim at the top of the knoll, but after our long walk in the dingy forest it was as if someone had switched on the stage lights and there was the chorus, lit up in brightest pink.

After a cheerful picnic among the rhododendrons, we climbed another 200m/650ft into curiously open forest with some fine specimens of *Picea asperata* and *Tsuga dumosa*, but little of the usual undergrowth of shrubs or bamboo. It made for better visibility and, while we did not expect to see pandas, we had been told that their digestion was inefficient and they have to eat large quantities of vegetation to get sufficient nourishment, with copious droppings as a result. Unfortunately we did not see any panda piles but we did see other mammal droppings which we characterized as coffee beans and black olives, probably musk deer and serow. On our return to the hut, our American friend was still sitting in the same position with the same book as when we left him! He said that he was having the day off.

Mature and young cones of Picea asperata *at Huanglongsi. This spruce is common in Sichuan.*

After another wet night it was still raining at breakfast, we were off up the valley to Balang Mountain with no further word of the pass being blocked by snow. It was an impressive drive up river with fine cliffs and side gorges, but there was a nasty rock slide where, just as our minibus was about to cross, rocks and boulders started to descend. We made numerous stops for various excitements and Peter was particularly pleased when large bushes of a white-flowered rhododendron turned out to be the newly described *R. balangense*. It reached 4.5–9m/15–30ft and is easily recognised from its persistent bud scales, winged petiole and a scurfy indumentum, buff when young turning to white. The loose truss is white or white tinged pink with small spots.[4] *R. galactinum* made more of a tree than *R. balangense* and the truss was fuller, the off-white to pink flowers having a distinctive purple blotch. There was a

We found Rhododendron balangense *in some quantity further up the valley at Wolong on a steep north-facing slope.*

conglomeration of Triflora along the roadside, including *R. lutescens*, *R. augustinii* and *R. ambiguum* and a range of hybrids between them. This stretch was richly forested, with very little human habitation. A small yellow-flowered daphne crept about the road edge and there were two primulas, both with magenta flowers. *P. polyneura* grew on steep scree slopes and rock ledges and *P. palmata*, which has deeply dissected leaves, grew on banks above the river. Soon the road crossed the river and started to climb up to the pass with the forest thinning out. Two more rhododendron species appeared, *R. watsonii* referred to earlier, and *R. prattii*. One plant of the latter had some pink flowers, which was unusual as it is normally white with spots.

Once the bare alpine pasture had been reached, *Meconopsis integrifolia* became plentiful with its lovely large saucer-shaped yellow flowers scattered over wide areas. As we neared the top, there was a robust and handsome Nivalid primula with violet or violet-blue flowers and a striking dark eye which we called

Rhododendron galactinum *is one of the most distinct and the hardiest of subsection Falconera. Confined to west and central Sichuan, we have found it in two other localities. Here it was with* R. balangense.

4. *Rhododendron balangense* was described by the Chinese in 1983 and apparently only grows in this valley. We found two good populations on a steep hillside, the second mixed with *R. galactinum* (CCH 4023). The leaves most closely resemble *R. watsonii*, which we found soon after, and there is some indication that *R. balangense*, while now a well established species, has descended from a hybrid swarm of *R. watsonii*, perhaps with *R. longesquatum* which does have persistent bud scales. It is doing well in cultivation but, like *R. watsonii*, is rather early into growth.

Omphalogramma species, probably O. vinciflorum, *on the Balang pass with a small* Corydalis.

P. melanops, now reduced to subspecies in the *P. chionantha/ sinopurpurea* complex. There was a fine collection of alpine plants with an omphalogramma, also with violet flowers, which may have been *O. vinciflorum*, a lovely little blue corydalis, a yellow draba, a mandrake and a curious *Rhododendron nivale* near to subsp. *boreale* with surprisingly glaucous foliage which may have been a different species.

Our next stop had to be our last – it was getting late and we had to reach habitation down in the valley on the other side of the pass. The actual top was covered in fresh snow and the road was deteriorating among mud and rocks, which our driver negotiated with skill. We measured the top at 4,300m/14,000ft rather than the official 4,400m/14,500ft but a bit of snowball throwing with Alphonso soon brought home the effects of altitude.

On the north-facing slope, the scrub and forest level was much higher but it was obviously drier with only small trees and much evergreen oak scrub. Primulas were in flower not far below the summit in half-melted snow and we swept rapidly down past a multitude of Lapponica rhododendrons. It was getting dark, bushes with pink flowers loomed past, and the country gradually got drier as we lost altitude, eventually reaching scrub-covered hillsides and apples cultivated in the valley.

We spent the night in a very rustic inn that must have changed little since Ernest Wilson's day, apart from one dangling light bulb that did not work. 'They only have electricity in the summer,' was the explanation, so we sat in candlelight round a single table in the tiny kitchen while dish after dish was prepared in the same wok: eggs, vegetables, strips of meat, potatoes and finally the rice came with sugar and a bowl of green peppers. 'Not hot,' they said. 'They are only young,' but they were sufficiently charged to leave us gasping.

Family came and went, visitors came to gaze and a three-year-old on the daughter's knee called Peter 'Grandfather'. I was flattered by being described as 'Ten Thousand Yuan Man' – apparently the equivalent of a millionaire – until I realized that at 6 yuan to the pound this made me worth £1,660. It was all very quaint and full of atmosphere. Mao Zedong had stayed there on the Long March and George Smith (of *Saxifraga* and *Androsace* fame) added botanical distinction. But as we went to our bunks we wondered if dinner would bring gastric retribution.

As we had missed a large part of Balang Mountain due to lack of time, we headed back up in the morning and our first stop was east of Rilong at the pink flowers we had seen by the road as it

A good form of Rhododendron concinnum *above the village of Rilong.*

Rhododendron vernicosum *above Rilong. This subsection Fortunea member is very widespread and variable, always having good flowers, but no scent.*

was getting dark. They were stunted bushes of *Rhododendron vernicosum* (CCH 3927) in a much hacked about area, although some were growing well in forest nearby. The leaves were narrower than those seen in Yunnan but the flowers were attractive, varying from a good pink to near white. Another common species was *R. concinnum* in shades of pinky-mauve and a variable flare but attractive and brightly coloured. A Lapponica was probably more *R. nivale* subsp. *boreale*, an upright and rather leggy bush, sometimes with good mid-blue-purple flowers. Other plants here were *Daphne retusa, Anemone obtusiloba* mostly white-flowered with only a few blue, a *Paeonia* species, probably *P. veitchii* which we saw in flower later and *Cassiope selaginoides.*

On the way back to the pass we found some surprisingly tall *Rhododendron primuliflorum* with pale pink to cream flowers, which grew as high as 1.8m/6ft, upright and often straggly. These tall forms are poor performers in cultivation as they usually take many years to flower and are always leggy. Peter managed to cross the stream where scattered rhododendrons included *R. przewalskii* and also *R. wasonii* (CCH 3926) with variable leaf widths and colours of indumentum.

Our top stop was back among the *Primula melanops* and

Paeonia veitchii *on a bank of mixed shrubs and herbs. Further east this species had white flowers. Easy to cultivate and very hardy.*

175

Girls in Xiaojin.

A fine specimen of Primula melanops *on the Balang pass. These high elevation primulas burst into flower as the snow is melting away from them.*

Meconopsis integrifolia, two plants of the highest class, although the fragrance of the primula possibly gave it the edge. Unfortunately in cultivation (when one can grow it at all) the meconopsis loses that restraint that makes it both delicate and flamboyant, yet never blowsy. Once again Peter braved the stream to look at three rhododendron bushes, perhaps the highest elepidotes on the north side of the pass. The first looked like *R. przewalskii*, the second *R. aganniphum* and the third half way between. There were many plants of the scarlet *Meconopsis punicea* which had flowered last year in among and even on the top of boulders. This species seems to be capable of growing in an astonishing number of different habitats, including bogs and alpine meadows.

On this part of the trip we always seemed to be on the wrong side of some riotous stream or river and, travelling back down the mountain, the opposite hillside showed groups of cream, white and pink rhododendrons. Some were probably inaccessible but one was just the other side of what was now a raging torrent, which we dared not cross, though if we had had more time we might have plucked up enough courage. On inspection through binoculars, this was clearly *R. bureavioides*. The leaves had indumentum on parts of the upper surface and dense cinnamon indumentum below, while the flowers were cream coloured and

Meconopsis integrifolia, *the lampshade poppy, on the Balang pass,* Wolong. *This superb plant occurs in scattered colonies above the tree-line.*

Opposite. We could not reach this Rhododendron bureavioides *owing to the torrent.*

larger than the *R. bureavii* in cultivation. Warren Berg collected *R. bureavioides* in 1986 near Mt Sigunian, the highest peak in the Wolong Reserve up the valley to the east of us.

We could easily have spent two more days exploring the Balang pass thoroughly but to do this it would be advisable to camp somewhere near the top of the pass, if permitted by the authorities. Good *Rhododendron sargentianum* has been recorded there, as has a more substantial population of *R. wasonii*, and we are sure there would be much more of interest as so many plants have very specialised habitats such as cliffs and ledges. In all we had found about twenty-four *Rhododendron* taxa in the Wolong

Reserve and a rich variety of primulas.

It proved to be a long drive and a dusty one down the valley to Xiaojin where we stayed the night, with everything getting drier and drier. It was a rather miserable place, a windswept little town at the junction of two rivers and several roads and set on both sides of the river, partly on steep slopes. But our rooms were not as bad as they might have been, there was an outside cold tap and even the outside public loo was conveniently close provided the wind was not coming from that direction. There was even television in our rooms and Peter's aerial sprouted beer tins on the end.

A good shrubby Lonicera *species near the Fubian river north of Xiaojin.*

A lovely pink form of Syringa tomentella *near the Fubian river north of Xiaojin. Seed of this species collected further south near Kangding in 1990 has given disappointing paler flowers.*

Mongbi pass

We were glad to get away early in the morning but puzzled as to where we were going next as no road going directly north was marked on our maps. However, one existed which eventually crossed the Mongbi pass and arrived at the sizeable town of Barkam. The road took us almost due north up the Fubian river and, to our surprise and delight, we had a most interesting day.

The valley was almost a gorge, its steep slopes covered with masses of deciduous shrubs. It started very dry and, as usual, the opposite bank looked better than our own. Our first stop was prompted by a very fine pink lilac, *Syringa tomentella*, in full flower and richly scented. We also found a dwarf yellow daphne and that fine daphne relative *Stellera chamaejasme*. It is

Our driver made an expert job of driving through this morass at Mongbi pass.

A shrubby Clematis *species found near the Fubian river north of Xiaojin. Only one plant was located and we have never seen anything similar again. The closest relatives,* C. angustifolia *and* C. longiloba, *are found in north-east China.*

The lovely Primula optata *at 3,650m/11,900ft on the south side of Mongbi pass. This rare species has never been in cultivation.*

invariably white or pink in Tibet and Nepal, but yellow-flowered in Yunnan and seed of it is very hard to locate. Amongst other plants there were species of *Abelia, Berberis, Cupressus,* and also *Potentilla arbuscula,* upright-growing with white flowers. At our lunch stop we all set off in different directions and found different things. The best trophy was Peter's single plant of a yellow-flowered clematis that was a shrub and not a climber, while David enthused over a variety of shrubby lonicera. By this time our plant presses were bulging, but as the road started to rise and we came to a wetter region, we had to stop again for no less than five primulas. *P. polyneura* was there again, a single plant of *P. sonchifolia* and the gawky *P. tangutica,* but the star was another Nivalid at 3,700m/12,000ft. Its flowers were a lovely blue-purple to lavender colour but with a dark eye instead of white and more pronounced petiole than the *sinopurpurea* alliance. The slightly nodding heads were finely scented. It was later identified by Hu Chi Minh as *P. optata* (CCH 4053). A clump of rhododendron had us puzzled as it seemed to be half way between *R. rufum* and *R. przewalskii.* Near to the pass were belts of rhododendrons, the slopes covered in *R. aganniphum* (CCH 4064) with near white indumentum but no flowers as yet, and in the valley bottom to our surprise, a mass of Lapponicas.

The Mongbi pass is high at just under 3,950m/13,000ft and has a bad reputation; the literal translation is 'Dream Pain' i.e. nightmare. Near the summit we ran into fresh snow and at the top the road twists through a narrow defile with a quagmire of snow melt and mud and high banks of snow on each side. We all got out but our driver successfully negotiated it, with wheels spinning and a bit of shoving. The view north from the pass was entirely different

– almost solid forest with an understorey of rhododendrons. Around the pass were more *Meconopsis integrifolia,* which appeared to be taller and finer here with more flowers per plant. The local people often picked them or dug them up to decorate their porches, window boxes and even themselves, and Peter went so far as to say that this plant was possibly his favourite of everything we had seen to date, including rhododendrons!

179

Part of Kha Jiao village, near the foot of the north side of Mongbi pass.

Decorated wooden panels on a house in Kha Jiao.

Near the top I spotted a fine looking yellow primula but it was one of the places where we could not stop and shortly after we had to negotiate a very bad and muddy section of the road which did not promise well for our hopes to return the following day. Dropping again, we came to the first villages and were particularly struck by one called Kha Jiao, to which we hoped to return. When we reached the main valley, we turned left for Barkam and to our surprise found the river here flowing west — as we learned later towards the huge Dadu river, which was just a short distance to the west.

Barkam was a sizeable place and we lodged in something resembling a hotel where, apart from the usual lorry drivers and travelling bureaucrats, some curious folk were staying.[5] In the morning, we set off back to the pass to find some of the things we did not have time for the previous evening, stopping on the way to take masses of photographs of the pretty village of Kha Jiao. With finely built houses of exceptional masonry work and colourful painted patterns around doors and windows, it had a prosperous air about it. We were told that of the twenty-eight families that lived there, twenty-four owned the 'hand tractors' that we saw chugging everywhere, belching smoke in the driver's face, and which cost 7,000 to 8,000 yuan.

Opposite the village was a meadow filled with the fragrant and pretty *Primula yargongensis* with its pink flowers held on long slender stems. Further up our fears of the driver refusing to negotiate the muddy stretch were unfounded and we arrived at the top where David and Peter searched *Rhododendron aganniphum* for capsules with only limited success – there had evidently been a frost the previous spring. In the meantime, I was delighted to find the yellow primula, a most refined plant with a beautiful scent, at first sight looking a bit like *P. strumosa* but obviously a Nivalid. Later this was identified as *P. orbicularis* from which seed had been collected in 1986, but it only had a short stay in cultivation like so many of its kin. Peter also looked in vain for the section Pogonanthum species *Rhododendron rufescens* which had defeated him in 1986.

We gradually walked down the road from the snow-banked pass through banks of *R. aganniphum* which, as one descends to the north, becomes mixed with and then is replaced by *R. phaeochrysum*. The two species showed no signs of hybridizing, however, as there appeared to be no overlap in their flowering time. It was now the end of May and the former was nowhere yet in flower while *R. phaeochrysum* was fully out, with flowers ranging from whitish to a good pink, always spotted. At lower elevations again *R. rufum* appeared in the form that used to be known as *R. weldianum* with a thicker indumentum and wider leaves than seen elsewhere, along with a poor form of *R. vernicosum*. *R. aganniphum* even popped up again, bigger and healthier at these lower altitudes. David found a hybrid between *R. phaeochrysum* and *R. rufum* and both these species

The most amazing coppery-red-flowered form of the marsh marigold, Caltha palustris, *on a moist slope in the forest on the north side of Mongbi pass. We found only one plant.*

had some black buds that looked identical to the bud blast fungus that we see at home.

In the forest we found two unexpected plants. One was a splendid group of *Primula sonchifolia* which obviously has a much wider distribution than we had realised. The other surprise was a single clump of a caltha with amazing coppery-red flowers. A search around revealed no more. This is evidently only a curious form of the circumpolar *C. palustris* which, of course, normally has yellow or sometimes white flowers.

Just above the villages, patches of forest had been felled and replanted successfully with spruce, probably *Picea asperata*, the species that is the commonest conifer here anyway. So far on our travels we had passed three tree nurseries, all looking well

5. Heading for the washroom in my pyjamas the next morning, I met a monk in full purple and red robes with shaved head. He greeted me in perfect English and we discussed the weather and other pleasantries; we must have looked an odd pair. Also sharing our guesthouse were two Austrians and an Israeli. The Austrians had been travelling the country on the cheap taking photographs for articles and they kept us entertained until late into the night with tales of the 'backside of China'. They had become experts on how to handle the local police and make use of any buses or trucks to get around. Minor bribery is rife, with packets of local cigarettes handed round as a preliminary to more serious discussion. We made a mental note to bring cigarettes next time, particularly western ones which are good currency.

Primula fangii, a recently described species in west Sichuan only, of the Aleuritia section (P. farinosa relative). Grows on steep, mostly shady banks.

organised with slat protection for the beds. We guessed that the reason for the prosperity of the villages was partly due to good management of the forests here. It was noticeable that no rhododendrons grew in the reforested plots. Either it was too low and they had never occurred here or more likely the foresters regard rhododendrons as weeds and remove any that reseed.

Our start the next day was much delayed by the Children's Day Parade in Barkam, which was nevertheless entertaining and large amounts of film were exposed. Squads of children, each group in different uniforms, marched about chanting slogans such as 'We must learn to work hard,' while the teachers blew whistles through loudhailers. Some of Mao's traditions obviously

continued, but it was a cheerful occasion with children dancing and singing and others playing musical instruments.

One of our principal objectives in coming to Barkam was to find *Rhododendron barkamense*, a species newly described by David, related to *R. lacteum* but smaller in all parts and with a cordate leaf base. As we had not seen any sign of it on our travels south of Barkam, we thought we should try heading north to reach the altitude of 3,800m/12,500ft at which *R. barkamense* had been recorded. There was a mountain called Kha'er Gu given as 4,498m/14,800ft on the map, so we headed up the Dadu river which rises in Qinghai. In the end we had an interesting day but, as expected, reached neither the rhododendron nor anything like the right altitude. In due course we turned up another tributary, the Jomojo, where there was an almost white *R. vernicosum* and I was delighted when we found a newly described primula, the very farinose *P. fangii* with magenta-pink flowers and a white eye on a tall scape up to 45cm/1½ft. The leaves were lanceolate with much greenish-white farina.

The drive through fine countryside with gorges, swift rivers and often good forest was longer than we expected. The architecture of the houses was most striking. They were tall wooden structures with the top floor protruding well out at the front; nearby there was often a stone-built tower of fine masonry with no mortar as high as 21m/70ft. We heard two versions of the towers' origin; one from the local Foreign Affairs officer that they were only a hundred years old or less and were built by a local village head as a gesture of his importance. However, the following morning an American anthropologist who was studying the local population told us that they were used for defense with a ladder inside to five or six levels at which there were slits for arrows. They certainly had a fortified look. He also told us that there is a great difference in the cultures in separate

In the town of Barkam we were delayed by a Children's Day Parade but it was well worth watching and photographing.

North of Barkam on the Jomojo river were the most extraordinary houses and towers. Our interpreter said they were purely decorative, but the American anthropologist said they were for defence, with ladders up the inside and slits for shooting arrows.

valleys in this area, in some cases matriarchal, others patriarchal. Relationships are loose with no formal marriages and a tendency to polyandry. There are no family names and each family tends to be known by the names of their house. The Han Chinese, who have moved into the area, attempt to force their culture on the 'Tibetans', causing much stress by fining them for children born outside marriage and resulting in a number of suicides. Our friend claimed he had saved a girl from throwing herself off a cliff and then got into trouble for saving her. He also told us that the local minorities are not true Tibetans, though they are classed as such by the Chinese.

In the morning two policemen, a female assistant and Alphonso invaded the room I shared with David, saying we needed yet another bit of paper for our permit for Hongyuan county. All was amicably resolved and we got our passes, but a procession of officials came and went. Our staff had decided that we needed a rest which really meant that they were demanding a rest for themselves. We had noticed that our driver went very slowly on the way out and roared along on the way home.

Our American friend led us a bit of a dance. He had dropped out of the computer world and was now a sort of self-appointed anthropologist living in a village at around 3,700m/12,000ft where he claimed there were three species of rhododendron, so we worked out a plan to go up there with him. After various delays due to buying his provisions, it turned out that he then expected us to carry most of them, plus a load of snooker balls! He was not fit and we ended by taking his backpack while he bicycled sedately along to Suomo, wheezing through a bad chest. Turning up the hill and after a stiff hike, we found ourselves in evergreen oak forest which was barren and apparently endless, so we parted company from our friend and trudged downhill in the rain, grumbling over the lost chance of *R. barkamense* and two unproductive days.

A fine pig in Suomo village. Very often pigs are slaughtered when very small and roasted whole.

Nomadic Tibetans come up to the high plains in summer to graze their livestock. They live in black yurts made out of yak skins. These yak herders are expert horsemen.

Another most attractive form of Primula optata *(see page 179) on the edge of the Hongyuan plain.*

Hongyuan and Huanglongsi

We now headed for the Hongyuan plain and hopefully for the Zhegu pass that we had failed to explore properly in 1986. We were off in good time but the road gradually deteriorated and endless road works including blasting and bulldozing delayed us for several hours. At one time we were towed by a bulldozer which broke off our front tow-bar. One section of road had had fine retaining walls newly built, only to be largely destroyed by a land slide. All the many stops and walks along the road proved to have limited interest but there was a good *R. vernicosum*, inevitably hanging over the far side of the river, some white-flowered peonies, a *Berberis* species for David and a particularly fine *Piptanthus*.

The wooded gorge gradually gave way to patchy forest and finally to grass. A truck that had turned on its side attempting to avoid a large pothole caused yet another delay. The contents were nothing but aubergines – who would eat all these in the middle of nowhere? In the mêlée of people Peter spotted a basket on a man's back and sprouting from it branches of what he thought was a small-leaved *R. phaeochrysum* var. *levistratum*, probably from the Zhegu pass. He pursued the man, plucking bits and pieces from the basket, much to the general amusement of the crowd.

Once clear of the forest, good plants appeared once more. Primulas included a paler form of *P. optata* with fragrant lavender cup-shaped flowers, still with a dark eye, and *P. fascicularis* which

we were to see in greater quantity the next day. As we dropped to the plain a new plant was *P. stenocalyx*, a dainty and fragile-looking member of section Pulchella with pale-purple flowers with a white eye, always bobbing in the wind. There was also a coarse corydalis with yellow flowers tipped purple, a tufted iris with a purplish flower with a white flare on the falls and more *Rhododendron rufum*, this time typical with less dense indumentum than on the Mongbi Pass. The flowers are usually among the smallest of the Taliensia in comparison with the leaf size, white flushed pink with small crimson spots. There were also a few *R. aganniphum* and plenty of the erect-growing early flowering Lapponica *R. capitatum*.

We had a beautiful evening driving on the undulating grasslands with yak, horses and sheep among the still pools and the black yak-hair yurts. To the south snow mountains rimmed the plain. This time the Red Grasslands were flushed with the green of spring and millions of buttercups and calthas stained patches with yellow. That night we found the bleak little town of Hongyuan had not changed much in three years, although the addition of toilets to our accommodation was welcome as one or two of us were in regular need.

In the crystal clear morning there was hoar-frost on the grass. Two Ruddy Shelduck with fawn-coloured wing coverts flew over

184

Primula tangutica *growing in a bog on the Hongyuan plain*.   Primula purdomii *on the southern edge of the Hongyuan plain*.

and later we saw a burrowing animal, about the size of a cat, with short bandy legs and a long bushy tail. Some truck drivers plus our driver spent ages trying to dig the poor beast out but its hole must have been too extensive for them to get it. We could not find anything like it in any animal book. There were also some terns with typical black heads and various buzzards, hawks, shrikes and larks. We were encouraged to ride a pony and our staff had a go but the pony shied at us, so we thought better of it.

Our driver amused himself but not us by swerving about at great speed attempting to avoid potholes, then landing in more than he avoided. He developed the most infuriating habit of getting up speed and then free-wheeling, often at top speed around corners. Later in the day we complained when he made an awful job of one such corner. This free-wheeling gradually became an obsession and he would do it even on a flat stretch of road by getting up speed, then switching off and then the same again. We wondered if he really thought he was saving fuel.

This proved to be a primula day. At one place there were no less than four species, including the curious *P. tangutica* with its dusky-maroon reflexed flowers and a strong musty smell.[6] A second species was the clump-forming *P. purdomii*[7] with flowers varying from bluish-purple to white, usually with a white eye. A third was *P. fascicularis*, which we had seen earlier, a

diminutive herb with bright pink flowers with a conspicuous yellow eye. All these enjoyed living on tussocks that stood out of the bog, but always clear of the water.

As we clambered over the pass 3,850m/12,700ft before the reserve of Huanglongsi, the scenery was absolutely staggering. On our previous visit here most of the mountains were hidden in clouds, but this time we were lucky. A long jagged snow-covered ridge was backed by other higher peaks. This was the Min Shan range, one of which we were told was called 'Icy Peak', over 5,588m/18,000ft. On the left were much lower limestone peaks with streaks of pyrites, while at the back in between an inky-black thunderstorm was raging. This was a truly awe-inspiring sight to which our photographs failed to do justice. We did not have time to stop for various plants of interest but we spotted a fine pheasant by the road with an iridescent breast, chestnut wings and a long tail like the traditional sporting bird.

Huanglongsi in 1989 was, frankly, a bit of a dump. The authorities were in the middle of constructing a chalet hotel in

6. This most unusual species belongs to subsection Maximowiczii of section Crystallophlomis (*Nivalis*) with narrow reflexed corolla lobes. We re-introduced this in 1986 but it lasted only a few years.

7. A well-marked form in the *Primula chionantha* / *sinopurpurea* complex as treated by Richards.

hybrid Swiss-Chinese style, but in a purely Chinese manner they had built everything other than the plumbing first; there was no running water, hot or cold, in our block and the toilet was a 70m sprint away outside. When you got there it was a kind of elevated urinal from which you could see the grandest of mountain scenery but privacy was in short supply as the walls were only waist high. A loo with a view, indeed.

Even this remote outpost in far northern Sichuan had television sets and we soon realised that something important was afoot as our staff were riveted to any screen they could find. This was the 4 June 1989 and we were witnessing something that shook the whole world. Through the open door of a cottage we watched fires burning and heard the rattle of gunfire. This was Tiananmen Square at the height of the battle between the pro-democracy students and the Chinese army. After a while the programme was suddenly taken off, no doubt when the authorities banned the television cameras.

After the dramas of the previous night we awoke in Huanglongsi to a lovely sunny morning which resulted in red faces and arms. Unlike 1986 we had the whole day to make our way among the catwalks and limestone pools up to the two temples and then up into the scrub below the great white peaks. We soon noticed that most of the flowers were damaged and poor, no doubt partly due to inclement weather. The plant that we thought was *Rhododendron anthopogonoides* in 1986, growing right at the edge of the pools, was now in flower and eventually we had to come to the sad conclusion that it was just common old *R. primuliflorum*, the

Primula orbicularis *on the pass above Huanglongsi. Its favourite habitat is on mounds in sludgy mud.*

most widespread of section Pogonanthum, in flower shades from off-white to a reasonable pale pink. This species continued up to 3,500m/11,500ft or more and we failed to find any other member of the section. Virtually all the *R. przewalskii* here lacked indumentum so should be called subsp. *dabanshanense*. *R. watsonii* was confined to the forest and the flowers seemed to be all in tatters, but eventually Peter found one good truss, pure white with a few crimson spots. This species is very slow growing in cultivation, partly on account of its early growth which often gets frosted, but at its best, the foliage can be impressive. *R. rufum* was also only growing in the more sheltered places. The last rhododendron found here was *R. oreodoxa*, its flowers over, but there were fine specimens to 7.6m/25ft tall. Hybrids occurred between all these species.

Beyond the top temple and limestone pools, *Rhododendron przewalskii* covered the mountainside in huge drifts. Some of these may have been *R. aganniphum* as a population on the road out proved to be a mixture of these two species with hybrids/intermediaries between them. We cut open some of the few *R. przewalskii* flower buds present and these were white. There were good clumps of *Meconopsis quintuplinervia*, 30–60cm/1–2ft across, and much smaller plants of M. *punicea*, alas, not quite into flower. It was observed that some of the latter species do die after flowering so even in the wild it is not reliably perennial.

Today was my birthday (I always seem to be having birthdays in China) so two bottles of Chinese wine were produced along with a birthday card from my wife Virginia and we were given a private room. The meal was followed by traditional Tibetan tea

Incarvillea compacta *on the pass above Huanglongsi. These incarvilleas with huge gaudy flowers look out of place on a windswept pass way above the tree-line.*

Opposite. The sectionalised natural limestone pools at Huanglongsi.

Rhododendron watsonii *at Huanglongsi with unusually good flowers for the hardiest member of subsection Grandia.*

taken in the housemaids' room. Hot water is poured on rye flour, sugar and a sort of chewy yak cheese in the bottom of a bowl and, with a little butter floating on top, it makes quite a meal, although nothing like as horrible as travellers' tales would have you believe. There is obviously a strong Tibetan culture here and they speak the proper language, unlike around Barkam where the locals cannot even understand Tibetan.

We made various stops on our way out and south. Large banks of *R. rufum* had off-white flowers as usual with indifferent small trusses. *R. capitatum* was more variable than we would have expected, both in leaf and flower colour, the leaves green to glaucous, the flowers pale lavender to blue-purple, some pinkish. But glamorous rhododendrons were not on the menu.

Among the flora of the upper reaches, we met some fauna in a group of girls making their way to the local market. They had been picking *Meconopsis integrifolia* and their baskets were filled with the bright yellow flowers. As the road wound over the top among patches of snow, the pink flowers turned out to be *Incarvillea younghusbandii*, so dwarfed and stemless at 3,600m/11,700ft that it appeared all flower. Also there was the yellow *Primula orbicularis*, another member of section Crystallophlomis, seen earlier but growing in fine clumps in and around a pool. The hills that day were all shrouded by the low mist which drifted around us.

Songpan did not look much different from 1986 and we headed on to Maowen for the night. This time we had been given the go-ahead to drive down the Min Jiang as the road was open, unlike 1986 when it was closed by mud slides. The turbulent river

ran through a fine gorge with a little forest down to the water level, but it was not wet enough to support any rhododendrons. Further down, the views became very impressive – fine peaks with knife-edge ridges, forested on the less steep slopes. Later the gorge became drier and drier with little in flower apart from spiraeas and a blue iris. Our driver carried on his dreadful free-wheeling habit with nearly fatal results, almost colliding with a truck and running down a road worker. After a bit I became exasperated but my outburst had little effect. There was the usual wreck of a truck down by the river that could so easily have been us. There were masses of logs in the river which is used as a timber transport system, some floating down but most stranded or piled up near the bank. The valley broadened out near the town of Maowen with fruit and other crop trees. The local minority known as the Qing wore a sort of white turban, but few of the young followed the traditional dress or even spoke their language.

We had hoped to make a high-level excursion from Wenchuan but a few miles out of Maowen clanking noises betrayed a broken spring, which was hardly surprising considering the potholes our driver had been vigorously assaulting the previous day. He was not a man of finesse either in driving or manners and his main redeeming feature was a sharp nose for a good kitchen. The inevitable delays lost us yet another chance to botanise. At least he was a bit more careful of his springs but we still had two more frights. The first was when a truck forced us to the edge above the river and we actually drove over a short void with only the momentum of the vehicle saving us. The second was when we met head-on a truck overtaking a mini tractor – how we avoided a

Rhododendron rufum *at Huanglongsi. This woolly rhododendron resembles* R. bureavii *but has no indumentum on the stems or leaf upper surface.*

crash, heaven knows. We heard bad news that Chengdu had been affected by the turmoil in Beijing and various buildings had been burnt. There was some doubt if we could stay at the Jin Jiang.

At lunch in Wenchuan, we noticed a lily in a container nearly into flower. This was the valley where Ernest Wilson discovered *Lilium regale* and after driving on again, we saw masses, mixed with *Eremurus chinensis* with white flowers. Wilson organised the collection of thousands of lily bulbs on two different expeditions, so it was good to see that there were still plenty left. Sadly virtually all were still in bud but eventually we spotted one plant with three flowers out. Jiang was agile and brave enough to climb up the cliff to collect it and it proved to be a magnificent specimen with thirteen flowers or buds (including some aborted) and stood 1.8m/6ft tall. Wilson's helpers must have risked life and limb to scale the cliffs gathering all those bulbs. Jiang took the bulb for himself. While most of the lilies were on the sunnier west-facing bank, there were quite a number facing east and these were much later with buds hardly formed.

After our trip down the river we spent the night in Guan Xian at a rest home for retired Party Cadres – less a sign of our age or respectability than the fact that the road into Chengdu was closed due to the upheavals. There were few people around but Professor Hu Chi Minh, the expert on Chinese primulas, was also marooned there, all flights having been cancelled. It was a splendid opportunity to get our dried primula specimens identified with great authority. David knew him well as he had spent no less than two years in the Edinburgh Herbarium working through the primula collections.

As we entered Chengdu we were struck by the unnatural quietness, but signs of the violence that had swept the streets three days earlier were all too evident. There were burnt-out buses and cars in the roads, now almost deserted apart from an occasional solitary bicycle. The People's Market where we had shopped before leaving had been completely gutted. Thirteen students, we were told, were still in hospital and 300 people had been arrested, most of them reputed to come from other towns and the countryside.

When we arrived at the Jin Jiang it was looking fairly battered, but had suffered less damage than the new hotel opposite where rioters had got up to the first floor and thrown the furniture out of the windows. Although some of the plate glass windows and doors of our hotel had been smashed, the staff and police had prevented the demonstrators from gaining entry, although they had looted and burned the shop in the grounds.

We crunched over broken glass in the foyer where a telex machine was still churning out world news. Communications were still operating and I went up to my room and astonishingly dialled clear as a bell through to Scotland where my wife Virginia and the other families had been anxiously watching the television reports for days. We learned that all American personnel had been advised to leave China, not through Beijing, the American Consulate had been closed and, although flights had been cancelled, our booking for two days' time would be leaving. It would be a scrum.

During the uneasy night that followed we could see and hear the truckloads of troops and police patrolling the streets

Lilium regale in the Min river gorge. The first flowers were just opening as we drove back to Chengdu on 7 June.

Growing with Lilium regale *on the very steep, dry, rocky banks was* Eremurus chinensis. *This species, the only one from so far east, does not appear to be in cultivation and Ernest Wilson does not even mention it in his books.*

Maddennia and Choniastrum and nutrition and poisonous substances in the flowers of *R. decorum*, *R. arboreum* and *R. simsii*, all of which are eaten as vegetables in China. *R. przewalskii* was being tested as a cough cure and other species were being investigated for medical or insecticidal properties. David was worried that there was lack of cooperation between Sichuan and Yunnan (Kunming) Botanical Institutes and that some of their work was of real value, but we were surprised and impressed by what they were endeavouring to achieve.

On the way to the airport the driver continued his infuriating habit of speeding and then free-wheeling, adding to the strain of an already tense situation. When we arrived, it was indeed a scrum, all elbows and shouting, and when I was asked at the customs if I had any specimens the professor bawled 'No!' before I had time to reply. There was a surge in the crowd and the three of us were propelled through the gate. We were out, we were on the first plane to leave since the troubles and we were very lucky. It even left on time.

We had witnessed the beginning and then the aftermath of one of the major events in recent Chinese history. Why did the Tiananmen Square uprising not succeed? The reasons are probably complex but many of our Chinese friends suggested that it had belonged to the intellectuals and the students and they had never engaged the vast masses out in the countryside, still the bedrock of China. And the farmers were no longer so discontented. After the tribulations and famine of the late Mao period, the market reforms of Deng Xiao Ping were starting to take effect, albeit under strict Communist order, and produce could be freely bought and sold. If it comes to a conflict between ideology and self interest, self interest usually wins.

with loudspeakers blaring. We were not allowed to leave the hotel but in the afternoon were taken to Chengdu University where once again the polite discussions over the traditional mugs of green tea about future cooperation had an air of unreality. We met five of the six members of Professor Fang's Rhododendron Group who were working on *The Flora of China* Rhododendron Section, with some involved in leaf waxes. There was also work being done on hybridization in

A burnt-out bus in Chengdu on 8 June, three days after the massacre in Tienanmen Square.

Opposite. The Min river near Songpan with logs being floated down. After the 1998 floods on the Yangtze, into which the Min runs, all felling of timber in Sichuan was prohibited, and in any case, most timber is now transported on trucks.

Chapter 8

WINTER COMES EARLY:
China 1990

Peter Cox

By 1990 China was really opening up, and over large areas it was possible to go where one wished, rather than where the Chinese decided. There were and still are sensitive places, often near international frontiers, and other areas which are not officially open to foreigners, although it may be possible to obtain a permit to enter. We gave the Chinese three different areas in order of preference: the Tsari valley in south Tibet, Muli in south-west Sichuan and, because of Roy Lancaster's enthusiasm about it when he was there in September 1981 and his frustrations at not being allowed to stop in certain exciting-looking places on route, the Gongga Shan / Kangding area of central west Sichuan.[1] Our expedition was planned for September–October and we heard only in July that Tsari was refused. Our second choice of Muli was officially not open and two months was too short a time to arrange permits, so we had to fall back on Gongga Shan / Kangding.

This expedition was organised through the Sichuan Mountaineering Association (SMA), a name that suggested

experience but meant very little. After our initial SBEC expedition (see p.62), it was very difficult to persuade the Chinese to organise camping. By now, with a little persuasion, some camping was possible, although the people who organised this and some subsequent expeditions, were very much beginners at anything to do with camping.

Kangding, formerly Tatsienlu, was well known to several of the plant hunters of the late 19th and early 20th centuries. Not only were many new plants found near the town, but it was used as a centre and as a stage for travellers. Wilson, Forrest and Rock all were familiar with this area, although not around Gongga Shan itself.

We were a party of six Americans and six British. Warren Berg and Garratt Richardson had been with us in Bhutan in 1988, both being great rhododendron enthusiasts, Warren

1. We had been told the previous year, when in Sichuan, that this area was now officially open to tourists.

having had one of the finest collections of species in North America. June Sinclair likewise has a great collection. Bill Stipe was then curator of the Meerkirk rhododendron garden. Jerry Broadus is a lawyer and his wife Clarice Clark has done much work for the Rhododendron Species Foundation. The British party was Ted and Romy Millais, rhododendron nursery people, Philip Bowden Smith, wholesale rhododendron nurseryman and his then girlfriend, now his wife Sarah Hanbury Tracy, and my wife Patricia and I. This was the first expedition that Peter and I were not on together.

We all met up in Chengdu on 18 September and had a

Above left: Viburnum betulifolium *between Kangding and Luding.*

Above: A Gongga Shan peak looking southeast from Laoylin.

Right: Romy Millais and June Sinclair.

The rampant climber Senecio scandens, *which flowers in autumn.*

Sarah and Philip Bowden Smith.

meeting with the people from the SMA, which seemed to go well and they were happy with being flexible over our camping and how long we were to spend in each place. The arranged time of leaving Chengdu of 8 a.m. was soon out of date and eventually we got away at 1.15 p.m! Our Chinese party consisted of Tan Jixin interpreter (reporter by trade), Gao Min guide and our three drivers. The vehicles were a minibus, 4WD vehicle and a truck to carry our baggage, food and so on.

We headed more or less due west from Chengdu, first across the endless plain with its stooked rice, then into low hills covered with cultivation including citrus trees and pine plantations. We were dodging all and sundry on the road, as usual missing everything by a hair's breadth. Finally we plunged down to the Chingye river, full of smoke from burning straw and then into the town of Ya'an for the night. Ya'an is quite a pleasant place with tree-lined streets.

Erlang Shan

Onwards once more, we started the climb towards Erlang Shan, which was one of the places that Roy Lancaster was not allowed to explore in 1981.[2] The wet east side of Erlang Shan was cut over forest, but over a deep ravine to the north were cliffs covered in enticing virgin forest that was totally beyond our reach. The first rhododendron was a *R. decorum* low down, then we saw *R. calophytum* and *R. argyrophyllum*. We were allowed a stop near the top where we found a puzzle and made a wrong identification. We thought we had found both *R. coeloneuron* with thick indumentum, which had not been introduced before, and *R. wiltonii* with thinner indumentum, but in the end we had to accept that all were variations within *R. wiltonii*. Other rhododendrons here were *R. concinnum*, *R. trichanthum*, *R. pachytrichum*, *R. orbiculare*, *R. lutescens* and *R. faberi*.

After an uncomfortable night at a truck drivers' flea pit

The approach to Erlang Shan. The trees are Cunninghamia lanceolata.

some way down the drier west side, we returned to the top of the pass at some 3,100m/10,200ft. Here we split into two parties to cover as much ground as possible but, owing to low cloud hiding any peaks there might be above us, we just had to trust to luck and head off into the unknown. Our party struggled through a damp dwarf bamboo and raspberry thicket on to a ridge. Here we found one small *Rhododendron watsonii* plus more *R. orbiculare* (C 5015)[3], *R. pachytrichum*, *R. faberi* and what we thought must be *R. sikangense*, a little different from what was grown in cultivation under *R. cookeanum* with narrower, somewhat recurved leaves and traces of loose indumentum. This *R. orbiculare* makes a fine rounded specimen with large leaves in cultivation and the flowers are a good rose. But best of all was to come, *R. dendrocharis* as an epiphyte on one of the few remaining firs on the ridge (C 5016). Clarice gave me a foot up to collect the one and only capsule. This produced sixty seedlings with good pink flowers and, being from 3,200m/10,500ft in Sichuan, these are perfectly hardy for us at Glendoick. The leaves are wider, have more shine and are less hairy than those from Emei Shan and Wolong. Other plants of interest here were pink- and white-fruited *Sorbus* (C 5018) (these have produced the same colour range at Glendoick), *Clintonia udensis* covered with black fruit, a red-fruited *Polygonatum* and a black-fruited *Lonicera*.

It was quite easy to push our way down to the road. Philip and I walked down to the next bend to look at what we thought might have been *R. strigillosum* but they were just more *R. pachytrichum*. Also plentiful here was *R. watsonii*. We walked down to our abode and found *R. davidsonianum* (C 5009) on the way. In cultivation this has rather pale flowers and a straggly habit. A small quantity of *R. racemosum* grew on a hillock by the guesthouse and also *R. decorum* (C 5003). These two species were actually a surprise here as we thought we were too far north for them, but they should be particularly hardy. Both indicate the comparatively dry conditions on this west side of Erlang Shan which was devoid of natural trees, although there were some forestry plantations and we found a nursery with nothing but spruce and poplars.

2. We were not much better off because this stretch of road was so narrow that there was a one-way system with several hours each way, so it was a question of having to carry on in case the traffic started coming the other way. On the way back we had a breakdown that delayed us two hours without being in trouble. There is now a tunnel through the top of the mountain.

3. C = Cox

195

The great Dadu river which ultimately runs into the Yangtze.

Hailuogou Glacier

We then travelled westwards down to the mighty Dadu river which, to our surprise, appeared to be substantially bigger than the Min and very swift. While descending, we were able to see the snow peaks of Gongga Shan, which we were heading for. We crossed the river, headed south, and then eventually branched off up a side valley to the village of Moxi (Moxixiang, pronounced Moshi). This village is in the most amazing position high up above the confluence of two streams, a little back up the V created by the rivers. The almost perpendicular banks are of soil, not rock, and appear to be eroding fast, which means that Moxi will eventually be washed away. The village is just one long street with every possible bit of ground around cultivated, mostly with maize and vegetables.

We walked down the northerly river where there was a small flood plain covered with shrubs such as *Cotoneaster, Elaeagnus, Clematis, Rosa, Berberis, Hypericum* and *Pyracantha* with bright red fruit, also a climbing blue *Aconitum*. The local girls are very attractive when young, especially when dressed in their Yi minority costume. We met one girl returning from school who gave us maize stem to chew, which was slightly sweet but very tough. We gave her some sweets, reluctantly received at first, and then she brought out her English teaching book and got in some practice.

We left the village at 9 a.m. ahead of our ponies, but they soon overtook us and arrived at 'camp one' one hour before us. All three 'camps' turned out to be guesthouses in what is now considered a tourist area. (There is now a large road up to 'camp three'). After leaving Moxi, a narrow path took us 91m/300ft down the cliff to rather an alarming bridge which bounced and swayed on crossing. At first everything was heavily cultivated or grazed and the only rhododendrons we saw were a few *R. decorum, R. davidsonianum* and the only *R. augustinii* of the expedition. There were a few other members of the warm temperate flora left such as *Populus, Schima, Cercidiphyllum, Elaeagnus* and *Sarcococca*.

As so often happens, find one and there are several species of rhododendron. After 'camp one' there was variable *Rhododendron floribundum* (C 5020), *R. argyrophyllum, R. polylepis, R. lutescens* and one plant of each of *R. longesquamatum* and *R. wasonii*. Where the forest had been long cleared near the path, the most fantastic impenetrable

A man waiting for customers in Moxi (Moxixiang)

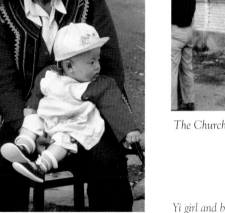

The Church in Moxi.

Cheerful old man in Moxi.

Yi girl and baby in Moxi.

The street in Moxi where we were able to hire horses to transport our kit.

The ubiquitous Chinese mini-tractor in Moxi.

197

Looking west from Erlang Shan towards Gongga Shan. Our road can be seen snaking its way towards the Dadu river.

Pyracantha angustifolia *in the gorge on the east side of* Moxi.

jungle of *Rubus* species and bamboo reared and plunged itself into a useless mass. So often, where the growing conditions are good, rampant weeds have taken over where forest has been destroyed. These smother any attempt of the natural forest to re-establish or any intended grazing for stock.

We did not stay at 'camp two' but carried on to 'camp three' for the night. 'Camp two' had a pool fed by a hot sulphur spring and beyond here the forest became magnificent with huge *Abies*, *Picea*, *Tsuga* and a few *Taxus*. *Rhododendron calophytum* (C 5021) became plentiful, often fine specimens, and *R. oreodoxa*. One *R. moupinense* presented itself by dangling over the path. Later we saw others, mainly terrestrial as small plants which appeared to be half way between *R. moupinense* and *R. dendrocharis*. There were also big *Betula platyphylla*, *B. utilis*, *Viburnum*, *Acer* and *Populus* species and numerous *Cardiocrinum giganteum* var. *yunnanense*.

Just beyond 'camp three' was a small dry stream bed area with an amazing collection of rhododendron seedlings about six to eight years old, including at least two species of *Lapponica*, a surprisingly large leaved *Pogonanthum*, *R. dendrocharis*, a

Opposite: *Pond and marsh between 'camp two' and 'camp three', with fine conifer forest beyond.*

Looking west up the Hailuagou glacier, one of the lowest in China, covered in debris.

Taliensia, a *R. wardii* (or possibly *R. souliei*) and *Gaultheria hookeri* and *Vaccinium glauco-album*. Very close by, heavily shaded in the forest, were *R. longesquamatum*, *R. watsonii*, *R. trichanthum* and very hairy *R. pachytrichum*. Thus ended a very good day with wonderful scenery, very healthy virgin forest and several 'new' plants, all in lovely sunny weather.

After passing the dry stream bed, we climbed up through fine forest with plentiful *R. watsonii* and *R. prattii*, both showing off their bold foliage well. Above was almost pure *Sorbus* (C 5028) forest, the small, spreading trees draped in moss, with an amazing mixture of red, pink and white berries (these have also come mixed in cultivation). Suddenly we came out on the most dramatic view over a broad valley with steep, bare sides. This was the valley of the receding Hailuagou Glacier which we looked straight down on. It was barely recognisable as a glacier as it was mostly covered with loose debris. Above was a lookout point with a hut, which we called the 'summer house', and above that was a cliff on which were numerous *R. longesquamatum* (C 5029), some as large as 4.5m/15ft high. This very distinctive species has dense shaggy brown hairs on the shoots, petioles and leaf midrib, plus quantities of persistent bud scales.

We waited for Tricia and Sarah for a while and, when they did not show up, we started off for the glacier with a guide. Part of the steep bank was covered with scrub, but the lower portion was newly

deposited moraine with pioneer plants such as buddlejas and some rhododendrons such as small *R. concinnum*. This part was very unstable with many cracks and anyone jumping on it could easily have ended up with a bump on to the glacier below. We slithered across the filthy surface of the glacier, carefully avoiding deep holes, often full of water, and crevasses which got worse as we neared the far side. We negotiated one nasty crevasse by cutting steps with my ice axe but then we were confronted with a more dreadful one. Most of us took fright and turned back to the 'summer house', while the youngest and fittest four brave members carried on over the rest of the glacier, up the steep bank beyond, and reached the top of a ridge. There they found *R. orbiculare*, *R. flavidum*, *R. nitidulum*, *R. prattii*, a large leaved *R. phaeochrysum* and the greatly sought after *R. rufescens*. This made a total of twenty-four *Rhododendron* taxa for Gongga Shan. Another interesting find was what appeared to be a *Gaultheria* species in flower with strongly scented flowers. Alas, they had no time to do any collecting.

In the meantime, the rest of us slowly returned to camp as we had plenty of time. There were great views up the glacier towards the several peaks making up Gongga Shan, including, we were assured, Minya Konka itself, which Joseph Rock once claimed to

Opposite. Hailuagou glacier wall smoothed off and left bare by retreating glacier.

be the highest peak in the world; in fact it is only around 7,590m/25,000ft. June and I hauled ourselves up the cliff above the 'summer house' to get at the *Rhododendron longesquamatum*.

I thought that Patricia had been painting with Sarah but a sad story was related. In a great hurry to disappear behind a bush, Tricia had left her camera on the path and when she came back minutes later, it had gone. The odd thing was that nobody else was seen on the path before or after. All the staff were told but it never turned up. Later, the minibus driver had all his clothes stolen out of his vehicle and I lost a woolly. There is no doubt that dishonesty has increased enormously in China since the iron grip of Mao ceased to exist. Tricia and Sarah did get some way out on to the glacier after the camera mishap.

I had been developing a cold and by nightfall my voice was reduced to a squeak. This also affected my stammer, often resulting in not even a squeak coming out! Romy was suffering from a fall and Sarah a kick from a pony, Ted now had the cold, Warren had a bad night – so we were a sorry lot.

That evening a party of Estonians arrived to study the glacier for six months. This is one of the most accessible and the lowest in China at 3,400m/11,000ft at its snout. The morning broke beautifully clear, perhaps a bad omen for what was to come, but we all rushed out to photograph the golden snow peak which lasted for just minutes. Warren took a particularly good shot. It soon clouded over and as we started off walking all the way back to Moxi, the rain began and became heavier and

Conifer forest picks a safe place among the glaciers and peaks of Gongga Shan.

heavier, resulting in us all being absolutely soaked by the time we arrived. Luckily our bags had arrived before us and the contents were quite dry. We had passed numerous awkward loads of equipment belonging to the Estonians as well as tourists, including a party of Japanese all on horseback.

We were staying in a room where the floor was strewn with coal grit and dust (which we learned was used to make into briquettes), so we wore our boots to reach our wooden bunks. It rained solidly all night and by morning our courtyard was flooded and the street awash. We had to wade past the pigsty to the loo, which was even more revolting than usual. We did not leave until 11 o'clock so as to ascertain that the road had not been washed away. As we were walking down to our

vehicles, we passed a wooden hut and a member of our party could not resist having a look inside – to find that a young Chinese woman was having a cold shower.

As with other parts of Sichuan such as Wolong, rhododendrons occurred only in scattered populations and sometimes as small groups and/or even single plants. We saw many favourable-looking rocks and slopes with no rhododendrons. Many flattish damp areas had mostly *Betula* species and also no rhododendrons. Ted had a pocket pH metre, perhaps not very accurate but near enough to indicate that the pH varied from 7 (neutral) in the subsoil down to 5.8. We were told that the rainfall is only 80cm/31½in, which sounded remarkably low, considering the fine forest trees.

The same peak goes on fire for a few moments at daybreak.

Kangding

We stopped at Luding (famous for its Iron Bridge associated with the Long March) on the Dadu river for lunch. After Luding, the road leaves the Dadu for its tributary the Kangding, which is extremely swift and much use has been made of this in the form of several small hydro-electric schemes. The banks above the river were rich in xerophytic shrubs, such as *Ceratostigma*, *Pyracantha* and *Coronilla*. The hotel in Kangding was an improvement on Moxi, with running warm water and some rooms had heaters, but not ours. Kangding had the usual mixture of ancient and modern buildings.

Our plan was to climb the slope to the east which rose directly behind the town. We could see a few buildings up the hillside. The first we came to was a pavilion, then an amphitheatre with a small monastery nearby inhabited by just one monk who took Jerry, Clarice and me around. The temple was recently redecorated and was adorned with fresh fruit and peacock feathers.

We decided to aim at the ridge near to some fresh snow. The first rhododendron was the inevitable *R. decorum*, followed by *R. davidsonianum*, *R. ambiguum/R. concinnum*, and our first finding of *R. bureavioides*, which I had seen in flower in 1989 but not close at hand. Warren said that it was very similar to a plant he collected near Mt Sigunian near Wolong in 1983. Further up there was a mixture of Lapponica, out of which no two plants looked alike. We picked samples to look at thoroughly in the evening with the aid of Philip's little

The temple in Kangding, a centre for 20th-century plant collectors.

A communal washing place in Kangding.

Meat in the market in Kangding, invariably covered in flies.

A local character in Kangding.

204

Looking down on Kangding (Tatsienlu), the virgin forest all destroyed.

A stupa above Kangding.

microscope. We reckoned that we identified *R. nivale* subsp. *boreale*, *R. thymifolium*, *R. nitidulum* and *R. intricatum*. This area is very rich in Lapponica rhododendrons and we were to have the same problems with identification a few days later. Best of all was our next find, a good population of *R. wasonii* var. *wenchuanense* (C 5046), equalling McLaren AD 106 which may well have been collected in exactly the same place. This was found at 3,500m/11,500ft, mostly on a north-facing slope or ridge and it carried on up the mountain for at least another 100m/300ft. It was obvious that there had been a severe frost when it was flowering and beginning to grow last spring as nearly all the flowers had been frosted and some of the growth was either distorted or all the young leaves had fallen off, leaving bare flower buds. This form has thick rufous, sometimes split, indumentum on the old leaves. Sadly, it was time for us to descend as the clouds were about to envelop us; we could have spent another hour or two going higher.

On the way down we found further species: some scruffy little *R. souliei* and *R. oreodoxa*, a really good *R. przewalskii* with a wide petiole and yellow midrib, some *R. prattii* and hybrids of it and *R. phaeochrysum* var. *agglutinatum*.[4] Arriving back at 5 o'clock, we were told dinner was at 5.30, which was annoying as we were wet and wanted a shower.

We had an excellent dinner in the huge dining room which that night was shared with a Tibetan wedding. We joined in toasting the bride and groom, took their photographs and finally sang 'Auld Lang Syme', which seemed to be a success. A very wet night produced more snow on the tops, ominous as we were about to set off for several days camping. Moon cakes for breakfast were not good, leaving a nasty aftertaste. The

The interior of a tiny temple on the hillside above Kangding.

Foliage of Rhododendron wasonii *var.* wenchuanense *(C 5046) above Kangding.*

4. There were many other plants of interest; *Pinus armandii*, *P. tabuliformis*, *Picea*, *Larix*, *Juniperus chinensis*, *J. squamata*, some deep blue gentians, probably *G. veitchiorum*, a poor pale *Cyananthus*, *Adenophora*, *Campanula*, *Gentianella* and a small *Viburnum* species.

Tibetan children at Laoylin, to the south west of Kangding.

Tibetans at Laoylin near Kangding

secretary of the SMA led the way in his jeep, taking us in a south-westerly direction past a factory called Laoylin and up a very bad road which our minibus negotiated successfully. We had a long muddy walk ending up in slush and snow and, after a rumble of thunder, down came more snow.

We walked up the valley through a long-since cut-over forest with a scattering of small *Picea likiangensis* var. *balfouriana* up the hillsides. There was an odd assortment of rhododendrons, including many hybrids and, to our surprise, it was mainly these hybrids that had capsules. The large proportion of hybrids was no doubt due to the demise of the forest some time ago. Most hybrids were within Taliensia with a mixture of *R. phaeochrysum*, *R. prattii* and *R. bureavioides*, those between the last two having very fine foliage, otherwise very indifferent foliage. *R. souliei* (C 5056) became quite plentiful, with some fine specimens, especially on steep banks which would give them good drainage. Also present was *R. oreodoxa* var. *fargesii* (C 5063) and this seemed to cross with *R. souliei*, which was unexpected as there is such a difference in

their flowering time in cultivation. Again, there were mixed Lapponica, including a very fine plant of *R. intricatum*. We thought we had found *R. flavidum*, but the scales were not quite right and when a seedling flowered, it was not yellow.

There were many plants of interest other than rhododendrons: a Candelabra *Primula*, an *Iris*, an *Allium* and *Lilium duchartrei* – Farrer's Marble Martagon – which we find rapidly makes a stoloniferous mass of stems and bulbs. Trees and shrubs included a flat-topped *Sorbus* (C 5054) with large white fruit and a lilac, *Syringa tomentilla* (C 5053), which has flowered at Glendoick with pale pink flowers. This was disappointing as we had hoped that it would be the same as we saw in 1989 with clear pink flowers. A tree of *Sorbus* (C 5054) at Glendoick has very fine large white fruit.

We camped at Jialzeca on 30 September and by the morning there was 15cm/6in of snow. Warren was the first up, digging channels around all our tents to keep the snow from flooding us late risers. More snow followed at breakfast, but it soon cleared and warmed up a little, except during spells of mist. The country looked beautiful with snow everywhere in the V-shaped valley. We did not walk much further up the track as the rhododendrons petered out. These were all *R. phaeochrysum* var. *agglutinianum* making rounded bushes of 2-3m/6-10ft, with concave leaves covered below with cinnamon-plastered indumentum. This contrasted with *R. phaeochrysum* var. *levistratum* lower down forming a more erect looser plant with paler, looser indumentum. Later we tried to reach the good *R. prattii* x *R. bureavioides* hybrids back down the track, but the snow came on again so we returned to camp. Ominously, we sensed snow falling on our tent all night and we periodically shook it off from the inside, creating some drips. By dawn we could see 40cm/16in of snow surrounding us, having spent over twelve freezing hours inside our tent. We ate a large late breakfast including 'porridge' and dismantled our tents to find that the snow under ours had melted and right in the middle was a large cow-pat. While we hung around waiting for the horses to be rounded up, the sun came out for a little, which at least partially dried our tents.

We hurried down, at first through deep snow, then horrible slushy mud. It was very noticeable that all the best rhododendrons were growing on the tops of large rocks in very little soil. We camped at the lunch place of the way up, eating only noodles with egg and the usual Chinese fish out of a tin. Rain soon started to fall, yes, rain and not snow at 3,200m/10,500ft. Dawn broke fine after more rain and it proved to be a lovely day. We decided to split into four parties. Bill went on his own up a scour track to Lapponica moorland in deep snow. Ted, Romy and Philip went off up one valley, got stuck in scrub and failed to reach the rhododendrons. Warren, June and Garratt took the ridge path, while the rest of us tried the nearby valley

Patricia Cox shoveling snow from around our tent at Jialzeca. The unexpected snowfall in late September forced us to change our plans and give up on crossing the pass to the west.

path westwards. We found some Lapponica and Triflora which soon petered out and further on there were other rhododendrons on rocky bluffs, but just the same as we had been seeing before. Tricia twisted her leg so she and Clarice sat down while Jerry and I struggled on through deeper and deeper snow and mud churned up by yaks and found nothing more of interest. Once again we had failed to find *R. rufescens* and so had the others.

Next morning there was over 5cm/2in of snow, but at least it was dry overhead with great views of the mountains including one of the big snow peaks that must have been out of sight above us at Jialzeca. The vehicles were a most welcome sight when we reached the road head and the hotel in Kangding felt like real luxury.

Our return to Kangding meant that we had to change our plans. We had intended to carry on up the valley beyond Jialzeca, go over a pass and then down on to the west side of Gongga Shan where we would have been picked up. The snow had spoilt all this.

Big rocks in rivers are inaccessible to animals and a favourite site for plants, provided they do not get washed away.

Zheduo pass

Our first effort again plant-wise was a day's excursion up the road to the Zheduo pass on the main road to Tibet. We passed where the road to Jialzeca and Laoylin branched off, went through an interesting-looking gorge and then up a gradual climb on a good well-graded road. Our first stop was at 3,800m/12,500ft where the snow was not deep enough to cover everything. Above the road was the usual mixture of the common Taliensia, but Warren found a group with an amazingly metallic sheen to the upper leaf surface which seemed to be *Rhododendron przewalskii*. Below the road near the stream was a boggy area with *Primula sikkimensis* and a host of different Lapponica rhododendrons on mounds in the bog. The most interesting was an erect plant with greyish-green leaves which had to be the rare *R. websterianum*, which is known only from around Kangding.

We drove up to the top of the pass in fine weather and got our faces burnt from the combination of sun and snow. There was too much snow for anything to be visible, so we turned

Gentiana veitchiorum at Laoylin. Due to the early snow, we missed seeing many gentians in flower.

The annual white Gentiana tongolenensis *at the foot of the Zheduo pass.*

The coarse Gentiana crassicaulis *below the Zheduo pass.*

around and dropped a little way down to 4,000m/13,000ft where, to our delight, we were able to see capsules of *Meconopsis integrifolia* (C 5119) sticking out of the snow and, even better, capsules of the rare *M. henrici* (C 5131) which has proved to be difficult in Scotland but relatively easy to grow in Tromsø in northern Norway above the Arctic Circle.

Our second stop was amongst scattered oak scrub at 3,500m/11,500ft. There were several *Rhododendron souliei* (C 5130) here and we were very much bearing in mind that the Chinese had described *R. longicalyx* from this very place, although the altitude of the type specimen was from 500m/1,500ft lower. Admittedly, the plants were perhaps not as typical *R. souliei* as we had seen at Jialzeca but really this is hair-splitting at its silliest. The calyx, supposedly very large in *R. longicalyx*, was very variable in size. On a return visit in 1992, I was able to examine more plants at a lower altitude with the same variation in calyx size so *R. longicalyx* is a synonym.

The third stop was just above some cultivation and now below the snow line at 3,200m/10,500ft. Here was an extraordinary mixture of plants. There were orange and red *Euphorbia*, dark and pale annual gentians, the remains of *Stellera*, *Sedum*, Lapponica rhododendrons plus one Pogonanthum rhododendron, leggy with long leaves and no rufous leaf underside, in other words just boring old *R. primuliflorum* and not *R. rufescens* yet again. The weather here was superb and we lazed around taking photographs of plants and scenery.

The last stop was in the gorge and it coincided with steering trouble. Growing on cliffs and rocks were numerous *Rhododendron bureavioides* with nice foliage and a very short petiole but not the indumentum to equal the best *R. bureavii* in cultivation. These plants had been horribly frosted with many aborted leafless shoots, almost no capsules and no apparent bud set for the next year. Admittedly many were heavily shaded by small trees and scrub. We crawled back to Kangding with no further trouble, having had a good day but it was very sad that, owing to the snow, we had not been able to see more than the odd gentian, which should by now have been at their glorious best.

Gisehai lake north of Kangding, with Sorbus *in autumn colour. There was a hot spring at one end and apparently no fish.*

To the lakes

Due to heavy snowfall, all thoughts of the west side of Gongga Shan had to be banished, so we asked for an alternative destination that was not likely to be snowbound. Apart from being told we were going north near some lakes, we knew nothing about where we were going. Soon after leaving Kangding, we turned left up a rough road through a valley, past some villages and cultivation that included crops on terraces up the hillside. The scenery gradually became wilder and less spoilt and, after a checkpoint, we entered a virgin area with fine forest showing good autumn colour from maples, mountain ash, berberis, etc. This was totally contrary to what I had expected, which was the edge of the Tibetan grasslands.

When we reached the end of the road, there was a very adequate campsite and what looked like a wooden store or shop. At first we were told that we had to camp half a mile up a path which soon became a mile, then that we could camp here but would have to walk the half a mile to a mile for meals. Finally our staff and a Tibetan with a fine tenor voice (a large powerful man), agreed to carry our bags without tents as there was accommodation. On the way were many fine old specimens of *Rhododendron oreodoxa*. The guesthouse rooms were quite nice in a well-finished building, obviously recently made for tourists. This overlooked Gisehai on which we could see paddle-boats waiting to be hired. The lake had sulphur springs at one end so there were no fish, but that did not discourage Philip from having a try with his rod and line.

Watching our porters cook their evening meal was a lesson in economy: one large saucepan for boiling vegetables, with two layers of bamboo sieves on top in which rice was steamed. After an early meal, we decided to hire two boats for Clarice, Ted, Warren, Philip and me to paddle across the lake to the

Usnea *near Gisehai lake.*

Rhododendron phaeochrysum *var.* levistratum *trunks, Mujizo lake. This variety grows much taller than the nearby var.* agglutinatum.

steep wooded bank on the opposite side. Ted and Philip took the first turn and we made a tricky landing near a stream inlet. By now it was raining steadily and getting dark so, while Philip attempted to fish (with no result), the rest of us divided into two parties, scrambling up the hillside to find huge *Rhododendron watsonii* (C 5075) to 6m/20ft or more high and masses of seedlings growing in non-sphagnum moss but with nothing much else. Warren began to get worried about darkness descending and started shouting and whistling for Ted and Clarice. Once gathered together again, Clarice and I attempted to paddle back, but my side had lost its pin so we went round in circles. Out of the gloom, we saw the Chinese people from the guesthouse rapidly approaching, who were aroused and worried by Warren's calls. The pin was replaced and off we went for home and it proved to be surprisingly hard work. We had had quite a little adventure for little reward.

By morning, we had more snow, this time only 5 to 8cm/2 to 3in. It started bright but soon clouded over again, obscuring any views and making photography difficult. It was dull and damp but very beautiful as we walked up a path by a rushing, plunging stream to the second lake, Mujizo, climbing about 300m/1,000ft. Ted and I found two magnificent specimens of *Rhododendron bureavioides* (C 5076 A&B), both with thick rufous indumentum. Mujizo was much bigger than Gisehai, being over 5km/3 miles long, and we could just make out what looked like a glacier at the far end. Everything looked entirely unspoilt by man and very picturesque. At the beginning of the lake was a boulder scree of small stones covered with *R. phaeochrysum* var. *agglutinatum* forming compact mounds. Right beside these but clear of the scree was a forest consisting of *R. phaeochrysum* var. *levistratum* making much taller bushes and the very handsome *Larix potaninii*

Foliage of a good form of Rhododendron bureavioides *near Mujizo lake.*

The Iron Bridge over the Dadu river in Luding, well known for its connections with the Red Army and the Long March.

over head. The south-facing slope was covered with Lapponica rhododendrons including *R. nivale* subsp. *boreale* and *R. intricatum*. Along the lakeside was a clearing in the forest where we found a pure population of the grey-green-leaved *R. websterianum* (C 5080), very erect to 90cm/3ft high with no other Lapponica present. It had a long style and a large calyx and capsule. This has produced pale mauve flowers in cultivation.

On the way back, Ted and I attempted to reach some south-facing cliffs but failed due to huge boulders. Binoculars only revealed junipers anyway. So we climbed on to a large rock instead and Ted had a fall which could have been quite serious. Later we found a *Notholirion*, three primulas, a lily with only one capsule per stem and a few gentians which we thought might be G. *farreri*. Near Gisehai were two nice *Sorbus* (C 5086 A&B), one with deep rose-pink fruit, the other pale pink. Seedlings have varied from white to deep pink. Not everyone had a good night's sleep because there were rats or mice running and gnawing upstairs, where Sarah had them travelling twice across her face. She seemed remarkably unperturbed by the experience.

A short stop on the way back to Kangding near a gorge indicated large-leaved rhododendrons on the opposite bank (as usual!) facing north. Binoculars showed exceptionally large leaves for what was almost certainly *R. galactinum* in a completely new location. They might just have been accessible

from the far bank but there were great bamboo thickets and it was very steep in places. On the way back to Luding we stopped at 2,500m/8,200ft at rather a good place with what we thought might be *R. denudatum* but it was only *R. floribundum* (C 5090), plus *R. decorum, R. trichanthum* (C 5089), *R. davidsonianum* and *R. lutescens*, plus one or two other Triflora. A great variety of shrubs included an *Actinidia* with yellow fruit and a fine red-fruited *Viburnum* species.

The hotel in Luding was probably built by the Russians, as were most of the polluting factories scattered around the country. It looked as though it was about to fall down with great cracks appearing on the balconies. The bathrooms were actually open but the contents were not to be recommended and drips came from the bathroom above. Tricia and I went for a walk over the Iron Bridge and its see-through walkway was not as terrifying as we expected. A hunt up the far bank produced the hoped-for *Lilium sargentiae* but we saw only immature plants, some with the characteristic bulbils in the leaf axils. We learned later that the bulbs are harvested and eaten.

That night was disturbed by a combination of barking and whimpering dogs, cocks crowing, the plumbing reverberating, people shouting and vehicles being revved up. To our surprise we actually got a warm bath. The plan for the next day was to do the Erlang Shan road more thoroughly and then stay the night at the foot of the road.

211

A mud slide on the west side of the Erlang Shan road held up the traffic for hours.

Traffic waiting for the mud slide to be cleared. This is a typical hazard in southwestern China.

The coalmine road

After a delay due to blasting, we soon reached a major hold-up below our hostel where we stayed on the way. Ted, Philip and I walked on up the road to see what the trouble was and found a still-oozing mud slide blocking the road and a great queue of vehicles waiting, with little hope of any progress for many hours. So we decided to turn around and try somewhere else, only to find the road blocked by stupidly parked buses and trucks. Eventually their drivers were persuaded to move these and we got through and tried the next road out of the valley to the south, which was said to be to coal mines. We were warned that there would be no forest and this was certainly the case. After winding up to 2,900m/9,500ft, we stopped to investigate relatively interesting country with a knoll with obvious rhododendrons on it.

We had followed *R. decorum* on the way up over a great altitudinal range and it was still occurring where we stopped. A cattle track led to the ridge and we passed the Triflora *R. polylepis*, *R. lutescens* (C 5100) and *R. trichanthum* on the way up. On the ridge were numerous *R. racemosum* (C 5099) and *R. concinnum*, *R. davidsonianum*, *R. pachytrichum* and small plants of *R. watsonii*. Both this *R. racemosum* and the one from Erlang Shan are a uniform deep pink in cultivation. There were calls for something to identify and there right out in the open was a fairly healthy plant of *R. galactinum* (C 5101), well to the south of any previous recordings, and several smaller ones were found too. Later *R. sikangense* and *R. floribundum* were also found, so the total in all for this desperately degraded site was eleven species. Also found here were *Ligularia*, *Lilium duchartrei*, a fine form of *Primula sinopurpurea* (now *P. chionantha* subsp. *sinopurpurea*), a very large berried *Cotoneaster*, *Incarvillea arguta* and *Veratrum*.

A stop on the way down revealed that we could see the traffic moving again on the Erlang Shan road, so back we went up to the truck drivers' flea pit for the night. We were fed a rotten meal of cabbage cooked in several different ways and this had followed a poor dry biscuit lunch. During the night

someone shone a torch into our faces through the window and was shouting and banging on the door. I grabbed my ice axe and shouted back and he eventually moved off.

The view in the morning was a pure Chinese painting with cotton-woolly patches of mist all over the valley below. Unfortunately the top of the pass was shrouded in cloud, so we had the same trouble as before in not being able to locate the peaks. The Americans headed off in one direction while the rest of us struggled again through seemingly endless thickets of soaking wet raspberries and bamboo. The going was so tough that we took it in turns to lead and push a path for the rest to follow. There were many rhododendrons, at first *R. sikangense* and *R. pachytrichum*, followed by *R. faberi* and *R. prattii*, often mixed together but distinct enough to easily tell apart. Towards the top there were small-leaved *R. oreodoxa* and then on rocky outcrops, *R. nitidulum* (C 5107), growing to 90cm/3ft or more in shelter, but making very fine compact specimens when exposed. All the plants of this species in the various locations where we found it seem to agree with the description of var. *omeiense* rather than var. *nitidulum* so the varieties should be scrapped. For freedom of flowering, we have found the Emei Shan plant superior in cultivation to what we collected on this expedition. Also up near to the top were a few plants of *R. intricatum*, not apparently recorded here before.

We headed downhill to find the road and this proved to be much easier, with clearings to walk through. *Rhododendron racemosum* was plentiful, plus the usual Triflora found in this area. What was new was a hybrid which must have been *R. racemosum* x *R. davidsonianum*. In all we found about ten remarkably uniform plants which seemed to flower freely enough, but there was no sign of them ever developing any capsules. That night was back again to the 'hell hole', with another dreadful meal and no *piju*. Once more we were disturbed, this time twice, by somebody shining a light through our window and shouting at us. Maybe he

Jerry Broadus examining a specimen of Rhododendron galactinum *surviving long after the forest had been cleared.*

was only looking for someone. Unusual in China, the staff here were very unfriendly, surly and unhelpful, giving strict instructions to have everything ready before breakfast, which I highly disapproved of; it was a bad place.

More than ever, thick mist and drizzle hung over Erlang Shan. We stopped at a place where there were more *Rhododendron wiltonii* (C 5110) with the thick indumentum. June and I scrambled up a bank with some success. Our staff would not allow us to stop further down, so once again we had missed much of the rich eastern flank. But vehicle breakdowns are another thing, and we came to a halt with apparent fuel starvation in the minibus. Sadly 1,500m/5,000ft was too low for the best plants and all we could find during a long delay were some *R. argyrophyllum*, a little primula on the sheer bank above the road and a large-leaved daphne.

Soon the minibus played up again, this time with the clutch gone. A mechanic was found who confirmed what Bill had been trying to tell them. Eventually a tow-truck turned up which proceeded to pull us up hill, then unhitched us to free wheel down any gradient. Again Bill came to our salvation as we were making desperately slow progress, and they were persuaded to tow us the whole way to Ya'an where even rather dilapidated mod-cons were a joy to us. We were offered catfish and snake, the latter all bones. We took

ages to get into Chengdu, with all the traffic having to cross one bridge, but our luggage took much longer as trucks had to queue separately and then obtain a permit to enter the centre of the city. Later we were told ours had had a breakdown too.

Our farewell banquet was in a private room in the hotel and very good it was. It was attended by the president and vice-president (female) of the SMA, who gave a long speech translated by Tan which included, 'Sorry we had difficulties with our harvest.' We eyed each other with expressionless faces! Professors Fang Mingyuan and Zhao (friend of Ted and Romy) arrived afterwards and we all discussed future expeditions, none of which came to anything. They told us that the early snow we had experienced was most unusual as it does not normally come until after 13 October.

Overall, it was a good expedition, seeing new areas and many plants, and although the snow had to make us change our schedule, it was all in the Chinese experience. We had seen two largely virgin areas, Hailuogou and the lakes, and we found the difference in plant populations and distributions of exceptional interest. It was disappointing to see so little re-afforestation after the promising efforts we had seen further north the previous year.

Chapter 9

Peaks and Plains in Spring:

China 1992

Peter Cox

In the vertical landscape of north-west Yunnan, a large plain at 3,200m/10,500ft is remarkable, to say the least, and the Zhongdian (Chungtien) plateau was to be our first destination in 1992. The small town of Zhongdian lies at the northern end of the plateau about 200km/125 miles north of our 1981 haunts around Dali. It was to be our first base in May 1992, moving north to the big-shouldered massif of Bei-ma Shan on the Mekong-Yangtze divide and then on into Sichuan to Da Xue Shan (Big Snow Mountain).

The plateau had been visited in 1990 by the Chungtien-Lijiang-Dali (CLD) group, who had collected much of interest, but the mountains further north had not been visited by westerners since before the Communist Revolution. So although the whole area had been explored fairly extensively by Forrest, Kingdon Ward and Rock and while few new species were likely to be found, there was a serious job to be done in reintroducing plants lost to cultivation or better forms.

It was a very Scottish group of five that arrived from the UK, and I brought my son Kenneth for his first trip out East. For me, it was to be the first of two trips to China in 1992, the first and last time I had done a double in a year, and I later admitted it was a bit too much! But it was a good team, with David Chamberlain from the RBGE adding some scientific distinction to the efforts of us two Peters (as he had in 1981, 1989, 1994, 1997 and 2000) and the group was completed by Ian Sinclair who was then second in command at the Younger Benmore satellite of the RBGE. On the Chinese side, we once again teamed up with the Botanical Institute of Kunming and we were delighted to have our old friend Guan Kaiyun (Clyde), the interpreter in 1981, as our leader.

Kunming gave us the sensation of a great nation in a great hurry. Some things were the same: the tide of bicycles flowing chaotically, the smell of brown coal burning and the use of sharp elbows in a crowd. But much was changing: there were many new

Above. Primula sonchifolia *above Napa Hai.*

Opposite. Limestone crags near Big Snow Mountain.

Terraced paddy fields in west Yunnan.

hotels, some very grand, and commercial activity was everywhere from department stores to the street traders forbidden under the Maoist regime. The stores were bathed in a greyish fluorescent light and, although the showcases were full, the goods had a dusty, second-hand look about them. That too would change.

We visited the garden of the Botanical Institute and saw *Rhododendron excellens* in flower. It had about four flowers per truss, in between *R. lindleyi* and *R. nuttallii* in size and shape of flower with a cream corolla fading to white with a yellow throat. The scent was less than that of *R. lindleyi*. We also saw a pale-pink-flowered *Magnolia delavayi* and were told that it can vary from white to as deep as purple. It was nice to meet up with some of our old friends of 1981, including Mr Ming Tianlu and professors Sun and Wu, and we celebrated with a nostalgic dinner.

The road west had improved with a dual carriageway for the first short stretch and plans to complete this to Dali (Xiaguan). We were told that the railway was being constructed all the way to Lhasa in Tibet, with the first part to Dali being completed in two years and to Lhasa in five. In 1997 we heard that plans had changed, with preference being given to the road construction (maybe following Margaret Thatcher!).

On the way we passed *R. arboreum* subsp. *delavayi*, *R. siderophyllum*, *R. racemosum* and *R. decorum* all in flower but they were just flashes past the window as Guan was determined not to stop. Xiaguan was surprisingly cool and damp on our arrival. As we drove up the Er Hai lake the next day, we passed familiar landmarks from 1981 and stopped at the north end to photograph curious huts on stilts over the water. Each farmer has a section of the lake for shrimping and fish and at night they sit in their huts to guard against fish poachers.

On the rise between Dali and the Lijiang valley, we passed some fine catalpas in bloom, and soon the tall bonnets of the Naxi women started appearing in the villages. We dropped down to the fabled Yangtze river, which neither of us had seen before, a grey swathe sliding between the mountains, still with some 8,000km/5,000 miles to go before reaching the sea. After crossing it we met a party of New Zealanders, many of whom Kenneth had met while lecturing in 1990 and I was to meet in 2000 in New Zealand. They had just been up to the Zhongdian plateau 'to have a look'. Before reaching the plateau, we passed through a gorge with many interesting plants, including the rare *Abies chensiensis* subsp. *salouenensis*. Clumps of the yellow *Primula forresti*[1] hung on rock ledges, and the sides of the gorge were spattered with quantities of pink- and white-flowered *Rhododendron yunnanense*. We were to find this species abundant in many places on this expedition with much the same colour range.

---

1. *P. forrestii* is a strange species in section Bullatae which has a woody base and grows naturally on dry rocky banks and under overhangs. It has been re-introduced several times recently but is not easy to keep going in gardens.

Co-dominating much of the plateau with Rhododendron hippophaeoides *is* R. racemosum, *which prefers the drier banks and flats.*

Zhongdian plateau

We came over the lip on to the Zhongdian plateau at about 3,200m/10,500ft, with mile after mile of dwarf rhododendrons interspersed with some grazing and a few cultivated patches – an extraordinary sight. There were only two species on the flat, *R. racemosum* and *R. hippophaeoides*, the former on the drier parts, the latter where it was wetter, especially along hollows and stream sides, and where they grew together, the combination of the pink and lavender-blue was most attractive. Low hills intersected the plateau, either bare or covered with pines and other conifers. Around the perimeter were higher mountains, many of which still had snow on them. We were told that there had been a late snowfall in March, the heaviest for thirty-two years, which made the crops late.

The next morning in Zhongdian town most of us woke with headaches, no doubt due to the altitude but it had been a bad night with the toilet block 36m/40 yards away from our 'hotel'. Spirits rose as we drove a short way to some low hills fringing the plain along with a stream of children heading for a school picnic. One hill was almost bare, others like Wu Fung Shan had a mixture of larch (*Larix potaninii*) and rhododendrons, mostly *R. rubiginosum* and *R. vernicosum* with *R. yunnanense* scattered

Rhododendron hippophaeoides *at 3,100m/10,300ft. This species prefers the damper areas, such as hollows and marshy stream sides.*

217

Young cones of Larix potaninii *on Wu Fung Shan, Zhongdian plateau.*

Iris ruthenica *var.* nana *at Wu Fung Shan on the Zhongdian plateau.*

Rhododendron rubiginosum *and Usnea drapes, Wu Fung Shan, Zhongdian Plateau. This 'Spanish Moss' is not actually a moss at all but a bromeliad (see photo [352] on page 209).*

A population of Primula chionantha/sinopurpurea *in mixed colours near Bi Ta Hai. Purple forms are much more common than the white in the wild.*

through it. They were not particularly good forms but draped with beards of *Usnea* moss, and with the fresh green of the larch foliage it made a delightful picture. There were good compact specimens of the gorgeous *Daphne aurantiaca* covered in its yellow flowers and a few *D. retusa* with no hybrids between them. The former species varies from being tight, almost prostrate (*D. calcicola*) to lax and leggy at lower altitudes. First introduced by George Forrest and re-introduced, it has proved to be slow and tricky to grow in cultivation and sometimes tender. We also found two species of *Iris* on Wu Fung Shan, one medium-sized

with generally purple flowers with small standards, the other the very dwarf *I. ruthenica* var. *nana*, hardly distinguishable from the matted grass until the pale or dark purple flowers emerged.

On 22 May we were taken to the reserve called Bi Ta Hai, a lovely unspoiled valley with a series of grassy meadows grazed by *dzo*, the cross between yak and cattle. We had to imagine the sheets of primulas and other herbaceous plants described by the CLD expedition as we were too early, but we did find robust clumps of *Primula chionantha* with creamy heads of scented flowers and the violet equivalent (*P. sinopurpurea*), surely just a colour form, which made up a quarter of the total. The only other primulas were *P. polyneura* making dabs of magenta in the thickets and a few plants of a muscarioides (*P. deflexa?*) with cone-shaped heads of deepest purple, almost black at the apex, contrasting with a little bright blue *Corydalis*.

The slopes enclosing the valley were clothed in virgin forest, a rarity even in this part of China. There was a complete

A Scottish Nationalist dzo near Bi Ta Hai.

Ian Sinclair lending his binoculars to a local man who wondered which end to look through.

Primula fasciculata *at Little Zhongdian. This very dwarf species loves to grow in oozing bogs.*

Podophyllum hexandrum *near Zhongdian. This woodlander, with large mottled leaves and large fleshy red fruit, is easy to cultivate.*

One plant stood out amongst the sea of Rhododendron racemosum, *SSNY 47, and seedlings have been remarkably even and similar to the high standard of their parent.*

Iris barbatula *on the south edge of the Zhongdian plateau.*

contrast between the south-facing, drier slopes which had pines, both *P. armandii* and *P. tabuliformis*, and an evergreen oak *Quercus semecarpifolia* that here made some decent trees in place of its usual scrubby self. On the other north-facing side the slopes were covered in spruce and larch (*Picea likiangensis* and *Larix potaninii*). The hand of man had been light on the valley and there had been little felling, but Peter counted the rings on a medium-sized tree which gave 125 years, so many of the larger trees must have been well into their second century.

After about 10km/6 miles the valley ended in a pine-covered ridge where, for the first time, we found *Rhododendron oreotrephes*, and crossing the saddle we dropped to the reed-fringed lake, an idyllic scene like much of this peaceful valley.

The next day we pottered around the fringes of the plain, enjoying the drifts of dwarf rhododendron backed by fine views of the Yulong Shan to the south and Haba Shan to the east. Near the village known as Little Zhongdian, Peter was delighted to find *Primula fasciculata* fringing the bog with

flowers bright as pink buttons against the black peat, with a yellow eye to set it off. We had last seen it on the Hongyuan, a delicate thing of only 3-4cm/1-1½in, and there was much squelching of knees in the bog as we knelt to photograph it.

We hunted among the *R. hippophaeoides* and *R. racemosum* for good forms, selecting SSNY 14 of the former and from a splendid form of the latter SSNY 47, which has produced excellent progeny in cultivation with rich pink flowers. Under a roadside tree we lunched on cartwheels of nan bread accompanied by tinned fish of great power and doubtful identity, and then explored a side glen among sunlit stems of birches, slender and white when young and crusted on the ancient ones with coppery bark peeling off in great sheaves. We lay in the sunshine at the top among emerging podophyllums looking even stranger than usual at eye level with a purplish green mop of unfurled leaves topped by a cup-shaped flower of startling pink. We also managed to find a new berberis for David, *B. lijiangensis*, armed to the teeth with

Stellera chamaejasme *var.* chrysantha *is a common herb on the Zhongdian plateau, often growing with euphorbias and* Daphne aurantiaca. *Related to daphnes, this fine plant is not commonly cultivated, partly due to the difficulties of procuring seed and of propagating it vegetatively.*

The magnificent fragrant Daphne aurantiaca, *a great feature of the Zhongdian area in spring, is at last beginning to become established in cultivation. It varies considerably in stature from tall and somewhat straggly to compact and low in* D. aurantiaca *var.* calcicola.

fearsome spines, and *Iris barbatula* nestled in the turf.

Our next excursion was up north to the pass beyond Napa Hai or Reserve, passing an amazing hillside covered with a combination of *Stellera chamaejasme* var. *chrysantha* and *Daphne aurantiaca* and nothing else. Napa Hai itself is a partially flooded plain at the north end of the plateau, which is the winter quarters for a flock of the rare black-necked crane. It is partially grazed and covers quite a substantial area. The road climbed past some splendid virgin forest but then into a large area where the forest had been clear felled some years earlier. We walked along a track and soon came to a cut over hillside with lots of rhododendrons including the usual *R. yunnanense*, *R. rubiginosum* and *R. vernicosum* (very variable but some very good, rich pink to pure white forms), plus *R. wardii* and later *R. selense*.[2] Among these were obvious hybrids between *R. vernicosum* and *R. wardii* with intermediate leaves and cream-coloured flowers which is sometimes known as *R.* x *chlorops* in cultivation.

2. The removal of the natural forest invariably encourages rhododendrons to hybridise. Several different species occur here, such as *R. wardii* and *R. selense*, and hybrids between them are now as common as the original species.

Rhododendron vernicosum *near Napa Hai in cut over forest.*

Rhododendron beesianum *to the north of Napa Hai.*

Rhododendron vernicosum x R. wardii *near Napa Hai.*

Fritillaria crassicaulis, *a close relative of* F. cirrhosa, *near Bi Ta Hai.*

As rain started falling, we followed a logging drag path and soon identified *R. uvarifolium* (SSNY 63), *R. beesianum*[3] and *R. heliolepis* (SSNY 66), and a probable hybrid between the first two species. The first had rather small trusses of medium-light pink or paler, often well blotched. There was a devastated look about the forest. The upper parts had been fir, the lower spruce and all had been cut off by axe 2 to 3m/6 to 10ft up, not by chainsaw, thus losing 10-15% of the timber. Even the bamboo was all dead, having flowered. Various plants other than rhododendrons were managing to survive the now completely open situation. These included *Primula sonchifolia*, which was suffering but still managing to reproduce, some *Notholirion* and, around a limestone rock pinnacle, numerous *Bergenia* and *Rodgersia*. There is little doubt the rhododendron hybrids that we saw would have been there before the forest had been cleared but the percentage of hybrids is now likely to increase and seedlings grown from seed collected here would vouch for that.

We were woken the next day at 6.30 with the usual blare of martial music from the loudspeaker system in the main street and the day continued as a bit of a disaster. Due to a rotten hired vehicle which had replaced our ailing minibus, our attempt to

reach higher altitude of some 3,800m/12,500ft to the north-east had to be aborted. After a brief excursion over old ground, Ian Sinclair, Kenneth and I, myself in high gloom, returned to base but David and Peter searched around the lovely river Shuo Dan Gang which flowed past the entrance to Bi Ta Hai, but would not have been out of place on Speyside. It was quite productive: an iris with plenty of seed turned out to be *I. chrysographes* and masses of our muscarioides primula poked their cones through the grass. They would have matched my purple trousers which I had had made by a tailor in Zhongdian, prompting Kenneth's remark that his father was unlikely to get lost now. Our first meconopsis showed white when we cut open the fat buds and we were surprised to find two fritillaries, the taller one of around 30cm/1ft with yellow flowers was probably *F. crassicaulis* and a smaller greenish-flowered one *F. cirrhosa*.

Peter was submerged with a cold the next day so stayed in the guesthouse, but the rest of us had a fairly productive time a little way beyond yesterday's area. We spotted a population of the indigo-blue flowered *Rhododendron russatum* (SSNY 83), unfortunately mixed with *R. hippophaeoides* resulting in hybrids with a mixture of transparent and brown scales on the leaf

Rhododendron rex subsp. fictolacteum *at Tian Bau Shan in a badly logged off area.*

Young cones of Picea likiangensis *at Tian Bau Shan.*

undersides. The former species normally has brown, the latter lighter transparent scales. We drove over a pass called He Shi Shan and some way down the other side, reaching a partially cultivated area called Tian Bau Shan where we found the finest *R. decorum* any of us had seen, more commonly white (SSNY 94) but also some good pink (SSNY 95). *R. vernicosum* was also there but some hybrids between it and *R. decorum* were decidedly inferior (SSNY 111). There were masses of *R. rubiginosum* at various altitudes and a fine bank of *R. yunnanense* among some rocks. Nearby was *R. wardii* (SSNY 99) with red to orange buds, one *R. uvarifolium* and further on some very good *R. oreotrephes* (this species is rarely poor) and *R. rex* subsp. *fictolacteum* (SSNY 90) with large leaves in a cut over area.[4] Climbing over a *Picea likiangensis* was a pretty *Clematis montana*, the sweetly scented flowers having a reddish flush on the backs of the sepals.

At the top of the pass at around 3,600m/11,700ft, we stayed for a two-hour walk. To begin with there was a mixture of *R. rubiginosum*, *R. oreotrephes* and *R. vernicosum* with *R. hippophaeoides* on the damper flats. Gradually *R. oreotrephes* and *R. phaeochrysum* took over as we climbed, and finally, there was only larch forest with *R. phaeochrysum* by the mile, as tall as 6m/20ft. The *R. phaeochrysum* (SSNY 108) was in full flower, mostly whites with the occasional flush of pink and a large flare. The rhododendrons were a promiscuous lot but it was odd that no meconopsis were seen and the only primula was *P. chionantha*.[5]

Rhododendron phaeochrysum *var.* phaeochrysum *occurred in vast quantities on the upper reaches of Tian Bau Shan. In 1992 this upper area had not been deforested.*

3. *Rhododendron beesianum* is very common in the wild, often the only species over wide areas, and the flower colour can vary from white to deep pink. On Napa Hai it had been drawn up to 7.6m/25ft when the forest existed and was now sick or dying. The flowers, of a good deep pink with a blotch, faded with age

4. Seeing plants just hanging on in a degraded habitat persuaded someone that this subspecies is in danger of extinction in the wild, and hence its inclusion in the IUCN Red Data Book of endangered plants and animals.

5. Natural hybrids seen were *R. russatum* x *R. hippophaeoides*, *R. decorum* x *R. vernicosum*, *R. phaeochrysum* x *R. vernicosum*, *R. wardii* x *R. vernicosum* and *R. rubiginosum* x *R. yunnanense*.

A good form of Rhododendron balfourianum *(SSNY 224) near Napa Hai. An isolated specimen, seed collected did not give any hybrids.*

The Yangtze looking south from Benzilan.

Tiny pockets of soil under cultivation north of Benzilan towards Bei-ma Shan.

Rosa sericea is a very common but nonetheless beautiful rose found in the Himalaya and western China.

Androsace bulleyana at the low elevation of 2,670m/8,700ft between Napa Hai and Benzilan.

Bei-ma Shan

On 27 May we set off for our five days on Bei-ma Shan. The country became very dry after Napa Hai when we dropped once more to the Yangtze, which was brownish and swifter than at our first encounter. On the way we saw various semixerophytic genera such as *Lonicera, Rosa, Deutzia, Indigofera, Berberis, Viburnum, Spiraea* and *Cupressus*. We arrived in Benzilan quite early and walked around this picturesque and unspoilt village. As might have been expected, the guesthouse was about as primitive as it could have been, and the loo so bad that we made use of the surrounding countryside. In the evening we played snooker with locals, being beaten in all three games.[6] That night in the Yangtze valley was hot and dream-filled and Peter woke to find the largest spider he has ever seen walking purposefully towards his bed; it must have been 5cm/2in across.

On leaving Benzilan we climbed immediately for the north, passing through dry almost bare south-facing slopes which probably never had much vegetation. North slopes had more with stunted bushes of the conifer *Platycladus orientalis*. Odd pockets of cultivation could be seen, often perched on distant mountainsides.[7] It is hard to describe the sense of bulk that these big dry hills give, leaning over the river valleys. Far above you can see paths, tiny scratches on the grey landscape, with occasional flecks of green from a settlement. Those who live there must be amazingly fit.

There are three summits on the road that leads over Bei-ma Shan to Deqin (pronounced 'dayjen', the Atuntze of Forrest's

6. Ian marched round the table, cheroot clenched between his teeth, and he and I suffered the indignity of losing on the black to eight- and ten-year-olds who could only just see over the top of the table! 'It's time this lot were in their beds,' said Ian grimly.

7. It is astonishing what tiny pockets of soil are cultivated even way up nearly precipitous mountain sides. It is very doubtful if the younger generation will continue to work these little plots, being more attracted to the easy city life or farm land workable by animals or machinery, leading to depopulation in remote areas.

Benzilan is a most attractive village with Tibetan-type houses with much carving, pot plants and hens.

The high peaks of the Bei-ma Shan range on the Mekong-Yangtze divide. The east side is comparatively dry, being in the rain shadow of not only Bei-ma Shan itself, but also the higher Mei Li range on the Salween-Mekong divide to the west.

and Kingdon Ward's travels), all at about the same elevation of over 4,000m/13,000ft. Even on 28 May, winter had barely left this altitude so there was little in flower, so we were at least two weeks too early. We were to spend two days on Bei-ma Shan, returning to Benzilan in between, which was a mistake as Deqin was nearer to the mountain and a better temperature. The central peak of Bei-ma Shan of 5,500m/18,000ft is surrounded by what might be considered as a plateau around the 4,000m/13,000ft level. While much of this plateau is covered with rhododendrons, several parts, especially on the east side of the road, are very barren with nothing but scree.

As might be expected, the country around 4,000m/13,000ft on Bei-ma Shan is above the tree-line and inhabited by many dwarf rhododendrons, including different species of subsection Lapponica. There have been disagreements as to what these species are, with some people claiming they are mostly *R. nivale* subsp. *boreale*, but we think they are wrong. The dominant species is undoubtedly *R. tapetiforme*, which forms tight mats with comparatively large leaves. This is accompanied by *R. telmateium* with considerably smaller leaves and the yellow flowered *R. rupicola* subsp. *chryseum*, while some may be *R. nivale* subsp. *boreale*. Other dwarfs are *R. saluenense* subsp. *chameunum* with shiny leaves and here rather pale flowers and *R. primuliflorum*, prostrate where exposed to 1.8m/6ft in shelter.

Among the dwarf rhododendrons were prostrate mats of *Diapensia purpurea*, here with pink flowers. There were some groups of primulas of the 'sinopurpurea' alliance at high altitudes that showed great variation in flower colour, dark eye or white and other features. But another much rarer Nivalid (Crystallophlomis) primula was *P. minor* which, although it occasionally took to the open ground, appeared most at home among screes of rock and cliff. It was a much more delicate thing, 5-7cm/2-2½in high, with pale violet flowers and a pronounced white eye borne on an elongated tube. On a lawn of closely grazed turf one of our prettiest primulas was appearing, *P. amethystina* var. *brevifolia* with its delicate stems and deep purple flowers nodding in the wind. It looked too fragile for these harsh uplands.

We gradually dropped back down the south side again, through plentiful *Rhododendron beesianum*, then down into a valley where *R. selense* was mixed with *R. wardii*, some in flower. Kenneth found a hybrid between these two species which David was delighted with as it undoubtedly equates with *R. erythrocalyx* and confirmed his theory of hybrid origin. It should now be written as *R.* x *erythrocalyx*.

Patches of larger species inhabited slightly more sheltered areas above the tree-line; these were all *R. aganniphum* higher up, while lower this was mixed with *R. phaeochrysum*. The

'Clint Eastwood' on the Bei-ma Shan pass.

Solmslaubachia *species on the high screes of Bei-ma Shan at 4,220m/13,600ft.*

Thermopsis *species on the Bei-ma Shan pass at 4,150m/13,400ft.*

Primula minor *on Bei-ma Shan. This is one of the smallest members of section Crystallophlomis (Nivalis) found on rocky slopes.*

Kagurpu, the highest mountain in the Mei Li range, 6,740m/21,800ft and unclimbed by 1992.

former was always low here with pale semi-plastered indumentum, the latter with darker indumentum, mostly fitting into var. *levistratum* and some with more rufous indumentum fitting into var. *phaeochrysum*. Amongst these were two other Taliensia. The first had indumentum inclined to split, which, although it seemed to fit into *R. aganniphum* var. *flavorufum* with a darker more split indumentum than var. *aganniphum*, it occurred only as scattered individuals amongst the others and definitely seemed to be a hybrid between *R. aganniphum* and *R. phaeochrysum*. The other plant with narrower leaves and pale indumentum, of which we found only three small plants, fitted best into *R. alutaceum* var. *alutaceum*. Field work since 1992 indicates that all *R. alutaceum* are natural hybrids involving *R. roxieanum* and that our find here would be *R. roxieanum* x *R. aganniphum*. Since our visit, several parties have explored a gully not far to the south of where we were that has *R. roxieanum* and *R. aganniphum*, plus *R. proteoides* with hybrids between them.

After our second day on Bei-ma Shan, we drove on and then down to the town of Deqin. On the way we had a breathtaking view to the west of the mountain range of Mei Li under blue skies with the glistening snow peak of Kagurpu surrounded by knife-edged ridges. Mei Li is made up of several peaks, with at least three over 6,000m/19,500ft, and Kagurpu, 'The Prince of Mountains' at 6,740m/21,800ft, has a lapful of snow spilling into a glacier which drops towards the Mekong. To our knowledge, Kagurpu has not been climbed yet and we heard that in 1991 eleven Japanese and six Chinese had lost their lives attempting it. We were lucky that the whole range was almost clear of cloud and we all agreed this was the finest view and most magnificent mountain that we had ever seen, even beating off the competition from east Nepal. Away below we could just make out the Mekong. There is little doubt that the whole of the Bei-ma Shan massif lies in the rain shadow of the significantly higher Mei Li range, and the resulting dryness means that Bei-ma Shan does not have plants associated with abundant moisture, such as large-leaved and Maddenia rhododendrons.

The town of Deqin (Atuntze) is situated in the foot of a valley at 3,300m/10,700ft, tucked around a shoulder, so there is no view of Mei Li and the Mekong. Like most outlying towns, Deqin is a mixture of old and new buildings, but by now most if not all the old ones will have gone. Much rebuilding had taken place between this visit in spring 1992 and my third visit in spring 1994. Most of the buildings are along the main street which is quite steep. Our 'hotel' was quite quiet but as usual lacked the basic facilities, and the rooms had a glass side to the passage without a curtain so we had no privacy. We ate in a restaurant up the street, one of the few in town on this visit, which produced on the whole quite edible food. All there was to sit on were tiny stools not far above ground level. By putting one on top of another, one could get up to a reasonable height.

On the first morning in Deqin we explored a valley close by which proved to be very rich in shrubs, some of which we could not identify but the list of those we managed between us included species of *Ephedra*, *Berchemia*, *Ribes*, *Berberis*, *Zanthoxylum*, *Prunus* and *Buddleja*. Few had any flowers or fruit

Schisandra grandiflora x rubriflora, a vigorous climber common in western China, in a little side valley above the Mekong at 3,040m/10,100ft. There are species with flowers of other colours.

The town of Deqin, lying in a sheltered hollow at 3,300m/10,700ft, serves a huge area as a shopping and marketing centre.

A typical form of Deutzia calycosa, *a common shrub on the Cangshan. It is easily grown and free-flowering in cultivation.*

which is quite often the case in the wilds of China, especially in virgin territory, perhaps because there is less pressure to reproduce.

Later we drove half way down to the Mekong and, after a grandstand view of the Mei Li, discovered a side valley which we christened the 'Mekong Glen. It was a delightful leafy contrast to the hot, dry countryside outside and contained great variety of trees and shrubs, with almost every one different from the next. Near the entrance was the lilac with heavily scented flowers that we had seen earlier, and a *Schisandra* in full flower got the cameras clicking. As we climbed, the frond-like foliage of *Abies chensiensis* var. *salouenensis* appeared, but the highlight was undoubtedly the maples, several species making trees of 18-24m/60-80ft, which they are rarely allowed to do in China. We collected an elm, later identified as *Ulmus bergmanniana* var. *lasiocarpa*, which has made a small spreading tree in cultivation, but one died at Glendoick in 2006, perhaps from Elm Disease. The understorey was equally assorted with several roses, two *Ribes* species one just like a gooseberry, a *Helwingia* species which bears its fruit in the middle of its leaf, *Deutzia*, *Philadelphus*, *Viburnum*, *Prunus*, *Cornus* – the list was endless and kept Peter, Ian and Guan fossicking away while the rest of us waited below with some impatience.

We drove on down to the Mekong, really just to see it. On the west side, where level areas permitted, there was cultivated land and a footbridge to cross to it from Mabandi village at 2,200m/7,700ft. We thought that we had been told that if we crossed over we would have been in Tibet, but later we were told that Tibet is some way on, which was disappointing. The Mekong was reddish brown with mud from the slopes further up and not as big as the Yangtze. Here, it was in an impressive gorge, which became exceedingly narrow just a little way below the bridge. It was very hot at the river at the time of our visit but when I came back later down river in 1992 and in 1994, there was a pleasant temperature with a wind blowing.

We looked up to the slopes of Mei Li to see much good forest with a surprising amount of snow still lying under the trees just below the tree-line, so we doubted if there would be much in flower now at that level. Also, we could not make out any colour from a mass of flowers but perhaps we were too far away to see any. On the way down the slope from Bei-ma Shan, a short stop revealed a hairy *Rhododendron selense* which was subsp. *dasycladum* and further down a probable hybrid that David thought might equal *R. calvescens*, which could be *R. selense* x *R. uvarifolium*, since the latter occurred near by.

After lunch, as Clyde urged us not to be late, David and Peter carried on to Zhongdian, but Ian, Kenneth and I stopped

again at Napa Hai pass and walked straight up the timber drag slope near the road. Suddenly I found, totally unexpectedly, a plant of *R. roxieanum* var. *oreonastes*, followed by a few more, all in flower though slightly frosted. I shouted to Kenneth and then immediately found *R. balfourianum* (SSNY 224) with nice pink flowers and then a *R. phaeochrysum*, all within a 46m/150ft radius. We soon found several hybrids of the *R. roxieanum*, probably crossed with *R. phaeochrysum*, *R. vernicosum* and *R. selense*. Back at Zhongdian, Peter and David were a bit peeved that the rest of us had had such a successful little exploration on our own without telling them where we were off to.

The Mekong, full of mud as usual. It is said to become less muddy during the winter when at its lowest.

Rhododendron roxieanum *var.* oreonastes *near Napa Hai, a favourite with its narrow leaves and compact trusses. We found this readily crossing with several other species.*

Truck fuel system making full use of the powers of gravity.

Da Xue Shan

We were now heading to the north-east to Da Xue Shan, Big Snow Mountain, and Little Snow Mountain. The 'snow' part we found a bit of a misnomer as these mountains are not very high and the snow had already largely disappeared. We started by going as far as Bi Ta Hai again, then straight on instead of right. We passed through some nice country, mostly well wooded, showing what pines can do if left alone and not repeatedly hacked. *Rhododendron hippophaeoides* was common in the wetter parts along the stream and suddenly Kenneth and I spotted something white amongst all the lavender blue and it turned out to be a pure-white-flowered plant of this species. I thought this was our best find so far (SSNY 229). We collected what capsules we could find, but there was very little seed so the chances of growing a white-flowered seedling seemed remote, especially as we managed to grow only two to flowering size. To our utter amazement, when the two seedlings flowered, both were white; perhaps some geneticist could tell us what the chances were of this happening. To us, this is potentially a better plant than other white Lapponica in cultivation though hard to propagate. We have heard that other plant hunters passing along this road spotted this white *R. hippophaeoides* and Bjorn Alden of Gothenburg Botanic Garden told me that they had raised between 5 and 10% of white seedlings. There were two fine white-flowered rosaceous trees flowering in this valley, the thorn *Crataegus chungtienensis* which grew to 9m/30ft and a very floriferous *Malus* species which made a slightly smaller tree.

A little further on David and I had stopped ahead of the rest of us at what David at first thought was more *Rhododendron primuliflorum* but which turned out to be *R. trichostomum* (SSNY 230), and we saw more on the way up Little Snow Mountain. This was growing in partial shade on a dry steep north-facing bank. The flowers were not yet full out but we could see that they varied from pure white to a good pink. We stopped here again on our way back and observed that this species was being pollinated by butterflies.

The forest on the south side of Little Snow Mountain had all been burnt off in a fire in 1984, leaving virtually nothing but some bamboo. We were told that the forest had been deliberately set on fire by Tibetans (who get blamed for anything that goes wrong in this part of China) to increase their grazing. The forest on the north side was better, with some *R. beesianum*. The view looking north was a spectacular array of limestone buttes (like in Arizona) and cliffs, which unfortunately were not easy to photograph due to the pine forest getting in the way. Some felling had been going on here and we saw a few timber trucks making their way south. We travelled some way up the valley before we started to climb again towards Big Snow Mountain through good forest and the usual rhododendrons. I climbed the slope north of the road and found in crevices the largest flowered *Diapensia* I had ever seen, with pink flowers, while Kenneth on the peak to the south found superb *Primula dryadifolia* with deep rose flowers sheltered by rocks and some *Rhododendron rupicola* var. *chryseum* (SSNY 270). After all eventually meeting up, we discovered a bank covered with magnificent *Omphalogramma vinciflorum* with deep violet flowers.

We passed by clouds of white crab apple flowering near the village of Geza and at the highest point before Zhongdian saw nasty rust fungus on both *R. decorum* and *R. vernicosum*, interestingly with no apparent spruce trees in the vicinity, which are supposed to be the alternative host to rhododendrons for this fungus.[8] Further on we found a mixture of *Paeonia delavayi* and *P. Lutea* Group with a variation all the way from deep red to yellow.

8. Diseases are often observed in the wild, including galls, powdery mildew, leaf spots (frequently) and, in this case, rust fungus on *Rhododendron vernicosum*. Certain diseases may be found on species that do not at present occur on those species in cultivation, so it is of the utmost importance not to introduce new species / strains of diseases on wild-collected seedlings.

The lady of the shop at Geza.

Only a thicket of bamboo replaces the forest where it has been destroyed by fire on Little Snow Mountain.

A mass of Rhododendron phaeochrysum *in flower on Big Snow Mountain.*

Malus species near Geza.

Rust fungus on
Rhododendron
vernicosum.

Primula dryadifolia *on
Big Snow Mountain.
This is one of the finest
high altitude species and
a favourite of George
Forrest.*

Omphalogramma
vinciflorum *on Big
Snow Mountain.*

Primula amethystina *var.* brevifolia *at Tian Chi, a small lake west of Little Zhongdian.*

A most unusual-coloured Primula sinopurpurea *below Tian Chi.*

Tian Chi

We pressed Guan to let us go to the peak to the west of Zhongdian but he stressed the impossibility of getting there and back in a day, so we planned to go to a lake to the south-west. Much of the area before we reached the lake had been replanted and there was a maze of forest roads which were going to have implications later on in the day. We walked up through a partly forested gully and then to a small meadow full of *Rhododendron complexum* (SSNY 296), a rare and tiny Lapponica, followed by a terrible area of dead forest. We questioned the Chinese on what had caused this and they said what we concluded were two different insects, the Asian Gypsy Moth, *Cosmotriche saxosimilis*, which ate the foliage and a weevil under the bark, *Lajonquiere*. The timber was all left standing as they did not want to cut and transport it for fear of spreading the pests. Even rhododendrons had evidently been devoured, as they were dead too.

By the time we reached the very attractive lake, Tian Chi (Small Heavenly Lake) we had escaped from the nightmare forest. There was a great mixture of Lapponica rhododendrons, some of which may have been hybrids. Some parts were pure *R. complexum*, others with larger leaves were probably *R. rupicola* but not yet in flower but other larger-leaved ones had

pale flowers coming out, so were not *R. rupicola*, and seemingly not *R. hippophaeoides*. If they had all been in flower, we might have been able to sort them out, but the snow had only just melted over some of them, which were still showing their brown winter foliage that would soon turn green again. On the driest exposed areas was *R. telmateium*. Amongst the dwarf rhododendrons were *Cassiope pectinatum* with its white flowers just opening (apparently not yet introduced into cultivation) and a small primula with nodding violet flowers dancing in the wind, *P. amethystina* var. *brevifolia*. This little gem has recently been re-introduced and in theory should be easy to keep because it divides up well.

Near the lake was a section of still healthy fir forest and below the trees was a mass of *Rhododendron beesianum* (SSNY 303), some still bent double or flattened under a mass of snow, others actually broken. To our delight though, they were all coming into flower as soon as they were free of the snow.[9] Out in the open and even right to the water's edge a few centimetres or an inch above water level grew *R. phaeochrysum*, and keeping very healthy too. If we tried to grow it in a similar position in cultivation, it would die instantly. Growing right under the rhododendrons was a striking primula with huge mauve-purple flowers, later identified

This is thought to be Primula boreio-calliantha *which was growing under the shade of rhododendrons near Tian Chi. Typically, this species has larger flowers, perhaps the biggest in the genus. It has never become established in cultivation.*

A fine form of Primula deflexa *below Tian Chi, in this case one of the best and most robust of section Muscarioides. Rarely cultivated.*

as *P. boreo-calliantha* which, alas, is one of these species that proves so intractable in cultivation (there is now some doubt if this is that species). Other primulas below Tian Chi included the richly coloured *P. sinopurpurea* and *P. deflexa*.

It was while we were among the *Rhododendron beesianum* that Kenneth, who was ahead, shouted to say he was going to the top of the hill, having agreed to meet back at the start of the dwarf rhododendrons at 3 o'clock. When he did not show up at the rendezvous, we went back to the vehicles, and still no Kenneth. After a while we found a local man who was asked if he had seen a white man with long hair and he said yes but could not remember when. So we split up and went searching in different directions; by

now we were getting worried. Our driver had a hunch that Kenneth had got a lift back to Zhongdian and, sure enough, reports indicated that this may have happened about 1½ hours ago. So we had to go back to tell the others and we were all absolutely furious. It transpired that he had got completely bamboozled by the roads in every direction and could not find the way back to our meeting place and perhaps wisely, he thought the best thing to do was to get a lift back. He was so full of apologies that we forgave him.

9. These varied in merit, some very fine with full trusses, others flat-topped, but it was the variation in flower colour that was so striking, from pure white to pink flushed deeper pink with a deeper blotch. It is such a pity that this species is not more amenable in cultivation.

The opening charge.

Zhongdian races

Guan decided that it would be good for all of us to have a day free of plants, so off we went to the Zhongdian races. This proved to be a tremendous gathering of everyone from many miles around. Before the races proper, there were many parades of local minorities including Tibetans and monks. Everyone was dressed up in their finest traditional costumes, many with musical instruments such as tambourines and drums, while others had demon heads or were inside dragons. We were given a VIP position and had many photographs taken of us. Taking shots of the procession proved very difficult for us as cameramen with TV cameras, videos, telephotos and ordinary cameras kept getting in our way, and we also suffered from a loudspeaker blaring away. We thought that we might be given a grand lunch, but all we were offered were dry biscuits and water melon, except Peter who was given the treat of jelly from pigs' trotters! The races were highly amusing with practically no rules. Many riders rode bareback, though some had stirrups. There were about eight races, two to five horses per race. To our left by the entrance was the sharpest corner and several of the horses ran out there, sometimes straight into the crowd and it did not seem to matter if short cuts were taken through the middle. Once a jockey was knocked off to be replaced by another who proceeded to win the race. Another competition was for riders to lift scarves off the ground; one rider fell off but the winner managed to pick up three scarves. The entertainment stopped at just about the right time.

In the evening we had a meeting with local council officials

Buddhist monks with their long Tibetan horns and 'Jimmy' holding the ends up.

The scarf-picking-up competition in which great skill was needed to lift the scarf without falling off.

An elderly lady in her finery.

Last-minute adjustments.

There were strange birds . . .

. . . and ogres bringing up the rear.

Lions chased tumblers…

. . . and even stranger animals

The parade.

Tired but happy people wending their way home from the races.

of the Zhongdian Prefecture. The assistant governor was very bright and clued up, but otherwise only the director of forestry had anything to say. We discussed such subjects as the sustainability and size of the forest reserves in this area, agriculture and also the possibilities for tourism. They told us two bits of potential good news – one that they are changing their policy from clear to selective felling and two that providing electricity with the new hydro-electric schemes is taking the pressure off cutting scrub for cooking purposes. Most of the second half of the meeting was conducted by candlelight, despite repeated efforts to mend the fuses. We came to the conclusion that the likely tourist season here would be very short, perhaps from mid-April to mid-June and then mid-September to mid-October. The latter might be too late in some seasons up on Bei-ma Shan due to early snow. Another meeting was arranged for 4 p.m. the following day at the forestry offices and nursery.

The Yangtzi river near Lijiang leading to the famous Tiger Leaping Gorge. The mountains are the very steep north flank of Yulong Shan which has been much less explored than the more accessible south side.

We get lost

Although this meant we could not have a full day, we decided to make a last visit to the ridge beyond Napa Hai on what was our final day in the north. I wanted to make the most of it. Peter said that I had a look of grim determination as I strode along the forestry road that sloped up among the shattered trees. Peter finally caught up with the rest of the party by taking a short-cut up a log slide and emerged into the sort of moorland we had come to know: dwarf Lapponica rhododendrons fringed with conifers and a skirting of *R. aganniphum* and *R. phaeochrysum*. There did not seem to be much new and we were due to be back at 2.30, so Peter made a circuit of the area, which did produce a good stand of solid *R. beesianum* from which he selected a good pink with a rounded truss (SSNY 323), also a new iris, and then set off back by the same route.

We were determined to go back along the ridge with the theory that we could then drop down directly to our vehicles. It was taking a chance and there was an argument between Ian (who had a compass) and I as to whether they should be heading south-east or north! In the end we struggled through some fairly dense hillside with bamboo brakes and then found ourselves in fine forest of the kind that had been destroyed on the other side of the mountain There was some good ground flora with *Bergenia*, *Actaea* and other herbs but we were getting desperately late and had little to show for our efforts, apart from a good form of *Rhododendron rupicola* var. *chryseum* found earlier and a fine plant of *R. balfourianum* (SSNY 322) in full flower.

On the other side Peter was taking the original route but, after slithering down various log drags, there was still 5km/3 miles to walk and he arrived half an hour late at the vehicles. After another half hour's wait and still no sign of the others, Guan and Peter decided to take one of the vehicles as we had an appointment to meet the Forestry boss for further discussions, a nursery visit and as it turned out, a dinner all of which had to be cancelled. Peter offered to do the apologies but Guan decided that one stray botanist was worse than none and did it himself.

A hillside of Rhododendron selense *subsp.* jucundum *on the eastern flank of the Cangshan above Dali. It is equally free-flowering in cultivation.*

However, our black mark must have been at least partly forgiven as we were invited to the annual Forestry Department Party that evening. It was a right old knees-up/ceilidh but with a team of Tibetan horsemen to act as compères, resplendent in pink shirts, high boots and fox-fur hats like mini-bearskins. There was a long dirge about Tibetan tea and its health-giving properties and, sure enough, we were given little bowls of the stuff, thickened with slightly rancid butter. The only other 'refreshment' was tiny glasses of colourless hooch which would have done nicely as a stain-remover and, as proceedings hotted up and the day's exertions caught up with us, thoughts turned to a long cool glass of beer.

It was the sort of party where one had to do one's piece and with Kenneth performing expertly on the drums, Peter and I hurled each other around in a doubtful version of the latter part of a foursome reel, uttering wild Scottish cries. This was all too barbaric for the gentle Tibetans whose dances are quite sedate with the men playing single string instruments and graceful movements. Fortunately, Ian rescued the Scottish reputation by taking a tall Tibetan lady as his partner for the Gay Gordons. This was an instant success and soon the whole room was full of Tibetans doing some amazing swooping and gyrations.

As we went home the streets were full of people dancing and partying and it was the early hours of the morning before we finished talking the night away with David Burlinson of Exodus Travel, a meeting which resulted in Kenneth leading several trips to Weixi and Tibet. But that beer tasted really good.

On our way back we stopped to photograph *Stellera chamaejasme* var. *chrysantha*, *Euphorbia* and *Morina* species, a fine large-flowered white *Salvia* and *Incarvillea zhongdianensis*, and a colony of the fine rich-yellow-flowered *Primula forrestii* on a cliff. We drove to the Yangtze and then down river a little to see the famous Tiger Leaping Gorge. This involved a walk of 3km/2 miles with fine views of the north side of Yulong Shan with its hardly explored limestone peaks and crags partially hidden in the cloud. These to us were actually more impressive than the gorge itself which we found a little disappointing, having seen parts of the Mekong and the Min rivers just as remarkable. In no way could a tiger cross there and were there ever any tigers in this area anyway? There was a prison at the entrance to the gorge which supplied labour for preparing the marble being excavated out of the road they were making in the gorge.

We stayed in an attractive but basic abode which had a courtyard nicely laid out with potted plants. The loo had a population of long-tailed maggots. This sort of place with reasonable mod cons would definitely appeal to western tourists. We were given a lesson on how to play mah-jong on a set that Ian had bought; we found it rather complicated and the drivers proved to be the most expert.

Cangshan

We stopped at the famous pagodas at Dali which we had last seen in 1981. There was a great change in the surrounds with new steps and rounded thujas encircling the pagodas. The south pagoda still had a tree growing half way up it and there was still no access up the big pagoda for the many tourists that come here. Dozens of marble sellers lined the way in, but there was not much change in the designs since our previous visit.

As for Dali itself, much of it was spoilt. Perhaps three-quarters of the old wooden buildings had gone, replaced with horrible modern monstrosities. There were not so many marble stalls in the main street but many more selling cheap knick-knacks. The most attractive locally made Bai minority clothes, table cloths, etc. were still ridiculously cheap and Kenneth must have bought up most of their stock!

Our last two days in the field on 9-10 June was spent up the road above Dali to Cangshan where so many people have been since our first visit in 1981. *Pinus armandii* and *P. yunnanensis* now covered a large part. We were blessed with another lovely day, only occasionally being threatened by mist and drizzle.

We soon noticed that pines were not nearly so heavily butchered as the trees on the lower slopes that had been lopped near to the ground. Some *Rhododendron neriiflorum* was still out, as was the yellow *R. trichocladum*. The latter has a huge altitudinal range from below the end of the road to very near the top. *R. rex* subsp. *fictolacteum* was nearly over, as was *R. selense* subsp. *jucundum* near the path with pale pink to deep rose flowers, but these filled the valley below with a pink sheen (see the endpapers of *The Encyclopedia of Rhododendron Species*). *R. cyanocarpum* was over at lower elevations but in

239

Rhododendron lacteum *covers large areas of the Cangshan just below and above the tree-line.*

reasonable flower higher up, with some plants extending above the tree-line. In mid May 1981, no larger rhododendrons had started to flower above the tree-line but being over three weeks later made all the difference. Our greatest joy was to see *R. lacteum* in full bloom, although it was not flowering all that freely, nor were the flowers in perfect condition, having been bruised by hail, rain, snow or wind.[10] The rich yellow colour was relatively uniform throughout the many plants we could see (a very few were paler) and the presence or absence of a blotch was scattered through the population.

Rhododendron taliense was also at about its best. The flowers of this species were mostly cream with some tinged pink or more pink and again a scattering of spots and blotches. Not far above the tree-line, this species reaches 3m/10ft plus. but is naturally more compact and attractive higher up. Where we could get a good view right up to the ridge, it was very noticeable that *R. lacteum*, *R. taliense* and *R. haematodes* occurred in belts all the way up, the last so covered in scarlet

flowers to look like rivers of blood cascading down the mountain side. Where the soil was thin, there were patches of *R. impeditum* (SSNY 354) with purplish flowers, while *R. campylogynum* (not quite out) was mostly ground cover under the *R. taliense*. Much of the foliage of this species was affected by a leaf spot. Some totally unnecessary destruction of rhododendrons had been going on, with branches lying all over the place. Some Chinese that we passed were carrying branches in flower and odd trusses littered the path.

As expected, the *Primula sonchifolia* and *P. calliantha* which were a glorious sight in the forest in 1981 were now over but the latter species was now in flower right up to the ridge. It is such a shame that this species is so hard to cultivate. On steep banks and cliffs in mossy crevices grew the diminutive tuft-forming *P. bella* with pale lilac flowers and also the two-toned yellow *P. serratifolia*, which I was to see at its glorious best on the Salween-Mekong divide in the autumn. The last primula was a few of the purple-flowered *P. amethystina* near the top. Purple-fringed flowers (without leaves) just emerging from winter resting buds turned out to be *Omphalogramma delavayi*. The architectural crucifer *Megacarpaea delavayi* with rich purple flowers grew to 30cm/1ft and a species of *Lloydia*, perhaps *L. delavayi*, showed off its dainty pendant yellow flowers near the radio station.

10. This superb yellow-flowered species is not the easiest to keep alive in cultivation, needing perfect drainage and a very acid soil; it is more likely to succeed if grafted. It was very noticeable that the depth of colour was much more pronounced in the wild than is ever seen in cultivation, though this does vary from season to season

After lunch Kenneth decided to go down to a boggy area to the south. so I lent him my compass in case the mist came down. He did not get very far before he shouted back, 'R. cephalanthum.' I shouted back 'Large leaves?' and the answer came back, 'Yes.' This was a great find of Kenneth's and something we had looked for in vain in 1981 and yet we must have passed within a few feet of it. R. cephalanthum var.

platyphyllum (SSNY 350) (formerly R. platyphyllum) was introduced in 1914 and was subsequently lost to cultivation. There were several plants on and mostly just below a very narrow ridge of rock, growing to 8in/20cm high with white flowers in a slightly flattened truss. To me, this was either the best or second best (to the white R. hippophaeoides) find of the expedition.

Omphalogramma delavayi *was just coming into flower near the top of the Cangshan. We have found this quite easy to cultivate in a peat bed.*

Rhododendron cephalanthum var. platyphyllum, *Kenneth's great find, had been lost to cultivation for a number of years. It was growing on steep, east-facing little cliffs and we must have walked within a few feet of it in 1981.*

One of the star plants we found in spring 1992 was Nomocharis pardanthina Mairei Group, *which was flowering in masses amongst scrub just below the end of the road on the Cangshan above Dali. Quite easy to grow from bulbs or seed, it is important to keep this form isolated, if seedlings are to be spotted like these. Also, it is susceptible to virus infection.*

At the foot of the gorge by the road, *Rhododendron brachyanthum* was in full flower with its dainty yellow bells on long pedicels. Up the gorge, the star turn was *R. dichroanthum*, also in full flower and all were excellent oranges. Also in the gorge were *Viburnum chingii*, covered with slightly scented little very pale pink flowers, the rare *Paris polyphylla* var. *yunnanensis* forma *alba* and *Trillium tschonoskii* with small white flowers. *Nomocharis pardanthina* Mairei Group was at its very best with its pale pink flowers spotted all over a darker pink; first seen on a rock at the foot of the gorge, it was plentiful amongst shrubs near by. Collected by SBEC in 1981, this has done well in cultivation and comes true from seed if isolated from other *Nomocharis*. Other good plants were *Rodgersia aesculifolia* in a good pink form, a coppery coloured *Hemerocallis* species and *Hypericum forrestii*.

The journey back to Kunming was thwarted by terrible traffic and took ten hours. While we Peters had various learned discussions in the Jeep, the others played a game with marks for the most hazardous overtaking, the worst being double fuel tankers and they did have two near misses. We Peters stopped when we saw small trees covered in white flowers. After some searching we managed to reach a diminutive specimen which, to our astonishment, was a rhododendron and one we had never seen before. It proved to be *R. hancockii* of section Choniastrum and the scented white flowers had a yellow blotch but, alas, it is probably not hardy enough for any part of the UK. Back in Kunming, as it was Ian's birthday, he was allowed to choose the meal in the hotel restaurant, but it turned out very indifferent with the duck just skin and bone and even the skin was tough! After a discussion on the archives in the RBGE, which Ian said were deteriorating horribly, Ian became belligerent on too much

One of the largest-flowered Hypericum *species, probably H. forrestii, just above Dali on the Cangshan.*

Opposite. A fine form of Rodgersia aesculifolia *near the end of the road on the Cangshan. Rodgersias appreciate a deep, relatively moist soil in cultivation.*

Hemerocallis species near the lowest scrub area above Dali on the Cangshan.

Chinese brandy. In the morning both he and Kenneth were suffering, and his summing up of the night before was, 'No more of that brandy.'

With a day to spare, we visited the Stone Forest which we had managed to avoid before. It is reckoned to be a 'must' for every tourist visiting Yunnan. Our British Health and Safety regulations would never allow people on to some of the more dangerous parts without handrails where there are drops of 9m/30ft from steep narrow steps.

Overall it was a good expedition with some exciting plants and fine country and, although I regretted not having reached more of the higher country around Zhongdian, we had had the bonus of seeing our old stamping ground of the Cangshan in fine flower with some valuable introductions from both areas.

Chapter 10

ON THE SALWEEN-MEKONG DIVIDE:

China Autumn 1992 / Spring 1994

Peter Cox

My second expedition to China was in the autumn of 1992, to the Salween-Mekong divide, the most exciting destination to date. This had been one of the best hunting grounds for Forrest, Kingdon Ward and Rock and only the Salween-Irrawady divide is known to be richer. Ted Millais, who had been with me in 1988 and 1990, was responsible for putting the expedition together. This time we were a party of nine: six British and three Americans. All had been on expeditions with me before except John Christie, owner of the great rhododendron garden of Blackhills in north-east Scotland. The rest of the party were Ted and Romy Millais, Philip and Sarah Bowden Smith and the three American stalwarts, June Sinclair, Warren Berg and Garratt Richardson. Ted and Romy and I returned to the same area in spring 1994 with David Chamberlain, Roger Hyams, David's then assistant from the RBGE, David Farnes, a retired dentist known as 'New Boy', two Americans who had been with us in 1990, Jerry Broadus and his wife Clarice Clark and the Australian Ross Hayter, a retired physician.

Our Chinese hosts in both 1992 and 1994 were The Institute of Mountain Hazards and Environment although we sometimes referred to them as 'Mountain Hazards and Disasters' as they later changed their name to Mountain Disasters and Environment! They were evidently involved in research into earthquakes, land slides, erosion and so on, and had a staff then of some 360. We were to find out that they knew little about the area to which we were going. In 1992, our Chinese staff were our leader Xiao (pronounced Chou) Jianping, so-called cook Chen Xiao, and our delightful little interpreter Huang Rong known to us as Rosie, plus our three drivers, while in 1994 we had Rosie's husband Lai instead of Mr Xiao and a new cook from Panzhihua, a decided improvement.

We flew Finnair both years, via Helsinki to Beijing, which seemed to work out the cheapest way but the plane was very full with no seats to stretch out on.[1] In 1992, we could not get on to the first flight to Chengdu, so took a mini-bus some way into town for lunch and a walk. I had been longing to see that

remarkable pine with the peeling bark, *P. bungeana*, which grows wild in north-east China and is planted around Beijing. We found several, those in shade being leggy, thin and unhealthy, but two in the open were fine with a much divided crown and most attractive bark all the way up to the side branches. At Glendoick there is one tiny plant that has been in for twenty-five years and is still only 1.2m/4ft high. Our climate is just not warm enough in summer.

Ted had been working on the best and quickest way to get to the Salween-Mekong divide from Chengdu but, despite endless correspondence with our hosts, we really did not know the answer until we reached Chengdu. Luckily, they had chosen what appeared to be the most sensible route, which was taking a train to Panzhihua on the Yangtze where we would be picked up by our staff who were to set off in advance. This worked well both years. In 1994, we converged on Panzhihua from four different directions, and all made it on time: Jerry Broadus and his wife Clarice Clark from USA, Ted and Romy from New Zealand, Ross Hayter from Australia, David Chamberlain and Roger Hyams from Chengdu and David Farnes and I from UK.

Above far left: The yellow Primula sikkimensis *and the puce P. secundiflora are often associated in flower together and yet no natural hybrids have been recorded.*

Above left: Nomocharis aperta *on the mountain north of Napa Hai. These nomocharis are so beautiful in their natural state, it is a shame to allow them to hybridise in gardens.*

Above: The village of Yongzhi sits on a tributary of the Mekong on the Salween-Mekong divide.

1. On the outward journey in 1992 we had to lug our luggage for great distances with no trolley or help. Kenneth often tells me that I take far too much kit while I reckon that I take an absolute minimum and can just carry it all at once. In 1994, David and I made the great mistake of taking a taxi whose owner/driver hailed us at the barrier without arranging a price. Including a stop at a ticket office for 35 minutes, we were charged $60US. From then on we always arranged a price beforehand.

The lovely Primula forrestii *near the south end of Gang-he-ba, the curious flat plain that lies into Yulong Shan, which is dry for most of the year, but flooded during the wet season in summer.*

Below. Arisaema *aff.* wattii *in a forest glade on the Salween-Mekong divide.*

A typical lunch as supplied by the 'Institute of Mountain Hazards and Disasters'.

Panzhihua is a horrible town with a huge steelworks and coal dump polluting the river. The area is famous for being the centre for wild camellias, although most must be remnants of what they were before much of the native flora was destroyed. The road to Lijiang passed through undulating country with several minor ups and downs but with no real virgin forest left. We stayed in the same hotel that I had been to in 1986, but by 1992 it had been greatly improved and was still being added to. In 1994 we stayed in a new and better hotel. As we were a day earlier than expected, we decided to spend the day on Yulong Shan and explore the fascinating area known as Gang-he-ba. This is a dry valley with no stream running through it, which is flooded in the wet season. It is just a short walk from the road to the valley, but on the way were some superb *Primula forrestii* and nice *Roscoea*. The valley stretches several miles into the hinterland of Yulong Shan with some of the big peaks rising at

Dipelta yunnanensis *is an attractive deciduous shrub, related to* Weigela.

Gentiana hexaphylla *on Bei-ma Shan. This species is identified by its short corolla lobes and short crowded whorls of leaves. A much deeper-coloured form was found on the Salween-Mekong divide. Rare in cultivation.*

resulting in arriving in Zhongdian rather late. It was after 9.30 when we finally reached Deqin with very tired drivers.

In 1994 we were delighted to see the great carpets of *Rhododendron racemosum* in flower again on the Zhongdian plateau, but *R. hippophaeoides* was mostly over. We had a prolonged stop on Bei-ma Shan, attempting to locate the GSP reading for *R. proteoides* that the Swedish KGB expedition had found in 1993.

The facilities in autumn 1992 at the old Deqin 'hotel' were even worse than in the spring, with the courtyard all dug up for new buildings and the only loos out in the street. To our horror, the gates were locked at night, so what did anyone do who was taken short in the night? Both June and John were still suffering from tummy upsets. In the morning we asked to be moved and were shifted a little way up the street, which at least had a loo up some outside steps with only hordes of rats to contend with. The restaurant up the street now had quite comfortable chairs in place of the tiny stools. What progress! We tried to make use of showers heated with solar panels but the result was lukewarm and only a few drips. Overall Deqin was a dirty and smelly little town with overflowing litter drums everywhere. By 1994, there

its head. On the way, we passed two recently made gravel and boulder 'dams' across the stony valley which had been constructed to stop the flooding from reaching some newly planted trees. Being 19 May and at first only at 3,100m/10,300ft, most of the rhododendrons, such as *R. cuneatum* and *R. rubiginosum*, were nearly over.[2]

In 1992, the first part of the drive from Lijiang to Zhongdian was new to me, passing through a plateau mostly cultivated, with quite a large lake. Between Little Zhongdian and Zhongdian, the other 4WD vehicle had a very nasty skid on wet tar, almost leaving the road, where it would probably have turned over. All the occupants looked thoroughly shaken up by the time we reached Zhongdian. Our driver was a trifle over anxious to please and stopped too many times for us to take photographs,

A dwarf Delphinium *species on Bei-ma Shan.*

2. There were some fine plants in full flower of the compact form of the Lapponica *Rhododendron telmateium*, previously known as *R. diacritum*, with some good blues. There was also *R. primuliflorum* with white flowers and others species seen were *R. vernicosum*, *R. decorum*, *R. yunnanense* and, eventually at the head of one branch of the valley, *R. adenogynum* (C 6502), sadly with its flowers over. The CLD 1990 expedition found masses of this species with white to pale pink flowers higher up these mountains. Seed gave us several natural hybrids with *R. vernicosum*, as did seed from a different Yulong Shan location collected in 1986. Known as *R. x detonsum*, this can have either *R. vernicosum* or *R. decorum* as the other parent, usually the former as they more often grow together.

Trigonotis *species on Bei-ma Shan. Related to* Omphalodes *in* Boraginaceae.

Pedicularis siphonantha *on Bei-ma Shan. There are many lovely species in this genus of* Scrophulariaceae *but they are all semi-parasitic, so difficult to grow.*

was a new hotel that at least had internal washing facilities, showers and loos, though the last were decidedly odd with the drainage channels set the wrong way. Our restaurant now had a new room added, so was really coming up in the world, no doubt due to the profits made from our previous visits!

In 1992, with much aplomb Philip took on the onerous task of negotiating the hire of our mules and their drivers. While he, Xiao and Rosie went down to the Mekong, the rest of us went back up to Bei-ma Shan again. Our two drivers had go-slow and speed-up modes, the former usually first thing in the morning

when they were recovering from a hangover. One had a nervous twitch when he kept looking over his left shoulder, usually at the most dangerous moments. This morning was definitely a go-slow mode as we drove up through low cloud. We stopped near the centre pass looking for a likely habitat for *Rhododendron proteoides* with no success, but there were lots of alpines in flower. A good collection was made of *R. tapetiforme* (C 6000), a rare Lapponica of which a well-distributed Forrest collection was wrongly named. This makes a low tangled shrub with larger leaves than most of its closer relatives.

Rhododendron tapetiforme *occurs in quantity on Bei-ma shan with yellow* R. rupicola *var.* chryseum.

Our first camp, at 550m/1,700ft, with the Mekong beyond.

The Mekong-Salween divide

Philip returned exhausted with not very great news. He was told that the mules and drivers could be out for a maximum of eleven days as they could not carry food to last for longer than that. We said that they could go back for more food. Our chances of being able to cross the Salween appeared to be out of the question and we might not even reach the river. Philip was told that the Doker La pass was too high, too difficult, too dangerous and very steep. Ted reckoned that these difficulties were exaggerated and so it proved. It is likely that we would have needed another mule team to take us to the Salween as ours would have been entering 'foreign' territory of a different minority who would own the grazing over the pass. Mule drivers are a law unto themselves and the ones we were to hire were no exception. Our staff kept saying that the drivers were asking for too much money and we said that the amount was very small compared with what our hosts were charging us. In 1994 the mules were organized beforehand and, apart from the local police attempting to bribe us for 300 yuan, we got off in reasonable time. We had the same head muleteer again so expected trouble.

In 1992 we climbed 550m/1,700ft up the hill from the bridge over the Salween to reach our first camp, with few plants of interest except an inferior leggy form of *Daphne aurantiaca*, and the usual semi-xerophytic *Euonymus*, *Cotoneaster*, *Berberis* and *Zanthoxylum*. It was a great relief to be camping and away from the smelly town. The campsite was rather hilly and we were invaded by several children and their

Daphne aurantiaca var. calcicola *is a very compact version of the commoner var.* aurantiaca *from which it differs in its decumbent branches and tiny narrow leaves. Rare in cultivation.*

We nicknamed this porter 'Smoky Joe'.

mothers. Our meal was noodles, green vegetables and spam and this proved to be all that we had with us apart from endless dry biscuits. Despite repeatedly reminding Xiao and Rosie that we wanted *piju*, orange and some variety of food such as quails' eggs, there were none of these until we sent our staff off for replenishments several days later.

Breakfast consisted of only dry biscuits and not even enough boiled water to do our teeth, let alone wash and shave. The Chinese needed to be sent to Nepal to learn how to look after trekking parties. The morning was dry after a wet and windy night. We climbed up to 3,000m/10,000ft and then, alas, down again, passing some mahonias; as soon as we changed direction up river, the vegetation became lush with large trees of *Lithocarpus, Populus, Ilex* and so on. Our campsite was by the river, Philip and Sarah pitching their tent right by the torrent, where, if there had been a flash flood, they would have been the first to be washed away. Rosie was feeling very homesick and temporarily fell out with the rest of our staff. Ted and Romy comforted her and Philip asked me if I would give up my tent to Rosie which I refused. Once I got to know her better, I might have been delighted to share it with her!

In 1994 we walked down the river, then up the gorge to the village of Yongzhi where we had to camp on the village square cum basketball pitch. As the track up the stream was impossible, due to a landslide, we had to climb 600m/2,000ft straight after breakfast, passing three Tibetan girls, one carrying a bucket full of *Mahonia* species (C 6509) fruit which they eat. Some distance on, away from the dry south-facing slope, we found a population of *Rhododendron lukiangense* with its upturned leaves with shiny undersides. This is a typical valley bottom Irrorata species which is really too tender and early into growth for Glendoick, as is another Irrorata, *R. anthosphaerum*, with narrower less upturned leaves, less shiny underneath. A third species was *R. augustinii* subsp. *chasmanthum* (C 6124) with glabrous petioles. In 1994, this species was nearly finished flowering, but we gathered a few small branches to photograph. Some were a goodish blue but many were a wishy-washy off white. In 1992 on a bank above the river we found a fine population of *R. edgeworthii* (C 6021, 6507) growing terrestrially for several metres and then no more. The soil here must have been

Various colour forms of Rhododendron augustinii *subsp.* chasmanthum *on the Salween-Mekong divide. This western form of* R. augustinii *has less hairy leaves than eastern subsp.* augustinii.

Trillium tschonoskii *is one of the few Asiatic members of this mostly North American genus. Widespread in western China, it is in the Red Data Book as apparently being threatened.*

extremely well drained for them to be here at all and making fine specimens to 1.8m/6ft high. We just missed seeing these in flower in 1994. Seedlings in cultivation have produced very large flowers but are less hardy than some introductions and the foliage is inferior to later finds of this species.

All along the valley were splendid virgin conifers including *Pinus armandii*, *Picea likiangensis*, *Tsuga dumosa* and the rare *Pseudotsuga forrestii* and higher up *Abies*, *Taxus* and perhaps a second *Picea*. We estimated some of these trees to be as much as 46m/150ft tall. Under the trees were a few *Trillium tschonoskii* with white flowers.

Later there were fine broad-leaved trees including *Sorbus aria* type, huge *Schefflera impressa*, *Betula* good to poor-barked, and a grove by our second bridge of huge maples growing to a similar size as our sycamore. This may have been *Acer caesium*. There were many *Rhododendron anthosphaerum* including one 10.7m/35ft high with a trunk 30cm/1ft in diameter. *R. rubiginosum* was common, also making large specimens. Soon we found a small *R. uvariifolium* on one side of the path and the related *R. fulvum* subsp. *fulvoides* on the other side. The former became very plentiful and was the only elepidote species for miles, with scattered plants in the largely deciduous forest. Getting higher as we approached our next camp, *R. fulvum* subsp. *fulvoides* took over.[3]

Our camp was near the river, once more, on a meadow with a shieling (mountain hut) called Zhuzipo nearby, known by us as the first cow farm. We had been a little disappointed not to find some 'new' rhododendrons by now but John and I went for a little walk beyond our camp really to see if there was a path up that side of the valley as the main one crossed the river here. There was no proper path but, when we came to a bank, we found the large-leaved *R. praestans* (C 6025) and *R. selense*

(C 6024, 6067). The former was very variable with the shiny plastered indumentum being bronzy to pale greenish and fawn and the buds red or green. While I investigated the path situation, John went a little higher and soon I heard excited shouts. Eventually he appeared with an arm full of material including three types of *R. sanguineum*, some large-leaved *R. eclecteum* and, best of all, *R. semnoides* with a winged petiole like *R. praestans* but the indumentum woolly and more like *R. arizelum*. Everyone went to bed excited about what else we might find in the morning.

The morning revealed a steep hillside covered in forest behind our camp and further along where a stream came down a more open area with bamboo and the smaller rhododendrons including *R. selense* and *R. eclecteum*. At the edge of the forest were a few *R. arizelum* with its woolly indumentum, non-winged petiole and peeling reddish pink bark, while *R. praestans* has a winged petiole and rough brown, occasionally silver, mottled bark. It soon became apparent that there was a host of plants varying all the way from the one species to the other which, at least in its intermediate form, equals what we know as *R. semnoides* in cultivation. We went back to the same camp in 1994 with a huge mass of snow filling the valley immediately below our camp and creating a snow bridge on to the opposite hillside. *R. eclecteum* was predominantly deep pink or flushed rose with a few cream and one really harsh rose-magenta. *R. selense* was covered in pink flowers over the stream and the few *R. arizelum* at the edge of the forest were cream, slightly tinged pink. The *R. rubiginosum* were of high quality including some deep colours and some with wide-open large flowers, in the form that we used to call *R. desquamatum*. *R. praestans* was mostly cream with a blotch but a muleteer brought in a magnificent truss with rose-coloured flowers and huge leaves.

Rhododendron eclecteum *is very variable in flower colour, from near red to white and also yellow. It is early flowering in cultivation.*

3. The indumentum of this subspecies is invariably inferior to subsp. *fulvum*, being paler, sparser and more granular, although the leaves are longer and some plants had better indumentum than others; subsp. *fulvum* has a more southerly distribution.

251

Gaultheria trichophylla *aff. on the Salween-Mekong divide. This has wider leaves than is usual for this very low-growing species.*

The tarn above what we called the second cow farm with Abies forrestii *forest behind. It was around this tarn that I first found* Rhododendron forrestii *including some with leaves with a crimson underside, typical of the original* R. forrestii *before* R. repens *was sunk into it.*

Cassiope pectinata *is a common species in north-west Yunnan. I have collected seed several times but have never managed to get it to germinate.*

I twist my knee

In 1992, John and I, who seemed to be the most energetic of the party, decided to climb up through the forest and see if we could reach above the tree-line. It proved to be tough-going with some bamboo, fallen trees, little cliffs and several large rhododendrons. One *R. rubiginosum* was about 7.6m/25ft high with a trunk diameter at breast height of 60cm/2ft. Some of the *R. arizelum* had trunks growing flat or twisted due to snow bending them down, as reported by Kingdon Ward. Soon the ground began to level out with a small stream lined with *R. sanguineum* and then a lovely little lake surrounded by rhododendrons. This proved to be a paradise for beauty and excitement. A rotten fallen tree jutted out into the lake and on it grew *Diplarche multiflora*, a dwarf ericaceous plant that is difficult to grow. At the edges of the lake were various other dwarf Ericaceae including several different *Gaultheria* species with lavender, black and blue fruits. *Cassiope pectinata* grew to 20cm/8in with broad hairless shoots. On a little peninsula was a mass of fruiting *Omphalogramma*, probably *O. vinciflorum*.

Creeping through the very damp soil was *R. forrestii*, a rhododendron that I had particularly wanted to find, here with both the reddish-purple and green leaf undersides, and *R. saluenense*. Another was *R. temenium* (C 6037), a close relative of *R. sanguineum*, but, alas, seedlings have all turned out to be hybrids, perhaps with *R. selense*. A few *Meconopsis betonicifolia* were the first meconopsis of the expedition. Beyond the lake over a little crest was an alpine meadow, probably cleared by man for grazing, with one *dzo* present. Multitudes of alpines dotted the grass, including a fine *Erodium*, a large-flowered *Anemone*, a tiny *Primula*, the near-black-flowered *Lilium souliei*, and best of all, a rose pink *Nomocharis saluenensis*.

John tried to start down again near a waterfall but I suggested retracing our steps around the lake. Even so we managed to drift too near the waterfall and landed in a terrible thicket of bamboo and *Rhododendron selense*. I slid on a cut bamboo and twisted my knee and then another bamboo whipped back across my eye. The eye soon recovered but the knee took many months to fully

We were so lucky to see late-spring-, summer- and autumn-flowering alpines in flower on the same hillside. Lilium souliei *is one of the strange lilies that resemble a fritillaria, especially in flower colour.*

An out of season flower (taken in mid-September) of Nomocharis saluenensis (C 6042)*, with longer lobes than the related* N. aperta.

Meconopsis impedita *does not seem to be one of the finest species in the genus. In cultivation it looked even worse than it looks here!*

recover. The jungle changed to bamboo with *R. eclecteum* plus fallen trees, the rhododendrons growing at right angles through the bamboo, tripping us up at every step. Eventually getting near camp, John and I waved and blew a whistle which was answered from camp only a few minutes before dark. It had taken us 3½ hours to descend. My knee was tightly bandaged by Warren, resulting in a huge swelling below the knee. It had been one of the most wonderful plant hunting days I had ever had, plus the toughest ever. John, who must have been really fit at that stage, appeared to be more tired than me, so it seemed especially unfair that I had to drag myself along behind everyone else for the rest of the expedition.

The next day's plan was to go to the second cow farm and, for those feeling energetic, on to the third cow farm. As my knee was decidedly sore, I would trail along after the others at my own pace. After crossing the stream and heading left, we walked through birch forest, all ring-barked so as to kill them and, no doubt, to increase the grazing area and to provide firewood. The chances are that nothing but useless weeds will take the place of the birch. The bark here was not particularly ornamental, trunks being mostly grey and dull. One would expect the ring-barking to force the trees to set seed heavily but it seemed that only the dullest ones had any seed.

The first rhododendron was *R. selense*, covering the knoll immediately opposite our camp, followed by *R. fulvum* subsp. *fulvoides, R. eclecteum* and *R. sanguineum* on the drier, more open places. Then there was a large population of *R. praestans, R. arizelum* and their hybrid *R. semnoides*. Before reaching the open area where the second cow farm was, the rhododendrons were restricted to *R. praestans* only. Turning the corner into the open, I could see the cirque where the others should have been. I was just above the level of the second cow farm and there seemed to be little of interest with everything heavily grazed. On the way, I had failed to find any primulas or meconopsis, but gazing around I spotted what looked like a meconopsis on a rock by the stream. Sure enough it was and a rare one too, M. *impedita*. On the way

down, I did find one little colony of *Primula sonchifolia* and two probable seedlings of *Meconopsis pseudointegrifolia.*[4]

In 1994, I somehow got left behind and lost the path, arriving near the second cow farm where the others were sitting on a knoll, as an island in the snow, surrounded by three lovely primulas in flower. Efforts to track down the names of two of these have failed, both probably being Nivalids, one rosy-purple with a divided flower, the other with bluer flowers and less divided lobes. The third species was the diminutive *P. hookeri*, very low with a whorl of leaves and white flowers looking like blobs of snow. Across the snow on some cliffs was that gem *Paraquilegia anemonoides*.

In 1992, Philip and Sarah passed me with a lovely bunch of flowers collected on the alpine meadows above the second cow

---

4. I spent some time here studying the big-leaved rhododendron population. There were comparatively few *R. arizelum* with the hybrids greatly outnumbering it, while *R. praestans* was the commonest. As observed earlier, *R. semnoides* varied all the way from one parent to the other. Leaves were laid out in rows to photograph to compare them. It was interesting that this population was all quite young with little signs of any having flowered yet and there were no older specimens nearby.

Primula hookeri (P. vernicosa), *the flowers of which resemble little blobs of snow. Richards has sunk P. vernicosa while Halda and Smith and Fletcher retained it on account of the flower size. It is difficult to keep going in cultivation and may not be worthy of great effort.*

A pink-bracted Saussurea *species of subgenus* Amphilaena *on the slopes near the approach to the Ding Zhulagu La above camp 4.*

Saussurea obvallata *is a widespread species with these strange inflated bracts.*

Rhododendron forrestii *opens its flowers as soon as the snow retreats.*

Saussurea obvallata *with the bracts deliberately opened up to show the reproductive parts in the interior.*

farm. These included *Primula sikkimensis* with very large flowers, another species, probably *P. serratifolia, Codonopsis* species with pale yellow or purplish flowers pinched in the middle, probably *C. tubiflora*, and a woolly *Saussurea* with flowers on the top. New rhododendrons were *R. campylogynum, R.* x *eudoxum* and Warren

found one plant of *R. haematodes* subsp. *chaetomallum*. John went over the top and, surprisingly, found nothing but *R. eclecteum*. It had been a fine day but rain threatened in the evening.

In 1994 we crossed the snow bridge and then climbed up a narrow gully running away up the hillside, getting steeper as we

We passed two lakes on the way to our fourth camp in spring, which proved to be an idyllic spot surrounded by mountains. The rhododendrons were disappointing, but the alpines were the best I have seen anywhere, even better than Tibet for variety. All the plants on pages 256 to 257 were found on the hillside in the distance.

went. The gully was still largely full of snow but along the sides were a few prostrate *Rhododendron forrestii*. I was thrilled to see this species in flower in the wild, opening its scarlet trumpets almost as the snow melted. It has always been one of my favourites and we saw only foliage in 1992. Alongside were dense tiny-leaved cushions of lovely rich pink *Diapensia purpurea* and further back in the scrub, deep yellow *Rhododendron mekongense* on straggly shoots with no leaves. Amongst these were a few of the evergreen *R. sanguineum* with deep almost black crimson flowers, therefore var. *haemaleum*. Away further up the hillside were conspicuous pink and white bushes which David C had already reached, being like a mountain goat in those days. I soon regretted that I had even tried to get up so far, but the bushes of *R. cephalanthum* were splendid large rounded specimens with tight little trusses of white to deep pink daphne-like flowers.

The food in 1994 was decidedly better than in 1992 and we were all delighted when Ross produced an enormous heavy, rich fruit cake which he very carefully cut into neat squares which lasted us the whole of our twenty-two days camping. A mule had injured its stomach on a sharp cut bamboo. Jerry and (Dr) Ross

went to examine it and alas, some of its intestines were hanging out and it had internal bleeding, so it had the *coup de grâce*. Later, we gave the bereaved owner cash to purchase a new animal.

In 1992, before leaving camp in the morning, Rosie gave me a pad for my knee made of supposed tiger bone balm mixed with mud! After the bridge, I got on a mule and soon very nearly fell off crossing a large tree buttress, but stayed on for 40 minutes in all, a record for me! The wooden saddle was most uncomfortable. Lunch was at another farm in a cleared area taken over by an *Aconitum* species and a large Compositae, so there was no grazing and there were a few more ring-barked trees here.

We entered a narrow valley up a steep path with the rhododendrons gradually changing. They started with *R. anthosphaerum*, *R. rubiginosum*, *R. uvariifolium*, changing to *R. selense*, *R. heliolepis*, *R. fulvum* subsp. *fulvoides* with several plants intermediate between the last species and *R. uvariifolium*. Eventually we passed through solid *R. beesianum* under fir forest with the occasional *R. saluenense* subsp. *saluenense* and *R. rupicola* var. *chryseum*. There were two small lakes with superb views of the mountains ahead, then a flat area carpeted with the last species. At last I spotted something different, which on first sight looked like

Though it was late September, snow had only just melted in some sheltered hollows and in one of these was a glorious group of Primula serratifolia *with its unusual deep and pale yellow flowers.*

Cremanthodium reniforme *or a close relative.*

Tiny Gentiana wardii.

A most attractive species of Saxifraga *in a rock crevice.*

Mat-forming Gentiana stragulata *with flowers constricted in the throat.*

Polygonum forrestii (*formerly* Koenigia forrestii) *is proving to be a useful groundcover.*

the usual *R. phaeochrysum* or *R. aganniphum*, but it was a splendid uniform population of compact bushes of *R. aganniphum* var. *flavorufum* (C 6070, 6516). This is very easily identified by its extraordinary heavily split indumentum on the old leaves, less so on the younger ones. The indumentum on the older leaves is invariably darker than that of *R. aganniphum* var. *aganniphum*.

In 1994, we camped before the first lake with an ominous amount of snow lying ahead of us. A reconnaissance proved we could not go any further, so we had to return to the main valley. Two years previously, after passing the lakes, we soon saw our camp in the distance and it was what looked like a perfect spot surrounded by hanging valleys with ample scope for at least two

Lomatogonium stapfii.

Gentiana phyllocalyx *with a large green calyx*.

Primula silaensis, *a tiny relative of* P. amethystina.

Corydalis *species with very pretty foliage and flowers, but obviously stoloniferous*.

days' exploration. We thought we had found our Shangri La. I wrote my notes sitting in my tent entrance on a fine, sunny evening with the background of wonderful mountains.

The Americans left camp first, heading up a stream, which is often much the easiest way through dense rhododendrons, provided there are no cliffs or waterfalls. Philip and I followed and were disappointed not to find any new rhododendrons, only *R. beesianum* and *R. aganniphum* var. *flavorufum*. Cliffs revealed nothing much, but a patch of yellow drew our attention. This was a drift of superb *Primula serratifolia* (C 6074) at its very best with masses of bicolour yellow flowers, its flowering being delayed by snow, which on 21 September had only just melted. While we find this species quite free-flowering and relatively easy to grow in cultivation, it never puts on a show like we saw that day. A Meconopsis species was in seed here, which turned out to be the recently resurrected M. *pseudointegrifolia* that has proved to be a better plant in cultivation than M. *integrifolia* itself. June told us that there were lots of alpines in flower further up and sure enough we found some superb plants including three dwarf gentians and two *Corydalis*. One of the latter had really good blue flowers and grew to 15cm/6in high, the other with blue and mauve flowers had most attractive glaucous foliage,

but it was obviously strongly stoloniferous, so might prove to be invasive in cultivation. There were many other alpines on a scree. In the meantime, Ted and Romy had stayed around camp and had found a population of *Rhododendron forrestii* on a flat area, an unusual habitat for this species. I have seen it in several locations since but always on steep slopes.

Potentilla longifolia *with large showy flowers*.

Trollius farreri var. major *(C 6091) proved to be very difficult in cultivation and was quickly lost as small seedlings.*

The outstanding seedling of Rhododendron forrestii *at Glendoick.*

The Ding Zhulagu La

On 22 September 1992, we set off for the Ding Zhulagu La, starting with the usual *Rhododendron beesianum* forest, giving way to steep alpine slopes. There were drifts of a good form of *Primula sikkimensis* just below a snow melt and many other primulas including *P. dryadifolia* and very varied Nivalids, perhaps covering three to four species, though John Richards may have sunk them all into *P. chionantha*. Other primulas were *P. serratifolia* and *P. amethystina* var. *brevifolia*.

Both Romy and I struggled to reach the place where the mules were waiting to carry us up to near the pass. Ted, Romy and I had rides and then walked the rest of the way. There were several *Meconopsis impedita*, very short with mauve flowers of limited merit and one plant of the prickly *M. speciosa* (C 6093), 38cm/15in high, growing in a rock crevice. Although seed of the latter germinated like mustard and cress, no one managed to get it to flowering size, hardly surprising considering its habitat. A lovely trollius, *T. farreri* var. *major* (C 6091), had orange, red and yellow flowers. Seed germinated but the seedlings would not grow away and were a magnet for greenfly.

The view from the top of Ding Zhulagu La at 4,400m/14,500ft was staggering. Snow peaks loomed out of the clouds in the distance, while in the foreground the land dropped away dramatically, giving Romy a bout of vertigo. The flora of this north-facing hillside was in complete contrast to the one we had just climbed up with its primulas and meconopsis. Not a primula was to be seen on the rib of ground running down below us, which contained an amazing collection of dwarf Ericaceae and other acid-loving shrubs. On the pass was a tiny *Cassiope* species, probably a diminutive form of *C. selaginoides* with very narrow shoots. *Diplarche multiflora* was growing in a very different habitat from that of the rotting log in the lake.

Ted, Romy, Philip and I spent some time on the ericaceous slope. *Rhododendron forrestii* (C 6100) was quite common and the

only capsules were on plants at the highest elevation, while those below had obviously all been frosted. Amongst the *R. forrestii* was another rhododendron which puzzled us at first. I was all for calling it *R. comistum*, which resembles *R. proteoides*, but then changed my mind to *R. codonanthum*, which is like a nearly glabrous *R. pronum*, but a further look at the specimens in the RBGE shot that idea right out.[5] Other rhododendrons on this bank were *R. campylogynum* (C 6095) and *R. saluenense* subsp. *chameunum*.

While the four of us were up on the bank, the others were down looking at a possible campsite half way down to the valley. Warren was always keen to press on while the rest of us wanted to return to the bank in the morning. In the end we won by outnumbering the Americans. It was a cramped site lacking accessible water but adequate for one night. Our staff attempted to shoot a squirrel but it managed to escape. The lack of wildlife, even in these remote areas, is all too easy to understand as virtually everything that moves is regarded as edible. Later, a raven was shot and we saw it skinned, ready to cook.

After a cold night at 3,900m/12,800ft, our highest camp, our breakfast was 'bread' rather than dry biscuits. That evening we had *piju* which went down extremely well. We had pressed hard for better sustenance, so a small party had been over the Mekong and back, following a more direct route down the main valley. When Ted, John, Philip and I went back up towards the pass, Philip suffered a disaster going across the slope. Searching for his binoculars, his camera fell out of his bag and bounced down the slope. The film came out and the camera was too damaged to take photographs. The descent to the valley was tough and quite hazardous in places. Then we had a climb of 200m/600ft or more up the valley to a good campsite just below the famous Doker La which Forrest, Kingdon Ward and Rock had all frequented.

Opposite: Mei Li from the Ding Zhulagu La. Even in late September, it is very rare to see high peaks clear of cloud.

5. Several seedlings have now flowered and, although extremely variable, most are undoubtedly *R. forrestii* x *R. aganniphum* (probably var. *flavorufum* but with a less split indumentum) (C 6099). Others looked like *R. chamaethomsonii* which were probably back crosses on to *R. forrestii*. Eventually these hybrids may stabilise and go through the process of speciation. One seedling at Glendoick is outstanding with large light red flowers that do not fade, nice foliage and attractive red buds.

Looking up towards the Doker La from the east side. It is just possible to see prayer flags on the ridge from this spot. Both in 1992 and 1994 our main goal was to cross this pass and both years we failed.

The Doker La

There was a mass of prayer flags by the river at the start of the climb to the Doker La as this is a sacred pass. Fine black cliffs marbled with white loomed above. Luckily my knee held up quite well on all the downs and ups. We had a camp fire for the first time and had a jolly evening with a singsong, which included several songs from one of our Tibetan muleteers.

As we expected, the path up to Doker La could no way be described as 'too steep, too dangerous, too much snow, cannot take mules'. It proved to be a well used route with constant traffic including livestock. People living on the Salween use it in summer to shop in Deqin, which takes seven days each way. Alas, by now it was too late for us to cross the pass and investigate the other side properly. If we had made straight for the pass from the Mekong, we could have got a long way down, perhaps even to the Salween and back.

Philip arrived at the top first and found a temple and a mass of prayer flags. The view showed a valley heading north-west towards the Salween, with side valleys going off. He found the attractive *Corydalis calcicola* (C 6114) with good purple flowers, an *Aconitum* species with very large pale blue flowers

and a purple-flowered *Cremanthodium* species. *Rhododendron forrestii* grew up there in small quantities but none of the hybrids we had seen on the Ding Zhulagu La. John followed Philip with Sarah lagging behind. I took the path in my own time. Near the foot of the pass was a fine berberis with red fruit and very glaucous foliage, especially on the leaf underside, *B. dictophylla* (C 6110), which has good autumn colour in cultivation. The forest soon thinned out and the pass could clearly be seen with its prayer flags and the zigzag path leading up to it. There was a quantity of the lovely blue *Gentiana hexaphylla,* including one almost white. The rhododendrons were the usual *R. uvariifolium, R. mekongense, R. heliolepis, R. selense* and some *R. aganniphum* var. *flavorufum* and further up a quantity of *R. sanguineum* (C 6111), including some with black indumentum which is thought to be caused by a fungus and does not appear on the seedlings in cultivation. There were two cassiopes, *C. selaginoides* and a prostrate species, perhaps *C. mysuroides* or *C. palpebrata.* I searched the side of the pass cirque for the elusive *Rhododendron proteoides* to no avail.

It was John's birthday and another fine evening allowed us to

have a camp fire again and an evening singsong that began with him singing a Scottish song. To everyone's astonishment, he produced a clouty dumpling, a Scottish dish with lots of dried fruit, which all voted a great treat. That night was very wet and we heard rock falls, including one which sounded like thunder quite near the camp and in the morning we thought that we could see where the rocks had come down. The whole valley is littered with rocks of all sizes so there must be constant falls, especially after heavy rain or frost. Kingdon Ward described hearing rocks falling here in *The Mystery Rivers of Tibet*.

Philip and I went a little way up the valley where there was a large flood plain covered with rhododendron seedlings all about ten years old, mostly *R. selense*, a second group mixed with *R. wardii*, while in a third area, there was solid *R. beesianum*. One surmises that every few years a landslide or avalanche comes down and clears everything in its path, leaving bare ground waiting for seed to germinate once more – hence the even age of

A 'holy' tree on the corner of the path heading towards the Doker La. We have rarely seen trees decorated in this way.

Our sixth camp was just at the foot of the famous Doker La, one of the main routes from the Mekong to the Salween. These Tibetans were about to cross the pass.

Just above our camp to the west was an obvious avalanche slope with this fine form of Rhododendron sanguineum *just surviving in the middle. All the branches lie down the hill.*

Just above the Doker La camp near the foot of the east slope was an area covered in rhododendron seedlings, all apparently of a similar age of about ten years, mostly R. selense *but a section of solid* R. beesianum *and some* R. wardii.

Rhus species in autumn colour on our way back to the Mekong in 1992.

this multitude of seedlings, the most I have seen on all my travels. We recorded that *Rhododendron uvariifolium* had an altitudinal range from 3,500 down to 2,800m/11,500 to 9,200ft which was a surprise. Down by the river we came across a curious plant that formed a straggly ground cover with long trailing stems on the higher areas of pebbles and rocks. It took us ages to find just a few seeds. My guess was a *Tamarix* species which could only be *T. chinensis*, but after reading descriptions, this was obviously wrong. Eventually a visit by Roy Lancaster solved the problem; it was a species of *Berchemia* (C 6120), perhaps *B. giraldiana*. While the parallel-veined leaves are quite attractive in a modest way, the flowers are insignificant.

A constant flow of traffic passed by us on its way to crossing the pass. Philip estimated that there had been at least a hundred yaks by 4 p.m., plus several whole families with their mules and even a flock of sheep. The date being 25 September, it is likely that both animals and people were on their last trip over the pass before winter closed in.

In the afternoon June and I explored the lower part of the flood plain between our campsite and the river. There was quite a variation in the leaf size of *Rhododendron primuliflorum* and the indumentum of *R. sanguineum* and a third rhododendron at first puzzled us but in the end proved to be just *R. lepidotum*, a remarkably widespread species that none of us realized at the time spread so far east. It looked very similar to plants found in south-east and south Tibet in 1996 and 1998. On the way down, Rosie, Sarah and Romy passed too near to a hornets' nest and got stung, so the rest of us gave it a wide berth, watching a herd of yaks go past, some obviously getting stung, shaking their heads and rushing by.

Returning to spring 1994, on the trek back to the main valley, we observed that the only rhododendron in flower was *R. beesianum*, nearly all pale to mid pinks and not as fine as those around Zhongdian in spring 1992. There were several primulas along the path side. On the cliff base were several *P. florida* with mostly pale lavender flowers and deep coloured *P. sonchifolia* which would be worth establishing in cultivation. There were also medium-purple *P. sinopurpurea*, plus *P. boreo-calliantha?* and *P. amethystina* var. *brevifolia*. Near the river we came across a curious area where a few plants of many rhododendron species had gathered together, most no doubt washed down as plants from above or having hitched a ride on an avalanche or even on a landslide from an earthquake. In an area of half an acre, I counted 15 taxa,[6] some of which would normally have large altitudinal differences and very different habitats. Many of them were in flower.

All the Primula sonchifolia *seen in flower in 1994 on the Salween-Mekong divide had very much darker-coloured flowers than we saw anywhere else. In one valley it was very common but all the plants were very small with a single inflorescence.*

6. These were *R. selense*, *R. temenium*, *R. oreotrephes*, *R. heliolepis*, *R. saluenense* subsp. *saluenense* and subsp. *chameunum*, *R. rupicola* var. *chryseum*, *R. mekongense*, *R. tapetiforme*, *R. brachyanthum* var. *hypolepidotum*, *R. primuliflorum* (white), *R. cephalanthum* (good pink), *R. aganniphum* var. *flavorufum* (about to fall into the river), *R. uvariifolium* and *R. anthosphaerum*.

Zhi Dzom La

On 31 May the news came back that the Doker La was still not open. Failing a second time was a terrible blow, especially for me as it was my second try, but some of the older members were in a way relieved, as the climb to the pass, down the other side and back, would have been quite a challenge even if conditions had been good, which they were not. This time we were satisfied that we were being told the truth, as obviously no one had yet crossed that spring. So we decided to try our luck with the much lower more southerly Zhi Dzom La (Chinsien La) which is only just over 3,750m/12,000ft. To save time, we went all the way back to Yongzhi and actually managed to get off at 8 the next morning. Our new campsite was on the edge of the river and a worse looking site would be hard to imagine, nothing but boulders and stones plus a strong wind blowing. Its only virtue was a tiny hot spring which we made great use of to cleanse our filthy bodies, hair and clothes.

News got around that Ross was passing blood and for a while we were all very worried about his condition. This is apparently known as 'marcher's disease' and is common amongst perfectly healthy soldiers over-exerting themselves without sufficient liquid and becoming dehydrated. Ross decided that after taking plenty of liquid, if it was not better by the morning, he would clear out back to Deqin and home. It had been one of those days when it was almost impossible to drink enough as we had walked a long way, mostly in hot, dry conditions. In the morning he was fine. We now set off for territory new to us all.

Rosie had managed to get some snippets of information from the locals. 'We' were paying our muleteers too much; there was no road from the north to Cawarang on the Salween so we could not have had a vehicle pick us up from there; the Tibetan for *Rhododendron* is 'damat' and for lepidote rhododendrons 'touke'.

The path led up the right bank of the stream coming in from the south-west. It was mostly a well-used path through

Rhododendron rupicola *var.* chryseum.

cultivation with some slash and burn on steep slopes, just asking for erosion. Most of the natural vegetation was evergreen oak scrub which indicates low rainfall. Soon *Rhododendron decorum* lined both sides of the path, white to pale pink, and regenerating freely, with a few *R. augustinii* subsp. *chasmanthum* and lots of *R. lukiangense*. I spotted one *R. coriaceum* (C 6531), new to us all in the wild, followed by a thriving population up to 9m/30ft high, often with much larger leaves than are seen in cultivation. Capsules were hard to find as this was virgin forest with dense shade, resulting in little flower. Soon we came to a bridge from which we could see thickets of rhododendrons, *R. praestans*, *R. coriaceum*, and *R. fulvum* subsp. *fulvoides*. One obvious hybrid between the last two was covered with rust fungus with the alternative host of spruce trees all around. Just by the path on a tree stump was a very neat plant of *R. megeratum*, alas finished flowering, and a thorough search failed to reveal any more. Further on the rhododendrons became monotonous with miles of nothing but *R. praestans* and *R. fulvum* subsp. *fulvoides*, and as it had been raining, leeches became active and we were all busy scraping them off our boots.

While plant hunting, I found a mule with one leg stuck in a hole and unable to move. Thinking it might have broken the leg, I returned at once to camp, told Lai about my find, who in turn informed the muleteers. All rushed to the place with me, got hold of the mule and hauled it out, none the worse for its ordeal. The way I was thanked, shaking my hand, patting me and giving me the thumbs up, just made my day.

We had now reached the point when we were to tackle the Zhi Dzom La pass and once again the head muleteer came up with excuses for not crossing: firstly the different ethnic people on the other side, then the fallen trees and snow. After a long argument, a compromise was struck: if we could get over, they would take our baggage; if we could not, we would return to our last camp. After a dough ball supper with no condensed milk, we all went early to bed, cold and wet.

We made an early start, hardly leaving us enough time to pack up our kit, but after a few bends up the steep path, everything came to a standstill and an examination of the situation forced us to admit that there was too much snow for the mules to proceed. David C had the last laugh as he was the only one who had left his tent up. We decided that all we could do was to walk up to the pass and return to the last camp. The going was difficult with deep patches of steep slippery snow but nearly everyone made it, including Ted and Romy.

Rhododendron fulvum subsp. *fulvoides* gave way to lots of *R. praestans* and *R. selense*, then *R. sanguineum* and *R. beesianum* then *R. temenium* with red flowers just opening and *R. rupicola* var. *chryseum* took over. There was a small peak on our left with *R. saluenense* subsp. *chameunum* and *R. cephalanthum*, the last

The top of the Zhi Dzom La is only 3,750m/12,000ft and yet in early June it still had large patches of snow, enough to stop our mules from crossing the pass. Right on the pass where the snow had cleared were some splendid primulas that have so far defied identification. Seed was collected but nothing germinated. All were of great merit.

with mostly pale flowers and then just snow. Beyond were the same glorious primulas that we had seen at the second cow farm in large quantities. Some of us went a little way down the west side of the pass, only to find some horrid erosion due to trees and shrubs having been cleared and over grazing. There were quantities of *R. eclecteum*, varying from creamy yellow, through pink to crimson. The others found more *R. temenium*, this time with bicolour cream and pink flowers, which might fit into var. *gilvum* or var. *dealbatum*.

As we were in no hurry, we took our time to return to camp, and this proved worthwhile as we found some unusual plants. There was a small population of *Rhododendron rex* subsp. *fictolacteum* with atypical foliage and the indumentum hairs not fimbriated, plus a possible hybrid between this and *R.*

praestans. There was a single non-flowering plant of *R. floccigerum*, an odd plant resembling *R. martinianum* with pendant deep pink flowers two to three per truss, but it was too big a plant for this species and the leaves were too long. We returned to camp after an interesting day but very disappointed that we had failed to get over the pass.

A further disappointment followed in an area which combined a huge bamboo thicket with a path through it which we called 'bamboo valley', followed by a snow field, all of little interest. One steep little side valley contained six plants of *R. floccigerum* with red to pinky-orange flowers, one of which fitted better into *R. sperabiloides* with bigger, wider leaves, thicker though still patchy indumentum and a less tapering ovary. Maybe the latter species should be sunk.

A grazed meadow near the Mekong river with quantities of the bright yellow deciduous Rhododendron mekongense.

Fine plants of Rhododendron saluenense *were mixed with the yellow* R. mekongense, *making a good colour contrast.*

The Three Sneezes Mountain

We now had to decide what to do with our last few days and we sought the advice of our staff. Our plans were to drop down so far towards Yongzhi and then head up towards the south-west, which would bring us on to the opposite side of the mountain behind bamboo valley. We dropped down across fields and then climbed up again, camping on the edge of the forest. I found that I had erected my tent directly in front of an *Aralia chinensis*, a spiny plant definitely not to be argued with, so my back door was forbidden territory! Perched on the crest Ted and Romy had a 'room with a view', looking back across the Mekong to Bei-ma Shan. I was surprised to find *Rhododendron augustinii* subsp. *chasmanthum* by the camp and up to 300m/1,000ft higher.

It was a long, steep climb up to our last high camp and most of us found the going tough, not helped by everyone taking the wrong route for a while and having to drop back before carrying on again. Mixed temperate forest gave way to birch, fir and thin bamboo, which was easy to walk through. The rhododendrons were just the same old boring *R. fulvum* subsp. *fulvoides*, *R.*

rubiginosum and *R. anthosphaerum*. On reaching an inhabited hut and turning the corner, the vegetation changed completely. There was a sea of the bright yellow *R. mekongense* (C 6544) in flower on a grazed meadow with no tree cover and a scattering of other species amongst them, mostly fine *R. saluenense* and *R. sanguineum* in full flower. Suddenly I found a different plant with paler yellow flowers. This was a superb form of *R. citriniflorum* with large flowers on relatively short pedicels. Ted and I reckoned it was the best find so far, but alas, many capsules did not give us a single viable seed. In actual fact, this plant was a one-off, so it is almost certain that any seedlings would have been hybrids. A later search here produced different variations of the *R. sanguineum* theme, such as var. *haemaleum*, *R. citriniflorum* yellow, cream and pink, *R.* x *eudoxum*, *R. temenium* plus a few *R. rupicola* var. *chryseum* and *R. saluenense* subsp. *chameunum*.

Beyond were some flattish but rather wet areas but one was just dry enough for a campsite. It was covered with *R. saluenense* and *R. sanguineum* but as the snow had not entirely cleared, they were not

Rhododendron proteoides *mixed with* R. aganniphum *and the hybrid between them*, R. x bathyphyllum. *The mountains behind are part of the Mei Li range.*

in flower yet. Roger and I had a fine pink *R. beesianum* just 3m/10ft from our tents with snow underneath. Amongst the rhododendrons were *Primula hookeri* and a beautiful *Omphalogramma* species, probably *O. souliei* with deep blue-purple flowers. The camp was at 3,800m/12,500ft so we had climbed 900m/3,000ft that day. We found out that night that this mountain was called Ah Tzi Chi Qiou which became known as 'The Three Sneezes'!

The mountain above us looked promising and we managed to start before 9.30. A dying bamboo area was full of *Rhododendron eclecteum* with the usual pale pink to deep rose colours, followed by fir forest, as often occurs, with a lower storey of *R. beesianum* and nothing else up to the ridge. Here we got a magnificent view of Mei-li, looking quite different than when we saw it in spring 1992 from across the Mekong (see Chapter 9), but no less formidable to climb. We crossed some snow, and on to a knoll which had lost its snow cover some time ago. Here there was a mixed population of *R. citriniflorum* cum *R. sanguineum* var. *didymoides* (C 6539, 6540) with flowers from pale yellow to yellowish pink. These two do seem to merge or create hybrid swarms in places. On the edge of the knoll from where we could look down directly on to our camp were *R. aganniphum* var. *aganniphum* in flower, actually the first we had ever seen in full flower as it had not been out in other places. The fine flowers varied from pale to a medium pink, sometimes with a deep blotch. It is a great pity that this species is not more amenable in cultivation.

We found a path that would take us higher, across some snow, then up a dry stream-bed and out into the open above the tree-line. David C and I simultaneously noticed something of extreme interest, a plant resembling our long-sought-after *R. proteoides* and then immediately next to it the real thing. Wouldn't Warren Berg be jealous! Species enthusiasts reckon this species to have the

I was in the lead when I found an excellent form of R. citriniflorum *with clear yellow flowers.*

The ridge with a snow cornice and a host of plants beyond. The mountains in the distance are the Bei-ma shan range.

most exquisite combination of neat small dark leaves with thick indumentum and perfect rounded plant form. Here it was taller and lankier than expected, up to 0.9m/3ft, with typical recurved leaves with rufous indumentum. Some flower buds were just showing colour, white flushed deep pink. We sat on *R. proteoides* (C 6542) to have our lunch, feeling a deep satisfaction. There were several plants of typical *R. proteoides* but nearby was *R. aganniphum* and in between the two were obvious hybrids.[7]

Ahead was a small cliff with a cleft, where, to the right, a snow cornice sat poised to crash down into the valley below. Sadly Mei-li was by now largely lost in cloud but away below we could just make out the village of Yongzhi, some 2,000m/6,500ft below. Beyond the cleft was a north-east-facing cliff with a host of plants in flower but none of us dared go too near. There were some *R. forrestii* and *Diapensia* but more things we could not identify. Why is it that the best plants are so often out of reach? Along the accessible cliff were lovely pure white and pale pink *Diapensia purpurea*.[8]

The rain soon stopped for our rapid descent to Yongzhi of nearly 1,800m/6,000ft in three hours. We had lunch at our uncomfortable hot spring and stone campsite and the muleteers were reluctant to move on. Nevertheless, we continued to a much better site near the foot of the gorge where the Yongzhi Jiang (river) debouches into the Mekong. There was a seemingly endless procession of livestock plus their owners heading up the valley, having heard that the Doker La was open at last, just before we had to leave. The food and *piju* back in Deqin were a joy after camping for twenty-two days.

A white-flowered Diapensia purpurea *was quite plentiful on a steep rocky bank facing east.*

7. David C was delighted to find these as they proved his theory that *Rhododendron bathyphyllum* (C 6541), which has always looked an unsatisfactory species, was a hybrid and here we were at its type location. Unfortunately most seedlings grown from seed collected off these *R. proteoides* turned out to be this hybrid. A second visit to further up revealed some *R. proteoides* in flower and others with larger leaves with thinner indumentum which were perhaps nearer to the little known *R. comisteum*. The going was so steep that *R. proteoides* was used for hauling oneself up the slope!

8. Towards the end of a wet and largely sleepless night, I dreamt that I took a few rhododendron trusses to the Royal Horticultural Society's Rhododendron Show without sending in the entry forms and was not allowed to enter them. I was absolutely furious but eventually, five minutes before judging was due, they relented and said I could go ahead but only had time to enter two. History does not relate whether any prizes were won!

The gorge just before getting back to the Mekong down from Yongzhi. The path was actually fairly wide and not nearly as frightening as many others.

Deep blue gentians near Litang.

Pale gentians between Batang and Litang.

Gentiana farreri *on the Zheduo pass.*

The long way back to Chengdu

On our 1992 expedition we reached Deqin on 27 September, on a very wet night with fresh snow on the surrounding mountains. It was still raining in the morning, too wet to attempt any climbing, so we discussed which way to go back to Chengdu. To our surprise, we were told that the northern route through Batang, which had been turned down on the way out, was now permitted. Our staff did not like the look of the weather, but as most of the route was on the main Chengdu-Tibet highway which they make every effort to keep open, we reckoned it would be all right. Eventually we won the argument.[9] Our evening meal was not so good. The aubergine was too spicy and the pigs trotters virtually devoid of meat, some bits looking like chicken's heads.

Our night was shattered by the opening of a new restaurant just under our rooms. Strings of firecrackers were let off at intervals, some tied to the balcony outside. Chinese people just love celebrating and this invariably means firecrackers *ad nauseam*. All of us had to make at least two visits to the loo during the night, wading through puddles and hordes of scurrying rats.

It took only one and a quarter hours to reach the Mekong. On the long drive up river, the hills became more and more arid with bare brown slopes, just waiting to be washed away. No wonder the river was so dirty, as just its swift flow, let alone rain, must constantly erode the banks. Being a relatively dry time of the year with little snow melt, the river was a little less muddy than on our arrival. Eventually the road left the Mekong where we had a glimpse through the cloud of a different snow range to the west. We travelled through partly wooded, partly cultivated country up to a pass at about 4,000m/13,000ft where there was a *Rhododendron aganniphum*, *R. phaeochrysum* mixture plus *R. vernicosum* and *R. wardii* and a Lapponica with very small leaves and purple-blue flowers with a short style, perhaps *R. telmateium*.

We descended into a long valley, again partly cultivated, with rye the crop. The flat-roofed, well-decorated Tibetan houses were surrounded by low, rounded hills, partly covered with junipers and spruce. In a way, it reminded us of the Southern Uplands of Scotland. Our driver's progress was pathetic, constantly looking over his shoulder, and ending up well behind the others, so we did not have time to stop at the next pass where there were many poor, straggly *R. primuliflorum*. Before reaching the Lhasa road, we passed through the village of Markam, and then crossed the broad and sluggish Yangtze once again, where we were not allowed to photograph the bridge. To our surprise, the traffic on the Lhasa 'highway' was hardly any more than on the road we had been on, nor was the road of better quality. We then entered what seemed like an endless gorge before the road branched up a side river. Soon the town of Batang came into view, quite a metropolis. The partly finished 'hotel' had internal loos (fair) and wash places but the couples had bathrooms and sit on loos

---

9. Xiao had an excellent map which Philip endeavoured to get a copy of, but all Xiao said what he would do was to copy the areas we had visited and send it to Philip which was not very satisfactory. Warren wanted to photograph it but was unlikely to get a chance.

The Buddhist stupas at Litang in 1992 with a thunderstorm brewing behind.

The old monastery at Litang.

The road from Yajiang to Kangding with whole hillsides of the ubiquitous Rhododendron phaeochrysum *in early October 1992. The autumn colour is a species of* Sorbus.

– amazing! Our plans were to stay two nights here and the idea of climbing the nearby mountain was approved. Philip was told that the river had trout in it so off he went full of enthusiasm.

Batang was full of modern buildings. We could not ascertain whether the old houses had been destroyed in a 1980 earthquake or during a Tibetan uprising when many of the inhabitants were killed. Numerous new buildings were being constructed, some on green field sites, others on cleared Tibetan areas. There was no doubt that many of these houses were for incoming Han Chinese, so they would outnumber the Tibetans in the town. But what would they do for a living? There was no sign of any (new) industry and the long, cold winters would make them wish they were back where they came from.

We were taken to a Tibetan fair outside town which was very poor compared with that of Zhongdian the previous spring. Our staff were determined to delay us there for as long as possible, with the need for maintenance as the usual excuse. The most likely explanation was hangovers. Ted, Romy, John and I managed to get a lift to a hydro-electric scheme well above the town near our intended mountain. The three older members soon gave up, finding it very hot, uninteresting, and the path deteriorating. John carried on, finding two Lapponica

rhododendrons, probably including *R. batangense* which the Phillipsons had sunk into *R. nivale* subsp. *boreale*. This has proved very fastigiate in cultivation and perhaps nearer *R. capitatum*. Philip caught no fish and reckoned there were none. Overall it was a lovely day but not very productive.

On a walk around town, we did find an old Tibetan area with tiny shops but could not locate any locally made clothes. Our supper included our first chicken for ages, but it was chopped as usual, with slivers of bone in every mouthful. I was delighted to have the ground rice and sugar mixture which Rosie said had pea flour added, the nearest to a pudding we ever had.

From Batang, it was a long steady climb up river to the pass. I was with the Americans that day and we stopped where there were obvious rhododendrons.[10] The pass was very high, perhaps higher than any of us had been before. The maps said 4,600m/15,000ft but Ted's and my altimeters said less while Warren's said 15,000ft. Both to the north and south were snow

---

10. These were the same old *Rhododendron phaeochrysum/R. aganniphum* mix, most fitting into *R. phaeochrysum* var. *agglutinatum*, plus two Lapponica, *R. nivale* subsp. *boreale* (*R. batangense*), *R. telmateium* and *R. primuliflorum*, all being very leggy and not garden-worthy.

peaks, presumably over 6,200m/20,000ft. Now we were on the real Tibetan plateau with the more sheltered ground covered in Lapponica rhododendrons, while the more exposed parts had very little vegetation except for scattered cushion plants, perhaps Draba species. There were a few *R. telmateium* with tiny leaves and no signs of flower buds or ever having flowered, perhaps at its extreme limits of altitude and exposure. Herds of yak and a few sheep could be seen away into the distance and yurts with multiple guy ropes plus piles of yak dung for burning, being the only source of fuel around. We passed carpets of rich blue gentians like pools of bright blue water and we stopped to photograph a mixture of shorter pale ones and slightly taller deeper ones.

Eventually we reached the small town of Litang at 4,000m/13,000ft, claimed to be the highest or second highest town in the world. We requested to see the monastery, walking past rows of flat-roofed Tibetan houses before reaching the old building, part of it 200 years old. They had been building a new one behind for three years and hoped to finish it in one more year. The main central hall had enormous wooden pillars which must have come from huge trees and we watched some craftsmen doing intricate woodwork. We were honoured by being given an audience with the head lama. It was a moving experience and we all gave money towards the new building. We had noticed threatening clouds before entering the monastery but missed the hail and thunder while we were with the lama.

In this remote place we were surprised to be plagued by Tibetans attempting to sell us beads, bracelets and so on and they even followed us into the hotel restaurant. John was a sucker for buying these things, which of course encouraged them all the more. Our meal was pleasantly good, but it included squid, tough and rubbery as usual and a long way from the sea. The shops were perhaps better than those of Batang but we still could not find good yak jackets for sale. John managed to ring his wife from here.

We spent some more time on the plateau before entering a more hilly area with valleys. Forest appeared once more but only on north-facing slopes and in the valleys. On one pass we could just make out the snow peak of Gongga Shan away to the south-east. We passed many horsemen all dressed up for some special occasion. The leggy *R. primuliflorum*, and Lapponica rhododendrons gave way to the dwarfer *R. intricatum*, *R. thymifolium* and *R. websterianum*, but all were suffering from over grazing with no sign of any young seedlings getting a chance to grow away. The *R. thymifolium* showed little evidence of having flowered or flower buds and was dying back with hardly any growth; it was going the same way as heather does in the UK if it is over grazed. The yak herders had a lucrative market in Russia for their stock but we wonder if this still continues. In a winter in the late nineties there were tremendous losses of yak in some

areas of the plateau due to extremely heavy snowfalls and this may have eased the over grazing at least for a while. There was no evidence that the gentians suffer from the over grazing; in fact they may take advantage of the elimination of larger-growing competition. The gentians were the glory of this plateau and somehow we did not do them justice, not stopping to study and photograph them nearly often enough. The Americans were really only interested in rhododendrons and as I travelled in their vehicle, other plants tended to be ignored.

Rhododendron phaeochrysum/R. aganniphum populations covered whole north-facing hillsides above the tree-line. There is no doubt that in this area these two species do merge; in some cases there is just one of the two, in others such as Bei-

Saussurea stella is a common but very strange plant, reminiscent of the Chilean Fascicularia *species.*

Gentiana szechenyii at over 4,000m/13,000ft on the Zheduo pass, north-west of Kangding. This was a very striking plant with large flowers.

273

Meconopsis pseudointegrifolia, *with nodding flowers and converging leaf veins, on Bei-ma Shan. This splendid plant is easier to cultivate than the related* M. integrifolia.

ma Shan they are distinct with apparent hybrids between them. These two species are dominant over huge areas, often with no other rhododendrons at this elevation. To the east they may change into *R. przewalskii* and appear to be predominantly white flowered, while to the west in south-east and south Tibet, they tend to be all *R. phaeochrysum* var. *agglutinatum* or *R. aganniphum* with fairly compacted indumentum and are predominantly pink flowered. In more favourable areas to the south in Yunnan and Sichuan, the varieties of *R. phaeochrysum* may be more obvious and a few to many other species of Taliensia may be present, such as *R. roxieanum* and *R. proteoides* though these require more specialised habitats such as north-facing cliffs.

As the road descended from the plateau into valleys, *R. vernicosum* showed up again, amongst beautifully colouring *Sorbus* species in all shades of orange, red and purple with fruit white to pink. The conifer forest gave way to scrub, too dry to

support rhododendrons and forest trees. Eventually we reached the Yalung river, almost as big as the Dadu, and Yajiang where we spent the night. Here we were able to buy strawberry jam to replace our long-exhausted honey and other jam supplies.

As we got nearer to more human population, signs of farming apart from grazing became more obvious. A crop of buckwheat was being harvested and laid out on the road for vehicles to thrash. In one part, all the forest had been clear felled with just stumps left, while later even the stumps had gone so it had probably been cleared many years before. In dryish areas where conifers have only just managed to exist, the chances of regeneration are much less than where it is wetter and, if grazing is intense, these dry areas will never return to forest unless planted. We did pass a fair-sized forestry nursery so hopefully some trees will be established if grazing animals can be kept at bay. There were flat-roofed Tibetan houses all the way up the valley approaching the north side of the Zheduo pass, which we had approached from the other side in late September 1990 when it was covered in snow. This year, 1992, in early October there was not a sign of snow.

We had been keeping a watch for the little known *Rhododendron bonvalotii*, said to belong to subsection Thomsonia but it may be *R. souliei* hybrid, and also for *R. longesquamatum*. Both have been recorded in this area but not even a suitable habitat could be seen. The most likely site would be in a sheltered gorge.

The metalled road started just before the village of Xinduqian and continued to Kangding, which was not that far away so we made frequent stops on the Zheduo pass, once seeing Minya Konka again, then a good view of a subsidiary peak. Although cloudy in places, it was a fine day and we were able to see well to the north too, including one sharp rocky peak, isolated from other snow peaks.

The summit stop at 4,300m/14,000ft seemed the most likely place for the long-sought-after *Rhododenron rufescens*. Even after climbing up another 90m/300ft we found only *R. primuliflorum* (C 6136) once again but a good compact form which has produced large pure white flowers. The dominant Lapponica was *R. nivale* subsp. *boreale* in its numerous guises. We found *Meconopsis henrici* plus M. *integrifolia* on the east-facing slope. There was a superb gentian with huge very pale blue trumpets, totally unlike any I had seen before. It may have been G. *szechenyii* or possibly G. *georgei*.

As we were running out of time that day, and we had a day in hand when we could return, we drove on to Kangding where, as expected, much new building had been going on since 1990. The showers by the hotel had gone with a large addition going up. Alas, 'our' good restaurant had gone too but we found another in an old quarter just over the bridge. Carp was very good but dried yak was too strong. Much of the old

Primula zambalensis (gemmifera) *on Bei-ma Shan.*

street still remained but it was being nibbled away and none may be left in another three years or so (from 1992). The small monastery was still there and looked like remaining with monks still in residence.

Unfortunately, it was a nasty morning with low cloud and even our lowish destination back up the Zheduo pass road was in cloud, so we had to guess as to where to stop, but luckily got it just right. We crossed two streams, probably just above their confluence. Everyone was complaining about the day, wet foliage and cold, but it could have been much worse. Finding *Rhododendron longicalyx* raised the question as to whether it has any significant taxonomic difference from *R. souliei*. The answer is surely no. The sizes of the calyces varied tremendously, even on one capsule, some lobes being to 20mm/¼ in long, others almost absent. We were still a little high for the location of the type specimen but that is most unlikely to make any difference. The second plant was *R. radendum*, another probable case of splitting. One plant was found with hairy stems and leaf margins which does not fully key with the description of the only herbarium specimen of *R. radendum* (Chang 1930), which is supposed to have recurved leaves, hairy above and below and a hairy calyx. Other plants had less recurved leaves and few if any hairs. This was the exact type location for *R. radendum* so I maintain that this is just an extremely hairy selection out of the *R. trichostomum* (C 6145) population.

Plants we found of the yellow *R. flavidum*, another lepidote species that we had failed to find in 1990, keyed perfectly with the description of this species and sure enough, when seedlings flowered in cultivation, they were all *R. flavidum* (C 6143) with yellow flowers. *R. ambiguum* grew here (plus perhaps *R. concinnum*) and plants evidently half way between *R. flavidum* and *R. ambiguum* matching *R. wongii* as we grow it. Cullen thought that *R. wongii* might be a synonym of *R. ambiguum* from the one scrappy herbarium specimen but was undoubtedly wrong. The sequel to this was that while my seedlings were all pure *R. flavidum*, Ted Millais's were a mixture of typical *R. flavidum* and *R.* x *wongii* as we saw it in the wild. The six plants of *R.* x *wongii* (as it should be written) in the wild were all covered with aborted flower buds or no flower buds at all and no capsules. There were no plants that matched so called *R. flavidum* white of which there are several clones in cultivation, nor were there any putative parents such as *R. yunnanense* which could be the second parent of that cross.[11]

I could have spent all day in that vicinity but what with the nasty day, Ted soon retiring feeling sick, accompanied by Warren and June, the pressure was on not to stay very long. We had lunch in the vehicles and then stopped at the *Rhododendron bureavioides* gorge, where it was so cold that even John would not get out. While Warren went to the *R. bureavioides*, Garratt and I walked further up to where the valley opened out and found *R.*

trichanthum (C 6149). In cultivation, this number has very varied amounts of hairs on the shoots and leaves.

We had intended to stop in the Kangding river gorge on the way to Luding, but we all somehow missed the place where in 1990 we had found several rhododendron species including *R. floribundum*. Philip was feeling very poorly on arrival in Luding. The combination of all the travelling, plus the drop to lower elevations had evidently upset his much reduced length of gut. The hotel was improved since 1990 with repairs to the bathrooms and the cracks on the balconies. No hot water until 19.30. This time, we had to pay the equivalent of 50p to cross the famous Iron Bridge over the Dadu river, which looked larger and swifter than ever. I walked out a few metres for John to take a photograph, then returned, at which point the bridge 'keeper' offered to take me over piggyback or hold my hand. I accepted neither offer!

After a slight hold-up at the 'fruit' village at the foot of Erlang Shan, we were off up to the pass. The traffic was as thick as ever, mostly logging trucks, then later a large army convoy (probably coming from Tibet) plus a few fuel tankers, jeeps, and so on. There were a few more hold-ups, mainly due to trucks being parked all over the road. The weather on the pass was as dismal as ever (as in 1990), with everything dripping wet. With the fug inside the vehicles plus the cloud, it was very hard to spot anything of interest but we were allowed one short stop for *Rhododendron wiltonii* (C 6140), with broad-leaves and thick indumentum. June and I hauled ourselves up cliffs to get at it.[12]

11. Other rhododendrons here were several other Lapponicas; probably *R. nivale* subsp. *boreale* again, *R. intricatum*, probably *R. thymifolium*, possibly *R. nitidulum* and *R. websterianum*. Apart from *R. souliei*, we found the following elepidotes; *R. phaeochrysum* var. *agglutinatum* with orange to brown indumentum and low, neat habit, var. *levistratum*, *R. prattii*, *R. bureavioides*, *R. oreodoxa* var. *fargesii* with very variable foliage and hybrids between most of these elepidote species. It is likely that this area was cleared of forest years ago which will have enhanced the number of hybrids and perhaps the quantity of species in that small area.

12. At this stage, we all thought that this was *Rhododendron coeloneuron* but it was quite different from what has recently been collected as this species in south-central Sichuan and adjacent north-west Guizhou. Other rhododendrons identified here were *R. calophytum* with a wide altitudinal range here, *R. pachytrichum*, *R. concinnum*, *R. trichanthum* and a probable hybrid between *R. wiltonii* and *R. pachytrichum*, which has appeared amongst the *R. wiltonii* seedlings in cultivation. This seems to be the same plant as grown under the name *R.* x *paradoxum* in cultivation.

A clear yellow Rhododendron wardii *growing just north of Napahai. Frank Kingdon Ward was lucky to get to China just early enough to discover this rhododendron and have it named after him.*

The relatively short distance back to Chengdu took ages due to many hold ups for no apparent reason.

Our dinner at the Minshan Hotel (opposite the Jinjiang) in a 'European style' restaurant was very good, finishing with a baked Alaska.[13] On our last day, we had a meeting with Mr Qiao and the people from our Institute's headquarters. We had no showdown on the poor food or pre-trek information. The plans for spring 1994 were to cross the Doker La, down to the Salween, up the river and then back north of Mei Li, with a minimum of eighteen days trekking. If we were to cross the Salween, at least four more days would be needed. The Institute of Mountain Hazards and Environment gave us one of the best Chinese meals I had ever had. Our goodbyes had Rosie in tears.

This had been one of the best Chinese expeditions, even though we failed to cross the Doker La, one of our chief objectives. The scenery had been amazing, the plants really special including splendid trees and super alpines and even the weather had been kind. One disappointment was the shortage of meconopsis; are they being wiped out by heavy grazing?[14] Our health was good enough when it really mattered and although my knee bothered me all the way through, I managed

somehow. The food while camping left a lot to be desired but should be quite easily improved with more guidance.

In 1994, we returned by the way we had come via Bei-ma Shan. The best surprise here was a few *Meconopsis pseudointegrifolia* in full flower. This was a case of two bites of the cherry as far as I was concerned as I had seen this species in flower before leaving home. There were plenty of the common primulas plus marvellous groups of *P. zambalensis (gemmifera)*.[15] Our last task on Bei-ma Shan was to try to locate *Rhododendron proteoides* where Bjorn Alden (KGB) had found it in 1993. To our horror, a jeep full of forest police was parked near to the gate we should have set off from and they asked for exorbitant

13. Afterwards we were taken to a fashion show in the Ginkgo Hotel which started with a singer and dancing. The models were all very tall (for Chinese) with elegant figures but with no discernible breasts. Some did not look typically Chinese but we were told that they were all local. The most popular clothes were black evening dresses but I preferred long red ones with black over one shoulder.

14. It is apparent that some species of *Meconopsis* are avoided by livestock and that heavy grazing actually benefits them.

15. A member of section Aleuritia or Pulchella, this species has been in and out of cultivation.

payments, 1,000 yuan each plus extra for herbarium specimens, leaving our cameras behind and having one of them accompanying us. After haggling for ages and getting nowhere, the decision was made to leave and carry on down the road. Nothing would induce our staff to stop again until well clear of Bei-ma Shan. This left Roger short of Taliensia material for his research. In a way it was a blessing in disguise as the *R. proteoides* was not that way anyway. We heard later that the road beyond the gate went on a long way, leading to a sanctuary for a rare monkey, and there was said to be some illegal cutting of timber which the officials did not want us to see.

As a sop to our disappointments on Bei-ma Shan, we were allowed three hours on the hill north of Napa Hai. After some searching we re-found the *Rhododendron roxieanum* and *R. balfourianum* that we discovered in spring 1992. In all we found fifteen to twenty plants of the former including several hybrids, some with *R. vernicosum*, others with *R. selense* and Roger was able to collect material off all of these. On the opposite side of the road we found some *R. decorum* with rayed blotches (C. 6548), something we had not seen before. In cultivation two seedlings are very vigorous with huge white flowers with no blotch.

There is or was a certain Mr Xuan Ke who must have trapped virtually every western tourist that has been in Lijiang in recent years, especially those that are plant-orientated and likely to have heard of Joseph Rock. Xuan Ke sits by a bridge in the middle of Lijiang and pounces on likely tourists. He lives in a little house occupied by Rock in 1931 and persuades visitors to come along to the house which contains Rock memorabilia including photocopies of Rock's book *The Ancient Na-kha Kingdom of Southwest China* 1947, which he sells. He has another ploy to amuse visitors and take more money off them by asking them along to a bi-nightly concert of Naxi (pronounced Na he) music which he says is dying out through lack of interest from the young. Some of the instruments are said to be hundreds of years old, and many of the musicians could be just as old! The music was rather monotonous.

While it was an enjoyable expedition and we succeeded in finding *Rhododendron proteoides*, and some fine sanguineums, it was a great disappointment not to be able to cross the two passes. A major lesson on a mostly camping expedition is to take ample large polythene bags to hold all clothes and bedding, as most rucksacks, sausage bags, etc. are not fully waterproof.

Below. *The old town of Lijiang, one of the few we have visited that the Chinese authorities are attempting to preserve. It was badly damaged in the earthquake of 1996.*

Chapter 11
'UNEXPLORED TERRITORY':
South Sichuan and East Yunnan 1995

Peter Cox

We were determined to find a 'new' area to go to and we knew that there were some rhododendron species from central-south Sichuan and neighbouring north-east Yunnan that had never been introduced. This was because the major collectors, Forrest, Wilson, Rock and Kingdon Ward, had not been to these parts. There are several possible reasons for this, the most obvious being that the mountains are not very high throughout this region and, therefore, were not considered likely to produce quantities of new, hardy plants. It is, in fact, astonishing that even a short distance east, such as from central-west Yunnan (Cangshan) to north-east Yunnan, affects the altitudes in which plants hardy in most of the UK are found, in this case we would guess a difference of 1,000m/3,300ft.

The hostility of the local minority people, the notorious Yi,[1] may have been a second reason for the major collectors avoiding this region. A third possible reason was the lack of natural vegetation remaining in those areas. Wilson often mentioned the long-term destruction of the natural forest in Sichuan and Hubei and, from our own experience, south-central Sichuan, north-east Yunnan and into north-west Guizhou have only tiny pockets left which, if not within well policed reserves, are disappearing at a most alarming rate, a fact that we mention repeatedly on this expedition in order to emphasise the importance of rescuing many species from extinction before it is too late. Several must have already gone.

Peter had become chairman of the Forestry Commission, so could not spare the time for the whole expedition. As we planned to spend the first half in Sichuan and the second in Yunnan, it was relatively easy for him to join us half way through. It was very nice to have Ted and Romy Millais with us once again as this was to be their last trip to China. We also had David Farnes, 'New Boy' no longer, and his wife Eileen, an alpine plant enthusiast, Dr Meg Weir from the UK and Steve Hootman of the Rhododendron Species Foundation from Washington State, USA.

For the first half we thought we would try the Sichuan Mountaineering Association (SMA) again, whom we had previously used in 1990, and then have the good services of the Kunming Botanical Institute in Yunnan. Mr Luo Dali was in charge, plus the drivers of the three vehicles. We had hoped to spend some time in south-central Sichuan around Leibo, and then move east to beyond Chongqing to Nanchuan and the amazing Jinfo Shan. In the end, permission was refused for Jinfo Shan, which in a way was just as well due to the distance involved.

On our arrival in Kunming, our old friend Guan Kaiyun met us once more, and it was nice to meet Mr Sun (pronounced Soon) Weiban and Dr Yang Zhenhong who would be accompanying us in Yunnan. We then flew on to Chengdu, and met up with Steve who had arrived earlier via Hong Kong. We managed to get away quite early in the morning but were not very happy with the look of the three vehicles, a small ancient hired truck, a 4WD Mitsubishi and the inevitable minibus. Our worries were well founded as all three kept breaking down or/and having punctures, but the drivers (Messrs Gow, Men and Tam) were adept at swapping parts over from one vehicle to another, which seemed to work for a while. The result was constant time-wasting as one

1. The minority are widespread in Yunnan, south Sichuan and into Guizhou. At the time of the early collectors they had a reputation for being brigands and murderers but now they dress well and live in better houses than many other minorities. They evolved an aristocratic society (even their slaves had slaves) and had a religion based on the reading of sacred writings. Nevertheless, one of our camps was raided and several items were stolen.

Above left. A fine Hibiscus radiatus *in south-central Sichuan, native to South East Asia. This is sometimes cultivated as a vegetable or medicinal herb.*

Above. Cliffs on Wumeng Shan, north-east Yunnan, looking up the valley. The large rounded shrubs on the right are Rhododendron sikangense *var.* exquisitum, *which is endemic to Wumeng Shan. Junipers in the foreground.*

vehicle had to keep waiting for another or going back to search. We found out near the end of our time in Sichuan that our truck driver had only been driving for one year.

The great Buddha at Leshan (see page 164) was our first stop and we started by driving up to the top of the cliff, walking down the narrow steps to near river level and then up again. It was quite hair-raising but as Romy had done this previously, I had no way out of it! The best view must still be from a boat. We crossed a low pass to the Dadu river and then had a long climb up a valley to quite a good camp site, as usual by a river.

This area was fairly heavily populated with crops on the hillsides. Many of the Yi women were dressed in their black hats and other finery, the men also with black hats like tam-o'-shanters and cloaks.

On the morning of 20 September I managed to find our first rhododendrons, a few *R. davidsonianum*, but it was some time before we found another. This was either *R. ririei* or *R. ebianense*, alas with no seed. It was a pity that we did not spend longer here as, compared with most of the areas seen later, it still had some decent forest.

Ted Millais, Eileen Farnes and Steve Hootman dwarfed by a Tetrapanax papyrifer, *an important source of fine rice paper. This shrub, used in gardens for its strong ornamental qualities, can create running, suckering thickets in mild climates with little frost.*

Yi men dressed in traditional cloaks in Meigu, south-central Sichuan.

Rhododendron denudatum *flowering in cultivation. This species appears to be closely related to R.* floribundum.

Members of the Yi minority (the pretty girl on the right wearing typical Yi dress).

A deciduous Euonymus *species with fruit not yet opened.*

The Yiziyakou (Chair) pass

We found several species of rhododendron going up the Yiziyakou (Chair) pass: *R. polylepis, R. argyrophyllum, R. augustinii* (CH 7008), *R. pachytrichum, R. decorum, R. rex* subsp. *rex* (CH 7003), one plant of *R. sikangense* (similar to the original *R. cookeanum*), *R. ambiguum* and an unknown Triflora. Other plants found around here were *Sorbus sargentiana* (CH 7002), which has turned out to be a fine form in cultivation, *Gaultheria hookeri* with large rich blue fruit and a small holly. Steve impressed us all with his knowledge of plants in general and his ability to climb trees (and later cliffs).

We found some *Rhododendron racemosum* (CH 7010) and, together with the similar (CH 7037) collected later, these turned out to be quite a distinct form with relatively small,

narrow leaves and uniformly pale flowers, white lightly flushed pink. Ted found one plant which none of us recognized, obviously related to *R. floribundum* but with wider rugulose leaves with floccose light brown indumentum. Later, when we reached Yunnan, Dr Yang said that it was *R. denudatum* (CH 7012). We will go into the quandary over *R. denudatum, R. floribundum* and *R. coeloneuron* later (see the footnote on page 286). We saw several plants that looked similar across the river, into which Steve at once plunged. He returned with a good haul and also found some non-fruiting *R. strigillosum*. Our truck had broken down earlier but, just as we were attempting to make ourselves comfortable in the minibus for the night with no kit, the truck turned up.

Rhododendron rex *subsp*. rex *growing on a tree stump on Daliang Shan where the forest has been all but completely destroyed. It was here that our camp was raided.*

Ilex fargesii *on Daliang Shan. This grew into a shapely columnar small tree.*

Daliang Shan

The river bank proved to be a good one for trees and shrubs, including a large-leaved lime, *Tilia* species (CH 7017), a fine large euonymus, *Cotoneaster atuntzensis* (CH 7020) (newly described) with dark red fruit and some maples. Above the Yi village of Hongxi was a scrubby slope with some pines, hazel, *Rhododendron racemosum* and *R. decorum*. After lunch at the village of Meigu, we drove on to Daliang Shan where we found a Lapponica (CH 7022) in what is very much an outlying area for this subsection. *R. tsaii* occurs a little further south in its type location across the Yangtze and the Sich Expedition of 1988 collected a plant just to the west of here, lying morphologically between *R. tsaii* and the related but larger *R. hippophaeoides*; this Lapponica was obviously the same thing. There was also a very neat *Pieris formosa* with small leaves and a compact habit, its flower buds often being red but seed collected did not germinate.[2]

We camped at 2,700m/9,000ft, having asked permission from the local people. They obviously thought that we had come here for their benefit as they raided our tents in the night. My muesli was stolen, Meg her trainers and most serious, Eileen's boots. We wondered what to do and after a lot of discussion, decided to risk another night. David and Eileen attempted to climb up the hillside above our camp and were chased off, while the rest of us explored the little valley below. Steve and I went together down the stream and found nothing much other than scrub. While sitting having our lunch under a *Rhododenron argyrophyllum*, we heard Ted and Romy calling out to say that they had found some *R. strigillosum* (CH 7035) up to 9m/20ft high. Near the *R. strigillosum* was a 'most desirable holly, *Ilex fargesii* (CH 7036), forming a small pyramidal tree with entire leaves and tight clusters of red fruit. In the densest shade by the stream was what looked at first sight like a bed of strawberry runners but in fact was a primula, *P. moupinensis* [3] (CH 7038). This has proved to be

easy to grow in cultivation in a shady situation, producing myriad runners, and is very pretty with pale lavender-pink flowers.

Gradually making our way back to camp, we found some *Paeonia mairei* (CH 7029), another winner in cultivation, with large long-lasting rich pink flowers. We then walked out into the open where we found three upright plants of *Rhododendron augustinii* (CH 7040), probably all that were left of a one-time substantial population. Both this number and CH 7008 have turned out to be much later flowering than all previously cultivated forms with lavender-pink flowers. They key out into subsp. *chasmanthum*. Nearby was a steep-sided narrow ravine, covered with quantities of *R. rex* (CH 7034), even though there was no shade. All that was left of the forest were a few scattered *Tsuga dumosa* and small *Abies*. Stumps were still there to indicate where the forest had been and, in some cases, *Rhododendron rex* had managed to grow on stumps. We were surprised that this species could still exist up here in full exposure at 2,700m/9,000ft. Another survivor was a large buddleja with white mealy young leaves, only white on the underside when mature, *B. nivea* (CH 7039).

After dark we heard ominous whistles around the neighbourhood and sure enough the locals visited us again. I kept awake for most of the night and thought they had gone. With hindsight, I had been very stupid to leave my sausage bag under my flysheet, even though the guys were pulled taut. In the morning I was horrified to find the bag gone. David shouted that it was lying on the bonnet of the truck and it was a great relief to find that not that much had been taken, only a towel, a pair of stockings and presents for our staff (tartan scarves).

2. This *Pieris* was found again in June 2007 and had very fine red young foliage. One seed germinated at second sowing in 1997.

3. Richards is now calling this *Primula hoffmanniana*, described by W. W. Smith in 1926.

A truck loaded with walking sticks made from the bamboo Qiongzhuea tumidinoda.

Leibo and Jin Pin Shan

After driving back to the main road we passed down a long valley, through a slightly moister area and stopped, purely by chance, where there were a few nice plants of *Rhododendron denudatum*. Eventually we drove down to the muddy Yangtze, down river a few miles and then a short way up to the small town of Leibo, built on a hill and consisting mostly of the usual modern buildings.

The 4WD and the truck had failed to turn up, so four of us (Ted, Romy, Meg and I) had a reception with local dignitaries and later ate a good meal without the others. Our 'hotel' was average with a bathroom with nothing that worked. Our plan was to spend another night in Leibo, drive a short way out of town, then walk some 2km/3 miles to where there were reputed to be 'several' rhododendrons. A short but rough drive took us well up the hill, past an artificial lake, to near a small hydroelectric station. We were allocated a guide, Mr Wan, who had the usual gym shoes and a polythene lunch bag. A short steep walk took us round and between some small but sheer karst peaks and then we walked some distance along the aqueduct, heading for larger karst mountains. After crossing the stream, the path gradually became steeper and steeper. The day was extremely hot and tiring and gradually members of our party dropped out, first Eileen (with no decent footwear) and David, then Meg and eventually Ted and Romy, but not before the first rhododendron appeared, *R. lutescens*, sticking out of a 'weed' jungle of bamboo, *Qiongzhuea tumidinoda*,[4] and *Rubus*, with a few constantly chopped hydrangeas, aralias, roses, and so on.

Suddenly, things started to get interesting: first some small shrubs and trees, sometimes chopped, including *Ilex pernyi*, *Magnolia sargentiana*, *Cornus kousa* var. *chinensis*, *Clethra* species and a *Cimicifuga* species and then several rhododendrons. Steve and I were in one of the most exciting

places either of us had ever seen and at one stage we were discovering something different with virtually every glance. All this excitement, and having eaten half our lunch, gave us a burst of much-needed energy to explore. This amazing gorge between two large karst[5] peaks that towered above us was covered in vegetation. The mountain is called Jin Pin, and what treasures there must be up there! The defile was full of huge blocks of rock that had obviously fallen off the peaks over the years.

The first rhododendron we found was a small-leaved *R. argyrophyllum* (CH 7044) with pure white indumentum, followed by *R. strigillosum* (CH 7047), *R. asterochnoum* aff. CH 7051) (similar to *R. calophytum* with varying amounts of indumentum), *R. concinnum* aff. (CH 7053) with small leaves, *R. huianum* (CH 7049) (*R. huanum* in the new *Flora of China*) with a glaucous leaf underside and a large cupular calyx, and a curious plant that may have been the commonest rhododendron here (CH 7050) with almost round leaves and round buds which invariably grew at right angles out of the sides of the rocks and cliffs. Subsequently, after consulting David Chamberlain, we came to the conclusion that this was a natural hybrid that might be undergoing the process of speciation. One small plant was of exceptional interest, its closest possible relative being *R. insigne*, with a wide rugose leaf with shiny plastered indumentum. Steve then found the best of all, *R. ochraceum* (CH 7052), which is related to *R. pachytrichum* and *R. strigillosum* but smaller in all parts and has an indumentum

4. *Qiongzhuea tumidinoda*, first described in 1980, is native to the Leibo area of south-central Sichuan (see *Travels in China* by Roy Lancaster, p. 89.) We saw a truck loaded high with walking sticks made from this bamboo, which are transported to Emei Shan where they are sold to tourists.

5. A karst region is one with limestone rock, in this case with sharp pointed peaks.

Jin Pin Shan to the north of Leibo. At the foot of one of these peaks Steve Hootman and I made our most exciting finds.

on the leaf underside. It was always growing upright on the top of rocks, with seed capsules already dehiscing. The last rhododendrons were single seedlings of *R. rex* and *R. orbiculare*.

In the shade amongst the rock blocks were small plants, again often of exceptional interest. We found more *Primula moupinensis*, plus another primula with much longer leaves and with thick runners (thin in *P. moupinensis*), which disappointingly proved to be only *P. pseudodenticulata* (CH 7060), and the *Shortia* relative, *Berneuxia thibetica* (CH 7061).

It is amazing to think that the heat and steepness nearly defeated Steve – and me too. So often the best plant hunting days require that extra bit of effort and this was a perfect example. Great care was needed to avoid falling, Steve fell once on to his thumb and I nearly fell twice. It took us two hours to get back to the vehicles where bottles of the best *piju* we had ever tasted awaited us. We were determined to go back if at all possible and we thanked the mayor of Leibo and his foreign affairs adviser for suggesting a place we would never have found on our own.

Alas, even this area was threatened, with branches of plants hacked off right in amongst the rocks. The valley below the peaks was heavily populated and the shortage of firewood was obvious. Surely it would be possible to plant quick-growing trees like eucalyptus to use for firewood? We advised the mayor of the need for conservation and he told us the cutting of trees is forbidden but little there could be classed as trees anyway.

The plan was to drive inland away from the Yangtze, which here was very muddy and steep sided with little or no habitation in sight. The local forestry department had obviously been ill advised on what to plant as we found larch growing poorly up to about 3m/10ft and then falling over. This was so obviously not conifer territory, the soil being heavy and sticky clay.[6]

We were taken up a terrible road to a logging station, Shuang He, with wooden buildings and, as all the rooms were apparently full, the occupants had to be moved out to make way for us. Our drivers did well to get us there and we could not blame them for getting drunk that night. The meal they gave us was astonishingly good with some excellent meat. The rats kindly kept to the rafters above our heads. The manager of the station turned out to be the brother of our mayor, so here was a case of Chinese nepotism if ever there was one.

The morning was dry so we walked up the continuation of the road up the mountain, getting a lift around a few bends on the back of a truck to where the road levelled out. This road through one of the few remaining areas of broad-leaved temperate forest had been there for five years and, although cutting the trees had not been done that quickly, it is presumably all doomed in time.[7] While some parts had been clear felled there were signs that below the road the davidias[8] had been left and some were rejuvenating from the trunks. We managed to find very few fruits of *Davidia* (CH 7057) and I was allocated two. To my great surprise, two seedlings grew from one and no less

Rhododendron ochraceum *flowering for the first time in cultivation at Glendoick in 2001. This was our best find at Jin Pin Shan.*

than five from the other. The large pinkish marrow-shaped fruit of *Rehderodendron macrocarpum* (CH 7056) were a different matter, seemingly impossible to divide without destroying the embryos, and only one germinated. After the wet night, earthworms 60cm/2ft long had come out on to the road and then we saw a huge toad and a land crab. There were quite a few birds in the forest and Meg thought she saw some hornbills.

The elevation was rather low for many rhododendrons, being only 1,700m/5,500ft, but we found three species, first what we took to be *R. calophytum* var. *openshawianum* (CH 7055), which made a large plant but the leaves were much smaller than var. *calophytum* and with only around nine flowers per truss. The second species was *R. lutescens* once again. The third was new to us, *R. longipes* var. *longipes*, which was quite compact with pale brown indumentum, but although there were flower buds, there were no capsules. A thorough search failed to locate any more plants. From the road and surrounding forest we could see the hills rising only a further 200-300m/660-1,000ft at the most and the undergrowth was too dense and the hills too steep for us to go far off the road.

On the way back to Leibo we had a look at the suitability of the Shanlenggang pass for camping the next day and it looked quite promising. On arriving back at Leibo, the news was that Mr Men's wife was very ill so he would have to leave first thing in the morning for the two-day journey back to Chengdu and would require the minibus. Steve and I took the opportunity to return to Jin Pin Shan while the others went to the proposed camp area seen the day before.

Steve and I were up at 6 and left with Mr Men at 7 o'clock. He was then to pick up the others in Leibo and drop them off at the pass on his way to Chengdu. It was a dull, humid morning with a few drops of drizzle, quite different from the sun and heat of our previous exploration of Jin Pin Shan. We started a thorough search from the lower rhododendrons upwards and failed to find any more of the *R. insigne* relative or *R. orbiculare* but did find two more *R. rex*. The commonest species here were *R. asterochnoum*, *R. argyrophyllum*, *R. strigillosum* and *R. huianum*

We did find two more clumps of *R. ochraceum* on rocks with the biggest growing to 3m/10ft. Steve's climbing abilities came into great use and we were satisfied that we had a good collection of *R. ochraceum* seed. This has so far done well in cultivation with splendid ball-shaped trusses of scarlet flowers but there was a percentage of natural hybrids, apparently all with *R. strigillosum*. As far as we know, we were the first to distribute both *R. ochraceum* and *R. huianum*. The growth of the former is late, so not vulnerable to spring frosts.[9] We also found a tiny creeping gooseberry, *Ribes davidii* (CH 7068), which, although remaining dwarf, is not staying prostrate in cultivation.

Steve made the mistake of carrying on too far down the hill in his endeavours to find more and had to come back to the path up an almost perpendicular slope, fighting his way through thorny climbers that attempted to hold him fast. Eventually he emerged, covered in scratches. I had a fall and thought I might need stitches but the wound was shallow. The steep path had been quite bad enough but if it had rained our descent would have been a nightmare. Despite the care we had to take in descending, we made good time and had to wait for twenty minutes for our transport, with an audience including three dogs. We had not expected to find much new on our second visit to Jin Pin Shan but it was worth going to consolidate our collections.[10] The others did not have a great day, having found nothing new.

A giant earthworm on the track through the Shuang forest.

6. They should have been planting native broad-leaved trees like *Juglans*, *Davidia*, *Tetracentron* and *Rehderodendron*, all of which we had seen in this area.

7. When we found out that most of the trees were *Davidia*, *Rehderodendron* and *Tetracentron*, at least two of which are on the Chinese special protection list, what hope is there for anything? Perhaps the no felling ultimatum issued for the province of Sichuan after the floods of 1998 may have saved at least a part of this forest.

8. I asked about the preservation of the davidias and they said they were leaving them, but this would be their answer anyway.

9. Peter Wharton got a few seeds of *R. ochraceum* in north-west Guizhou in 1994, the first to be collected, and the two seedlings grown from these are more compact and hairy than our own but with darker red flowers in more open topped trusses.

10. During the day we saw a pheasant, like our British one but with a shorter tail, a hoopoe, lots of small birds and we thought that we heard a troop of monkeys on the peak we passed on the way back.

The last tree of Magnolia sargentiana *var.* robusta *near Yongshan in north-east Yunnan. We were proudly shown this tree by the local dignitaries.*

Shanlenggang pass

A suitable campsite near the pass turned out to be too close to a Yi settlement, so we camped lower down near the road, planning to spend just one night here and then return to Leibo for our last night in Sichuan. The area was roughly to the west of Jin Pin but slightly lower in elevation, being around 2,300m/7,500ft at the highest point. The plants were a mixture of the two last places, Jin Pin and Shuang He, but it had all been horribly cut over with no more than remnants of what must have been beautiful forest. Steve soon found several *Rhododendron longipes* (CH 7072) with plenty of capsules, which now completed good collections of our major rhododendron species that we were hoping for in this area. There was also more *R. huianum* and some *R. calophytum*. We had crowds of friendly Yi around our camp in the evening, but we took all possible precautions to avoid more losses.

In the morning we split into two parties, Steve, David and Eileen going lower and the rest of us higher, above the Shanlenggang pass. The only rhododendron our party collected was *R. huianum* (CH 7073), which had much more pronounced calyx lobes than our Jin Pin collection. But we found a bonanza of trees and shrubs including more *Rehderodendron*, *Magnolia sargentiana* var. *robusta* (from which only one seed could be found which did not germinate), two *Acer*, *Styrax*, *Viburnum cylindricum*, *V. longiradiatum*, *Enkianthus*, *Symplocus*, *Juglans* and a *Celastrus* with bright yellow fruit. The other party found *Rhododendron coeloneuron* but not much else and returned early.[11]

Near the end of our party's wanderings Meg, who had been in the lead, was very upset suddenly to discover that her legs were covered with leeches, sixteen on one leg, eight on the other. Ted and Romy had a few, while I, having been mostly at the back, had none. I had taken the precaution of wearing leggings in addition to stockings and socks and there is no doubt that a leader is the person most likely to suffer, not that I had kept to the back intentionally!

Yet again, the mayor and his sidekick accompanied us, plus the latter's son. After driving some way down the Yangtze, we came to a very new-looking suspension bridge, which, much to our surprise, we were allowed to photograph. Before leaving for China, we had had much correspondence concerning the whereabouts of a bridge along this stretch of the river as they seemed to be very few and far between. Heaven knows how far in either direction we would have had to have gone if this one had not been built. We had noticed that the Yangtze has very few tributaries entering it on this stretch, hence the few suitable valleys for roads.

Crossing into North-east Yunnan

The Yongshan rendezvous was not far from the bridge and we got there just after 1 o'clock but Peter and the others from Kunming had not arrived. They turned up at 3 o'clock, having been held up by major road works and bad roads, so it had taken them two and a half days from Kunming. Sun Weiban, an expert on Magnoliaceae, was leading the party, accompanied by Dr Yang, a botanist from Kunming. At last we were able to get rid of the hangers on and say goodbye and thank you to Mr Luo Dali, Mr Gow and Mr Tam, who had really done as well as they could, considering the poor vehicles. Even new tyres might have been punctured on those rough roads.

No sooner were we out of the clutches of one set of local

---

11 There is little doubt from our observations on this trip and on seedlings in cultivation that *Rhododendron floribundum*, *R. denudatum* and *R. coeloneuron* are closely related, despite the last having been placed in subsection Taliensia. What we collected here at Shanlenggang and later in Yunnan seem to be the same as Peter Wharton collected in north-west Guizhou and Edward Needham collected on Jinfo Shan in south-east Sichuan. All three species would be better placed together in subsection Argyrophylla and possibly *R. denudatum* should be sunk into *R. floribundum*.

dignitaries than we were into the hands of County Magistrate Wang and his acolytes. They had everything planned for us for the next day, so we just had to go along with it. We had already emphasized that we wished to get as high as possible, but we were soon to realize that in north-east Yunnan this does not necessarily mean good plants or even any wild plants at all.

We were able to lay out our seeds to dry in the Yongshan hotel as we had permission to collect from Kunming and the Sichuan people had obviously accepted that we were collecting, probably because they knew we would be leaving the country from Yunnan and not Sichuan.

Our first stop was of some interest with a large quantity of *Rhododendron simsii*, one with a large red flower, and a few *R. spinuliferum*, well outside its recorded distribution. The second stop was much longer and a disaster plant-wise. There was more *R. simsii* which the local dignitaries kept on pointing out to us until we could have thrown them in the bushes. We walked on miles of slippery mud paths (made worse by rain and pulling out timber) and even a camellia just turned out to be a tea bush! The only other rhododendron was *R. racemosum* – just a few small plants. The third stop was on an absolutely bare tree-less waste of a mountain of 3,000m/10,000ft, admittedly the highest in Yongshan County. Higher still we went for a walk. Peter went one way, finding *Ilex pernyi*, possibly the only worthwhile plant of the day, with a *Sarcococca* species and *Ligustrum compactum*, plus the ubiquitous *Rhododendron lutescens*. The rest of us went another way, finding *R. polylepis*. All that could be said for these was that they were new records for us as no western collectors had been here before. A dismal day at least ended with an excellent banquet.

Yiliang, Xiaocoaba and beyond

On 4 October we planned to do a long drive to Yiliang. Everything and everyone fitted into the 'new' minibus from Kunming, with the back row of seats removed for luggage. We spent most of the day driving up and down spectacular gorges with very few stops, perhaps missing some rhododendrons at the top of one pass. We did see some very large lilies and managed to find six enormous capsules and bulbils in the axils of the leaves. It has now flowered in cultivation and is *Lilium sargentiae* (CH 7099) in an excellent form. To our dismay, we found that some of our Yongshan officials had been following us and would no doubt pass us on to their opposite numbers in Yiliang.

We had another good banquet with the Yiliang officials, including local spirit made out of orchid roots. After dinner, instead of cleaning seeds, Meg, Steve and we two Peters went out on the town and found a night club with an entry of '2 yuan, which was quite amusing with couples doing a sort of waltz shuffle to very slow music. Peter and I left before the other two, leaving Meg circulating with our driver, and we noticed that we were being followed back. We were getting into bed as our door opened

A small gorge in the Xiaocaoba Forest Reserve as the mist descended.

and in came our floor lady, keys jangling, with a girl whom she indicated was her daughter. She looked no more than 13 or 14. She was obviously being offered to us or rather to Peter who must have looked the sexier of us two! The girl looked amazingly cheerful at the idea but we were not so keen and eventually we got it over that we did not want her. Shortly after, a man came in, presumably to check on what had happened. He said he was from Beijing (in English) and asked if we were tourists and then left. Under our mosquito nets, we pondered on the meaning of all this.

We then set off for Xiaocaoba which is to the fore in *Rhododendrons of China* Vol. 2 as a place to see rhododendrons. First stop was to see *R. irroratum* Ningyuenense Group (CH 7100) which has fine creamy yellow flowers. This made nice neat bushes but it may be tender as the elevation was only 1,900m/6,200ft. Other interesting plants here were an azalea, probably *Rhododendron microphyton*, some *R. yunnanense*, an *Indigofera*, and *Euscaphis japonica* (CH 7103), an attractive

Euscaphis japonica in Xiaocaoba Forest Reserve. This curious Staphyleaceae deciduous shrub has so far survived well on a sheltered wall at Glendoick but has not flowered.

deciduous shrub with scarlet fruit containing black seeds, and a *Cotoneaster* species, probably the newly described *C. leveillei*.

Most of the area between Yiliang, Xiaocaoba and beyond was covered with little conical karst hills, the less steep often cultivated well up their slopes. We stopped at a picturesque village with thatched cottages but, overall, there was terrible pressure from the local population on any natural vegetation. Our lunch stop was one of the most degraded places we had ever seen, with over grazing and hacking. *Rhododendron calophytum* (CH 7116), *R. strigillosum* (CH 7108) and *R. huianum* were there. We then moved on up a very rough forest track into the so-called Xiaocaoba Forest Reserve. This was better forested with dense shrubs and small trees. Dr Yang had been here before but he had difficulties in finding the best places.[12] We did find a very fine *Sorbus* (CH 7122) with large panicles of smallish bright red fruit and up to only nine large pairs of leaflets. There have been various efforts to identify this, starting with *S. harrowiana*, which it obviously was not, then *S. sargentiana*, but Hugh McAllister's latest thoughts are *S. wilsoniana*. It is growing well in cultivation and looks promising, with colouring leaves that shed late. We found more *Rhododendron coeloneuron* (CH 7118) but not as good-looking as that of Shanlenggang, possible *R. longipes* var. *chienianum* (CH 7126A) with silvery-grey

indumentum, though this may just be *R. argyrophyllum*, and plentiful *R. lutescens* (CH 7124) which has so far proved to be more compact than usual in cultivation.

We went back to Xiaocaoba Forest Reserve the next day and this time picked up a guide who apparently had been here before with Dr Yang. It started fairly clear but mist and drizzle set in, so photographs were impossible and plants hard to see. The minibus stopped beyond the previous day's place and we walked on past dripping cliffs and waterfalls. We found two immature, non-flowering *Rhododendron ochraceum* on the roadside and a few *R. huianum*. Dr Yang said that there had been many large specimens of *R. huianum* below the road so they must have been chopped, all we could find there being *R. strigillosum*. After a while Dr Yang said that there were no plants further on so we turned back. He also mentioned that *R. ochraceum* was extremely rare, with possibly only around 500 plants in existence. Steve crossed the river and disappeared for ages up the vegetation-covered cliff, which appeared through the gloom to be the same as that illustrated in *Rhododendrons of China* Vol. 2. He did find some small *R. ochraceum* (CH 7126B) but, alas, could find none in fruit. He also found *R. moupinense* aff., this form later being introduced by Alan Clark from here. It has proved to be an inferior form with small off-white flowers. Steve also made a very surprising find, a dwarf Maddenia with hairy leaves and funnel-shaped scented flowers which should prove to be reasonably hardy. It is almost certainly an undescribed species.

There were many other plants of interest along the cliffs and roadside including a *Paris* with brilliant red fruit, *Corylopsis*, *Fagus*, *Carpinus*, *Hydrangea*, *Berneuxia*, *Parnassia petitmenginii* and apparently the same *Primula pseudodenticulata* as Steve and I had found at Jin Pin Shan. There were also some immature *Davidia* and *Magnolia*, probably not *M. sargentiana* var. *robusta*. We had a packing, pressing and cleaning seed session before bed.

Paris polyphylla in fruit in Xiaocaoba Forest Reserve.

12. In *Rhododendrons of China* Volume 2, pages 30-33 show magnificent *R. ochraceum* in flower at Yiliang which we took to mean Xiaocaoba, but we did not have time that day to investigate further along the road.

A three-hour hold-up on the way to Wumeng Shan.

David Farnes emerging from wading a river. Some of us were given a piggyback by a local man.

The road to Qiaojia

Our plan was to drive the short distance from Yiliang to Zhaotong and then make the longer drive to Qiaojia near the Yangtze, where there is an isolated peak of 3,400m/11,000ft that is known to have several rhododendrons and is the type location of the Lapponica *R. tsaii*.

Soon after leaving Yiliang the road climbed up to 2,800m/9,200ft on a hilly landscape pitted with small coalmines and spoil heaps, which probably prevented it from being farmed. We suddenly saw a rhododendron with large leaves and at first sight I thought it was perhaps a queer form of *R. calophytum* but, once we had seen it properly, we realized it was something we had not seen before. Dr Yang at once said it was *R. glanduliferum* (CH 7131) in a new location (he had previously found it on two sites further east in north-east Yunnan). We had slipped up completely and did not even have it on our possibilities list. It and its neighbours had all been cut over so there were no specimens more than around 1.8m/6ft high. The large leaves were glaucous below and there were five to seven large capsules per truss. A local coalmine worker said

that the flowers were white and scented, as would be expected. This was a great find and an exciting new introduction, and seedlings are doing well in cultivation with huge leaves. The only one that has flowered to date at Glendoick has fine pale pink fading to white scented flowers in July.

Peter found a smaller-leaved rhododendron here and moving on, we found many more of the same species, in fact the largest population of rhododendrons we had seen so far in north-east Yunnan. This new find, while obviously a member of subsection Fortunea (CH 7132), was a puzzle as it had almost round leaves, looking closer to *R. wardii* at first sight. Ted and I then decided on *R. vernicosum* but, to our surprise, Dr Yang said it was not *R. vernicosum*. As these were all cut over bushes too, they had not been flowering much and it took us a long time to find any capsules. Seedlings flowered very young in cultivation, which was strange, as those in the wild, though up to 1.5m/5ft tall, were so shy flowering. As soon as we saw the flowers in cultivation, we knew it had to be *R. decorum*, and as it retains the ability to flower very young from seed, it is a really good introduction. The *Flora of China* indicates that this should not be called *R. decorum* subsp. *cordatum* as the petioles are too long. Two other rhododendrons here were small plants of *R. calophytum* and *R. coeloeuron*. Alan Clark's party, who passed this way later that autumn, said that they found *R. insigne* here (no capsules) but we have seen no foliage to give us a chance to confirm this. It could be the same plant of which Steve and I found one seedling at Jin Pin Shan.

Accidents and mudslides

That night we stayed in Zhaotong but then, after various road hazards that culminated in a serious mud slide, we gave up on Qiaojia. Instead we left for a 3,000m/10,000ft peak to the west of Zhaotong, but hold ups and dead ends continued to thwart us. Once we tried to get round a truck stuck in porridge-like mud in the middle of the road by driving into a field, only to get bogged down ourselves. A common flat-bed truck hauled us

An under-wear stall in a village in East Yunnan.

out in no time (for a fee). We tried to find any high ground with natural vegetation but without much success. Fields of potatoes are now planted up to 3,000m/10,000ft on any ground that is level enough for cultivation. One place looked promising but we ran out of time, having just found some of the common rhododendrons for this area, as well as *Clerodendrum trichotomum* with pale maroon sepals enclosing blue-black oval fruit, a *Cephalotaxus* species, a pretty pink gentian, G. *rhodantha*, and the ubiquitous *Incarvillea arguta* (CH 7147) at a surprisingly high altitude

By now it was 10 October and everyone except Steve and I had to leave for home on the 15th, so we had to get on to Wumeng Shan as soon as possible. Another hold-up delayed us for three hours. Some 30m/100ft below us a lorry lay on its side in a ravine. Beside it was a small makeshift tent which contained the driver, alive or dead we never learned. Another truck was skewed across the road and leaned drunkenly from a broken axle. Some queue barging helped us forward but there was nobody in authority to take charge and get things sorted out. Three policemen in a car were totally useless but eventually a fat man attempted to take charge and some grit and other rough stuff was added and things eventually got moving. A lady in red with high heels decided that this state of affairs might be lucrative and took bribes for allowing vehicles to the front of the queue!

As we travelled south there were more of the tree-clad hillsides that were totally absent in far north-east Yunnan. We noticed that a well wooded hill would often be right next to one that was completely bare, even though the topography was the same. It would seem that some villages are conservation minded while others are hell-bent on burning everything. There are huge areas which are nothing more than very poor grazing, which could be utilized for tree planting, either for long-term timber or short-term firewood production.

Wumeng Shan

We had a substantial lunch including *piju* in the next village, where we were warned that the road ahead had two breaks. We thought to hell with it, we have nothing more to lose if we are completely stuck once more, but the road proved to be excellent and led right up to a shoulder in the mountain at 3,150m/10,400ft in good time. To our great surprise, ponies were gathered in record time and we were told that we were setting off up the mountain immediately. This would have been fine if we had not just eaten a large lunch and not been virtually immobilized sitting in the bus for most of the last two weeks. So we were all totally unfit for a substantial climb. David and Eileen decided to camp at the road end and amuse themselves round about while the rest of us started off. Some of us were horrified that several ponies had saddles so were waiting to transport us up the mountain. We did not know one end of a horse from another and were nervous of both ends! Ted and Romy rode most of the way, while I rode for a while and then got off. Poor Dr Yang was seen to slowly fall off his pony in a circular motion as the girth slipped. Even Steve, the youngest of us by far, admitted that he felt almost as though he had a heart attack after walking the whole way.

Wumeng Shan is known for its special forms and varieties of well-known species and the first rhododendron we came upon was *R. heliolepis* var. *fumidum*, which seems to lie taxonomically between *R. heliolepis* and *R. rubiginosum*, then *R. sikangense* var. *exquisitum* in a heavily grazed area. Eventually we reached a rough stone path just as it was getting dark, and out there it gets dark quickly. We were told it was 100 yards to our destination, but it seemed ten times as far and the darkness intensified as we plunged into forest of *Abies georgei*. Peter and Meg pushed on as fast as they could to send help back with a torch, but then Steve produced no less than two torches out of

A Leontopodium *species in north-east Yunnan. Most species of edelweiss are found in south-east Asia and are seldom cultivated.*

Cliffs on Wumeng Shan, looking down the valley.

his rucksack. I looked after Romy as well as I could, while Steve took charge of Ted, a valiant warrior of 78 and finding the going difficult in the dark and at 3,400m/11,000ft. There were quite a few tumbles along the way.

The camp proved to be a group of chalets surrounded by rhododendrons at 3,750m/12,200ft. Steve and I shared a hut. By the time we ate it was very late and extremely cold, and I was right off my food, which was a shame as they had produced a very good and large meal. Both Peter and I took Stematil and we felt a little better in the morning. A misty start soon cleared to give us a lovely day for once. The plan was to stay around camp before having an early lunch, and then whoever wanted to could make for the top. We were told that the real peak of Wumeng Shan was some way off and had to be approached by a different route and involved several days climbing and camping. The part we were on was called Jiao Zi Shan, meaning Sedan Chair Mountain, from its shape. Facing the camp was a semi-circular cliff that looked impregnable but there was a narrow cleft running up it at an angle which proved to be steep but not difficult.

If we had not been told what we should find by Alan Clark who was there in 1994, we should have been utterly astonished with the rhododendrons growing on Wumeng Shan. In addition to the two species already mentioned, *R. sikangense* var. *exquisitum* (CH 7166) and *R. heliolepis* var. *fumidum* (CH 7165), there was *R.*

There is one way up these cliffs – through this cleft.

Dr Meg Weir with a very vigorous form of Rhododendron lacteum, *which occurs in quantity on Wumeng Shan.*

We were lucky to find one plant of Primula faberi *in flower on the meadow above the cleft.*

lacteum (CH 7164), *R. sphaeroblastum* var. *wumengense* (CH 7157) and *R. bureavii* (CH 7158). When the overall distribution of these five species is looked into excluding the varieties, other locations for them are scattered in all directions. They are all at least 225km/140 miles away and only *R. lacteum* and *R. heliolepis* are found growing together elsewhere, in this instance on Cangshan in west Yunnan. This is the sort of case which makes study of the distribution of plants so enthralling.

On Wumeng Shan *Rhododendron sikangense* var. *exquisitum* makes a huge bush, often wider than high. Its leaves are wider than the population at Muli, south-west Sichuan, and much wider than the Erlang Shan population in central-west Sichuan. The flowers are white with a red blotch on Wumeng Shan. *R. heliolepis* var. *fumidum* has purplish-red flowers. *R. lacteum* is more vigorous with larger leaves on Wumeng Shan than the Cangshan plants but is just as susceptible to root rots in cultivation. We were careful to select seed from only the best plant populations. Of all the species *R. bureavii* was the most typical of its kind, but even then most seedlings have been disappointing in cultivation. *R. sphaeroblastum* var. *wumengense* is a fine foliage plant with the young leaves often glaucous and Steve who revisited here in spring 2005 says the flowers are a very attractive pink. Most of these species are inclined to grow mixed together on Wumeng Shan, resulting in numerous natural hybrids, including many *R. sikangense* x *R. bureavii*.

Around the camp growing in the shade of the firs and rhododendrons were several other interesting plants. There were two gentians, one with blue flowers, probably an annual, another clump-forming with dense flower heads, the flowers hardly opening, even in the sun. The evergreen *Berneuxia tibetica* carpeted moss-covered ground in dense shade while

Meg admiring thickets of Rhododendron sphaeroblastum *var.* wumengense. *It is endemic to Wumeng Shan, on the plateau.*

more in the open was *Cremanthodium campanulatum* (CH 7156) with pendulous yellow composite flowers.

Meg, Steve and we two Peters plus Dr Yang, Sen and a guide set off for the higher reaches of the mountain, crossing a stream, up the cleft and out on to a plateau with wet meadows, tarns and rhododendron-covered banks. Just beyond the cleft was a meadow with primulas. *P. moupinensis* occurred in patches in shade, while a Muscarioides species was widely scattered in the open. Then we found another primula with foliage very like *P. amethystina* and luckily Peter found one in flower, which, to our surprise was yellow with tubular flowers. Consulting our reference books at home soon revealed this to be *P. faberi* (CH 7162).[13] A fourth primula was a small Nivalid.

We climbed up the bank above the meadow to the right where *Rhododendron fastigiatum* (CH 7159) was common, a few flowers showing the usual range of shades of blue-purple found

13. This member of the section Amethystina has so far proved not that difficult in cultivation, flowering over a long period into autumn, and has set good seed. It is also found on Emei Shan in Sichuan.

A good form of Gentiana arethusae *was plentiful on the Wumeng Shan plateau.*

on Cangshan. Some selected seedlings have outstanding glaucous foliage. The common Hymenanthes species up here was *R. sphaeroblastum* var. *wumengense*. The other two 'species' recorded high up on Wumeng Shan are *R. pubicostatum* and *R. montiganum*, both of which are almost certainly hybrids. Alan Clark found a small population of *R. campylogynum* up here which looks similar to the Cangshan plant. A lovely dwarf clump-forming gentian, *G. arethusae* (CH 7160), with erect dark to light blue flowers with darker striae on the outside, was common on the plateau. It is undoubtedly closely related to *G. sino-ornata* and may be a form of that species.

There was a small peak at the top of Jiao Zi Shan which we did not have time to climb but, as it was only a little higher than the plateau, it is doubtful if it would have yielded anything new. We reached just below 4,000m/13,000ft and were shortly able to descend by a different route, which was easier and less steep than the cleft. On our way down was a very fine stand of *Rhododendron lacteum* but it was infected by gall fungus on the leaf undersides. Some of the galls were large

white ones but there was another type forming almost round knobs, which might have been caused by some gall-forming insect. We returned to the huts in good spirits having had a very good day and excellent weather.

After a cool night we had a clear morning without a cloud in the sky. We became split up on our descent back to the bus. Steve, Peter and I all managed separately to take a wrong path and got on to a ridge south of where we should have been. We ended by having a climb to get back to the road ending. This meant that we missed the chance to find another rhododendron reported by Alan Clark which I was sure I had seen in the distance on the way up. This was a big-leaved species which was reported to Alan by local inhabitants to have yellow flowers, but seedlings of this from Alan's collecting look like typical *R. rex* subsp. *rex*, thus extending its known range quite a long way south. Just below the car park was a group of *R. arboreum* subsp. *delavayi* (CH 7178) which should be reasonably hardy from 3,150m/10,400ft. Seedlings produced their first excellent scarlet flowers in 2005.

Our group before we broke up and went our own ways. Left to right: Sun Weibang, Yang Zhenhong, from the Kunming Botanical Institute (both accompanied us in north-east Yunnan), Eileen Farnes, a Chinese lady, Ted Millais, Peter, Romy Millais, David Farnes (at front), myself, Meg Weir, driver Wen Lee and Steve Hootman.

Rhododendron sinofalconeri in *fruit on Lao Jing Shan. This has cream to yellow flowers to rival* R. macabeanum.

The distinct Rhododendron valentinianum *var.* oblongilobatum aff. *(CH 7186) was a good find on Lao Jing Shan, near Wenshan.*

Lao Jing Shan

While the others flew home from Kunming, Steve and I stayed on for a short trip down to south-east Yunnan, quite near the border with Vietnam, especially to find *Rhododendron sinofalconeri* but not until we had been to the Golden Temple which none of us had seen before. The temple itself was surrounded by an extensive stand of *Cunninghamia* and *Keteleeria evelyniana* forest and there were various gardens which Dr Yang advised on. The Camellia Garden was very shady but the sun here was obviously strong enough to ripen the growth and form flower buds. There were several greenhouses full of ferns, begonias, house plants, palms and so on, and then we visited the 'Azalea' Garden with *Rhododendron*

pachypodum, *R. excellens* (CH 7180), *R. molle* subsp. *molle* (CH 7181) and best of all, *R. vialii* (CH 7182) with lots of capsules. The last must have been too immature as only one seed germinated for me. This red-flowered member of section Azaleastrum comes from low elevations in south and central Yunnan and flowers early. We are attempting it outside at Glendoick on a sheltered wall. We also saw plants of *R. hancockii*, *R. protistum*, *R. sinofalconeri*, *R. maddenii* subsp. *crassum* and a queer relative of *R. valentinianum*, probably the same as Steve and I were to see later.

On our journey south, we passed through some karst country with limestone pavements and pinnacles, some with rocks on top of rocks, like a small-scale Stone Forest. Later there were miniature karst peaks, some rising straight out of a flat plain. We stayed at Wenshan, a sizeable prefecture town. Efforts to buy some ethnic crafts came to nothing, presumably because this was not a tourist area.

In the morning we were off westwards to Lao Jing Shan just after 8 o'clock. A metalled road changed to dirt, then finally became a forestry / military road which was exceptionally bad in parts, right to the top of the peak where there was a military outpost. Sun became extremely nervous and we drove back down a little before searching for plants. Most of the forest near the road had been cut over but away from the road there was still some virgin broad-leaved evergreen forest. This area had or was about to become a reserve, so perhaps the rest can be saved. Dr Yang said that there had been larger specimens of *Rhododendron sinofalconeri* (CH 7183) but what we found were very healthy, despite being in full sun, and there were plenty of seedlings. The foliage, while being bold and handsome, is not as impressive as *R. falconeri*, but the yellow flowers of some may rival *R. macabeanum*.[14]

Dr Yang told us that we would find the *R. valentinianum* aff. that we saw in the temple garden and sure enough it was growing there in some quantity, both on steep banks and as an epiphyte on large broad-leaved trees where they still existed. Steve and I reckon that this plant may warrant specific status, being much bigger in all its parts than the long cultivated *R. valentinianum* from the Shweli-Salween divide. In cultivation it is much later flowering with generally an upright habit and is so far doing well outside. We were calling it var. *oblongilobatum* (CH 7186) but David Chamberlain says it is not but should be given a new subspecific status.

Rhododendron valentinianum *var.* oblongilobatum *at the Rhododendron Species Foundation, Washington State, USA.*

The third rhododendron we found was obviously an Irrorata which Dr Yang was calling *R. irroratum* itself. Despite its narrower leaves, the flowers are quite typical of this species.

The fourth species was clearly a member of subsection Fortunea and looked to us closest to *Rhododendron hemsleyanum*, which is known only away to the north on Emei Shan. Similar wavy-edged leaves are less wide than in *R. hemsleyanum*, the habit is more upright and it is exceedingly vigorous. The scented flowers are white with no blotch. We failed to find any capsules but the Chinese, who were ahead of us walking down the road, found some and kindly shared them with us. After much debating, at first wondering if it could be *R. chihsinianum*, David Chamberlain has come up with the name *R. serotinum*, which is thought to have been collected originally by Delavay near Mengtz, a little to the west of Lao Jing Shan, although there is no wild collected herbarium specimen. Flowers of the described cultivated specimen have a blotch and similar plants have been found in Vietnam and Laos. It has been flowering at Glendoick since 2006 in July-August.

The last two rhododendrons we found were of less interest. *R. siderophyllum* is one of the lowest elevation and tender members of subsection Triflora, a bush of which was in full flower. The other was *R. arboreum* subsp. *delavayi* which had a more spongy indumentum than plants we are familiar with from Cangshan and around Shillong, India.

Sun was still nervous of the military and especially so when a jeep passed us, but his fears seemed unfounded, as the occupants waved and smiled at us and did not stop. If we had been allowed more time, we would surely have found many more different plants but perhaps no more rhododendrons. We did find a *Clethra*, almost certainly *C. delavayi* (CH 7184), *Gaultheria forrestii*, *G. hookeri*, a paris and a very fine *Schefflera* species (CH 7190).

We took a longer route back to Kunming, partly to look for plants to photograph and collect seedlings for the Institute garden in Kunming, the elevation around 1,500m/5,000ft being far too low for the UK, and partly to look for *R. hancockii*, which is or was plentiful in this region, but with no success. Nearing Kunming, we passed restaurant after restaurant which specialized in 'Crispy Duck', a special dish of this area. Eventually we stopped at one and I was disappointed – it was not as good as Peking Duck and not even crispy, but I may have been unlucky in getting poor bits of meat. As in many 'superior' restaurants in China (including Hong Kong), fish and birds are kept in cages for guests to choose which they would like to eat. Here there were tailless but otherwise ordinary pheasants and little doves. We ordered a pheasant, which was killed, plucked and cooked within half an hour.

In the morning we went to the Institute garden, of which

Schefflera species (CH 7190) on Lao Jing Shan. This is growing robustly at Baravalla but a hard winter might test it.

Guan Kaiyun was director and Sun Weiban vice-director. We asked to see Magnoliaceae and rhododendrons and, overall, were most impressed with what we saw. There was an amazing number of *Michelia* and *Manglietia*, of which several lots were planted too close together but were being thinned out by being sold for street trees and to hotels. The rhododendron planting was mostly in too much sun and the soil lacked organic matter. Two plants of interest here were probable *R. orbiculare* subsp. *cardiobasis* from the province of Guangxi with leaves having a slightly cordate base and a queer *R. rex* perhaps nearest to subsp. *fictolacteum* from Wulian Shan towards south-west Yunnan.

A shade house was planted with rhododendrons dug up from the wild of which three-quarters were dead but some might have come away all right. We saw their method of growing rhododendrons from seed, which was to sow on to a raised bed divided into sections with soil containing a fair proportion of organic matter. We then went on to a shaded nursery with species seedlings in considerable numbers, mostly healthy. These were being looked after by the son of Professor Feng Guomei (our leader in 1981) who was evidently 'making a good job. Rhododendron species noted (amongst many others) were *R. sinogrande*, *R. rex* aff., *R. sidereum*, *R. valentinianum* var. *oblongilobatum* (collected off a different peak from Lao Jing Shan), *R. hancockii*, *R. stamineum* and *R.*

moulmainense. I suggested that quite dense high pruned shade trees would create the best environment for rhododendrons from south Yunnan and Vietnam plus low elevation species from elsewhere. Sun fully realizes that alpine rhododendrons are just not worth attempting in Kunming, which is at only 1,800m/6,000ft and with quite a dry climate.

Although we had had much trouble from the weather wrecking the roads and creating all sorts of hold-ups and diversions, it had been an extremely successful expedition covering a wide variety of locations which resulted in rich collections of plants.[15] Most of these are under severe pressure for their survival in the wild and we brought them into a relatively safe horticultural environment.

14. I say 'may' because the plant that flowered for the first time at Glendoick in 2005, though it had splendid trusses, was definitely cream and not yellow. In 2007 this plant and its neighbour flowered, this time with superb pale yellow flowers. Its elevation was 2,800-2,900m/9,200-9,500ft and so far it has proved much hardier than was originally guessed at by the compilers of the old rhododendron handbooks.

15. Probable new introductions or special forms into cultivation from the first part in Sichuan: *Rhododendron asterochnoum* (could be just a form of *R. calophytum*), *R. coeloneuron*, *R. denudatum*, *R. huianum*, *R. longipes* var. *longipes*, *R. ochraceum*, *Primula moupinensis*, now *P. hoffmanniana* (stoloniferous), *Berneuxia tibetica*, *Ribes davidii*, *Philadelphus subcanus* var. *magdelenae*, *Paeonia mairei*, *Cotoneaster atuntzensis*. Probable new introductions or special forms into cultivation from the second part in Yunnan: *Rhododendron sinofalconeri*, *R. valentinianum* subsp. nov, *R. serotinum?*, *R.* subsection Maddenia sp. nov. *R. decorum* forma, *Cotoneaster froebelii*, *Primula faberi*, *Sorbus wilsoniana*.

297

Chapter 12

PEMAKO: THE PROMISED LAND OF KINGDON WARD:

Tibet 1996

Peter Cox

To get to Tibet and follow in the footsteps of Frank Kingdon Ward, Frank Ludlow and George Sherriff had always been my most cherished goal. My son Kenneth had jointly led an Exodus trip there in spring 1995 which I had been very tempted to go on but feared that it would be aborted at the last moment, like so many previous efforts to get to this enchanting land. However, the trip had been a great success and 1996 was to be mostly a repeat of 1995, missing out the Nyima La, but going further east into the Bomi (Pome) area. Kenneth had the then director of Exodus, David Burlinson, as co-leader, who also had his Chinese right-hand man, He Hai, who did much of the negotiating with the Chinese authorities.

Our party was fourteen plus the two leaders: Michael Baron, Franz Besch, Raymond Bomford, John Durran, Philip Evans, Dr Peter Hartrey and his wife Bathsheba Pradhan (originally from Sikkim), Helmut Prinz, June Ross, John Roy, Chris Sanders, Professor Ernst Sondheimer, John Vaughan and myself, plus David Burlinson and Kenneth. All were more or

less interested in plants with about half really keen. I was average age at 62, the oldest being 72, the youngest in their 30s. Most had experience of trekking or serious climbing. Our Nepalese staff were Himal, Ladeh and Tsering.

We flew via Bangkok to Kathmandu where we stayed in the relatively new Blue Star Hotel, which was fine but in a rather grotty area with little of interest nearby. It was just as well that we had to be at the airport two hours in advance of our flight to Lhasa, as panic set in when we were told that our group visa needed a stamp. The Chinese Embassy was closed for the day and the next flight was not until Saturday and this was only Tuesday. It came to light that this rule had been introduced only two to three weeks earlier, to make some extra cash for the local head of the Chinese Embassy, and Beijing had not even heard of it! The combined effort of David going off to the embassy and Kenneth pushing from the airport end eventually did the trick, and thankfully the plane had waited for us.

The flight from Kathmandu to Lhasa is dramatic, with

298

superb views of Mt Everest on the left-hand side and Kanchenjunga on the right (heading north). (It is worth sitting on the same side of the plane coming back to get the reverse view.) The vehicles which David had organised to drive us in Tibet soon arrived, five Toyota Landcruisers with Nepalese drivers and cooks and a truck. The road starts along the Yarlung Tsangpo (Zangbo) river,[1] very dry as far west as this, with

xerophytic flora including masses of the pale blue and occasionally white *Sophora davidii* (syn. *moorcroftiana*). We then had to go over a high pass, before returning to the river. Our first night in Tibet was spent in Chusum, which lies below some peculiar mud cliffs that must get seriously eroded when it rains here. This village is on the way up to the pass, the Putrang La (Gama La, Podo La),[2] and it was here that some discomfort – both external and internal due to the high altitude and a lack of mod cons – hit newcomers and old hats alike. We had a surprisingly good meal with sugared bananas to finish up with.

The Putrang La, at some 4,600m/15,000ft,[3] was very bleak with masses of tattered prayer flags fluttering in the wind and

1. The Yarlung Tsangpo rises in west Tibet and flows eastwards until it hits the Himalaya, which it cuts through in a great arc, almost completing a circle, and then turns more or less south into India. Before turning, it enters a tremendous gorge, passing between the great mountains of Namche Barwa and Gyala Peri. In India it becomes the Siang (Dihang) and then, when it joins the Lohit, it becomes the Brahmaputra which flows west into the Ganges.

2. This high pass, rising to 4,600m/15,000ft, has to be crossed on the way down the Yarlung Tsangpo, as there is no road due to a gorge. The route north-east from Lhasa goes equally high.

3. The sudden rise to this altitude was some test for those prone to altitude sickness and we all suffered to some extent, with or without Dimox, but nobody was seriously affected. I had a loss of appetite for a week which I partly put down to taking Dimox, but two years later, with no Dimox, I had the same trouble.

Above: The Yarlung Tsangpo often know as the Tsangpo (which means river in Tibetan) in the drier part not far from Lhasa.

Above left: Androsace aff. muscoidea on the Putrang La (Podo Gama La).

gave the first warning that we were here in a later season than 1995. There was lots of *Rhododendron primuliflorum* which James Cullen insisted in placing in the merged *R. kongboense*. This was mostly an indifferent pale pink, occasionally white, dwarf on the top, but up to 1.8m/6ft high down the east side. *R. nivale* subsp. *nivale* was also common, with larger flowers than I expected. The only elepidote rhododendrons were *R.*

Rhododendron principis *on the Putrang La.*

Paeonia ludlowii (P. lutea *var.* ludlowii).

aganniphum with quite woolly indumentum and usually pink flowers and the usually pale pink *R. principis* with narrower leaves and a greater stature. The latter species is often found in the valleys where it is too dry for most other rhododendrons, its presence always a sign of at least a partial rain-shadow.[4] There was the very dwarf pink *Primula tibetica* plus the rich reddish-purple *P. calderiana* and the bluer *P. macrophylla* var. *ninguida*.

Soon we were back on the banks of the Yarlung Tsangpo and, as we travelled east, there were encouraging signs of a wetter climate. The first wild tree was *Cupressus gigantea* growing on the sides of a gorge with a line of them not far above the water.[5] Then we came to *Pinus densata* forest with the usual understorey of *Quercus semecarpifolia*. Forest could be seen up the mountainsides but only on north-facing slopes to start with. The scenery along the valley was much more varied and beautiful than I expected. Numerous sand dunes were a surprise, some being quite extensive, and easy to get bogged down in, even in a Landcruiser. Kingdon Ward and Lord Cawdor suffered from this sand blowing in the cold winter winds of 1924-25. Patches of level ground near the river were planted with fruit and other trees. The mountains behind were often dramatic with knife-edge ridges and sharp points and here and there were villages or monasteries, often at strategic positions.

On a scrubby bank was something with purple flowers and Kenneth at once said *Rhododendron bulu* (CC 7501) as they had stopped and investigated this in 1995. This previously not introduced Lapponica is one of the largest in the subsection, growing as high as 3m/10ft. Another halt was at a vigorous colony of *Paeonia ludlowii* (formerly *P. lutea* var. *ludlowii*) with its fine deep yellow flowers.[6] Eventually we made the village of Miling for the night. Above the village were lots of *Rhododendron triflorum*, here without the peeling bark found further west, with mostly pale yellow flowers but some heavily marked mahogany. Later we saw this species in several places and it was always yellow or blotched to a variable extent. Invariably free-flowering, the mixture is very attractive for those with enough space in their garden. This Tibetan form is hardier than those from Nepal to Bhutan and is often referred to as *R. triflorum* 'Mahogany' or *R. triflorum* var. *triflorum* Mahogani Group.

4. *R. principis* was previously known by the name *R. vellereum*, which refers to its soft fleecy indumentum.

5. *C. gigantea* makes an upright narrow tree, a typical cypress growing to about 18m/60ft. Young seedlings are very glaucous and trees from a Ludlow and Sherriff introduction of 1946-7 still had juvenile foliage up to 1987 (*Conifers* K. Rushforth).

6. We found two populations of this strong-growing tree-peony, both very near to human habitation, so it is likely that it has or had some medicinal use. There was some difference in the size of flower between the two populations. Recently it was given full specific status by the Chinese.

The view south from the Doshong La into the valley that ends up in India. At 4,000m/13,000ft, this is one of the lowest passes over the main Himalayan range and yet it is one of the wettest. We were the first to cross the pass that spring and had to wade through fresh snow covering old snow.

The Doshong La

The river gradually increased in size as more tributaries joined it. Just before the village of Pe (Pei), which leads up towards the famous Doshong La, we had to ford a tributary, the vehicles nearly getting carried away mid-stream. From Pe the track took us to an excellent level meadow for our camp and just below was a sea of yellow *R. wardii* (CC 7514) in full bloom, these all unblotched. Wherever we went, this species was at its glorious best and was undoubtedly the star of the expedition for sheer flower power. On one occasion we could even see great patches of yellow away up on the tops of a ridge with the naked eye. David and He Hai left us to do a recce of the Dokar La in Bome (Pome), which we were to go to later.

Here we had another example of the lateness of the season, *Iris chrysographes* being not nearly out, and even a week later just before we finally left this camp, there were only one or two flowers. Last year there had been masses. We were taken up to the top of the road and just below is a boggy area where Kingdon Ward camped before crossing the pass. We were lucky to be able reach the top by vehicle as the previous year there were fallen trees which necessitated them having to walk round the last two bends. Around small ponds were many plants of interest. *Rhododendron cephalanthum* Nmaiense Group (CC 7521) with yellow flowers was just opening its thinly textured daphne-like flowers, and the evergreen *R. viri-*

descens (CC 7531), which was recently re-instated as a species after having been wrongly sunk into the deciduous *R. mekongense*. Both these species occurred here in quantity and were extremely easy to tell apart, as, other than the presence and absence of leaves, the former flowers very much later that the latter. The *R. mekongense* here was often tinged red, in contrast to those of the Mekong-Salween divide, which were always pure deep yellow. Another rhododendron here was *R. calostrotum* subsp. *riparium*, not yet out. Near the water's edge were primulas, the little *P. hookeri* with a blob of white flowers, easily mistaken for a little lump of snow, contrasting with the tall orange of *P. chungensis* with flowers in tiers.

As we walked back to camp through the forest, there were numerous rhododendron species and many hybrids between them. This area may be the only place where *R. wardii* and *R. campylocarpum* meet in the wild and it is odd that here *R. campylocarpum* grows at higher elevations, even above the tree line, while *R. wardii* is very much a woodland plant. In the middle they appear to merge / hybridise. Other elepidotes between the end of the road and the camp were *R. uvariifolium* var. *griseum* (CC 7506) with silky white indumentum, *R. cerasinum* (CC 7510) here all the pure red 'Coals of Fire' form, *R. faucium* with pink flowers and peeling bark, *R. phaeochrysum*, *R. dignabile* (CC 7509), a close relative of *R. beesianum* with almost no indumentum and,

301

nearer camp, the pink-flowered bristly *R. hirtipes*.[7]

In the forest were several handsome herbaceous plants. *Meconopsis betonicifolia* was opening its first clear blue flowers, *Podophyllum hexandrum* was just producing its remarkable mottled leaves and *Rodgersia aesculifolia* its large palmate leaves.

On the last day of May we had a trial run up to near the top of the pass. The day started with a little drizzle which appeared to clear and it was quite still. We were driven once again up to the end of the road, soon meeting deep snow, which proved to be the steepest and worst bit. To our left were black beetling cliffs, while to our right the valley was largely full of snow. As the snow was too soft for crampons (which most of us had brought), those of us who had ice axes were instructed how to use them if we had a fall on steep snow. We followed in each others' footprints as the weather conditions became worse and worse with rain turning to sleet and the wind hitting us straight in the face. I had no goggles (only dark glasses) or gloves with me and my hands became numb and my eyes were watering and sore. On top of that I had an aching tummy and bouts of nausea. Under the circumstances plants coming into flower were ignored as all one could think about was surviving in atrocious conditions. The relief was tremendous as I reached the shelter of a large rock where there were some Nivalid primulas coming into flower that marked the end of our struggles for the day. For the return to camp David very kindly lent me his gloves, which took ages to pull on to my completely numb hands.

Going back down again was much easier than expected. It helped to dig one's heels into the soft snow and now it was better to avoid the old foot-prints. As we descended plants were just beginning to start into flower on 'islands' in the snow. The previous year's party had been in raptures about these little raised areas where the snow melted or was blown off first, as was Kingdon Ward when he crossed the pass in 1924, calling it 'Rhododendron Fairyland'. This pass must have one of the richest collections of ericaceous plants in the world but in 1996 we were too early to see them at their best.[8]

After that day's experience, I was dreading the crossing of the pass on the next, but in the morning I was feeling decidedly better, in spite of a night disturbed by barking dogs. Michael was feeling poorly with a severe cold, so his friend John Durran nobly said that he would stay behind with him. All the way up to the limit of the previous day's climb was much more pleasant, with little or no rain or sleet and much less wind, and I was better prepared anyway. As we carried on up to the top of the pass, the snow became deeper and deeper, and our boots sank through fresh snow up to a foot, which made walking very hard work, and for a short time we had a white-out. Eventually we all reached the bleak top with its array of prayer flags. This is actually one of the lowest of the passes over the Himalaya at only 4,100m/13,500ft, but being one of the wettest, means that it gets more snow than most. We were the first people to cross the pass that spring.

Into Pemako

We still had to negotiate the most dangerous part of crossing the pass which was steep snow-banks with rocks below, and in fact, looking back up to this part from the valley below, it looked like an unscalable cliff. Several people did have falls but luck must have been with us as there were no injuries. We soon re-found the path but it frequently disappeared under patches of snow. The weather on the south side of the pass in Pemako must be one of the most continually damp places on this earth. It may not have an exceptionally high rainfall but its persistence is most depressing and it hardly let up during the 60 hours we spent there. We gradually descended towards the flats where our camp was already set up on rather a boggy area of ground, but there is little else over here. Kingdon Ward used the same camp. There were some very tired people that night.

We were of course there primarily to see plants and such wet conditions generally mean a great variety and also endemics. The multi-coloured *Rhododendron parmulatum* (CC 7518) was certainly showing us what it could do and the variety was amazing. It varied from a slightly bluish red, carmine pink, yellowish flushed pink, white flushed pink, almost orange, pale yellow and almost pure cream. Most but not all were spotted, sometimes heavily. At least we saw this species in better bloom that they had in 1995 but no plants were actually covered in flowers. Even here in little disturbed country, there were natural hybrids including one obviously between *R. parmulatum* and *R. chamaethomsonii*, a low plant with flowers more tubular than the former species and the colour more of a bluish red than *R. chamaethomsonii*. Another rhododendron only known from this valley is *R. cinnabarinum* subsp. *xanthocodon* Concatenans Group (CC 7517), Kingdon Ward's famous 'Orange Bill'.[9] We found it to be quite plentiful on rocks and cliffs, very uniform in foliage and flower, and consider it worthy of some botanical status. Other species found here were the

Mandragora caulescens, the mandrake, is a curious poisonous plant.

The beautiful Primula falcifolia, the daffodil primula, has only been found on the south side of the Doshong La and was introduced once by Ludlow and Sherriff but soon lost from cultivation.

Arisaema *species on the south side of the Doshong La.*

lovely white *R. leucaspis*, only found by us on the rocks and cliffs just by our camp, and *R. exasperatum*, a Barbata with large handsome bristly leaves and the occasional tight truss of light red to scarlet flowers.[10] Both these species have recently been seen in different locations in Arunachal Pradesh.

There were several other rhododendrons on the south side of the pass, not found on the north. *R. megeratum* (CC 7527), here always epiphytic on the trunks of firs, all had cream-coloured flowers with a small yellow blotch. The early *R. lanigerum* (CC 7526), all red-flowered here, was, for some reason or another, wantonly hacked about by the locals. *R. heatheriae* (*arizelum* aff.), with pink, sometimes fading flowers, had petioles always winged to some degree. This has also been found to the east of the gorge on the Dokar La by Keith Rushforth who named it after his wife. Up on the hillside just above the trees we could see a pink sheen and we knew at once what it was, as some of the 1995 party had found it too. This was *R. imperator* (CC 7530) with narrower leaves and larger flowers than the closely related *R. uniflorum* which Kingdon Ward found a bit higher up where it would be still under snow, though the latter may be a hybrid. *R. imperator* had been found only once before in Upper Burma. This made a beautiful sight along the hillside but has not proved amenable in cultivation.

Rhododendron cinnabarinum *subsp.* xanthocodon Concatenans *Group is Kingdom Ward's 'Orange Bill'. This photograph was taken in 100% humidity with a fogged lens.*

R. glischrum subsp. *rude* (CC 7524) with a hairy leaf upper surface was a good pink with a blotch. Apart from *R. imperator* it is difficult to enthuse about the rhododendrons here because they had so few flowers. Evidently they are so happy growing in that soaking climate, living to a great age, that there is little need for them to produce a lavish amount of seed.

The fittest members of the party were Chris and Kenneth and they went further down the valley than any of the rest of us. This wide U-shaped valley loses altitude very gradually, so it is necessary to walk some way down before the plants change. They found four more rhododendron species, *R. sinogrande*, probably as far west and north as this widespread species has been found, *R. fulvum* subsp. *fulvoides*, *R. keysii*, *R. leptocarpum* and what Kenneth thought might be the not then in cultivation *R. monanthum* with just one capsule per inflorescence. On a preliminary visit on behalf of Exodus in 1994, David went on down the valley and got too close to the Indian frontier, resulting in being arrested by the Chinese Army and marched back to Pe.

We were too early to see the primulas at their best. The very

7. *R. campylocarpum* (CC 7541) varied from a good yellow to creamy white and it hybridised readily with *R. cerasinum*, some being rather muddy coloured, others a prettier apricot. *R. dignabile* made a large handsome bush, flowering (as does *R. beesianum*) with snow lying under the branches. Its flowers vary from white to pink, any reported as being yellow are likely to be hybrids. It has proved to be exceptionally slow-growing as a small seedling and difficult to satisfy.

8. Rhododendrons just coming out were *R. forrestii*, *R. cephalanthum* (mostly yellow, one pink), *R. fragariflorum*, *R. mekongense*, while those identified still in bud were *R. pumilum*, *R. chamaethomsonii* and *R. aganniphum* (*R. doshongense*). There was a complete gradation between the prostrate *R. forrestii* with one (to two) flower(s) to the mounded *R. chamaethomsonii* with one to five flowers per inflorescence, with the latter growing in the more sheltered positions.

9. Kingdon Ward made a great story of finding this in flower and just managing to collect the seed later in the snow.

10. I say occasional, as after a long search, Philip and I only managed to find four of that year's trusses on about fifty plants and only three where it had flowered last year, all on one plant. Luckily it is freer flowering in cultivation. Seed was so scarce that only two seeds germinated and these had no vigour and died off in infancy. This species is very fastidious as to where it grows, always being found on rocks from which it hangs outwards and downwards.

The cliffs on the south side of the Doshong La looking towards the pass. Traversing the path was not as difficult as it looks apart from where there was still snow and this was very steep.

variable yellow, cream, purplish-blue, pale mauve yellow-centred *P. dickieana* was nothing like as good as they had seen it in 1995 but there was enough of the fabulous *P. falcifolia* to see how beautiful it is. Its daffodil-like flowers and very narrow leaves make it very easy to identify and it would be easy to be fooled into thinking that it is not a primula at all. This species and its two equally gorgeous relatives, *P. agleniana* and *P. elizabethae*, have so far proved impossible to keep in cultivation. Other primulas seen here were more *P. hookeri*, the diminutive *P. rhodochroa*, a lovely little thing with comparatively large purplish-pink flowers, and *P. tanneri* subsp. *tsariensis* with rich purple flowers.

A rare tiff occurred when June accused Bathsheba of picking a rare primula (*P. rhodochroa*) as we had only seen two or three. Luckily, on the whole we all got on fine together, although playing bridge late into the night proved to be a bone of contention with some non-playing members of the party. Even over here we had our generator, porters having nobly carried it all the way over the pass.[11]

We spent the two days in Pemako exploring as much as we could, but leaving the path to go any distance was sadly impractical. Once we tried to get up the side valley just north of camp, but leaning rhododendrons made progress too arduous. We went back up the path to study *R. parmulatum* (CC 7532) and

here there were open patches which made access easy. The 100% humidity made photography very difficult as lenses kept fogging up. Believe it or not, there was a little shop down the valley where in 1995 they had managed to buy some *piju*, but this year there was none. The litter around the shop was appalling.

Perhaps we should have been more careful not to venture out in small parties as the native population of Pemako has a reputation for murdering visitors. Due to the steepness of most of the terrain and the dreadful weather, Pemako is very sparsely populated, but there are occasional villages, even in the Yarlung Tsangpo gorge between the great mountains of Namche Barwa and Gyala Peri.

Bed tea was at 6.45 a.m. and we were off back over the pass in reasonable time. One of the worst aspects of living in a continually damp climate is that all one's clothes get saturated and putting back on wet stockings, socks and boots was postponed until after breakfast. I was one of the last to set out and, to my surprise, was the third last to get back to the waiting vehicles, having thought that I had travelled at some speed, and without many delays taking photographs and collecting seed. The weather was as good as could be expected and was actually dry more than wet. I found it easier than anticipated, with the long steady climb through deep snow to the pass being

The Nyang Chu, which flows into the Yarlung Tsangpo from the north, with blue-flowered Sophora *in the foregound.*

the worst. I skipped across the snow where the decline was gentle and then slid down part of the steeper bit, but stupidly braked too much with my ice axe, thus losing momentum and had to walk much of what others had successfully glissaded on.

As usual, there was a wind on the north side of the pass and it was very windy when reaching camp. Despite a few drops of rain, this wind enabled us to start drying everything out, and it was a joy to see some blue sky again. It was Philip's birthday and, to our astonishment, our staff had made a cake in Pemako and brought it back over the pass. It had a thin sticky chocolate icing. We drank duty-free cognac and whisky to celebrate.

In the morning, we all set an example to future campers on this site by systematically picking up rubbish, including that left lying by previous occupants. Chris and the eccentric Raymond dug an enormous hole, the latter admitting that he likes digging and digs holes about 1.5m/5ft deep through clay for his trees and shrubs. We doubted if our staff even noticed what we were doing and, if they did, considered us to be mad foreigners. The driver of the Toyota that I was in was too timid in attempting to cross the tributary and very nearly got stuck in the deepest part. It is important to cross these fords early in the day, as later on snow melt increases the volume of water.

We drove up the Nyang Chu, a beautiful river divided up over a flood plain, to Bayi, a horrible modern town developed for the Chinese army, which has barracks all around the town. We had to walk the streets while the vehicles were refuelling and we noticed that every second shop was a brothel. It was a relief to escape and stay in the neighbouring village of Nyingche, situated under a steep hillside. Through our binoculars we could see white, pink and yellow flowers on the top, most likely all rhododendrons. Here we met a party of four intrepid Americans who were on their way home after exploring the Yarlung Tsangpo gorge for the fifth time, and they told us that it was quite easy to get permission to enter the gorge, provided the Chinese in Lhasa were bribed enough. Kenneth stayed up half the night drinking with them, discussing the gorge and the area in general and exchanging addresses.[12] David and He Hai arrived late from their recce of Bome and they reported a lot of icy snow but no other problems.

11. I had not played bridge up to now as there always seemed to be so much to do, but later we learned to have cards always at the ready, as there is nothing like a game for passing the time when there is an annoying delay. We even played across the aisle in the plane on the way home! We did have a limit as to how late we played in camp as our staff slept in the mess tent.

12. Thus was hatched Kenneth's plan to re-do Kingdon Ward's book *The Riddle of the Tsangpo Gorges* (published 2001).

305

The super little Primula baileyana *grew on little cliffs in the forest on the east side of the Sirchem La.*

Cassiope selaginoides *in the Rong Chu near the foot of the Sirchem La. Cassiopes often occur in woodland on rocky outcrops as in this case.*

The Sirchem La

After a slow start, we were off up the Sirchem La, a pass of 4,400m/14,500ft, which took us into the Rong Chu (valley). We passed a fine blue *Meconopsis simplicifolia* on the roadside and then stopped further on near some small shady cliffs on which grew quantities of the lovely little *Primula baileyana* (CC 7544) with delicate lilac flowers with a yellow eye. This grew mostly under overhangs, making it all but impossible to keep going in cultivation. There was still some seed which germinated but their demise was horribly inevitable. Kenneth once came out with the remark that these difficult primulas are really best left to be seen in the wild as we cannot simulate the conditions that they are found in. Other primulas recorded on this pass were *P. atrodentata*, *P. tanneri* var. *tsariensis* and *P. macrophylla* var. *ninguida*.

The west side of the pass had plentiful *Rhododenron nivale*, mostly not out yet, and what we took to be *R. laudandum* var. *laudandum* (CC 7545), which looked close to *R. primuliflorum* with the same upright habit, and white, pale pink (mostly) to a clearer pink flowers, but with a chocolate-coloured leaf underside. Further on we found some with pale undersides which could only be *R. primuliflorum*.[13] The top of the pass was still dead to this world and very cold with hailstones. Here grew typical *R. laudandum* var. *temoense*, which is a different plant altogether, being much lower, with shorter, darker leaves, and a deeper leaf underside. It is our opinion that var. *temoense* should have the specific status and that var. *laudandum* should be placed with *R. primuliflorum*, perhaps as a variety, so it should be *R. laudandum* and *R. primuliflorum* var. *temoense* if that is allowed in botanical circles.

The widespread *Rhododendron lepidotum* started occurring at 4,000m/13,000ft with small leaves which became larger at 3,600m/11,700ft, resembling *R. baileyi* but definitely not that species as the flowers were just one per inflorescence. Large 4.5–9m/15–20ft *R. principis* covered the hillside with its pale pink flowers nearly over, and again *R. wardii* was superb with some great specimens overhanging the road. We had seen and passed a small quantity of *R. hirtipes* on the west side, but here on the east were dense colonies with pretty pink campanulate flowers, often associated with *R. dignabile* with which it hybridised. For some reason or other Helmut was mad keen to see *R. hirtipes* (CC 7549), which he had missed earlier and thought he was sure to see if he got a lift down the road and, in doing so, missed it again. Kenneth refused to let him have a vehicle to take him back up again but honour was eventually satisfied when Helmut found plenty on the Dokar (Showa) La.

Shouts came back up the road, 'Is my father there?' Kenneth's eagle eyes had spotted a small scruffy plant away ahead leaning over the road and recognised at once what it was, *R. lanatoides*. Much searching failed to reveal any more. This was a great find as the 1995 party had sought it in vain and had actually passed along this road too.[14] Nearby was a bank free of trees which must have been felled some years before. This had encouraged quite a collection of different plants to grow and it proved to be worthwhile spending some time there. There were two slipper orchids, *Cypripedium tibeticum* and *C. flavum*, both just coming out, a fine blue *Cynoglossum* species, and a few excellent *Cassiope* covered in their little white bells.

Just before reaching the Rong Chu valley bottom was another rhododendron and this proved to be a bit of a puzzle. Kenneth thought it was just *R. oreotrephes* (CC 7550), a common species in north-west Yunnan, and specimens collected around the Rong Chu have been placed in this species in the RBGE herbarium, but I was not happy with this state of affairs. The more tubular and deeper colour of the flowers point towards a relationship with *R. cinnabarinum* subsp. *xanthocodon* Purpurellum Group, and I reckon that this plant lies half way between. It has produced much paler flowers in cultivation and David Chamberlain has passed it as an aberrant form of *R. oreotrephes*. Incidentally, Purpurellum Group should be reinstated, so as to have some botanical standing, but that is another story.

Along the side of the grazed valley were tall *Rhododendron*

A rhododendron with reddish-purple flowers at the base of the Sirchem La in the Rong Chu Wa produced a startling show of colour in the forest. It seemed to be half way between R. oreotrephes *and* R. cinnabarinum.

Primula alpicola *var.* alpicola, *the moonlight primula, flourishes in damp meadows, scenting the air all around.*

Podophyllum aurantiocaule *on the south side of the Doshong La.*

A fine pink-tinged Clematis montana *which David Burlinson (a non-plants person) first spotted.*

nivale covered in blue-purple flowers, contrasting beautifully with creamy yellow *Primula alpicola* var. *alpicola* growing amongst it. We camped in the valley near the river where there were some fine banks of *R. triflorum* and the large gentian relative, *Megacodon stylophorus*. On the way east, we had one very good stop where David had also halted on his recce in preparation for our visit to Bome and, though not really plant-minded, had spotted two fine clematis, both of which have been introduced into cultivation. One was a white-flowered *C. montana* f. *grandiflora* with huge flowers 15cm/6in across and another *C. montana* with a distinct pink flush.[15] A third clematis was *C. barbellata* with pendulous flowers, red inside, paler outside. A strong climber, *Schisandra neglecta* had white pink tinged flowers with a very good scent. There were also plants of the winter-flowering *Lonicera setifera* here which we have found several times in China.

We passed through a fine gorge with splendid virgin forest on both sides of the river. The road descended to around 2,000m/6,500ft near where the Po Tsangpo runs south to join the Yarlung Tsangpo in the gorge. Kingdon Ward and Ludlow and

Sherriff had found the Maddenias *Rhododendron scopulorum* (CC 7571) and *R. nuttallii* (*R. gorerii*) here at Pilung. Davidian described *R. goreri* as being less bullate than *R. nuttallii* but it is doubtful if it warrants specific or any status. On the way, we found only *R. scopulorum* growing on roadside cliffs and, in a drier area, there was nothing but the heat- and drought-resistant *R. virgatum*. A bank of a rhizomatose iris with pale mauve flowers on a long stalk stopped all our vehicles. There was also a small-flowered but pretty form of *Deutzia corymbosa* and *Philadelphus tomentosus* with a sickly perfume. The multi-flowered *Podophyllum auranticaule*[16] with white flowers was very fine and there was the pretty *Streptopus simplex* with pendulous flowers.

13. We found both *Rhododendron laudanum* var. *laudanum* and *R. primuliflorum* again on the nearby Temo La towards the end of the expedition.

14. By 1997, this little plant had disappeared, the victim of a landslide.

15. David was able to remember where he had seen this clematis and from then on it became known as 'Burlinson's Blush'. Alas, it has not proved to be very hardy in cultivation.

16. This striking plant was introduced by a member of our party and is now becoming well distributed in cultivation.

Jhulong peak to the east of the Po Tsangpo.

The Dokar (Showa) La

Eventually we reached the village of Showa where the Dokar (or Showa) La starts. The vehicles turned off down a narrow track to a footbridge over the Po Tsangpo. Our luggage was taken across to a pretty campsite near the village with views of the river and the mountains to the south of Namcha Barwa. Along the roadside banks and cliffs were masses of *Lilium wardii*, which unfortunately would not be in flower for another month. This stoloniferous species is closely related to *L. lankongense* and *L. duchartrei* with pink spotted Turk's cap flowers.

We were very late in starting for the Dokar La due to doubts about porters, so a bridge four got playing while we waited. Several women and teenagers carried our gear, some of which was so heavy that we could not even get it off the ground. Our walk started through fields of barley and then into pine forest, in which there were a few clearings full of weeds or shuttlecock ferns. After a few ups and downs, we camped in a weed-infested open area at only about 420m/1,380ft higher than Showa. Our porters re-built a shack to stay in. We were surrounded by fine undisturbed forest with some huge conifers and old multi-stemmed *Betula utilis* with papery cinnamon-coloured bark.

Perhaps the outstanding plants of the day were orchids, *Calanthe tricarinata* with yellow flowers and another, less common *Calanthe* species with white flowers. There were fine trees of *Acer caesium* var. *giraldii* with large leaves, *Tsuga dumosa* and *Pinus wallichiana*. *Rodgersia aesculifolia* had huge leaves and

the royal fern relative *Osmunda claytonia* with spores on special fronds, which are much smaller than the sterile ones. *Cardiocrinum* looked to be half way between *C. giganteum* and var. *yunnanense* with green stems but cordate leaves. My plant of the day was *Sorbus filipes* (CC 7568) with, to our astonishment, red flowers. This species is actually quite widely distributed into China and I have seen a shrubby introduction with the same red flowers in the Gothenburg Botanic Garden, Sweden.

The new rhododendron for the day was the tender *R. ramsdenianum* (CC 7567), which had finished flowering but we could just make out the remains of a red flower. It is closely related to *R. tanastylum* from further south. The *R. oreotrephes* here had more funnel-shaped flowers and rather long non-glaucous leaves. *R. viridescens* (CC 7557) was often well into new growth but with no flowers showing, while *R. uvariifolium* var. *griseum* had a wide altitudinal range with some huge specimens.

We moved to a higher camp at 3,200m/10,500ft, which gave us magnificent views of the mountains. One peak with an altitude of over 6,500m/21,000ft had the Chinese name of Jhulong and was quite splendid with incredible ridges and cornices, Chago being another smaller peak. Jhulong looked extremely difficult to climb and probably never has been conquered. We all took lots of photographs, although there was invariably a little cloud hanging around the peak.

Our walk to the higher camp started through *Rhododendron*

Omphalogramma elegans *var.* tibeticum *on the Dokar La (Showa La) in Bome. This was the furthest east we reached this year. We could not get near the actual pass due to the depth of snow still lying.*

A very fine pink form of Rhododendron primuliflorum *on the Dokar La. Other plants were less good.*

faucium and deciduous forest, passing *Meconopsis pseudointegrifolia* on the way. The camp was again in a man-made clearing with shuttlecock and royal ferns plus weeds and another ramshackle hut. We explored the forest beyond the camp and found some *Rhododendron sanguineum* (CC 7562) sprawling on the forest floor with dark red flowers but not as dark as var. *haemaleum*.[17] The *Shortia* relative *Berneuxia thibetica*, forming a carpet in the mossy forest, was just coming into flower with pretty pink buds that opened to disappointing small white flowers.

After walking through some dull birch forest, June, Philip and I reached the tree-line and crossed a patch of snow to an 'island' where we found *Omphalogramma elegans* var. *tibeticum*, *Rhododendron calostrotum* subsp. *riparium* (CC 7563) just opening its purple flowers, very good dwarf *R. primuliflorum* (CC 7559) with clear pink flowers and *R. forrestii* with a few red flowers. We went back up the ridge to look at *R. wardii* and something purple which turned out to be only *R. oreotrephes*, and there was *R. lepidotum* on a cliff. The three of us then headed towards the river and we found ourselves getting gradually into worse and worse territory, at first down a stream bed which narrowed into nothing, then into a thicket of birch scrub with *R. wardii*, plus berberis, roses and brambles which endeavoured to halt our progress and scratch us from head to foot. It was with great relief that we hit a cattle path that led us back to camp. Our first lunch had been Kendal Mint Cake, dried apricots, bananas and fruit pastilles; arriving back to have a proper lunch at 4.15.

In the meantime Chris and Kenneth had climbed higher and found *Rhododendron pemakoense* (CC 7561), a really good discovery with darker flowers than those in cultivation but it is proving to have even more bud-tender flower buds. They also found a few plants of a Petiolares primula with very serrated leaves and a sessile capsule. *Rhododendron wardii* was scattered all over this area and it was very noticeable that here it was of a uniform poor quality with small flowers and trusses, compared with what we had seen earlier and were to see later. We had found hybrids between *R. sanguineum* and *R. wardii* and some were of poor muddy colours. We noticed that the flowers of *R. sanguineum* were often attacked by birds, presumably for the nectar, as they do

sometimes with red flowers at home. Another rhododendron both in and out of the forest was *R. charitopes* var. *tsangpoense*, a low plant with purplish flowers, also found on the Doshong La.[18]

We had had a lovely day, mostly sunny and warm enough for shirtsleeves, but it became cold as soon as the sun went down behind the mountains. We realised that there was too much snow for us to go further up the Dokar La, and we never found out exactly where the pass was, which is reputed to drop down extremely steeply on the other side into the Yarlung Tsangpo gorge.

We were allowed to spend the following morning up here before the return descent to Showa, which would not take long, being downhill all the way. Philip and I went back up the previous day's cattle path, searching for primulas, to a meadow where decidedly unfriendly yaks were grazing, which obviously did not appreciate us invading their privacy. Luckily there was an excellent supply of rocks which we hurled at the yaks until they retreated. Hidden in the birch scrub was a quantity of *Rhododendron calostrotum* in full flower and the combination of this, *R. wardii* and the background of partly snowy mountains made an unforgettable sight. The adjacent area which we thought might be marsh was a disappointing rocky area covered with thorny caragana scrub. So our hunt for primulas was in vain.

The river was too large to cross so I scanned the opposite bank with my binoculars which revealed only the same rhododendrons – *R. sanguineum*, *R. wardii* and *R. calostrotum* – but there was a lily with a flower bud on top which looked different from *L. wardii*. In the meantime, June had ventured up a steep gully above our camp and also found a lily which she photographed and picked for us to see. Great was the excitement when Kenneth identified this as the fabulous red lily, *L. paradoxum* discovered by Ludlow and never introduced into cultivation. Was the lily Philip and I had found in bud the same?

17. Here, *R. sanguineum* var. *haemaleum* was almost confined to the forest which is unusual as elsewhere it occurs on forest margins or above the tree-line. This is the furthest north and west that this species has been found and was previously recorded here by Ludlow.

18. Other plants here were *Diplarche multiflora*, *Adonis brevistyla*, *Cardamine macrophylla* and *Cassiope selaginoides*.

View in the upper Rong Chu showing peaks still covered in snow in mid June on the divide between the Rong Chu and the Yarlung Tsangpo.

The Rong Chu

We left Showa for the Rong Chu, stopping on the way at a bridge over the Rong Chu near where it empties into the Po Tsangpo. David and Franz went off together on a ploy of their own down the river, hoping to get to Gompa Ne in the Yarlung Tsangpo gorge. The rest of the party walked down the river a little way, while I walked along the main road. I soon found *Rhododendron nuttallii* (*R. gorerii*) (CC 7570) on a cliff with three flower trusses recently gone over, and several more smaller plants further on. There was another rhododendron here, which was a great surprise, with rather narrow leaves and thin grey-plastered indumentum, indicating that it is in subsection Argyrophylla. All I could find were two immature plants in shade, so not flowering, and despite walking along the road for some miles, no more were to be found. Keith Rushforth and Alan Clark have also found this plant, but apparently Ludlow did not. Kingdon Ward may have done so and his specimens may have been wrongly identified as *R. uvariifolium* var. *griseum*. It is obviously close to *R. coryanum* from north-east Yunnan and adjacent south-east Tibet and was recently introduced by Alan Clark. The altitude was remarkably low at 2,000m/6,500ft, compared with 3,700–4,300m/12,000–14,000ft for most known *R. coryanum*, and it is proving to be tender in cultivation.[19]

Having returned to our vehicles, we passed enormous road works where there had been a land-slip and they were building up concrete all the way from the river at least 200m/660ft below. People working at river level looked like ants from the road. That night was spent in the wider part of the Rong Chu on a hard-grazed meadow where the patches of *Rhododendron nivale* were past flowering and our tent became frozen stiff. Heavy thunder-showers passed on both sides of us towards evening, missing us completely. The Rong Chu valley is behind the main monsoon rain influence that affects Pemako, with a high ridge between it and the Yarlung Tsangpo, culminating to the east in the huge peak of Gyala Peri of 6,800m/22,300ft.

The sides of the Rong Chu valley are comparatively gentle by Tibetan standards, so all are easily exploited for their timber, which is being extracted in several places. We started our explorations up a logging track, probably the beginning of the Tra La, and heard at least two chain saws in action. The valley has obviously been inhabited for a long time, and there were clearings within the forest that looked as though that had been used for grazing for generations. A fierce-looking yak bull roared at us, so we had stones at the ready, but he did not charge.

There were lots of good *Rhododendron wardii* of considerable size in full flower and on one plant all the flowers were frosted. Kenneth shouted out 'R. lanatoides' (CC 7574, 7577), and we soon found several, including one with a flower truss not yet over. Kenneth went off exploring on his own and found a gorge full of this species including more in flower. Seedlings are now growing well in cultivation.[20] *R. principis* was growing up the slope near to cliffs where Philip and I found a few hybrids / intermediaries between this and *R. lanatoides*, which may originally have evolved from *R. principis*, although at the moment, the two are placed in different subsections, and it is also related to *R. circinnatum* which is common around Tsari further to the west.[21]

Philip and I attempted to reach the cliffs above but failed to get there through lack of time. On the way we came across a clearing full of tall, straggly plants of typical *Rhododendron kongboense* growing to 1.8m/6ft and more, and these looked identical to what we grow at home under this name. The nearly red flowers are attractive though very small and need to be seen closely to appreciate them. The foliage is very aromatic with a strawberry-like odour. Much of the forest in this immediate vicinity was *Juniperus recurva*, growing into large trees some 25m/85ft tall, all covered with moss, but it was too dry for epiphytes. We found probable *Primula sonchifolia* here, plus *P. tanneri* subsp. *tsariensis* and

A landslide below a notoriously bad stretch of road along the Po Tsangpo in Bome. Note the 'ants' starting to construct a 'wall' perhaps 300m/1,000ft below, which looked to us to be an impossible task.

Primula chungensis, *an easy candelabra that can naturalise in gardens, flourished in shade in the Rong Chu, forming colourful drifts.*

Prayer flags at the village of Tumbatse in the Rong Chu where Kingdon Ward had his base on the 1924 expedition.

masses of the orange candelabra P. *chungensis* in drifts in clearings and under the trees. *Meconopsis betonicifolia* was coming into flower, usually growing in fairly damp sites near streams.

In the afternoon we went back to the foot of the Sirchem La road to see cypripediums where the one plant of C. *flavum* was now fully out. On the way back to camp we stopped to look at the unspoilt Tibetan village of Tumbatse, in which Kingdon Ward and Cawdor had made their headquarters in 1924, the flat-topped houses being just what we imagined Tibetan houses should look like.[22] We were asked into a house with a very nice family to whom June gave presents and they reciprocated with Tibetan tea. Back in camp, Kenneth and John Roy entertained the local children playing the fool. That evening we stopped playing bridge at 10.20 as it was so cold, and even Kenneth complained with all his many but thin layers of clothes on.

David and Franz did not turn up that evening but arrived in the morning, having failed to reach their goal. They stayed the first night in a headman's house with all his best rugs laid out. The Americans, whom we met earlier, and some Japanese had stayed there too. Unfortunately they met up with police who charged them some large undisclosed sum for being in a place

for which they did not have a permit. Going on to Gompa Ne would have involved a climb of 600m/2,000ft, then a substantial drop down into the Yarlung Tsangpo gorge, and then back, which would have taken an extra day.

The next day, our last in the Rong Chu, proved to be our dullest day, but these poor days are inevitable, even in the richest country. There were only a few *Rhododendron wardii*, R. *uvariifolium* var. *griseum* low down and many R. *principis* (unusually) higher up, including very big specimens, some of which were in flower. In the meantime, Chris had gone up the valley beyond our camp and came back with an armful of R. *wardii*, all with blotches deep in the throat, rather than just on the upper lobe, taken off different plants. Alas, he could not find any good seed.

19. Other plants of interest at this low elevation were a huge *Pieris formosa*, *Acer sterculaceum* with large leaves and fine red new growth and the endemic *Mahonia pomensis*, also with large leaves and reddish young growth.

20. Since 1996, this species has been found in several locations.

21. It is my opinion that R. *lanatoides*, R. *circinnatum* and the closely related R. *luciferum* are only distantly related to R. *lanatum*, if at all, and they grow into much bigger plants. There were numerous other hybrids including R. *hirtipes* x R. *wardii*, R. *hirtipes* x R. *lanatoides* and probably also crossed with R. *phaeochrysum*.

The top of Temo La, which we crossed to get back to the Yarlung Tsangpo valley.

The Temo La

The following morning looked good for our climb over the Temo La, which in 1995 they had approached from the south side, only very few reaching the top, and no one crossing over.[22] John Vaughan, Philip and I started off first, crossed the bridge, then followed the stream up what was at first a good path. After a while the path deteriorated and virtually vanished into the forest and we began to get somewhat alarmed, so we stopped and wondered what to do as we seemed to have come the wrong way. Luckily we were still just in calling distance of the others on a still morning and heard Kenneth shouting a long way off, and soon after we made out Himal's whistle. We had lost one hour and twenty minutes but had done almost no climbing. The proper path had turned sharply up hill a long way back. Moral: do not start towards unknown territory without a guide.

The path climbed steadily with masses of *Rhododendron lepidotum* and *R. triflorum* up the path side, later *R. principis*, *R. uvariifolium* var. *griseum* and *R. wardii*, the last as usual in full flower. Some were slightly blotched but nothing like Chris's of the day before. There was lots of apparent *R. laudandum* var. *laudandum*, all shades from white to good pink but poor trusses. All had wider leaves than the *R. kongboense* of two days ago, and all but one of dozens examined had chocolate indumentum. This does seem to merge with *R. primuliflorum*. *R. laudandum* var. *temoense* (CC 7581) did not appear until near the top of the pass, while *R. fragariflorum* (CC 7580) started a little lower. Also near the top were plentiful *R.*

phaeochrysum, nearly all having good pink flowers, contrasting with those of Yunnan and Sichuan which are mostly white. The dwarf rhododendrons were still largely in bud so there was not the mass of flower seen here in 1995.

We passed several plants of that excellent berberis, *B. temolaica*, named after this pass, which has beautiful glaucous young leaves, purpling with age. Its young foliage contrasts well with its pale yellow flowers, which are followed by egg-shaped red fruit with a white bloom.

The climb to the pass at 4,150m/13,500ft was relatively steady and easy and we all made it without too much difficulty. We stopped for a while on the top amongst the inevitable prayer flags, admiring the view in both directions and having our lunch. To the east, we could sometimes make out the great peak of Namcha Barwa and the less impressive Gyala Peri to its left. In between there was the long undulating ridge between the Rong Chu and the Yarlung Tsangpo, still with patches of snow here and there. To the west, we looked down right into the Yarlung Tsangpo valley over 1,000m/3,300ft below us.

Some of us went searching for more plants on a little path that carried on up the ridge to the south of the top of the pass. I found a pure white *Rhododenron nivale*. Cushions of *Potentilla microphylla* adorned the screes with its silky leaves and yellow flowers.

Just over the pass on the south side on small cliffs with fairly dry gravelly soil grew quantities of the unusual *Primula cawdoriana*, just starting to open its pendant tubular pale blue

A *beautiful blotched form of* Rhododendron wardii *on the south side of the Temo La.*

Meconopsis betonicifolia *on the south side of the Temo La. It was from the Rong Chu in 1924 that Kingdon Ward first introduced this now so well-known blue poppy.*

flowers from velvety rosettes. This has been cultivated with some success but is by no means easy. It was named after the Earl of Cawdor who accompanied Kingdon Ward in 1924. Those who reached the top of the pass in 1995 saw it in full flower, as they did quantities of cassiopes which also were still in bud.

The path dropped steeply to begin with and then became less steep, but it seemed a long way down into the Tsangpo valley. We passed some of the best specimens of *Rhododendron wardii* yet seen; one clear yellow plant in particular was perhaps the finest specimen I have ever set eyes on, and below it was an excellent blotched one like Ludlow and Sherriff 5679. We passed some good blue *Meconopsis simplicifolia*, and then lower down two good clumps of M. *betonicifolia* in flower. Near the foot were masses of berberis in full flower, unfortunately not B. *temoliaca*, but none the less very showy, perhaps B. *aristata*. Near our camp was a fine group of *Paeonia ludlowii*, this time with larger yellow flowers with no red markings. Perhaps the first lot were P. *delavayi* Lutea Group (or *Paeonia delavayi* var. *delavayi* f. *lutea*.).

We stopped at our proposed camp, only to find that our drivers would not bring their vehicles up that far due to rocks in the track, so we had to walk some distance more. John Durran and Ernst looked especially tired. We had an entertaining evening with quantities of local Tibetans milling around us.[23] It was about here that the 1995 party had their worst night due to dogs barking non-stop, so we were relieved to have quite a peaceful one.

In the morning, David reckoned that he had 'flu and certainly looked under the weather. The drive to Bayi was rough, passing another attractive Tibetan village, and luckily, we did not have to stop in Bayi this time. We noticed Communist red flags on the occasional house in these villages. We were to go to Lhasa by the northern route, thus cutting out the high Putrang La road. Our vehicle had a puncture, but the tyre was very quickly changed by our driver, the nicest of the bunch. We camped on a sort of island near Gyanda Gongpo on the way to the Pa La, our last pass of the expedition. Chris was delighted to see a pair of a rare plover on the river, which he had not seen before. We had all signed a card for John Roy on his birthday and he also had a cake made for him plus 'flambé' bananas. We had our usual audience of locals, both evening and morning.

Philip and I climbed up the dry north-west-facing hillside above the camp and found a very fastigiate *Rhododendron nivale*, yellow-flowered *Euphorbia wallichii* and *Stellera chamaejasme* with white and pink flowers that indicate western influence (it is yellow flowered in China). There were bushes of a very neat erect form of *Potentilla fruticosa* var. *parvifolia* with small leaves and the brightest of small yellow flowers. There were also the last few bushes of *Rhododenron phaeochrysum* up on cliffs before conditions became too dry for it to survive.

A typical Tibetan house in a village near Bayi.

22. The climb from the south is much steeper than we had to accomplish. In 1995 the dwarf rhododendrons were at their best, but in 1996 the season was later, and they had only just started to flower.

23. I have hardly mentioned the Tibetan people who I have always admired. I met a few that the Sherriffs had to stay at their home Ascreavie in Angus. Many Tibetan girls are most attractive but they age quickly, no doubt due to the harsh climate and hard manual work. Carrying heavy loads from a young age is hard on the human body, and men and women alike soon look very much older than they are.

Alpines on the south side of the Pa La included this very narrow-leaved dwarf form of what otherwise seems to be typical Meconopsis integrifolia.

The gaudy flowers of the prostrate Incarvillea younghusbandii look out of place on the bare Tibetan plateau.

On approaching the Pa La, we saw sheets of carpeting pink flowers, Androsace graminifolia, which seems to be little-known in cultivation.

Chionocharis hookeri was at its glorious best on the Pa La. There are many splendid alpine plants in the world but few rival this one.

The view south from the Pa La.

The Pa La

As we approached the pass, the hillsides became drier and drier, especially those facing south. For a while the north-facing ones were covered with *Rhododendron nivale* subsp. *nivale* as are the best hillsides with heather in eastern and central Scotland, though the colour is different, here creating a blue-purple haze, which petered out by the pass. We had numerous stops on the way to the pass, too many in fact, as the top proved to be the best place of all, and our time was limited there. The earlier stops produced many interesting plants. *Clematis tibetana* subsp. *vernayi* had flowers ranging all the way from yellow to almost black and *Spiraea canescens* (CC 7595) had flowers white to a good pink. At another stop there were sheets of the bright pink ground-covering *Androsace graminifolia*, the extraordinary looking sessile *Incarvillea younghusbandii* and a fine blue Gesneriad *Coralodiscus kingianus*.

The 4,600m/15,000ft Pa La (Mangshung La is the Chinese name) proved to be very different from anywhere else we had been, although a few plants were in common with the less dry Putrang La, our first pass. This was the first time I had seen a species of that highly rated alpine crucifer with the extraordinary name, *Solms-laubachia*, in this case *S. ciliaris*, with rather washed-out grey-blue flowers, growing on eroded ground only. A lovely *Meconopsis* species was just coming out, obviously closely related to M. *integrifolia* but with very narrow leaves and large yellow saucer-shaped flowers.[24] Other plants were a white *Androsace*, yellow-flowered *Oxygraphis*, an *Arenaria* with the usual white flowers, a very dwarf blue *Corydalis* and a tiny pink *Primula*. But the star turn was *Chionocharis hookeri*, a close relative of the fabulous *Eritrichium nanum* and perhaps even more desirable. This formed tight cushions, often up to 20cm/8in across, with grey foliage covered with the most stunning clear blue (sometimes blue-purple) flowers imaginable. It was later voted plant of the expedition. I had rushed over the back on to the north-facing slope as I had spotted these enticing alpines from the vehicle. Before long, Kenneth was shouting that we had to go, but I rebelled and refused to go until I had seen and photographed everything. Some of the others were slower off the mark to the north slope and hardly saw anything as they had obeyed Kenneth's summons.

On the way down from the pass, the Toyota that June, Ernst, Franz and Helmut were in very nearly toppled off the

24. *Meconopsis integrifolia* is only supposed to occur further east, while M. *pseudointegrifolia* takes over in the west. It could be that the former is more of a dry country species and the latter a wet one.

We saw a fine population of Arisaema flava *around the Potala in Lhasa. This is one of the smallest members of this genus of aroids and is invariably found in dryish areas, sometimes in full exposure.*

is obviously still much as it was, the lack of the Dali Lama's physical or spiritual presence, and the commercialism, gives only a little more atmosphere than the average museum. Photography is permitted inside, but only at a price, and each room is charged for separately.

The Johang monastery was in complete contrast to the Potala. Very small in comparison, this was still occupied by monks and used as it should be. All of us admitted to feeling something special which, as far as I was concerned (I am normally an atheist), was very pleasant and humbling.

We had a very good meal on our last night in Tibet but the food was hardly Tibetan. David, Kenneth and Ernst all made speeches and Ernst's was outstanding. We voted on the best plant of the expedition, won by *Chionocharis hookeri* as stated earlier. On reflection I thought *Rhododendron wardii* should have had it and other serious candidates were: *R. imperator*, *R. parmulatum*, *Primula falcifolia*, *P. chungensis*, the two forms of *Clematis montana*, *Meconopsis integrifolia* aff. and *Podophyllum aurantiocaule*.

We spent nearly three full days in Kathmandu, due to there being so few flights out. The Thamel district with its narrow streets is a great place to shop, and we spent a lot of time there,

road, just missing a fuel truck that swerved when avoiding a pothole. There was a drop of about 7.5m/25ft and they could have been seriously hurt, especially our oldest member Ernst who was on the corner nearest the drop. As usual, a bunch of locals soon appeared out of nowhere and, with some army fuel drivers, they bodily lifted the front back on to the road. The driver was the one who came to be known as the 'Whinger'. We stopped for lunch at a cafe where we had excellent yak soup with tender bits of meat, and good Tibetan tea.

The last 20km/12 miles of road to Lhasa was paved. On the way in we had a car wash, like the one we had on the way into Chengdu. Lhasa as a whole is now just like any other Chinese town with very few old buildings left. We stayed in the Tibet Royal Hotel where we were able to have good showers, but Philip's and mine had to be cleaned out. We had a meal in a restaurant in view of the Potala (pronounced without any accent on any syllable) which is one of the most magnificent buildings in the world and fully lived up to its photographs. The tour of the interior, however, filled one with sadness and a sense of the complete loss of religious atmosphere. Although it

Lilium nepalense *coming into flower on Pulchoki peak.*

The Potala in Lhasa.

especially at Pilgrims famous bookshop. One day we went to the old town of Bhaktapur, which is well worth a visit, and another to Pulchoki, a 3,000m/10,000ft peak behind the Botanic Garden. The chief object of this was to find *Lilium nepalense*, in flower, we hoped. Five of us hired a 4WD vehicle. As soon as we reached the mountain and started going up the hairpin bends, we realised that our driver had obviously never driven up hills before and that the vehicle was equally incapable of climbing. Stupidly, we all got out and wandered along a path out of sight. When driver plus vehicle disappeared we panicked, remembering that some of us had left our little rucksacks in the vehicle and the driver could have scarpered with the lot. But he soon appeared, having driven a little way and then walked back. He actually seemed quite decent and had a nice smile. Twice more the vehicle failed, so we had to get out and walk up hill, but eventually we made the top.

Although it was undoubtedly at least second growth forest, there was no sign of any recent cutting. We found some *Daphne bholua* and a fair number of *Rhododendron arboreum*. The latter were at first the typical low elevation type with a silvery indumentum, then near the top, it turned into subsp. *cinnamomeum* var. *roseum* Campbelliae Group with brownish indumentum. We did find *Lilium nepalense*, mostly in bud, but one splendid stem full out with two flowers. This stoloniferous species is easy enough to grow if it is kept free of virus, but not always easy to get to flower. Among the trees and shrubs seen were *Lithocarpus*, *Quercus*, *Schima*, *Mahonia*, *Luculia* and *Deutzia*.

We left for home early on the 21 June, stopping in Dubai, where I bought a 75–300mm zoom for my Canon, the same as David had, but probably did not save much money. The journey passed quickly for the bridge players, playing across the aisle without too much difficulty.

This had been an excellent expedition with remarkably few hassles, good organization, company and food and splendid scenery and plants, not forgetting games of bridge to pass idle moments.

Chapter 13

TSARI, A VALLEY TOO FAR:

Tibet 1998

Peter Cox

The Exodus expedition to Tibet in 1998 was to a totally different area from the 1996 one, which others followed in 1997 when I went up the Salween. This time we were going to the Tsari valley, which Ludlow and Sherriff had found so rewarding. Our party included many people I had travelled with on previous occasions.[1] In contrast to 1996 when I was about average age for the party, this time I was the third oldest, with only Raymond and June being older. Age does not actually matter too much as everyone can do things in their own time, and age does not seem to play any part in susceptibility to altitude sickness.

Just a few weeks before we were due to leave home, the Indians tested their A-bombs, and at once I guessed that this would cause trouble with the Chinese. In Chapter 2 we explained about the disputed territory of Arunachal Pradesh, and it so happens that Tsari is right on that border with India.

On 5 June we flew Qatar Airways (Qatar for those who do not know is a Gulf Emirate) via capital Doha to Kathmandu. Kenneth and I had made the mistake of not getting Nepalese visas at home,

and had to wait in a queue for ages at the airport. We stayed in the Royal Singi Hotel. While most of the first comers went to Bhaktapur, the rest of us chose Patan, where it was good to see several of the old buildings being repaired, with money from Austria, we were told. We had a meal in the Annapurna Restaurant where they were having a Mexican Week with two Mexican chefs dressed up in traditional costumes. Kenneth was able to converse with them in Spanish. The second night we had a good meal, Nepalese style, sitting on low cushions which was very uncomfortable. We were greeted with fire-water poured out of a long spouted kettle from a height, with great expertise.

When we got back to our rooms, the unwelcome news I had half expected came through that the Chinese were being difficult, restricting us to the north-facing slopes of the mountains overlooking the Tsari valley and withdrawing our permit for the valley itself. David offered us the choice of going home or just making the best of what we are allowed to do. Everybody wanted to carry on, having got this far.

318

We had an excellent flight over the Himalaya with very clear views. After our arrival in Lhasa, we started with some trouble with the Peoples' Security Bureau (PSB) (more of them later) and we heard that the Chinese were on the point of sending in troops and tanks to the frontier. We stayed in the same village as the first night in 1996, Chusum. I began to suffer altitude symptoms and, by the morning, several of us were reporting feeling ill, even Kenneth spending the morning in bed. We played bridge and found that we had enough players for two tables. The Leathers, particularly Fiona, proved to be formidable players. Some of us walked to a scrubby wood nearby adorned with the common yellow-flowered *Arisaema flavum*, *Clematis tibetana* subsp. *vernayi* and *Primula tibetica*.

We made several stops going over the Putrang La where there was a good amount in flower but nothing much that we had not seen in 1996. We camped at a low elevation (for Tibet) shortly before reaching the Yarlung Tsangpo once more. In the morning, there was much discussion about where to leave the main road for the Bimbi La, various locals being asked. There were several villages up our road, including one with timber trucks but with very little timber to harvest on these mostly dry slopes. I did notice one hillside with different exposures that

1. I had been with half our party in 1996: Chris Sanders, John Roy, June Ross, Raymond Bomford, Peter Hartrey and his wife Bathsheba Pradhan and our leaders David Burlinson and my son Kenneth. Steve Hootman had been with me in 1995 and 1997 in China. Anne Chambers and Richard Lilley had been to Tibet on years that I had not, and the following had never been: Dr John Welton and his wife Dr Ann Welton, Graham Rugman and Jane Milson and Jay and Fiona Leathers. Our Tibetan and Nepali staff included some of the same members as in 1996, Tsering, Myingma, Akal, Shuma, Choedak, Dorje, Shen Tao and last but not least, David's Chinese right-hand man, He Hai.

Above. View across the Yarlung Tsangpo looking east with sand dunes covering extensive areas.

Above left. Stellera chamaejasme *on the Putrang La. This is the typical Himalayan form as opposed to the yellow Chinese form.*

319

Orobanche *species make no chlorophyll themselves, depending on the roots of other plants.*

The amazingly coloured Thermopsis barbata.

had larch, pine and spruce or fir. We passed an old Tibetan kings' burial site with large flat-topped mounds.

Arisaema flavum followed us all the way up to the village of Layi which was the end of the road at 3,800m/12,500ft. I reflected that this was higher than anywhere we reached in 1997 in Yunnan and here we had not even started. There was the pretty but prickly blue *Onosma hookeri*, mats of the little scroph *Lancea tibetica*, which at first sight resembled a roscoea, and an ugly parasitic *Orobanche*. The locals brought in specimens of *Rhododendron aganniphum*, *R. nivale* and *R. primuliflorum*, which indicated that rhododendrons were to be found locally.

It was good to hear that the Tibetans of Layi had plenty of ponies, and that they were very friendly and willing to help us. The ponies were scattered all over the hillsides, so it would take them a day to catch enough, which actually suited us fine, as it gave us a chance to acclimatise and explore the immediate vicinity. In the morning we set out in a westerly direction, at first through fields and grazed meadows with many berberis in full flower, and then after we turned the corner on to a north-facing slope, we found forest, *Sorbus*, *Betula*, *Larix* and *Abies* and, of course, rhododendrons. Of these, the first three were *R. principis* (CHC 8509), *R. aganniphum* (CHC 8501)[2] and wishy-washy *R.*

primuliflorum. There were masses of *R. aganniphum* in full and excellent flower, mostly pink to deep rose, a few white, and Kenneth and Steve reckoned that some fitted into Glaucopeplum Group (CHC 8502). Then there was *R. wardii* (CHC 8503), only just coming out, all of which appeared to have blotched flowers and were good specimens, except for one large one that had the poorest flowers we had ever seen on *R. wardii*. In the more open spaces, there were quantities of splendid *Cassiope fastigiata* covered in little white bells. Kenneth and Steve went on further than the rest of us and found yellow to cream-flowered *Rhododendron phaeochrysum* aff. (CC 8504) with semi-plastered rufous indumentum. My Ludlow and Sherriff field notes of the Bimbi La have two numbers, one lemon-yellow, the other pale lemon cream, but there were no specimens to go with those numbers in the herbarium at the RBGE. So here we were with the same plant recorded in 1936, which was never introduced or given any botanical status.

With my head and tummy troubles I had an awful struggle to get up anywhere that day. Poor June, who had been so fit in 1996, admitted that she had made no preparations for this trip and was also not feeling up to it, with trapped nerve problems in addition.

2. CHC = Cox, Hootman, Cox.

A fine pink R. aganniphum *on a north-facing slope behind the village of Layi. It was to prove to be very plentiful on the Bimbi La.*

The fine Euphorbia wallichii *was plentiful on disturbed ground near the villages above Layi.*

One of the many attractive Pedicularis *species, perhaps* P. oederi.

Coloured young foliage of a rhubarb, Rheum moorcroftianum.

Bergenia purpurescens *on a steep bank on the way to the Bimbi La.*

Tibetan woman at the village of Layi at the end of the road and where we started our trek up the Bimbi La.

The Bimbi La

On 13 June off we walked at 10 o'clock on the start of our trek towards the Bimbi La, beginning with a gradual climb, followed by a descent along a cliff, finding ourselves lower than when we set off. We passed various plants of interest or beauty. Ranunculaceae were well represented with blue *Anemone wardii*, *A. trullifolia* with flowers white above and bluish below or yellow, *A. trullifolia* var. *linearis*, *A. obtusiloba*, yellow *Caltha scaposa* and the neat *Trollius pumilus*. There was a pretty blue *Dracocephalum* at the foot of the cliff and two species of *Androsace*, *A. biscula* or *adenocephala* and the common pink *A. geraniifolia*. The long-named *Gueldenstaedtia himalaica* was a nice little purple-flowered alpine but the plant of the day was the almost black-flowered *Thermopsis barbata*.

We walked along damp meadows before turning left up to the Bimbi La. There was one short but fairly deep patch of snow which nearly floored the horses, but all got through without any accidents. The pass itself at 4,500m/14,700ft was very bleak, as they often are, and we camped just over the pass at 4,400m/14,500ft, the highest I have ever camped.

On the way up to the pass at 4,100m/13,500ft plus, we were delighted that the yellow *Rhododendron phaeochrysum* aff. (CHC 8512) was up here in large quantities, and with the flowers at their best. It was most attractive with surprisingly large flowers, always with a blotch, large or small. Sometimes it was on its own, covering

Our pack horses crossing a small snowfield. Horses have difficulties in walking through deep snow.

Rhododendron laudandum (R. laudandum *var.* temoense) *is a lovely and distinct species.*

A pale-flowered form of Meconopsis simplicifolia *growing in a thicket. Any in the open are munched off by livestock.*

Oreosolen wattii, *a member of* Scrophulariaceae, *is one of several high alpines that produce flat fleshy leaves as a way to reduce transpiration and keep the plants out of the wind as much as possible.*

A beautiful pink from of Diapensia purpurea *on the Bimbi La. Oh how we wish this plant was easier to grow.*

large areas with sheets of pale yellow, at other times it was mixed with the contrasting pink R. *aganniphum*, which made a delightful mixture. Although they flowered together and are assumed to be closely related, there was no evidence of hybridity between the two. Up here, R. *primuliflorum* was much dwarfer, wider than high, with some very pretty pink forms. R. *laudandum* here all fitted what is officially called R. *laudandum* var. *temoense* with dark leaves, shiny above, with chocolate 'indumentum' below, and white to pale pink flowers.[3] There were a few intermediate plants with brown indumentum. R. *fragariflorum* had flowers varying from pink to more mauve. All three of these dwarf rhododendrons were in full bloom and made a splendid sight.

The alpines were perfection, in great variety, and we definitely hit them at their peak. The following were the ones that impressed me most. It is obviously too dry here to have many different dwarf *Ericaceae*, but there was fine *Cassiope selaginoides*,

and also *Gaultheria pyroloides*. There were lovely cushions of *Diapensia purpurea*, all pink-flowered and the curious *Oreosolen wattii* with fleshy flat leaves with sessile yellow flowers in the centre. Another oddity with an appropriate name was *Pycnoplinthopsis bhutanica*, which had long, strap-like leaves and white flowers and always grew in shallow water. The widespread *Fritillaria cirrhosa* (CHC 8544) was always yellow here and grew associated with its cousin *Lilium nanum* with single nodding pink flowers. *Meconopsis horridula* (probably one of its resurrected relatives, M. *racemosa*)[4] was amazingly variable, both in shape of

3. R. *laudandum* var. *temoense* is endemic to south-east Tibet and the true plant was not in cultivation until 1995. It is proving very slow and difficult to grow and does not flower at an early age, which is a great pity as it is a lovely and distinct species.

4. Dr Chris Grey-Wilson is in the process of revising the genus *Meconopsis* and reinstating many of the species sunk by Sir George Taylor.

323

This is me near the Bimbi La.

A strange member of the family Cruciferae with the incongruous name of Pycnoplinthopsis bhutanica. While Polunin and Stainton say it grows on rocks, screes and cliff faces, we always found it in little pools of water.

Primula glabra *on the Bimbi La.*

Primula ioessa *on the Bimbi La. There was a great variation in the flower colour, lilac-blue, through pink, yellow to white.*

Mats of Primula jonardunii *plastered the rocky banks on the Bimbi La.*

A Saussurea *species, perhaps* S. obvallata, *on the Bimbi La.*

Saussurea medusa *aff. on the Bimbi La.*

Primula macrophylla *on the Bimbi La.*

flower and its colour, varying from a clear pale blue to purple, while M. *simplicifolia* was disappointing, being dirty purple to pale lilac. There were scattered plants of that extraordinary rhubarb *Rheum nobile* with cream, sometimes flushed pink columns, which, unfortunately for them, are eaten by the Tibetans. Matching the rhubarb was a woolly *Saussurea* and a *Bergenia* had round leaves and pink flowers (CC 8519). For me, the primulas stole the show. There were masses of P. *tanneri* subsp. *tsariensis* all the way up to the pass, P. *ioessa* in all colours from white, yellow and pink to violet,[5] and the gorgeous P. *jonardunii*, which is sometimes treated as a subspecies of P. *dryadifolia*, but is dwarfer and separated geographically.

Our camp was situated above a little tarn on a roughish piece of ground, the only almost flat area available, with us stumbling through undergrowth to get from our tents to the mess tent. Beyond the tarn was a steep mountain side which was particularly rich in alpines and many of us spent hours photographing there. The plan for the morning was to carefully make our way down towards the Tsari valley without being seen by the Chinese army.

There only appeared to be the one path that we had come

up, which carried on almost on the level. As our object was to descend as far as possible, we overruled the guides who, it turned out, had never been over the pass themselves. The mountainside appeared to be quite open, so we started to drop down opposite our camp, only to find ourselves getting deeper and deeper into rhododendron thickets, with no hope of getting any further. So we were all quite exhausted by the time we had extricated ourselves and got back on the path.

Steve and Kenneth were determined to get at least some way into the valley, so went ahead. Fiona and I joined up and followed Steve and Kenneth, while the others dilly-dallied behind. There was not much new for a while until we came to a rock which had an overhang where the Tibetans placed stones as a religious act. Under the overhang grew the most beautiful little pink primula with a yellow eye, P. *caveana*,[6] covered with meal and sweetly scented. This grows at the highest altitudes of all

5. *Primula ioessa*, a P. *sikkimensis* relative, is not nearly so vigorous or so common as that species and its distribution is apparently confined to the Tsari district.

6. This super little plant has the distinction of having been found at 5,600m/16,300ft, higher than any other primula and higher than most other flowering plants.

Huge drifts of Primula sikkimensis *covered these Bimbi La yak meadows, sometimes accompanied by the purple* P. *tanneri* var. tsariensis.

Primula sikkimensis, *with* Rhododendron aganniphum *behind, on the south side of the Bimbi La.*

326

Primula caveana *growing on a tiny Buddhist shrine to which people evidently keep adding slabs of stone, thus spoiling the primulas.*

primulas, so is understandably hard to grow. We then came to a sea of primulas in full flower. There was a long argument as to whether these were *P. sikkimensis* or *P. alpicola* but in the end, the former won. This was accompanied by *P. tanneri* subsp. *tsariensis*, and the contrast of the yellow with the purple was very striking.

Looking down to the next level, Fiona and I saw Steve and Kenneth taking what was obviously a considerable interest in some rhododendrons, so we reckoned correctly that it must be something different. So we carried on down to another smaller primula meadow where there was the great combination of a pale mauve *Erigeron*, the yellow *Primula sikkimensis* and, at the back, fine pink bushes of *Rhododendron aganniphum*. We soon came across the object of our endeavours, some tall rhododendrons with thickish woolly indumentum, and cream-coloured flowers just going over. This was *R. circinnatum* (CHC 8518), which was discovered by Kingdon Ward on this pass in 1935 but never introduced. This is closely related to the generally more westerly *R. luciferum* which has narrower leaves with a thicker indumentum. Kenneth thinks they are the same thing.[7]

By the time Fiona and I got back to the upper primula meadow, most of the rest of our party had reached there, and were very pleased that they had. After a lovely day, we all reached camp happy but tired, especially Steve and Kenneth.

I woke up with a splitting headache which paracetamol eventually alleviated. It was an easy day as it was all down hill, apart from the initial short climb back to the pass. From the pass, we had a great view of snow peaks to the north, and we planned to spend an extra day (two nights) on the way down exploring a side valley, and perhaps reaching a glacier. We heard three explosions which seemed to come from the Tsari valley and we wondered if the Chinese and Indians were shooting at each other. We stayed at the same camp as on the way up.

We crossed the river coming in from the west, then walked up the north bank of the Zumdung valley along a cliff, but the path was good. We had lunch at a clearing where we thought we were going to camp, but no, we were going on. We attempted to play bridge in a shower under an umbrella but David's plastic cards

stuck together! A little further on we came across Kenneth lying stretched out in the shade feeling very giddy. A staff member was sent to find Dr John who was ahead, and the medical kit and a horse were sent back. He soon recovered and was able to eat that evening. As most of our staff had to go back to the village for provisions, we helped to erect tents, and luckily just after we had finished, down came the heaviest rain of the expedition.

Our plan for the next day was to split into two parties, one to go south up another valley, the other north-west towards the glacier. Steve, Raymond and I started up the south Ydok valley, followed by Jay and Fiona. Steve and I carried on when the rain came on, but the others returned to camp. The valley widened, and climbed only very gradually, a mere 180m/600ft to the scree at the top end. The first part was a shallow lake with a pair of ruddy shelduck, and there was evidence of other wildlife with many burrows made by marmots or pika. Beyond

Rheum nobile *and our local guide in the Ydok valley. This rhubarb stands out like a beacon in the landscape, which often leads to its demise, as the locals chop it down and eat it.*

7. On examining herbarium specimens, it is evident that *R. luciferum* occurs to the west up the Chayal Chu and east on the Lo La.

327

Cassiope fastigiata *is mid-way in width of shoot between* C. selaginoides *(narrower) and* C. wardii *(broader). It is apt to become straggly in cultivation and rarely flowers as well as seen here.*

The yellow-flowered Taliensia rhododendron that seems to be related to R. phaeochrysum.

the lake was a stony flat with water running through it, and beyond the scree there was snow.

Low down the valley was a fine group of good blue *Meconopsis simplicifolia* but further up were the usual washed out mauves. The others found good blue ones too. The primulas seen were similar to the Bimbi La except there were no *P. jonardunii*. The yellow *Corydalis conspersa* was growing on the water's edge and the blue *Lonicera syringantha* had very small leaves and flowers. Both parties saw *Cassiope fastigiata*

and *C. selaginoides*, while we had plenty of *Fritillaria cirrhosa* and the others had few.

The rhododendrons were in particularly good flower for Steve and me, with some huge bushes of the yellow *R. phaeochrysum* aff. (CHC 8524 and 8527),[8] and lovely mixtures of the other species. I thought I saw a dwarf yellow rhododendron in flower near a waterfall and we plunged into a thicket to reach it. The distance had fooled us and it was just more *R. phaeochrysum* aff. In the thicket were some sprawling

A 'gardened' mound in the Ydok valley with Rhododendron fragariflorum, R. laudandum *and a* Rhodiola *species.*

Looking north across a patchwork of ripening tiny fields to the village of Layi, towards the Yarlung Tsangpo, over which a storm is brewing.

plants of *R. dignabile* aff. which appeared to be somewhat different from what we saw in 1996, especially in their almost ground-covering habit. The other party failed to reach the glacier and did not find anything new.

On 19 June we set off back to Layi. By now most of us were getting fit and used to the altitude. I found the ups and downs surprisingly easy. It was hot and sunny most of the way, then after lunch, those of us who lagged behind got caught in a heavy shower, while the others in front had missed it and were already playing bridge. The view to the north after the shower was staggering. Towards the Yarlung Tsangpo an inky-black thunder storm was rumbling away and to the right were gleaming snow peaks. In the middle distance was a patchwork of ripening fields of grain scattered over the hillsides, while in the foreground were masses of flowering white roses and clematis. More wildlife was seen by most of the party. Large hares with long back legs sprang around a meadow and Kenneth saw a stoat-like mammal which might prey on the hares. A few eagles soared overhead.

We were welcomed by the jolly inhabitants of the village who seemed happy to have us there. Jay and Fiona had brought a bag shower, which was enjoyed by most, but it was hardly adequate to wash more than a single part of one's body. Our plans were to make for the Sur La, another high pass to the west overlooking the Tsari valley.

Expertly carved new windows in Layi, with a proud craftsman standing by.

8. Seed of *R. phaeochrysum* aff. germinated poorly and the seedlings are very slow-growing. It is better grafted. CHC 8504, 8512, 8524, 8527.

329

Incarvillea longiracemosa *growing on dry scrubby banks.*

The Sur La

On 20 June it was Ann Chambers' 60th birthday and she started it by complaining that she had had only two hours' sleep due to the noisy bridge players. The road up so far towards the Sur La was very rough and on the way there were shouts of 'Stop' when a really exciting plant appeared for the first time. Growing on dry scrubby banks from 3,500 to 3,800m/11,500 to 12,500ft, we found numerous plants of what we took to be *Incarvillea lutea*, but after getting home, we consulted a recent article by Chris Grey-Wilson which indicated it was the more westerly distributed *I. longiracemosa* (CHC 8533). There were two fine plants about 50cm/20in tall in full bloom, and driving on we saw no more. We camped on a small site at little above river level in the village of Beru, at the confluence of two rivers. This looked a poor village compared with those of the valley below the Bimbi La and the people looked surly and untrustworthy. Our tents were carefully secured and heavily guarded. Ponies were hired from another village higher up where the people were much more friendly. We suspect people from Beru got us into trouble after we returned from the Sur La.

The river right by the camp was dirty, perhaps due to some development such as a new road upstream, while the other one which we were to follow was clean. After a short but pretty

gorge, we came to a large yak meadow which would have been a perfect campsite. All along the hillsides, *Incarvillea longiracemosa* became very common, and to our great surprise, all the old seed-bearing plants were dead, indicating that this species is monocarpic. This is apparently unique in the genus *Incarvillea*. The seed was held tight within the capsule like a strong spring and it took brute strength to release it.[9] Anne Chambers has flowered it in her garden near Glascaw. It is indeed a handsome plant in full flower and as incarvilleas are poisonous to livestock, it was never eaten, and probably benefited by competing herbage being grazed off.

We turned left by the village of Zhong up a dryish valley with plentiful *Juniperus indica*, *Rhododendron principis* and 1.8-3m/6-10ft leggy *R. primuliflorum*. The valley narrowed with almost pure birch forest on the slopes and *Cypripedium tibeticum* in full flower in semi-shade near the trees. Most of our

Meconopsis racemosa *on the Sur La was very variable in flower size and colour and on our way back west on the Putrang La (see page 335) the flowers were a clear pale blue.*

Lloydia flavonutans *is a delicate little member of* Liliaceae *with a distribution west to central Nepal.*

party drooled over these, even though they had seen plenty before, and at the end of the expedition, it was voted the best plant we had seen. *Rhododendron lepidotum* was common on drier banks in the clearings, with yet more *R. aganniphum* and very small-leaved *R. nivale* with bright rose-purple flowers.

This valley is reputed to be one of the most beautiful in Tibet with its string of four lakes, but as it lacks spectacular mountains in the immediate vicinity, such praise may be a little overdone. It is, though, most attractive with forest-clad slopes often down to the water's edge. We passed the first lake and then crossed the stream on stepping stones to camp on a small rather rough meadow by the second lake. We had had showers on and off all that day.

As with the Bimbi La, the Sur La is not at the head of the valley but off to the west in this case. There was quite a steep climb up through the forest. We were surprised to find two populations of the *Rhododendron dignabile* aff. with *R. aganniphum* in between. Though the flowers of the former were mostly over, there were enough left to see that the corollas were small in flat-topped trusses but some were nicely flushed pink. There were also several large *R. circinnatum* to 7.6m/25ft with cream-coloured flowers with no markings.

Above the tree-line were the usual dwarf rhododendrons,

Just above our lake-side camp in the forest were tall specimens of R. circinatum *with some good flowers still hanging on.*

R. nivale, R. laudandum, R. fragariflorum and *R. primuliflorum*. One plant had wider leaves and pinker flowers than *R. primuliflorum*, looking more like the Himalayan *R. anthopogon*. An exciting variation of *R. fragariflorum*, of which we saw two plants, had white flowers with yellow calyces, with some pale pink ones nearby. *Primula sikkimensis* followed us right up to the pass and *Meconopsis racemosa* was again amazingly variable

9. While seed is easy enough to germinate, growing on the seedlings is not so simple, and they may take as long as ten years plus to flower.

Our ponies wading the river near our camp below the Sur La. We were able to cross on the stepping stones.

The eastern end of the sacred Tapka Shelri was all we were able to see of this beautiful mountain.

At the top of the Sur La we were right above the forbidden Tsari valley and every now and again the mist cleared enough to see parts of the valley floor, including the village of Chosam to the west.

with a few pale sky-blues, through good blue-purples to purple. *Lilium nanum* was common and there were several large *Fritillaria cirrhosa*, while there was a pretty dwarf *Cremanthodium* with the usual nodding heads of yellow flowers. Most of the *Rheum nobile* had already been eaten. Overall, the flora was not nearly as rich as the Bimbi La with no dwarf Ericaceae other than the rhododendrons.

The climb was relatively easy until near the pass where there was a short but steep final assault. We passed a high mountain lake on the left, bigger than the one by the top camp on the Bimbi La. Only nine of us reached the top and I was pleased to observe that I was the oldest to make it. Fiona had ridden most of the way, but husband Jay took it all in his stride, having finally got over his altitude sickness. The 4,785m/15,500ft pass was perched on the top of a steep drop straight into the Tsari valley with little apparent soil or vegetation immediately below. We sat there for some time eating our lunch and, when the mist cleared, getting tantalizing glimpses of the valley and the opposite hillsides and valleys, and longing to be down there ourselves. The sacred snow mountain, Tapka Shelri,[10] was opposite but it never cleared enough to be worth a photograph. We scanned the valley with our binoculars to see if we could spot any Chinese army but were not sure of locating any. The village of Chosam could be seen clearly, slightly to the west, while to the east was the wide part of the valley known as the Senguti plain.

It drizzled a little on the way down, but we were lucky to avoid a heavy shower which must have drenched the top of the lake valley. On the way up we had passed a *baku* (hide tent) guarded by a fierce Tibetan mastiff, which as usual was on a long rope, and woe betide any stranger who ventured inside the radius of the rope. In 1999 John Vaughan (who had been on the 1996 trek) failed to observe the length of a rope and received a nasty bite. On this occasion, the dog (bitch) had puppies, and Choedak bought a puppy for 80 yuan to take back to his mother in Lhasa. Both Fiona and June drooled over this puppy all the way back.

The walk down from the lake camp to Zhong was easy. Again we were lucky, as no sooner were our tents up than the rain came down. We played lots of bridge after supper with two tables, including Raymond, who said that he had not played for thirty years. Near our camp were masses of primulas in boggy ground near the stream. These were vigorous yellow *P. sikkimensis* and the contrasting little pink *P. tibetica*. *Rhododendron lepidotum* had opened a few flowers, all with the typical, rather small plum-purple flat-faced corollas.

It took some time to get a name for this curious composite, Bolocephalus saussuroides, *the specific epithet meaning like a saussurea. It has only been found in the Tsari area.*

Persicaria amplexicaulis *is like* Bistorta affinis *but with drooping flowers.*

The lovely Anemone rupicola *filled a clearing in the scrub on our way back.*

10. For Buddhists the trek around this mountain is considered a great accomplishment. Not long ago the pilgrims were liable to be attacked by Lopa tribes people.

The Drepung monastery near Lhasa.

Arrest

It was an even easier walk across the meadows to where the Land Cruisers and the truck were waiting for us. After a bumpy ride down the track, we reached the main road, where we had expected to turn left towards Lhasa, only to find that we were forced to turn right into a hotel compound. Here we found ourselves under virtual arrest by the PSB. Evidently the nasty people of the village of Beru had reported us; no doubt hoping to share out the cash that the PSB would squeeze out of us. First, they wanted to see any drawings that we might have made of the topography; both Dr Ann and Bathsheba had painted some. Bathsheba's (her first ever landscape) was removed while Ann's were blotted out with more paint. Ann told us later that hers were imaginary, with the skyline just something like she had remembered it! The next thing they wanted was our films, eventually accepting one from each of us, with nearly all of us handing over unexposed film! What they really wanted was print film which could be processed immediately. Then they demanded $400 each. He Hai spent four hours arguing with the six of them; a more dreadful-looking lot no one could imagine, with a Tibetan 'traitor' who had an almost square head. Eventually they realised that He Hai had friends in high places and we got away with paying almost peanuts each. What a stupid lot! They evidently suspected us of being Indian spies

sent to photograph the undersides of bridges. It would be entirely beyond their comprehension that people should want to go all the way to Tibet just to look for plants.

We had deliberately not contacted the PSB on our way to the Sur La as they would have insisted on us staying in their hotel, saying it would take a week to arrange porters and horses, charging us four times the amount, and putting the balance into

A post truck hurtling down the muddy road on the Putrang La on its way into the ditch.

The peculiar fleshy-leaved Phlomis rotata *on the Putrang La.*

Pale blue Meconopsis racemosa *on the Putrang La.*

Potentilla parvifolia, *a relative of* P. fruticosa *that is smaller and neater in all parts.*

their own pockets. This sort of local corruption is becoming all too prevalent in China as a whole, and is difficult to avoid.

We returned to our riverside campsite before re-crossing the Putrang La. The site was decidedly damp and, after a wet night, the loo tent hole was full of water. The way up to the pass was a dreadful mess with various groups of workers attempting to build walls and generally repair the so-called road. Delays gave us extra plant forays, and at one, a post truck came roaring down the hill and went straight into the ditch. The other (dry) side of the pass was fine. Our last incident was when swerving to avoid a truck, we landed in a sand ditch and even the 4WD would not get us out. We wandered off to the river and were greatly embarrassed to see the occupants of the following vehicle pushing ours back on to the road.

Back in Lhasa, those that had been to the Potala before went to the Drepung Monastery to the north-west of the city.[11] In the afternoon we went to the Sera Monastery, north-east of Lhasa, again in the foothills. I was quite moved by the religious atmosphere there and others felt the same. We were told that there were 500-600 monks and we saw one large group at a sort of question time. They repeatedly slapped down their arms. This is for pushing sinners down to hell while the lift upwards afterwards is to help them to repent. It was nice to see the monastery with very few tourists or beggars.

There was apparently still a threat that we might have our films confiscated by the PSB but He Hai managed to banish that threat. David was determined to make use of Exodus's tourist importance to get the PSB off our backs. We finished the day with a good meal but some members of the party ate a raw yak meat dish with not unexpected results.

It rained all night and into the morning with very low clouds. As conditions like this are practically unheard of in Lhasa, the airport has little in the way of navigational instruments to guide planes in and out during periods of poor visibility. We arrived there to find it very crowded. David told us that planes never take off from here after 3 p.m. for some unknown reason, and although it started to clear about mid-morning, the plane we were to catch had never left Chengdu. My nearly new roll of loo paper came in very useful for wiping down some wet chairs and a table (the roof leaked), in preparation for playing bridge.

In the meantime we transferred to the Airport Hotel which was cheap but not too bad with reasonable rooms. Steve and I had a loo which made churning noises like bull frogs and efforts to silence it failed. David had been back to Lhasa, and returned with a welcome supply of more Dynasty, one of the few palatable Chinese wines. The following morning, 28 June, brought yet more rain, and again the plane did not leave Chengdu. So our chances of connecting with the Qatar Airways flight from Kathmandu were now nil. Eventually three planes came in one after the other and we got away on a very quick turn around. As the Qatar Airways flights from Kathmandu were only twice weekly, we had to stay another three nights in Kathmandu, thus getting home three days late. The flight was an all day one, which was good, as we were able go to bed at the normal (for home) time, and get over jet lag quickly.

It had been an enjoyable expedition, despite our failure to reach the Tsari valley, and seeing only about half the plants we were hoping for. As in 1996, the first few days were partly spoilt due to the altitude problems of loss of appetite and morning headaches, only Fiona being able to eat her food properly. But we shall never forget the wonderful plants on the Bimbi La.

Our arrival home was somewhat disturbed by reporters wanting a good story on our arrest by the PSB. The resulting articles were so exaggerated, despite our more or less accurate reports, that it makes one wonder how much of what one reads in the papers is true.

11. Drepung was the largest monastery in Tibet with 10,000 monks in the time of the fifth Dalai Lama, 1617-82; now it houses 50-60. One huge sleeping-praying hall could hold 7,000 monks.

335

Chapter 14

A VOLCANIC PROFESSOR OF GLACIOLOGY:

Guizhou 1999

Peter Hutchison

It had to happen to one trip and our 1999 trip to Guizhou was somewhat eccentric, prone to misunderstandings with the Chinese and rather unproductive. But with all its oddities, which are best put down to experience, it had its lighter moments and it was certainly memorable.

Among our pre-trip problems was the dreadful bombing by NATO forces of the Chinese embassy in Belgrade with the loss of three Chinese lives, followed by a wave of demonstrations outside the American and British embassies with dire warnings from the Foreign Office to intending travellers to China. Gradually people dropped out from our original party of five and I have to admit that at one point I thought of giving up.

So it was just the two of us that finally boarded the plane to Beijing, each clutching our bottle of duty free, in my case Islay malt and for Peter his traditional Sauternes that somehow lasted the month. Then on from Beijing to Chongqing in the south of Sichuan, a vast city straddling both sides of the Yangtze with a population of 30 million, although this apparently includes many of the surrounding districts. Negotiating the scrum at both these airports, where push rapidly gave way to shove, left us wondering at their relatively small and undeveloped state, given the burgeoning Chinese economy.

In Chongqing we were met by a Chinese party of four, including Mr Fan Ting MA, very much the new China and busy in a suit with a mobile phone permanently attached to his ear which, with his round face, earned him the name of 'Moon face and Mobile'. He left shortly after but more important to us was the Professor from Chengdu's Institute of Mountain Research who was to be our leader, and also our excellent driver Liang Jian Hua. The hotel was also very much new China, all marble and glitzy chandeliers, but due to a shortage of common language dinner was a fairly silent affair, punctuated by the very old China sound of noodles being suctioned off the end of chopsticks.

Our principal objectives were the mountains of Jinfo Shan in south-east Sichuan before crossing the border for Fan-jing-shan in north-east Guizhou. We had mentioned both of these in our correspondence before leaving, with no objections or caveats being made. We had been inspired by accounts of the trip which Jim Russell, John Simmons and Hans Fliegner undertook in 1985 to Fan-jing-shan,[1] but they collected only on the south side of the mountain and we wanted to explore the rest of it. Jinfo Shan had been very little plant hunted by foreigners.

Above: The startling cliffs of Jinfo Shan viewed from just outside the reserve.

Above left: The sweet-scented Rhododendron stamineum *was common at Dashahe. It has proved to be quite hardy but shy-flowering in Scotland.*

1. Jim Russell's privately printed version of the trip is one of the most entertaining in all the literature of plant-hunting.

Jinfo Shan

It was hot and hazy as we left Chongqing on the morning of 19 May, heading for Nanchuan, the nearest town to Jinfo Shan. But it was good to get into the teeming Chinese countryside, almost subtropical here with fountains of giant bamboo sprouting among the terraced fields, maize on the slopes above, rice paddies below and ducks dabbling their beaks in the fishponds. Here China feeds its people.

It did not look far to Nanchuan but detours and an appalling road made it a longish journey. As we plunged through rocks and mud, the Professor told us that this was fossiliferous country, 'Making roads is good to find dinosaur,' he said and it seemed entirely possible that we might come on a Plesiosaur as the landscape turned Jurassic. Then as we approached Nanchuan and rose to 600m/2000ft, the hillsides showed pines, cypresses and *Cunninghamia lanceolata* with a surprisingly temperate collection of shrubs, such as *Viburnum, Rubus, Rosa, Pyracantha* and our old and variable friend *Lyonia ovalifolia*.

Rhododendron platypodum had, alas, just finished flowering. This evidently failed to produce good seed that autumn.

The Professor announced that a feast had been laid on with local dignitaries in Nanchuan that evening, with the usual speeches and toasts. Among the great variety of food was a dish of what looked like lumps of scaly fish, which turned out to be snake. It was a mass of tiny bones and the general sensation was of eating stewed knitting – with the needles left in. Since we had seen a large snake on the road that afternoon, the Professor was anxious to explain that this was a farmed one. It was clear that he was quite keen on the social side of our trip as he made good use of my malt whisky as well as the local liquor (surprisingly they were about the same strength, Bunnahabhain 43% against Mau Tai 45%). His background was as an ecologist and glaciologist, but unfortunately there are no glaciers in Guizhou; nor did he know the names of any plants and his interest in them was minimal, which was to cause problems later.

Jinfo Shan has long been out of bounds for foreign plant explorers, largely due to its very rare conifer, *Cathaya argyrophylla*, the Silver China Fir, which has only been found on a few mountains in Guizhou, Guanxi and Hunan, in addition to Jinfo Shan, and usually grows on limestone hills and pinnacles.[2]

The disadvantage of having a substantial minibus with only four of us in it became clear when a posse of six, including our council friends and the 'mayor', turned up the next morning to join the party going up to Jinfo. Some no doubt came for the ride but we had been warned by Edward Needham that the authorities would keep a close eye on us and so it proved. The road goes over a spur at 1,200m/4000ft and then drops down again along a river valley. There were some interesting plants on the spur, but they would have to wait until our return as we could not stop with this contingent on board. The spectacular peaks of Jinfo appeared, with sheer limestone cliffs rising from the cultivated slopes beneath, and we were soon climbing again. When we reached the gates to Jinfo Shan Park a suspicious-looking old man unlocked them and forms had to be filled in. The vegetation thickened and the road dived through a cleft in the cliffs with pinnacles above bearing names like 'Candlestick Peak', 'Stone Person' and 'Penholder Peak'.

The Professor gave us a lecture on being tourists and how we must be careful not to be seen collecting anything. Off we went for a walk towards the high ground, accompanied by a rather athletic young man, while desperately trying to give an impression of casual disinterest in anything resembling a rhododendron. We observed, nevertheless, *R. longipes* var. *chienianum* and *R. calophytum* in the form that the Chinese call var. *pauciflorum*. The former was a straggly plant with surprisingly small leaves for an Argyrophylla, with reddish-brown indumentum, and even smaller white or pinkish flowers. The *R. calophytum* also had smallish leaves and flowers and David Chamberlain thinks it is doubtfully different from var. *openshawianum*. In contrast to this rather undistinguished pair we spotted a plant of *R. platypodum*, a fine rhododendron not yet introduced and one of the species we most hoped to see. Then a heavy wetting mist came down that was to be with us for the rest of our stay on Jinfo.

There were sounds of machinery in the mist ahead, apparently from a new hotel being built, and we stumbled on piles of bricks until we came to the entrance to a cave. It was shut but it turned out that the Professor had an obsession with caves so we would come back tomorrow to see what was interestingly called 'Fairy Maiden's Hole'. However, our interest was caught by some bushes on the steep rocks above the cave; they were superb specimens of *Rhododendron platypodum*, alas too late for the flowers but we could clearly see the remains of the inflorescences, which looked huge with long racheae and pedicels.

On the way back a sign saying 'Stone Forest' led us into a karst landscape with a labyrinth of paths among upright columns of stone. These rocks carried many *Rhododendron platypodum* and a new addition in *R. ochraceum*, although the scarlet corollas were littered on the ground and once again we could get no photographs. The karst habitat was very similar to that in which Peter had found *R. ochraceum* near Leibo in 1995. Then I found another puzzling rhododendron, usually epiphytic, with very scaly obovate leaves and an elongated upturned style. Luckily I found a broken bit on the path (the Stone Forest is obviously well used by tourists) and when I showed it to Peter he thought it was *R. valentinianum* var. *oblongilobatum*, which he had also seen in 1995. However, David Chamberlain in Edinburgh later identified it as *R. changii*, described by W. P. Fang as recently as 1983.[3] It was obviously frustrating being unable even to examine these novel rhododendrons without our 'shadow' popping out from behind rocks, and there must be others we did not see; a guidebook to Jinfo refers to there being forty-eight species of 'Azalea'.

Back at our lodgings, a sort of bamboo ranch by the gate, we had a convivial evening with a delicious dinner of strips of various meats in a good sauce, excellent aubergines, peppers and bamboo shoots, and over a tot of whisky we played patience with some pretty girls who looked after the place. Unfortunately the 'mayor' provided a raucous background of hawking and spitting, an unhygienic habit which used to be widespread and the Chinese government had tried to stamp out, obviously not entirely successfully. It was a bad night with doors banging until 2 a.m., the whole structure creaking and groaning and some incredibly loud snoring coming through the bamboo. When I came down blearily for breakfast the Professor was loudly berating the council hangers-on who were standing round the door. It was the first time we had seen the Professor fully aroused and it was impressive: he followed them out into the courtyard, bellowing with full megaphone wrath, and they melted away into the dawn, never to be seen again.

The weather was miserably wet that morning so the suggestion of visiting local caves was not unwelcome. But the first one, not far from our lodgings, was not what we expected and we found ourselves descending a narrow vertical shaft in the limestone by a series of bamboo ladders and scaffolding. To take my mind off rotting bamboo, I counted the rungs; there were 283 of them and assuming 23cm/9in between them that would mean a drop of over 60m/200ft. It eventually levelled out into a series of interconnected caverns – 14km/9 miles of them in all – but after a short distance thoughts of *R. platypodum* came over Peter and me and we clambered up, leaving the Professor to his underground explorations.

Rain or not, it was a relief to get out into the open again and we set about having a good look round, unhindered by hangers-on. When you are on the rolling wooded plateau of Jinfo, it is easy to forget that it is propped up by massive limestone cliffs all round. There was a good selection of classic tree genera, *Castanopsis, Lithocarpus, Quercus, Acer* and *Sorbus,* and beneath them we saw several species of *Arisaema,* a dwarf *Uvularia* and a delicate and pretty *Disporopsis.* We visited a rather sad monastery with decaying Buddhas. It was deserted but a bowl of recently burnt incense indicated that a few of the faithful still came.

Cliffs and plants go together. We several times came on a sudden abyss and on one occasion we looked over the edge to see masses of rhododendrons lining the crags below. All three of our Stone Forest species were there and we noted how straggly *R. changii* could become. We also saw a substantial new hotel being built on the cliff edge with a twin cable car being used to carry building materials, which no doubt would add to the flow of tourists in due course. By 1999 China was entering a boom in mass tourism for the first time in its history and it was the Chinese tourists rather than foreigners who were fuelling it. Their fascination with natural features is bound to put a heavy burden on the most popular sites.

After lunch at the ranch we returned to the cave that had been closed the previous day and I took photographs of the *Rhododendron platypodum*[4] over the entrance. The Professor found a plant with a few flowers left in one truss and there is no doubt that the leaf and flower sizes recorded in *Sichuan Rhododendron of China,* and by Davidian and Chamberlain, are all far too small. The racheae were up to 7cm/2¾in and the pedicels to 5cm/2in long. It has large oval leaves which are amazingly thick with widely winged petioles. The fine pink open-campanulate flowers are in trusses of around twelve. Overall it is a splendid species.

Rhododendron platypodum *over the entrance to the cave.*

The cave itself was astonishing. After a narrow entrance it opened up into a vast domed cavern which could have held three football pitches quite easily and the roof was high enough for rugby goalposts. Out of it a vaulted passage ran for half a mile or more and five cars could have driven down it side by side towards an exit in a sheer cliff, shaped like an open mouth and a hundred metres wide or more. My morning cave-aversion vanished in awe at this monster.

That evening was warm and jolly – a mixed crowd of eighteen grouped round a hot stove with a metal table on top and a kettle in the middle so wet boots and trousers were soon steaming. Cards were being played in one corner and there was a Mah-Jong school in another where Peter, who is no slouch at cards but had never played this before, was soon giving advice to our bus driver. The Professor presided over this scene in fine humour, with a glass in hand containing a mixture of whisky and Mau Tai.

On our way back the next day, and freed from the restrictions of the Park, we stopped several times to collect on the spur we had crossed on the flank of Jinfo Shan.[5] A nice stand of lily stems, probably *Lilium sargentiae,* bore only empty capsules but we took seed off a hydrangea and two deutzias, one being the evergreen *D. denudatum* which unfortunately is tender. There were some fine scheffleras but the best find was a splendid Gesneriad with purple flowers, which Bill Burtt later identified as *Chirita eburnea.*

2. It was discovered in the 1950s and the Chinese have been very jealously guarding this conifer from would-be collectors. We understand that it has recently been legitimately introduced to the west.

3. It produced pale yellow flowers in 2007 much earlier in the season than *R. valentinianum* var. *oblongilobatum.*

4. In case readers wonder why there should be so much interest in this particular species, I quote Peter's opinion that this was probably the finest hardy rhododendron not yet in cultivation.

5. It is worth noting that the mountains of eastern Sichuan and Guizhou are all quite low compared with those of western Sichuan and north-west Yunnan. The highest peak of Jinfo Shan is a mere 2,250m/7,300ft; Fan-jing-shan, the highest mountain in Guizhou, is only 2,500m/8,250ft. These comparatively low altitudes should not be too much concern as anything over 1,200m/4,000ft can be hardy, as can some items coming from even lower.

Karst cliffs in the Dashahe reserve, north-west Guizhou.

Daozhen and the Dashahe Reserve

We set off for Daozhen, just north of the village of Yangxi and the county town of the region we next wished to explore. Peter Wharton of the University of British Columbia Botanic Garden in Vancouver had been to the area around the Dashahe river in the autumn of 1994 and had found it very rich in plants and we had come on his recommendation. It was a roundabout sort of route and we deliberately made a detour to avoid Nanchuan as we were afraid the council officials might be less than welcoming after the Professor's outburst on the first morning. Although our driver handled the greasy roads with skill, it was 7.30 p.m. before we arrived and were faced with another dinner with local

Pigs on leads, probably on their way to be slaughtered, in Daozhen.

dignitaries. However, they were much more friendly than the Nanchuan squad, the dinner was genial and the Professor was pleased, announcing in a hoarse whisper 'Tomorrow Number One come!' He also announced that tomorrow, Sunday 23 May, was a rest day ('From what?' Peter muttered).

We took a walk round Daozhen which was very much New China. We were told that in 1980 the town had been little more than a village with a single street but now there were new apartment blocks everywhere in a tasteful combination of white sanitary tiles and windows of blue glass, which seemed to be the fashion. Obviously, there had been a big increase in population that the Professor put down in part to the local Miao minority being allowed two children instead of just one. Throughout the day there was a sporadic rattle of firecrackers and I asked why. 'Some pippuls is dead,' the Professor said with finality. He also told us the very bad news that Fan-Jing-Shan, one of our main objectives, would not be possible. First we were told it was too far and then the reason was that we would need a travel permit. Our argument that it had been on our schedule from the beginning got us nowhere and we began to suspect that a degree of idleness was playing a part.

Dinner in the evening with Number One (and Numbers Two and Three and most of Daozhen) was a genial affair and even when the question came as to why NATO had bombed Belgrade they seemed to accept our explanation. We were pleased to meet Mr Jiao Zhuo, retired head of the Daozhen Forestry Bureau, who was to accompany us on our travels and who seemed a kindred spirit. The Professor also seemed pleased. 'Local pippuls is vay wum [warm],' he announced the next day, although he himself had got fairly hot on a mixture of anything that was going. But the result was that we set off the next morning for the village of Yangxi and the reserved area around the Dashahe river. This time our followers included Mr Jiao of the previous evening, natty in a beige suit and tie, brown tinted glasses and a flashing smile, the assistant mayor who plagued us by putting food into our bowls and pushing buns our way on the minibus, the round-faced 'minder' who had accompanied us around Daozhen and a reporter/photographer with lemur spectacles and a huge video camera who skipped around in the mud ambushing us at awkward moments. Luckily the message eventually got through that we did not want to eat buns every half hour.

We spent four days exploring the limestone country around Yangxi with patches of cultivation, some commercial forestry mostly planted by Mr Jiao, cut-over scrub and sometimes the kind of limestone pinnacles that one associates with karst. Unfortunately, although it had some deciduous shrub cover of interest, rhododendrons were few, and altitudes were lowish at around 900–1,500m/3–5,000ft.

On our first day we found ourselves on a kind of limestone pavement with tiny patches cultivated between rocks; imagine the Burren in Ireland with two or three maize plants growing in each gryke. Later it became more hilly with planted forest of *Cunninghamia lanceolata* and then secondary growth natural forest, often mixed with cultivation. This habitat obviously provided a perfect combination for pheasants, of which we saw several cocks and heard many more. All were ring necked as in our domestic pheasant but a bit darker and browner than our average bird.

Higher still among limestone cliffs and karst peaks, we went for a walk, crossing and re-crossing a shallow river, which the Chinese embarrassingly led me across as though I was an old crock and which the Professor used as an excuse to suggest we turn back. In fact, the water was rather pleasant after hot boots. Being around 1,200m/4,000ft, there was a mixture of what we would consider hardy and not so hardy trees and shrubs, many of some interest. Three rhododendrons were in full flower, one being the section Choniastrum member *R. stamineum* which Peter finds relatively hardy at Glendoick though it rarely flowers. Here it made a loose upright evergreen shrub to 4m/13ft or more, the flowers being spidery in effect with a long tube, white with a yellow flare, and sweetly scented. While the individual flower is not that showy, the overall effect of the massed flowers of around twenty per shoot gave a great display and it stood out in the forest from a long way off. The second species was a plant of *R. simsii* in dense shade with its usual red flowers. The third species, a member of subsection Fortunea, we describe later.

We passed a monument with some planting around it

Peter and I are waiting for potatoes to be cooked for lunch.

including the rare conifer *Amentotaxus argotaenia*, the Catkin Yew, named for its male pendulous catkins, with leaves much larger than our native yew. Later two trees of the Silver China Fir, *Cathaya argyrophylla*, were pointed out to us up on the hillside. The mature tree was quite large with a straight trunk up to a multi-branched head. We were not greatly impressed with our only sight of this exceptionally rare tree. As we had been warned, it had a generally rather scruffy and disorganized appearance.

Along our shallow river were some delightful shrubby areas which for some reason had not been hacked in the usual way. A *Styrax* species made an elegant small tree of 6m/20ft or so, hanging with white pendant flowers. *Viburnum plicatum* had typical flat heads of sterile and fertile flowers but lacked the tabular form usual in cultivation. Surprises were *Kerria japonica* and an attractive *Dipelta* species. *Neillia sinensis* had bright pink cones of flower arranged along arching stems.

For the next day we had asked to get to as high an elevation as possible and were taken up a very rough track until the vehicle finally got bogged down in mud. We got out and walked, but it was a bleak place with partially grazed hillsides and no nice cliffs or screes. We came to the conclusion that this had to be the world centre for species of *Rubus* and *Viburnum*. *V. rhytidophyllum* was

341

The second rhododendron we found in quantity at Dashahe was R. fortunei subsp. discolor, again scented. Growing to 10m/33ft with white flowers, it was easily located in the dense forest.

Rose hips.

probably the most interesting with older stems of industrial black but new ones a bright furry russet. We did our best to look keen and full of the joys of the place. The best find was *Decaisnea fargesii* with peculiar strings of green flowers and a handsome *Mahonia* that had no ripe fruit. We had been told that we could collect specimens provided they were not something very rare. Yet the next day, there they were, digging up every *Cypripedium* in sight. The Professor made it quite clear that he was missing his large restaurant lunch and refused to eat any of the food we had with us.

We asked to be dropped off about a mile or two short of Yangxi as there were some interesting looking limestone cliffs, and indeed it was much more exciting than where we had been, although the altitude was only 1,040m/3,250ft. *Rhododendron stamineum* was again common and Peter got a little seed, as was *R. simsii*, here long finished flowering. A third rhododendron was the deciduous azalea *R. mariesii*, which is of limited ornamental value and too tender for central Scotland. We saw a vigorous climber with hanging flowers of deep crimson which was later identified as *Actinidia coriacea*. Another climber was the semi-evergreen *Lonicera similis* with pink and white tubular flowers, which is used by the Chinese to make an infusion for chest and throat infections.

That evening we were given new potatoes and were told that they are much more expensive than rice. Hosts in China like to give their guests the best and most expensive food first, so they always finish a meal with rice and watery soup. After pressing our specimens and writing our notes, we were called to have special local tea with pressed vegetable oil, not unlike Tibetan tea, and more of the potatoes with which they are traditionally consumed. We found out that our nice round-faced 'minder' was in fact a policeman; very much plain clothes!

They now informed us that the best rhododendrons were too far to reach in a day so that camping would be a necessity but we should reach some tomorrow. Somehow we suspected that, given an early start and a packed lunch, we could have achieved very much more; our Daozhen people did seem to do their best for us but the Professor would have probably vetoed the idea.

On 26 May we returned to the same area as the first afternoon. Before leaving Yangxi, we noticed that Mr Jiao had

been buying various edible items in the shop owned by the same people as our guesthouse. When we stopped on the way at a small village, out he got with his provisions and started handing them out to some children. There was much ribald laughter in the back of the bus, and when we inquired what the joke was, we were told that the children looked remarkably like Mr Jiao! Apparently he had lived here off and on for some years while he was in charge of the local tree planting.

We stopped near some small karst outcrops and descended steeply before climbing again into a gap between two peaks. Mr Jiao indicated that this had been an excellent place for plants, but although there were still some fine trees including a *Magnolia* (*Michelia*), most had been chopped. We passed a subsection Fortunea rhododendron with old capsules (no seed germinated) but no flowers and noticed a big one in flower in the forest just above. We went back to the road and picked up a local girl who took us down to her family's farmhouse for lunch. She said we would have 'some good potatoes'. It was an idyllic place with karst mounds and rocks and a gully in the middle where they grew their produce. Peter amused himself by imagining making this into a garden. The Professor remarked, 'Pippuls vay poor, girl not work here, work in town', a refrain we had heard many times. The Chinese are mad keen on posed photographs and we had a session here with a rock as background and later we were asked to pose with various groups of local dignitaries, all of which wasted a great deal of time.

Blobs of white flowers in the forest were usually either *R. stamineum* or *R. fortunei* subsp. *discolor*, most of them being the former, although once or twice we were fooled into thinking they were the latter. Time was running out and Peter was determined to get to a plant of subsp. *discolor*; he persisted and finally set off with the policeman against the wishes of the Professor (and, I have to admit, myself) to the plant seen in the morning. The path had dried up so they made very good time until they had to struggle through the thicket, only to find it was a tree of 10m/33ft with all the flowers well out of reach. Without a moment's hesitation, our policeman shinned up the bare trunk, broke off a branch and dropped it down. Peter and policeman reached the road triumphant with a polybag full of collapsed trusses, having taken only one and a quarter hours.

Rosa multiflora *was very vigorous and common.*

Rosa roxburghii *was common over much of the country we travelled through.*

Later photographs were taken of the flowers arranged together in a simulated truss on the balcony of our guesthouse. The pure-white scented flowers were similar to those of *R. decorum*.

I decided to get my big camera out, known as the Hassle, and concentrate on roses on the way down. The Chinese farm the countryside with such intensity that anything must be vigorous to survive, able to regenerate after hacking and browsing, and preferably well armed with spines or thorns. Some survivors are good garden plants, such as the *Pyracantha* species and the *Cotoneaster integrifolius*. A number of roses fall into this category and *R. roxburghii* had followed us through much of our journey on the drier banks, with flowers of carmine to pale pink. One of the musk roses, probably *R. helenae*, could produce enormous shoots with panicles of white flowers reaching 6–9m/20–30ft, sometimes into the planted *Cunninghamia* forest where it showed well against the dark foliage. A third rose that intrigued us had arching sprays of what appeared to be yellow flowers due to the large boss of stamens, and a heavy scent. Then there was a shell-pink rose with a strong Old Rose fragrance that was not so competitive and was often chewed to unhappy fragments. I also found a gully full of *Cardiocrinum* nearly into flower.

Peter later spotted a *Cardiocrinum* in full flower growing on the edge of a bottomless sink hole and an even better one grew on the opposite side. The Chinese kept on saying 'very dangerous', which was all too obvious. As it was so dangerous, there were numerous plants growing all around the sides, untouched by the devilish hand of man or his livestock. One was the pink rose mentioned earlier. The *Cardiocrinum* was identical to plants at Glendoick collected by Jim Russell on Fan-jing-shan, with darker stained, closer packed flowers than the usual var. *yunnanense*.

The plans for the next day were to visit a gorge and take in some local history. We crossed the biggest river in the area, the Fulung Jiang, and then turned up a side stream into the gorge. This was certainly impressive. A rhododendron look-alike grew on the cliffs, resembling *R. protistum* in foliage, there was a wisteria-like climber with pink flowers and two beautiful gesneriads with pale mauve flowers; none were close enough to photograph. Beyond was a monastery, said to have two monks, set away up on precipitous pinnacles, rather like the famous

Tiger's Nest in Bhutan. Then we looked at the ruins of walls reputed to be the remains of old Daozhen, which was abandoned 300 to 400 years ago. Apparently the son of the ruler jumped into the river and died and the ruler was so distraught that he ordered the town to be moved to its present site.

We had a farewell meal in Daozhen, supposedly very special, but almost completely inedible. Snake was all bone, terrapin similar plus slime, black chicken had nothing on it, some curly things from cattle innards were all gristle, very hot beans and 'cucumbers' were too hot, mushrooms were tough and tasteless but there were some delicious little hot bananas; luckily we were not hungry. More posed photographs in the hotel garden and great hand shaking all round. Two Miao girls dressed up in their finery posed in the garden for us to photograph.

After more farewells in the morning, we were off, but to where? We had long since had to accept very grudgingly that we were not going to get to Fan-jing-shan and the Professor said that we were now finished with plants and could not collect anything else. We were furious, of course, saying that our only objective in coming to China was to look for plants, but we were in his hands and could do nothing much about it. He was delighted to get away from Daozhen, saying that the entertainment and drinking had been too much for him, but he still managed to drink more 'white lightning' at lunch.

Until we had a chance to stop and examine this rose, we thought it had yellow flowers, an illusion caused by the large boss of yellow stamens.

343

Fine specimens of Cardiocrinum giganteum *var.* yunnanense *growing around the edge of a karst sink hole between Dashahe and Daozhen.*

Two girls of the Miao minority in Daozhen dressed in their tribal finery.

Part of old Daozhen.

Khan kui Shui and Baili Dujian Reserves

Heading for Zunyi, the second city of Guizhou, the Professor made an effort to find somewhere in the area where there were good plants and enquires revealed that there was a forest reserve back up the road some 30km/20 miles. Driving up a cultivated valley, the scenery became more and more dramatic with large caves in the cliffs that rose straight out of the paddy fields, followed by the road climbing up the cliffs. We came out on to a plateau of rounded, heavily forested hills, rather like the top of Jinfo Shan. This was Khan kui Shui Nature Reserve with its headquarters further on in a well-kept tea plantation. The road got up to nearly 1600m/5,250ft with quantities of bamboo and fine broadleaved trees and shrubs. The only rhododendron was *R. stamineum* again but outside the reserve headquarters there seemed to be a different planted species from section Choniastrum. There were very fine trees of a *Styrax* species in full flower, which also appeared to be planted. To our dismay, three of the tea workers hitched a lift, but the second time we stopped, we got well away and were able to do some botanising. There were the usual umpteen species of *Rubus* and *Viburnum* and some nice *Acer*, *Cornus*, *Decaisnea* and what we took to be the Chinese sassafras, *S. tzumu* with its curious irregularly lobed leaves. We collected some seed from a *Meliosma* species. The cliffs were surprisingly disappointing for plants, with only the occasional *Lilium*, *Cardiocrinum* and *Arisaema*.

Some wildlife was observed for once. The day before we had seen a hare cross the road in front of us, swim a paddy field and disappear amongst maize. Today there were several egrets, two small brown herons and one 'ordinary' heron, plus a brown pheasant on the way down the cliff. It was nice to see plentiful swallows and cuckoos and we heard new bird noises from the forest. There were various reports of a few tigers in this forest but what do they eat? Or had they all been eaten?

We went on to Zunyi, staying on the way at the rather attractive town of Suiyang with tree-lined streets and a market full of live produce such as terrapins, eels and catfish that were climbing out of their buckets. Zunyi is a large industrial city with a huge factory making minibuses like our one and its own brand of small taxis painted white and green. It was a pleasant town by Chinese standards with decent modern buildings, a river running through with a backdrop of mature forest, some nice parks and tree-lined streets. Zunyi is famous for being the place where Chinese Communism was launched in 1935, aided and abetted by Russia. In the building known as The Meeting Place, a house previously owned by aristocrats, Mao Zedong took over the leadership of the Red Army and won an important battle in the civil war. He also delivered his famous speech in a Roman Catholic church which was now closed. The Long March started from here and, after crossing several rivers, headed for Yunnan. Deng Xiaoping was here too as a

Meliosma *species*.

young man. Mao must be turning in his grave to see so much apparently successful capitalism in Zunyi.

Both of us were pretty fed up and determined to get to somewhere worthwhile before returning to Chongqing. The Professor was clearly wondering what to do with us for the rest of the trip now that he had stated that botanising was finished. It was 1 June, we did not fly away until the 11th and he certainly did not intend to sit in the bus while we scrabbled around the countryside after plants. He offered an assortment of temples, even to visit his home in Chengdu. We tried to get him to look into a visit to the Baili Dujian Reserve near Dafang on which James Ogilvie, who came with us on our 1997 trip, had written a report. I had lent this report to the Professor and quite obviously he had never even glanced at it. 'Maybe road not so good,' he said. 'Dafang not open by Government…vay difficult to go place…you change mind…too many place…no rest day…Government says must have rest days…you make my foot not well.'

Eventually after a series of tantrums and our threatening to fax Chengdu with complaints about the treatment we were getting, he agreed to look into going to Qiangxi, Dafang and the Baili Dujiang Reserve. The next morning, with a long face and as much dignity as he could muster, he announced that after innumerable phone calls, enquiries, discussions and the like he had arranged for us to go to Dafang for two days.

It was a long drive, starting at 10 a.m. We arrived at Qiangxi at 5 p.m., having asked many people in uniform the way.[6] The road was obviously hazardous as a surprising number of vehicles had fallen into paddy fields and we saw one man wandering around swathed in bloodstained bandages. Qiangxi was mucky, the rest house was smelly and damp and the town had been rebuilt in the latest fashion of blue glass and tiles,

6. There are few road signs in China and many uniforms; the trouble is that you never know whether they are police, army or waiters.

345

only the tiles here were in shades of Alarming Pink as well as Sanitary White. It did not bode well.

After a ridiculous argument the next morning about which town was nearest to the Reserve, we drove the 2½ hours to Dafang. It had been agreed that we would be able to spend two days around the Reserve if we went back to Chongqing by the circuitous route that the Professor wanted. It has to be said that after we finally reached the Reserve it was a disappointment. Baili Dujian actually means '100 Li of Rhododendron' and a li is half a square kilometre, but James Ogilvie reckons that the area is nearer 200 sq km than the 50 this would produce. The altitude varies from about 1,400 to 2,000m/4,700ft to 7,000ft. There are said to be eighteen species of *Rhododendron* and eighty varieties.

A request to stop for a particularly attractive pink and

Zunyi Communist Meeting room, where Mao Zedong took control of the Red Army.

The grim-looking Communist headquarters in Chongqing.

white rose outside the Reserve was studiously ignored and signs (in Chinese) were pointed out to us as prohibiting picking of plants; in fact, they were directed at local farmers grazing their animals. First we saw dollops of a fairly robust form of *Rhododendron decorum* in full flower and then suddenly we were in the tourist area of massed rhododendrons; *R. arboreum* subsp. *delavayi*, *R. irroratum* and masses of hybrids between the two, some involving *R. decorum*. Presumably this accounts for the 'eighty varieties'. Although at flowering time they must have made a striking display, they involved some of the commonest species and were of little interest to the specialist. Certainly the 10,000 people said to visit annually had left an appalling amount of litter.

It was on the second day at Dafang that 'the Eruption' occurred. The Professor was complaining about his sore ankle, which he clearly thought was our responsibility due to having to move stones when the vehicle bogged down the day before, but we set off nevertheless with the aim of photographing *Rhododendron decorum* and, we hoped, finding something new. We made a few stops and the Professor hobbled around, clearly feeling sorry for himself but unable to follow us to make sure we did not collect anything. We were about two-thirds of the way back to Dafang when Peter spotted a promising looking ravine and asked to stop. 'No!' shouted the Professor. 'No! No! No!'. And when Peter asked why he stormed up and down the bus calling us 'foreign pigs' and shouting other stuff about human rights and how he hoped we would get caught by the customs in Beijing. He was making an awful racket and I told him – probably unwisely – to sit down and shut up. This set off another torrent of abuse and things seemed to be getting close to violence. He was jabbing his fingers a few inches from my face and shouting 'I am heeting you.' Whether he meant 'hitting' or 'hating' was not clear but neither seemed a good idea.

We sat tight, looking grimly to the front, and by the time we reached Dafang things had quietened. But it happened to be my birthday and I really felt I could not sit down to dinner with this man, being wished a happy birthday a couple of hours after he had been hurling abuse at me. So I stomped off to our room in dignified dudgeon (I hoped), leaving Peter who was marginally less out of favour to act as mediator. From then on it became pure farce. Peter discovered that a celebration had been arranged with singing and dancing and including the hotel staff. A highly decorated cake was produced but the date on it was wrong so it went back and did not appear again for two hours. Meanwhile, Peter was working hard to mend fences downstairs and various overtures were made to get me to join in. Eventually, as I was consuming Virginia's packet of mushroom soup, along with a large Glenfiddich, there was an apologetic door-tapping and the Professor entered. 'Some pippuls from hotel wish you happy birthday, ' he said, and the

The busy Yangtze river in Chongqing.

whole staff entered in full song carrying the cake which was flaming so vigorously that the whole hotel seemed about to catch fire. Eventually the cake was extinguished, some *piju* appeared, a journalist from the *Dafang Reporter* set about the cake with chopsticks and the remains of my Glenfiddich dwindled rapidly. Honour was restored.

It was now just straight back to Chongqing via Xuyong and Luzhou. It was an uneventful journey through undistinguished countryside and the Professor, relieved that civilized life would soon return, was charm itself. Two incidents remain in the memory. One was when a man in rags with what the Victorians would call 'an evil countenance' stepped straight into the path of the vehicle and held up his fist with two fingers extended. He had positioned himself so that we could not get past and was demanding two yuan. Eventually he was bargained down and we threw the one yuan note out of the side window, driving past as he came to pick it up. On reflection it was quite a neat bit of highway robbery.

The other was a memorable dinner given by an old friend of the Professor who was now a senior General. I seem to be writing a lot about eating, but the whole trip seemed to consist of meals with short intervals between. This was a lavish and stylish affair with gold-plated bowls and chopstick holders and the food was outstanding. But the star turn was an attractive girl in local costume who filled delicate porcelain cups with flowery tea from a vessel like a watering can with a pencil thin spout that must have been 60cm/2ft long. The tip of the spout never touched the tea bowl but filled it with an arc of boiling water. And she never spilled a drop.

In Chongqing we immediately tried to alter our tickets to an earlier flight but they were unchangeable. The Professor, however, who had acquired a decorative lady friend and a sudden air of geniality, took us on some interesting excursions to fill the time, including a trip on a battered ferryboat, all jostle and honking. We also visited the former Headquarters of the 8th Red Army, dating from the late 1930s when there had been an uneasy alliance between the Communists and the Guomintang of Chiang Kai Shek against the Japanese invaders. The austere, black-painted buildings still reeked of suspicion and spy holes, secret entrances and coding equipment were everywhere, even bowls of quicklime on the stairs to throw in the face of invaders.

Our own uneasy truce with the Professor prevailed until the time came to depart. Rather meagre presents were handed over and we slipped something extra to our driver, the nice and stoical Liang. Relief was probably mutual as we pumped hands, but we could not quite bring ourselves to thank the Professor for one of our least successful trips to China. I still have a souvenir from the Red Army Headquarters – a key ring with a bullet on the end. It may be needed if I ever return.

Chapter 15

THE ANGRY RIVER:

The Salween, Autumn 1997 and Summer 2000

Peter Hutchison

In what has come to be known as the Gorge Country of Western China, three of the greatest rivers of Asia come within 160km/100 miles of each other in parallel rifts north and south: the Yangtze, the Mekong and the Salween. In this crumpled corner of the earth's surface the Salween has claim to be the most impressive of them all. It also has an astonishing diversity of plant life, particularly in the corridor along the Burma border from the 25th parallel up to the marches of Tibet.

So it was not surprising that Peter and I should set our ambitions on the Salween. The British American Salween Expedition (BASE) made an autumn trip in 1997,[1] with seed

collecting the main objective, and a second one in May and June 2000,[2] with the primary aim of seeing the upper slopes of the mountains in flower. On both occasions we benefited from the help and guidance of Guan Kaiyun (known to us as Clyde), former director of the Botanic Garden at the Kunming Institute of Botany, who had been our interpreter in 1981 and leader of our spring 1992 expedition. We were also fortunate in having cheerful and enthusiastic companions with between them a great knowledge of plants. Complaints were few, expertise was generously shared and a collective sense of humour got us through the bumpier moments.

1. **1997: UK:** Dr David Chamberlain, taxonomist RBGE; Peter Cox, Glendoick; Philip Evans, former editor of the RHS Yearbook; Peter Hutchison; James Ogilvie, Forestry Commission; Brian Poett, farmer/forester. **USA:** Steve Hootman; Co-Executive Director & Curator, Rhododendron Species Foundation; Garratt Richardson, physician and traveller.

2. **2000: UK:** Hugh Angus, Curator, Westonbirt Arboretum; Peter Catt, nurseryman; Dr David Chamberlain; Peter Cox; Maurice Foster, plantsman; Tom Hudson, horticulturist; Peter Hutchison, Chairman, Forestry Commission. **USA:** Steve Hootman; Garratt Richardson; Bob Zimmerman, plant photographer.

Above. While native to the area, this clump of the striking Lycoris aurea *appeared to have been in a previously cultivated area that was now a park.*

Opposite. The Pula river and the new road to the Dulong valley from Gongshan on the Salween.

The beautiful richly scented Luculia pinceana, *a very desirable but tender shrub, was flowering in the autumn on the Dasheyao pass between the Salween and Tengchong.*

We found one bog full of Primula prolifera (helodoxa) *in the Shweli valley in spring 2000.*

Peter's Preliminary Excursions

Both in 1997 and in 2000 Peter led shortened parties on preliminary excursions for a week each. In 1997 two peaks towards south-west Yunnan were chosen, Ailao Shan and Wuliang Shan, both around 3,500m/11,500ft, with the fair-sized town of Jingdong in between, where they stayed. Heavy rain had warned them of the inevitable mud slide on Ailao Shan so they tried Wuliang Shan, but there was no access to the higher elevations. Various roads yielded only *Rhododendron arboreum* subsp. *delavayi*, very fine in one area of virgin forest,

R. pachypodum, R. irroratum, R. decorum and *R.* x *agastum*.

So the decision was made to try the Shweli-Salween divide, though with the time left there was little hope of achieving much, and so it turned out. On the top of the pass they divided into two groups and Steve's party found an amazing little population of *Rhododendron edgeworthii* (CCHH 8016) on top of a rock, perhaps the furthest south this species occurs. The indumentum was thick and deep rust in colour and the number of seed capsules had to be seen to be believed. At home the

Rhododendron simsii, *the principal parent of the indoor azaleas, was common in the Shweli valley.*

flowers have turned out to be pure white. Other rhododendrons there were *R. moulmainense* and some fine plants of the narrow-leaved *R. arboreum* subsp. *delavayi* var. *peramoenum* (CCHH 8036) with leaves almost as narrow as *R. roxieanum* var. *oreonastes*.

The following day the party set off on a day's trek with the promise of huge rhododendrons, presumably *R. protistum*, but it was thought to be too far south for that. This area has been made into a reserve and previously inhabited parts of it were reverting to nature. They found autumn-flowering *Lycoris aurea*, which looked as though it was planted, although it is native to China. There were masses of conical trees of the evergreen *Schima wallichii* or *S. yunnanensis* with its white camellia-like flowers. Eventually the large rhododendrons were found but they were only *R. arboreum* subsp. *delavayi* some 24m/80ft high which had been drawn up into the forest.

In 2000 the advance party had again one week, the idea being to reach the top of the Shweli-Salween divide and to find the little known *Rhododendron shweliense* of the subsection Glauca, plus some species which are rare in the wild such as *R. valentinianum*, *R. lepidostylum* and *R. meddianum* var. *meddianum*. A map in the hotel in Tengchong in 1997 had shown the way to get to the divide, so they returned to Tengchong, this time by a new road further south and then drove north and east back over the Shweli river. While travelling up the valley they kept looking out for *R. griersonianum* which has only been found in the Shweli valley. But there is little forest left and they doubted if they were in the right place anyway. It is a plant that could easily be nearing extinction in the wild. Only *R. simsii* was around, in full flower and quite common. They were told that eventually the intention is to build a new road to link with the route over the Pianma pass.

Approaching the Gaoligong Shan, the massive ridge dividing the Shweli from the Salween, the valley was rich in trees and shrubs, including fine deutzias and *Decaisnea fargesii* with both upright and pendulous green flowers, which must look striking in autumn with its fat blue seed pods. There were several groups of fine *Cardiocrinum giganteum* var. *yunnanense* with white trumpets tinged yellowish green and a maroon throat, slightly pendulous and wider spaced than the Guizhou form.[3]

(In 1997 we also made a day excursion up to our old hunting ground on the Cangshan to see it for the first time in autumn colour. The pictures from this excursion are shown on pages 90 to 91 in Chapter 3.)

3. It would appear that there may be intermediates between the Himalayan *Cardiocrinum giganteum* var. *giganteum* and the Chinese var. *yunnanense*, this *C. giganteum* var. *yunnanense* perhaps falling more into the former variety with its whiter, more pendulous flowers that appear to open first at the bottom of the inflorescence.

Magnolia delavayi (CCHH 8026) *on the Shweli-Salween divide in spring 2000. Seedlings of this magnificent evergreen (from seed collected off the same plants in 1997) are growing very vigorously against a wall and cliff at Glendoick.*

Decaisnea fargesii *in flower. This shrub is common at low elevations in west Yunnan, but proves quite hardy in cultivation.*

A *fine spike of* Cardiocrinum giganteum *var.* yunnanense, *with greenish-tinged flowers that apparently open first from the top of the inflorescence, on the edge of the Shweli valley. A very variable plant; compare it with that on page 344 in Guizhou province.*

Cardiocrinum giganteum *var.* giganteum *on the Pula river. Compare this with the one found on the Shweli-Salween divide.*

They had to climb up a steep narrow ridge with many low elevation rhododendrons and other *Ericaceae* and then plunge down again to a stream, followed by a moderate rise through splendid broad-leaved temperate forest which included the rare *Emmenopterys henryi* among many interesting trees. It transpired that the main reason for taking the party to this place was to see the giant *Rhododendron protistum* and that evening they went to see it just a short distance from camp. Apparently there had been two large specimens but one had been chopped, possibly the very tree that Forrest had had cut and then recorded in his famous photograph. Certainly the remaining tree would be several hundred years old. It was a great specimen, much bigger than anything we would later see in the north, but it was nothing like the 30m/100ft tree reported by Forrest. There were very few younger plants round this giant and the inclusion of this species in the IUCN Red Data Book may be based entirely on this relic population, perhaps the farthest south of what is still quite a common species further north.

A promise to take them higher in the morning had Peter's party all excited. A wet night meant everything dripping in the morning and the leeches were excited too. Starting on the same track, they cut up a side stream, but walking proved extremely difficult, criss-crossing the slippery stream and then up a dangerous cliff path. Everyone had some falls and near accidents and eventually they decided that they were never going to get near the top, having climbed only 260m/850ft in three hours. Few rhododendrons were found – some large *R. tanastylum* var. *tanastylum*, as usual with no seed, one *R. megacalyx* seedling and a curious one of *R. arboreum*. So Peter felt they had failed to achieve anything worthwhile. There must be a relatively achievable way to reach the Gaoligong Shan as George Forrest climbed up on several occasions, but to make sure of success it would be advisable to make the ridge the principal goal of one expedition.

The big bend on the Salween below Gongshan in sleepy mode.

A rapid on the mighty Salween.

To the Salween

The whole party met up in Baoshan on both occasions. From there as you drive north to Liuku the valley starts to narrow and the hills rise on each side until, after the town of Fugong, you are in a deep cleft with serried ridges rising thousands of feet on each side. There is an increasing sense of drama and on our first trip it was heightened by the shifting mists that outlined first one ridge and then another, sometimes with a single fringe of trees that gave it a curious lace-like look. This theatrical landscape reaches its climax in the Marble Gorges north of Gongshan where vertical cliffs plunge 300m/1,000ft into the river and where, until now, no road had penetrated.

All rivers have their individual character and 'powerful' might be the best word to sum up the Salween. The Chinese in these parts give it a different name, the Nu Jiang Lu, or Angry River, and angry it often seems when it is surging over hidden boulders or ploughing a ravine where the rocks have pressed it too close. But the overall impression is of power, a mass of grey water in a hurry to reach the sea.

Both in 1997 and 2000 we had set our minds on getting to the Pianma pass and over to the Burma side of the dividing range between the Salween and the Irrawaddy catchment. The border between China and Burma (or Myanmar) follows the

353

Rhododendron monanthum, *which we came across lying on the roadside in autumn 1997 on the east side of the Pianma pass.*

crest of the ridge, and the pass at a little short of 3,000m/10,000ft forms one of the few breaches in this formidable obstacle. The Chinese have established by treaty an enclave on the western side of the mountains, so there was no question of crossing into Burmese territory.

We had been told that it was a good road but, as with the whole of our 1997 trip, we were dogged by landslides. Even by the standards of this rain-soaked part of the world, it had been an exceptionally wet year and we regularly found ourselves bumping and grinding over the detritus shed from the slopes above. At around 2,000m/6,500ft both driver and minibus had had enough and refused to go on. There was nothing to do but walk and anyhow we were told that the summit of the pass was only 10 miles (16km) away. After about 6 miles we had made little altitude and doubts began to arise. Fortunately a passing jeep was persuaded, with the help of 300 yuan, to give us a lift and the driver dropped us at 2,700m/9,000ft where they were blasting the road and we could go no further.

The rain was easing and our spirits lifted as we started to look around. Familiar and less familiar rhododendrons abounded; R. sinogrande loomed out of the mist, R. decorum subsp. diaprepes, R. edgeworthii and R. zaleucum were seen with R. annae, R. araiophyllum and a curious small-leaved Maddenia. But seed was very hard to come by. It often happens that the best finds are dumped on the road for you and Brian Poett and I who were ahead of the group found a neat bush of 60cm/2ft or so with yellow bell-shaped flowers which had come down with the collapse of the bank above. It was *Rhododendron monanthum* (CCHH 8041) – which had not previously been introduced – and better still it had a few capsules. By the time the others arrived it had been combed over with the sort of detailed

attention given to a suspect head of hair on a schoolboy.[4]

Our journey back looked like being quite a walk, although downhill we reckoned that the abandoned minibuses must be fully 24km/15 miles away and it was getting dark. Fortunately Professor Cheng spotted a lorry in a backyard and, having located the owner, negotiated with him to take us the final stretch, a cavorting and exhilarating ride on the back of a Chinese truck.

Back at Liuku on the Salween we were billeted in the 'best' hotel in town which sported a brass plate: 'Designated for the Use of Foreign Tourists.' Elephantine sofas in leatherette decorated the marble entrance and dinner took place in a hall that would have housed a People's Congress. A plate of fried bees complemented the meal. They looked like bees too, but more grub-like and larger than decent little furry British bees.

Bee larvae, tasty, crunchy and enjoyable!

Rhododendron facetum *on Zhi Bei Shan on the Salween-Mekong divide. We saw plants of this species in full flower here, both at the beginning and end of our 2000 trip, so it has a long flowering season.*

354

Rhododendron calostrotum *subsp.* calostrotum *in a damp meadow on the top of Zhi Bei Shan.*

They tasted of Chinese cooking oil and crunched like croutons.

The following day it was still raining and we split into two groups; Peter took one party to try the Pianma pass again, while I took the other one south-east to a forestry track in an area called Zhi Bei Shan. It was a day of unremitting and penetrating rain and the vehicle had again to be abandoned on the track, which had turned into a minor torrent. Nevertheless, we found a good collection of berried things including a *Sorbus* with brilliant scarlet fruits and a *Malus* with carmine crab apples. There was also a giant buddleja with drooping racemes 30cm/1ft long, now just brown husks, but we wondered what colour it had been and whether it would be as tender as it looked when growing in British gardens. It was quite a productive day.

We were able to return to Zhi Bei Shan on our way home in 2000. There is a road right to the top at 3,000m/10,000ft which was impassable for our own vehicles, but we were able to hire a truck that took us all the way – not exactly a comfortable journey clutching on to the back of the cab for dear life and ducking one's head to avoid low branches. The long-lasting flowers of the superb scarlet *Rhododendron facetum* glowed in the forest at lower elevations, while along a stream bank were numerous trees of a *Pterocarya* species, perhaps *P. stenoptera*, with large pinnate leaves and amazing hanging catkins 30cm/1ft or more long. At the top of the peak was a plateau where much to our surprise the big-leaved *Rhododendron basilicum* (*R. gratum*) occupied the higher ground. The dwarf *R. calostrotum* subsp. *calostrotum* (BASE 9716) which covered the lower slopes and boggy flats was a glorious sight covered with comparatively large rose-purple flowers. Many of the rhododendrons were the same species as we had seen up the Salween, but we were able to collect seed of the newly described Maddenia, *R. pseudociliipes* (BASE 9697) with small leaves.

A most attractive form of the climber Schisandra chinensis *on Zhi Bei Shan.*

4. *Rhododendron monanthum* is one of the very few species that always flowers in the autumn and takes a year to ripen its seed. In cultivation indoors, it blooms from June to January.

We were thrilled to be the first to re-find the rare Rhododendron mallotum *just above the top of the Pianma pass.*

Pianma

Meanwhile the other group attempted the Pianma road. They tried to hire a 4WD but when they told the owners where they wanted to go the vehicles were all fully booked. Eventually someone agreed to take them but they were told they would have to wait as the car was being repaired, a bad sign. Ages later a totally clapped out old banger arrived with virtually no windows, no wipers and an engine that made alarming grinding noises from time to time. James Ogilvie took one look at the vehicle and suddenly remembered that he had lots of notes to write. How wise he was!

To their surprise, however, the party somehow negotiated the hill and in the pouring rain reached the previous day's bad landslide to find a continuous stream of flowing mud. They watched rocks the size of footballs hurtling by for a while and then decided that discretion was better than valour and returned to Liuku.

When we returned to the Pianma in June 2000 on our way

south, we encountered no such problems and swept up to the pass and over, although the crest was shrouded in thick mist and guard posts loomed out of the fog. We scrambled around the summit and there was an interesting selection of plants with some surprises. *Rhododendron sidereum* we had seen before and it was plentiful, although only one creamy truss of flowers peered out of the fog at us. *R. basilicum* was betrayed by a well-winged leaf stem or petiole although it was past flowering. But one of the best finds of the whole trip was *R. mallotum* (BASE 9672) perched on the slopes above the guards' accommodation block. It must have as a fine an indumentum as any rhododendron, a splendid rusty red and deep as a pile carpet, and it made a bush of neat habit and good foliage. It was originally introduced by Euan Cox and Reginald Farrer in 1919 and rarely found since – it appears to have a very limited distribution. It flowers early so its rounded crimson or scarlet truss was well past flowering. But for Peter it was a happy connection with his father. We were at only 3,000m/10,000ft so it was a surprise to find a dwarf rhododendron, *R. campylogynum*, which hugged the sides of rocks and pinnacles with cushions of foliage and held its thimble-shaped flowers perkily above on an upright pedicel. The colour was variable but mostly of a bloomy plum shade with a red interior. Perhaps we should not have been surprised to find it as Kingdon Ward had also remarked on finding it at this low altitude, describing it as *R. myrtilloides*, which is now regarded as one of the Groups of this variable species.

Apart from the rhododendrons there was a sense of being overwhelmed by the profusion of trees and shrubs, which were mostly evergreen, rarely in flower and for the most part unrecognisable. There was a *Euonymus* with showy crimson-maroon flowers 20mm/¾in across and two viburnums, one with maple-like foliage but, all too often, on examination the vaguely familiar turned into the totally unknown. Many fine deutzias were found in flower in spring 2000 and one on the Pianma pass, possibly *D. purpurascens*, was particularly choice, and is also looking good in cultivation. We were by no means the first plant enthusiasts here, although most of the early Europeans had come from the Burma side, then under British control. Indeed Kingdon Ward had described it as 'probably the most collected spot on the frontier' and as far back as 1919 Euan Cox had done pioneering work with Reginald Farrer when he recorded a similar gloom at the unrelieved luxuriance of the vegetation, writing, 'the truth is that the whole country is overgrown: it is nothing more than a gigantic propagating bed'.

What had changed completely since the days of the early travellers was the political scene and the economic imperatives. On 10 June 2000 we again drove over the pass and through the small town of Pianma to the place where in 1960 Chou En-lai signed the agreement whereby this patch on the Burmese side of the range was leased to the Chinese 'in perpetuity'. The scene in Pianma itself was very different from that which must have greeted British travellers arriving at Hpimaw Fort. The whole place had become an enormous logging camp. Timber extraction was obviously going on at a grand scale[5] and we were told that Chinese entrepreneurs were buying concessions to whole hillsides from Burmese villagers. Massive butts of conifers, mostly *Abies* subsp. two to three hundred years old were on some of the lorries, so harvesting of old growth forests on the high slopes was obviously taking place but we also saw stacks containing hardwoods. Later we visited the small museum dedicated to the defeat of the British in 1911.[6]

5. As Chairman of the Forestry Commission in Britain at that time, I took a professional interest in the sprawl of sawmills, woodsheds, timber yards and piles of lumber covered in striped tarpaulins. I actually counted 72 timber lorries in the short distance between the town and the frontier.

6. The museum had portraits of tribesmen – Lissus, Dulong, Nu, etc. – in heroic combat armed only with crossbows and poisoned arrows. In one panorama a bloodied British soldier lay dead, a torn Union Jack on the ground beside him to emphasise the point. Just in case our American colleagues were getting uppity about British military adventures around the world, we were taken outside to see the shell of a wrecked DC3 which had come down in the last war, possibly simply running out of fuel rather than shot down. The world's frontiers are littered with the debris of these disputes, sometimes exercises in real power, sometimes cock-ups from a General's miscalculations.

A *fine form of* Rhododendron campylogynum *growing on a mossy pinnacle to the west side of the Pianma pass.*

A *deutzia, possibly* D. purpurascens, *on the Pianma pass in spring 2000.*

The 'levada'

North of Liuku, the next town is Fugong, an unprepossessing collection of Mao-period concrete blocks on the banks of the great river. We were halted there on our 1997 trip by the news that yet another landslide had blocked the road further north and, as a government delegation had taken over the 'best' hotel in town, we were lodged in an old-style accommodation block with very basic facilities.

The resourceful Mr Cheng quickly arranged for us to make an excursion up the mountain known as Biluo Xue Shan, which rises steeply behind the town and becomes in effect the divide between the Salween and the Mekong rivers. The following morning a motley collection of porters assembled on the street and we set off in the rain. It was a serious hike on slippery paths in incessant rain, climbing at first between fields, then bamboo brake and finally scattered forest, until we came to a rock shelter where we were to spend the night. We had climbed over 1,200m/4,000ft and were tired, soaked and hungry.

On our way we had traversed one of the more alarming features I have ever encountered in the Chinese countryside, which we called the 'levada'. During the great famine Chairman Mao had decreed that new irrigation systems should be created (although why water should be in short supply in this sodden countryside escaped us) and on this mountainside a channel had been incised across a massive cliff face. In section it was like a capital letter 'G' with water running in the dip at the bottom and our path on the little platform above the tail with the channel on one side and a sheer drop on the other of several hundred feet. Neither Peter nor I have much liking for heights and in places the gangway was only a couple of feet wide, the stones were often loose and the surface was littered with debris from the cliff above. One side a soaking, the other oblivion and for more than a kilometre or about three quarters of a mile we kept our eyes grimly focused on the ribbon ahead.

The rock shelter had a Palaeolithic look about it and the blackened roof told of many centuries of travellers who had sheltered there. There was no place to pitch tents among the huge rocks, but the porters soon had several fires going and hot noodles restored us until we unrolled our sleeping bags on any level space we could find among the boulders. Garratt Richardson and I were not quite covered by the rocks above but an arrangement of umbrellas kept most of the drizzle at bay. Although a waterfall from the cliff above rattled noisily into a polythene sheet, sheer fatigue won and we slept soundly.

The following morning the rain had turned to snow and 30m/100ft above us the forest was quite white. It looked most unwelcome after a wet night, but we made an excursion into

Snowflakes against a waterfall. We gave up shortly after this!

what was obviously a very rich area with some giant evergreen oaks, including one veteran over 7.6m/25ft round at breast height and at least 36m/120ft high. It was largely an evergreen forest with scheffleras, *Lithocarpus*, several *Ilex* species, including a very broad-leaved one, and numerous rhododendrons including such softish species as *R. anthosphaerum*, *R. lukiangense* and *R. edgeworthii*, but *R. fulvum* subsp. *fulvoides* and *R. glischrum* were also there. *Dipentodon sinicus* was one of the few deciduous items, a small tree with fruits carried in bunches on upright pedicels that stand in soldierly rows above the branches.

It was a chilly spot and we were not sorry to set off down again, although we were dreading the 'levada'. In fact, the cliffs around the channel were rich in epiphytes and, once past the worst section of gangway along the cliff edge, the rhododendron enthusiasts gathered round some exotic species, with *R. nuttallii* (CCHH 8077) and *R. megacalyx* (CCHH 8076) in evidence and, perched above, were *R. chrysodoron*, *R.*

Opposite. Our rock shelter above Fugong on Biluo Xue Shan where we spent the night huddled together with some protection from the incessant rain.

The Moon Mountain on the west side of the Salween seen through a telephoto lens, with cultivation right up to the hole.

The Moon Mountain from the north, its precipitous hillsides covered in vegetation.

xanthostephanum and scarlet-flowered *R. kyawii* (CCHH 8078, recorded for the first time east of the Salween).

Most travellers on these hill paths have at some time had a private debate with themselves as to whether going up or down is worse and the answer usually depends on which you are doing at the time. My notes for the day read: 'In wet and slippery conditions going down is certainly worse. You never seem to take a normal human stride and the jolting, crab-like descent is tough on knees and calf-muscles alike.' We had dropped 1,330m/4,500ft by the time we reached the Salween and, in spite of its basic provisions, our Fugong hotel seemed welcome. That was until David Chamberlain appeared pale and wide-eyed and started muttering about corpses. We rushed down the passage and found in the washroom what did indeed look like a rather messy murder. Bright red smears were all over the tiled walls and in the corner a man lay face down in a pool of his own blood. In fact he was drunk rather than dead and in due course his mates removed him, but the blood remained until we left, making a visit to the loo even less appealing than usual.

We had a welcome rest day in Fugong. Mr Cheng, resourceful as ever, arranged for the Municipal Baths to be closed so that we could take showers without the usual audience. There were few tourists in Fugong and our clothes

had aroused some curiosity, so perhaps they wondered if we looked equally odd without them. Brian Poett, who took a military man's interest in communications and weather matters, heard on the World Service that the monsoon had officially ended – not before time in our view. Sure enough the clouds started to break and so, showered and washed and with the first blue sky we had seen on the trip, we set off north towards Gongshan, which was to be our base in the north for both our trips in 1997 and 2000. Life was looking up.

Driving along the Salween on our way to Gonghsan, we stopped to take photographs of Moon mountain, an extraordinary natural feature that can be viewed from both sides, and passed through the picturesque village of Leshadi where the women wore beaded headdresses. Further on, a wire rope crossing of the Salween gave some of us a breathtaking experience to rival any fairground ride. Gongshan is, or was in 1997, the end of the road, a cheerful terminus for travellers perched above the Salween in a bay in the mountains. An adequate guesthouse provided Peter and me each with a large room filled with enormous velvet sofas and an assortment of plumbing that worked intermittently. The town had been open to foreigners for only a month and we were warned not to wander around late at night or go anywhere near Christian churches. By 2000 a new hotel had been built with bathrooms attached to all the rooms and we had an almost luxurious base from which to make our sorties.

Hugh Angus paired up with a local man to cross the Salween the quick way.

A typical village scene at Leshadi in the Salween valley.

The women of Leshadi village wear these attractive beaded headdresses.

An excursion to the new road in 2000

We knew about the new road that the Chinese authorities were building north and west into the Dulong valley, indeed on our 1997 trip we had been bombarded with rocks as they exploded bits of the hill opposite to make it. Even the mules had run as stones rattled off the cliffs above and to say we were relieved that we did not have to traverse it was a great understatement. So it was with some anticipation that we set off by bus to drive as far as we could. This was new territory that the great collectors of the past regarded as hostile in the extreme and, with the exception of Heinrich Handel-Mazzetti, had left largely untouched.

The road had been open only a few months before a section had collapsed into the valley below and this seemed likely to be its regular fate. The slopes must have been 70 degrees in places and the thin skim of soil was held together by the vegetation. Dodging the alarming cracks that were opening in the road's surface, we drove the 32km/20 miles to the breach and then edged nervously across the landslip to continue on foot. The view was magnificent. Ranks of blue hills, some still tipped with snow, stretched towards the Burma border and, from the horizontal scratch that was the new road, cascades of detritus ran to the valley below while darker lines of forest rose between the cliffs and crags.

There were also some memorable plants. On the way up we had admired a *Deutzia* species with the purest white flowers, as yet unidentified, and a fine stand of *Magnolia rostrata* with elephantine foliage was so regular and good that we debated whether it could have been planted – but for what reason? Medicinal use was a possibility. *Rhododendron megacalyx* had a pinkish flush to its heavily scented cups and *R. taggianum* (CCHH 8108) added its fresher fragrance. Further up than these tender species we found several rhododendrons that we were not to see anywhere else: *R. coryanum*, a rarity in the wild as well as in cultivation, *R. glischrum* and *R. coriaceum*. There were some embattled old warriors among the conifers that had wedged themselves into these vertical slopes. The hemlock, *Tsuga dumosa*, had a few historic specimens and a spruce, probably *Picea brachytyla*, sometimes reached 30 to 36m/100 to 120ft in height. *Pinus armandii* grew lower down but the usually disappointing *P. yunnanensis* had straightened its back and grown into a decent tree.

It had been a fine sunny day among good plants and, as we made our way back to our comfortable hotel in our comfortable bus, we mused on the road that had made possible our intrusion – but at what cost to the wilderness?

Above: The path up a crumbling bare hillside to the new road being built from Gongshan on the Salween westwards in 1997. Even the mules were frightened.

Left: Crossing loose shale in 2000 after the new road had fallen away.

The Marble Gorges of the Salween, with tiny figures visible below the cliff.

The Marble Gorges and beyond

On our earlier trip we had little opportunity other the Fugong excursion to explore the east side of the river where massive slopes rise to form the divide between the Mekong and the Salween. Recognising this, Mr Cheng organised a five-day trip north and then east on what had been the old route into Tibet. It was to take us through some remarkable contrasts in scenery, from the grandeur of the Marble Gorges to some of the best farming countryside we had seen and finally into fine primary forest. Throughout it all, however, there was a sense of

foreboding that things were about to change. The young are reluctant to take on their father's farms and are ambitious for city jobs, as they are in rural areas all over the world. And in the gorges periodic explosions signalled that a road was being driven through and the Chinese engineers were in the grip of the historic urge that drives engineers to 'tame nature'.

We drove the final 40km/25 miles north of Gongshan to where the road currently ends in a village called Bin Zhong Lo, which earlier travellers had told us was a bit of a dump but had

Steve Hootman defending US honour at the village of Ni Da Dang. He lost.

Cypripedium henryi (probably).

obviously been tidied up for impending tourists. Our ponies had not yet arrived so we set off ahead through farms and fields fringed with banks of a tumbling creamy flowered rose which Maurice Foster was calling R. brunonii although it looked similar to what we had earlier been calling R. helenae. Maurice had a great knowledge of the lowland shrub flora and his enthusiasm was infectious. He was particularly excited by a pretty white deutzia that he thought might be D. monbeigii, which had been found only once before.

The gorges are every bit as impressive as our reading of the early

explorers had led us to believe, but nothing like as difficult to traverse. For the most part it was an easy walk along the overhung shelf that the road makers were blasting. The cliffs, absolutely sheer for the best part of 300m/1,000ft to the river, are indeed marble with occasional intrusions of slate or shale and, although the surfaces have darkened with exposure, the excavations have spilled out giant sugar lumps of dazzling white or occasionally pink. These were not too bad to scramble over, but traversing the shale slips was a gingerly business with the Salween swirling below. From time to time a faint shout would be followed by an explosion and we would

Cymbidium species.

Our mule man. Despite treacherous parts of our route, our mules had no apparent difficulties in traversing them.

take cover as chips of marble spattered the river surface. The Chinese enjoy bangs. They invented gunpowder and no Chinese party would be complete without firecrackers.

We bounced over a suspension bridge to the east side of the river and followed a short track up to a village called Ni Da Dang. Wooden buildings surrounded a courtyard where the ponies gathered and before long Steve Hootman was playing table tennis with the local schoolchildren on a concrete table. Steve had been on several trips with us before and is a skilled plantsman in the field, but he had to work hard to defend America's honour at China's national sport. We were lodged in the upstairs schoolrooms among the desks and dust and it was a magical evening as we sat on the veranda enjoying a tot of whisky while the night came on us. The village had no electricity so there were no lights apart from a few candles, and there was no noise other than the rushing of the distant river but, as memories of past trips were shared, foreign laughter trespassed on the Chinese night.

The school at Ni Da Dang is at an altitude of only about 1,650m/5,300ft so we were obviously going to do some climbing to reach a more interesting flora. We rose steadily all day, first through attractive farmland and past the Nu village of Shi Na Tung, then up the Qi Na river until we found ourselves in magnificent forest. We passed under some large trees of the rare conifer *Torreya yunnanensis* with yew-like foliage and fruits shaped like olives which unfortunately were not ripe. A little further and the forest cleared for what had been a farm for medicinal plants called Yao Cai Di, though little remained, which was to be our camp for the night.[7]

On 25 May we set out from Yao Cai Di to reach the pass. The old road into Tibet showed little sign of recent use and it was hard going. We had little assistance from our guide, whom we called Shades on account of his wraparound dark glasses. He was rather pleased with both his glasses and himself and disappeared into the damp forest as we struggled to find our way up the river bed. There was only an occasional slippery log to indicate where a bridge might have been and we all fell in from time to time – coming round a boulder we found Maurice Foster and Peter Catt pink from the waist down and wringing their trousers out before putting them on again.

The mossy crowns of boulders held some interesting plants. A fine *Rhododendron edgeworthii* in flower matched the foaming river

Our camp at Yao Cai Di, an old medicinal farm, now just a bed of weeds.

Rhododendron edgeworthii, *one of the loveliest epiphytic species, with a wide distribution from Sikkim to central Yunnan.*

7. The area was rich in conifers. With the aid of binoculars we could see around the camp and on the hillside opposite were no less than eleven species. Apart from the *Torreya* that we had passed, there were two spruces, *Picea brachytyla* and *P. likiangensis*, two firs in *Abies* aff. *delavayi* and *A. chensiensis* var. *salouenensis*, two pines in *Pinus armandii* and *P. yunnanensis*, as well as *Larix griffithii*, a proper yew in *Taxus yunnanensis* and at least one juniper, *Juniperus recurva*. Like those seen on the west side, the *Pinus yunnanensis* was straight stemmed and we were told that the Chinese had themselves collected seed there for forestry purposes. Lists make dull reading but it must be unusual to say the least to have sight of an inventory like that from within one spot.

The Roman Catholic church at Shi Na Tung, reputed to be 150 years old.

but the prize was *R. fletcherianum* (BASE 9577), a neat bush with creamy yellow flowers that had been collected only once before by Joseph Rock and was known as *R. valentinianum* aff. until it was named after the Regius Keeper of the RBGE at that time.

We turned uphill from the river zigzagging up an almost vertical ascent to over 3,400m/11,000ft with blobs of *Rhododendron floccigerum* (BASE 9579) as a companion in motley colours from pinky-orange to full red. A handsome column of juniper stood out from the forest and Peter counted eighteen species of rhododendron, many of which were common but *R. eclecteum, R. selense* and *R. megeratum* were all

Rhododendron fletcherianum, *only its third finding, twice previously by Joseph Rock, supposedly at much higher elevations.*

there and *R. crinigerum* (BASE 9583) had particularly fine foliage. Near the top the land levelled out but there was little new and the rain was becoming persistent and heavy. We knew the river would be rising below and, hurrying down, we finally reached camp soaked and exhausted.

The following day we made our way back to the Salween, first through the forest we had admired and then through some beautiful farmed countryside, unusually serene and pastoral in such rugged country. We passed two Nu villages where the wooden farmhouses are constructed as in Scandinavia from crossed and notched timbers. They sit well in the countryside with their broad eaves, tiled with large slabs of slate from the gorge and shaded by enormous walnut trees. In the village of Shi Na Tung there was a small Christian church. It stood above the village square in best Catholic style at the head of a rise of steps, but it was a modest building and peering through the cracks in the door we could see a curious blend of Chinese style and Christian iconography.[8]

We were beckoned into one farmhouse and given bowls of home-brewed beer.[9] It was fascinating to see inside, the ceiling tarred a shiny black by the open hearth, with only an apology for a hole in the roof to let the smoke out. There was a faded picture of Mao and a finely made basket, which we were told came from the Dulong, hanging on the wall. We sat on tiny stools while Shades, who had miraculously reappeared, gave the beer good measure and was rapidly approaching the singing stage.

Outside they were harvesting the barley, some of which would no doubt go to make the beer. Men and women were up to their waists in the long corn, cutting the heads first and then the stalks in a separate operation. We asked Mr Cheng about ownership of the farms and he told us that the government leased them to the families for a long term – it can be a hundred years or so – and they can be passed on from father to son.

We then went down to the dusty classrooms at Ni Da Dang for the night with our ponies wandering about in the courtyard and the children nipping in and out to collect schoolbooks. The next day the Salween was still surging milky-grey out of the hills beyond, the blasters were in full action in the gorge and there were uncomfortable moments when all eight of us were lined up on a pile of unstable shale, waiting for the next explosion and eyeing the river below. We returned to some comfort and a welcome hot bath in Gongshan.

8. The Chinese government is understandably sensitive about the extent of Christianity, some 60% of the local population is said to be Christian so the missionaries of a century and more ago who often came to an untimely end did not die in vain. Mr Wang told us that the church in Shi Na Tung was 150 years old, which would make it one of the earliest established by the French priests; it had been smashed during the Cultural Revolution in 1958 and rebuilt in 1988.

9. Such potions are brewed organically rather than hygienically and can have a drastic effect on the bowels, so I donated mine to a potted plant.

Peter just beyond a cliff that was being blown up to create a new road up the Salween. These explosions were among the worst hazards we encountered.

Rhododendron xanthostephanum. *We found this to be quite plentiful on both sides of the Irrawaddy-Salween divide. Sadly, it is usually exceptionally tender in cultivation.*

Dimalo

We made some one-day excursions out of Gongshan, which was surrounded by interesting and plant-rich country on both sides of the Salween. The only problem was getting access to it. Apart from the main north-south road which followed the Salween, occasionally changing sides, public roads were non-existent and we had to make use of forestry tracks and the like wherever they happened to be.

One such excursion in 2000 was to the Dimalo area to the east of the river. We crossed the suspension bridge to the north of Gongshan and wound up into the hills. It was not a good track, the bus started to fall behind and then the Mitsubishi decided it was too difficult. So we walked – a long way – although we climbed only about 300m/1,000ft. It was at about 2,200m/7,300ft when two corollas of *Rhododendron nuttallii* lying in the road, bruised and empty, gave notice of better things to come. The last time Peter and I had seen this improbably beautiful plant in flower in the wild was in Arunachal Pradesh in 1965. Steve made heroic efforts to collect it and got a few capsules. Then by a waterfall there was a very fine group of *R. xanthostephanum* (BASE 9594) with extra large bells of a lovely yellow.

A few hundred feet higher we entered some magnificent old forest, although there had been some selective felling among the old warriors. Many of the major genera were represented: lime, elm, ash and a bewildering variety of maples. *Tetracentron sinense* (BASE 9595) was scattered through the forest, as was *Davidia involucrata*, neither of which could be said to be rare in spite of their Red Book status. There were innumerable seedlings of *Magnolia rostrata* where there was a clearing, along with some M. *mollicomata*. As for rhododendrons, R. *protistum*, R. *sinogrande* and R. *lukiangense* were all there and we would see them again on the other side of the river.

We came to a halt at 2,630m/8,500ft where a herd of goats was tearing into a mass of *Cardiocrinum giganteum* var. *yunnanense*, reducing it to shreds, so we did not feel bad about removing some seed before they ate it (BASE 9599). *Rodgersia aesculifolia* (BASE 9598) and a nice *Stachyurus* species were also collected there. A little lower down I was pleased to find two *Agapetes* to collect, one with tiny leaves which is hopefully A. *lacei* var. *glaberrima* (BASE 9596) and another with larger leaves (BASE 9597).

The Mitsubishi had braved the rest of the road so as to drive us down, which Mr Li performed with great skill. It was a narrow shelf road, the surface greasy and muddy and only a few inches of leeway to an instant chute of several hundred feet if anything went wrong. We were very silent on the way down and shook hands with the driver after our safe arrival. Meanwhile Peter Catt had been a little shaken by an uncontrolled slither on a steep slope; the need for a little caution all round was the thought of the moment.

Saxifraga fortunei *on a damp shady bank near Dimalo on the east side of the Salween.*

Ye Niu Gu

For those who find the name a little difficult, it helps to know that Ye Niu Gu means 'The Field above the Valley', but, whatever the name, it was for us a logging camp perched above a sawmill. We made two excursions there on our 2000 expedition, the first being on 22 May before we left for Ni Da Dang and the Marble Gorges. Like Dimalo it was on the east bank of the Salween and had a pretty rough track, no doubt used by timber lorries. Although the minibus had difficulties, the 4WDs had no problems and we were decanted at the sawmill at 2,400m/8,000ft to walk up to the logging camp.

There were some good trees and shrubs in the area, many now becoming familiar such as the 'big band' of rhododendrons, but there were new things as well. We had passed on the way an attractive *Indigofera* species possibly *I. nigrescens*, *Enkianthus deflexus* (BASE 9548) and a new white-flowered *Deutzia* species (BASE 9550). A petiolarid primula close to *P. moupinensis* (BASE 9547),[10] but with very rugose, deeply veined leaves, grew on a mossy bank; there were no signs of runners. The star turns, however, were *Philadelphus tomentosus* (BASE 9553), which launched out from the banks in a cloud of scented white flowers, and *Rhododendron hylaeum*, which was voted plant of the day. It grew on the banks of the small river at the foot of the valley and the most striking feature was the big, bony branches and trunk with bark that peeled back to reveal a smooth, hard to describe colour, a sort of pinky grey buff. Peter says that it is close to *R. faucium* and

---

10. This has been named *Primula odontocalyx* by Richards and is proving difficult to cultivate.

Waterfall and snow at Ye Niu Gu.

the true species may not have been in cultivation, so he was particularly pleased with the find.

On our second visit to Ye Niu Gu after the Marble Gorges we hired a third 4WD vehicle to get us beyond the logging camp and up into our hoped-for collecting ground at higher altitudes. We

Schefflera species on the road to the logging camp at Ye Niu Gu near the east bank of the Salween.

Pileostegia viburnoides, a relation of the hydrangeas, climbing up a tree on the Dulong-Salween divide.

The last old warrior fir above Ye Niu Gu, with a yellow-flowered epiphytic Rhododendron sulfureum *flowering in the tree.*

succeeded in getting a considerable length up the valley and were surrounded by staggering scenery with snowfields still hanging on the higher slope and cascades of water coming down to huge piles of snow still making triangles of white at the foot of the cliffs. Added to this it was a brilliant sunny day, and David, Maurice, Tom Hudson and I had use of the very comfortable Toyota Landcruiser, complete with blue tinted windows so dark it might have been the Arctic midnight. David complained that it made everything look blue until we suggested he wind down the window.

Although the forest had taken a bashing from the loggers there were still fine trees above the camp and the maples were particularly rich, perhaps eight or ten species in all. Ahead was a south-facing hillside drenched in sun and looking rather dry. I called it Sunny Bank and the others set off with sweaty enthusiasm on a track that could be seen etching diagonally up the hill. I took the view that one sometimes sees more and does a more thorough job at a slower pace – at least it seemed a good day for that philosophy – and I meandered up the hill, poking around

and finding yellow things. There was *Rhododendron trichocladum* at the base of the hill and higher a superb species of *Scrophularia*. A battered old *Abies* was standing alone on the hillside, perhaps left by the loggers as a seed tree, more likely because the timber was no use. It reminded me of one of those shipwreck films where the masts and spars are all broken and the sails torn and hanging, except that here it was draped moss instead of sails and no dangling ropes – we were too high for lianas at 3,600m/11,700ft. Then I spotted a splendid bush with bright yellow flowers perched in the crook of a branch. Obviously an epiphytic rhododendron, but the height was surprising – what could it be? It was probably *R. sulfureum* which the others also spotted.

Meanwhile, Peter's party had got bored with the endless *Rhododendron arizelum*, but higher up eventually reached some *R. haematodes* subsp. *chaetomallum* and a forest of *R. praestans* with *Trillium tschonoskii* scattered beneath. A surprise was *R. edgeworthii* perched on little islands in the stream; surely some of these forms should be relatively hardy.

370

The west bank and Dan Zhu

On 31 May we made another excursion, this time to the west of the river in the direction of the Burmese border. Not for the first time the road was badly rutted and we spent a bit of time filling in the ruts to avoid grounding, but one vehicle soon gave up entirely and the Toyota complained a lot. We took to our feet eventually but did not gain much height, perhaps around 2,600m/8,500ft at the most.

With woody wreckage all around,[11] there were sufficient remnants of old forest to keep us interested and some magnificent old trees festooned with epiphytes. I collected two *Agapetes* species with corky tubers. *Rhododendron seinghkuense*, draped profusely among the moss, has the look of a neater *R. edgeworthii* with smaller bullate leaves and yellow flowers, although these were not yet showing. *R. leptothrium* was a pretty companion

Davidia involucrata *near Ye Niu Gu. The Handkerchief or Dove tree has a much wider distribution in the wild than was previously thought.*

Rhododendron seinghkuense *(CCHH 8106) in cultivation. With a much lower growth habit and brighter yellow flowers, this is quite different from the original Kingdon Ward introduction.*

The tender evergreen Magnolia nitida *is evidently rare in the wild and this was the only tree we saw.*

along the way with airy growth and massed pink flowers, spotted on the upper lip. Peter caught sight of *R. xanthostephanum* in full flower up a side valley and with it were *R. maddenii* subsp. *crassum* and *R. seinghkuense*, here growing on a bank. Steve Hootman claimed another yellow in *R. chrysodoron* (CCHH 8116, 8126), which we had seen on the Dulong expedition in 1997.

With the trees, however, we had a real bonus. An elegant small tree was recognised by Tom as *Huodendron tibeticum*. The stem was slender and a smooth slate-brown, and young shoots of the evergreen foliage were marvellous shades of bronze and copper, even red. One tree was in flower with masses of small pendulous flowers. Tom and I shared memories of an article by T.T.Hu in the *New Flora and Sylva* that described exciting new trees from China and had kindled our urge to go and look for such treasures ourselves. *Magnolia nitida* was there with its lip-gloss leaves, as was the strange *Dipentodon sinicum*, and by a bridge a huge *Davidia involucrata* had littered the track with discarded handkerchiefs.

11. The loggers use the streambeds as chutes to send huge fir and spruce logs down to the road from hundreds of feet above. They were also rolling them down and we had to dive for safety as one came crashing through the forest. I counted the rings on one huge log and buried my ice axe at the 200th circle. It was less than half way to the centre and the tree must have been between 450 and 500 years old. The Tudors were on the throne in Britain when that tree was a seedling and it had managed to survive the years until the voracious appetite for resources to feed 'development' felled it at last.

A *fine flushed-pink* Rhododendron megacalyx *on the new road to the Dulong.*

Paris polyphylla *in fruit near Gongshan.*

Hedychium gardnerianum *flowering in the autumn. A very invasive plant in suitable climates.*

To the Dulong and the Nam Wa pass

On both trips we made major excursions west of Gongshan, five days in October 1997 and six in the summer of 2000, to the pass over to the Dulong valley. Here the Chinese border with Burma breaks west to include the Dulong river, the Taron of Kingdon Ward's explorations, which feeds eventually into the Irrawaddy. It must contain one of the most cut-off populations in China with a thousand people living in the valley with no communication with the outside world except across the 3,600m/11,700ft Nam Wa pass that we were to visit. In October 1997 we followed, with a procession of mules, a lone telephone line that wobbled over the pass on posts bent by snow, but by 2000 the posts had been cut and the line no doubt replaced along the new 'Road in the Sky' which currently seemed to spend much of its time at the bottom of the valley.

The route follows the Pula river, a boisterous affair tumbling among the rocks and as cheerful as the Salween is sombre. The first stage on the ancient mule track took us to a staging post called Qiqi and on our first trip we had been advised, on account of 'very many bugs', to camp below the forestry huts rather than

using them, advice that we forgot 2½ years later and paid for with several days of scratching. Although the track is not difficult, it goes up and down without making much altitude and Qiqi is at only about 2,000m/6500ft. Parts of the track had been paved at one time, we were told on the instructions of Chairman Mao, but it had deteriorated into a jumble of stones and progress was slowed by having to hop from stone to stone. However, at about half way we found ourselves in very rich forest with many epiphytes perched on the trunks of trees and mossy rocks. Various *Agapetes* species with corky tubers dangled from the moss, also rhododendrons such as the neat *R. vaccinioides* and its rarer and larger cousin *R. emarginatum*.[12] I was pleased to have persuaded David Chamberlain that it was indeed a distinct species! But the star of the upper storey was undoubtedly *R. nuttallii* (CCHH 8104), sometimes perched away up in trees,

12. This has flowered at Glendoick and identified as *Rhododendron emarginatum* by Dr George Argent. The flowers, single or in pairs, are very small but of the brightest possible yellow.

with large wrinkly leaves and urn-shaped corollas of creamy white with a yellow throat which advertised its presence with a luscious, spicy scent. The most impressive rhododendron had to be *R. giganteum*, well named but unfortunately now demoted to a synonym of *R. protistum*. It can reach 20m/65ft or more in the wild and George Forrest was uncharacteristically enthusiastic, calling it 'assuredly a magnificent species'. Although the leaves are not as big as *R. sinogrande*, which we were to see a little further up the trail, the flowers of rich rose-crimson are larger, with corolla tubes as much as 10cm/4in long. Alas, we did not see this precocious grandee of the rhododendron world in flower on either trip.

The magnificent Rhododendron nuttallii, *alas too tender for virtually the whole of the UK, but suitable for parts of Australia, New Zealand and the California coast.*

The trunk of a huge Rhododendron sinogrande, *the species renowned for having the largest leaves in the genus.*

Taiwania cryptomerioides (syn. flousiana), *the tallest tree in China, towering above the rest of the forest.*

With *Rhododendron protistum*, *R. sinogrande* and *Magnolia rostrata* scattered along the track, this was an area with plants of great stature and one of the most interesting discoveries of the whole trip was *Taiwania cryptomeriodes* (*flousiana*), a conifer of distinction and rarity. Scattered trees towered above the canopy of the forest with mists shifting around them. Individual trees can reach 60m/200ft, although 46 to 55m/150 to 180ft is a more usual height at maturity, and while ages of 1,000 years have been claimed, Kingdon Ward suggests 200 to 400 years as more normal. It is lucky to survive that long as the wood has always been highly prized for its durability.[13] It has an extraordinary disjunctive distribution, with its only other location being Taiwan. Unsurprisingly it is on the IUCN Red Data Book.

The stage from Qiqi to our next camp brought a new variety of plants as we gained a little altitude, although many were still of suspect hardiness for British gardens, other than those on the west coast. Fine foliage was seen to right and left of us in

Rhododendron genestierianum,[14] which has tinted young growth and mature leaves that are startlingly grey underneath. We were particularly pleased to find *R. gongshanense* (CCHH 8110), recently described by the Chinese as a new species. It made a vigorous and handsome bush and the slender leaves have deeply impressed veins which gave it a corrugated look. Unfortunately, it was long past its flowering time, which is March. *R. seinghkuense* (CCHH 8106) hugged the rocks with its bullate leaves and we found an old friend in a curious holly, *Ilex nothofagifolia*,[15] that we had last seen thirty-two years previously in Arunachal Pradesh and introduced from there. One of the stars of the area was a herbaceous plant, a species of *Smilacina*

13. Kingdon Ward gives an interesting account of its commercial value for the coffin trade in *Burma's Icy Mountains* although it was Handel-Mazzetti who discovered it in this remote north-west corner of China.

14. The name honours Père Genestier of the French Catholic Tibetan Mission, who accompanied Kingdon Ward to the Marble Gorge in 1922 and whose parish base was Khiunaton, which may well be the same as the village of Shi Na Tung with the church where we peered through the doors.

15. This holly gets its name from the crisp little rounded leaves, not unlike some *Nothofagus*, which are held on tiered horizontal branches.

Opposite. I am standing next to one of the huge trunks of Taiwania cryptomerioides (syn. flousiana).

Our path to the Dulong valley beneath a fallen giant, Taiwania cryptomerioides (syn. flousiana).

(now *Maianathemum*), with the purest of white flowers that lit up the forest gloom, which would be a great asset to the woodland garden if it can be successfully introduced.

The valley widened for our next camp at 2,900m/9,500ft, and we hurried to pitch our multicoloured tents among the scattered scrub before darkness fell. Above and around we were enclosed by the high slopes that led to the pass into the Dulong and to our left to the Burma border. We had made some altitude at last. Food in camp was simple and contained few surprises. All meals, including breakfast, consisted of a cauldron of boiled rice and another cauldron of a kind of watery soup with lumps of pork or bacon fat floating in it. The Chinese are very fond of bacon fat. But most of us carried some comforts: Peter travelled with a jar of honey, which could be used to improve most things, and I had a large pot of marmalade that reminded me of British breakfasts. There was always a huge blackened kettle on the wood fire which could produce a palatable drink.

We were now within an easy march to the watershed of the Nam Wa pass. On the 1997 trip it was 4 October when we set off on this final stage, so we were much too late for any rhododendrons in flower but hoped for some gentians and a few alpines. In the event, the gentians were disappointing, given the twenty-nine or so species recorded from the area, and the only 'traditional' gentian with blue trumpets held its flowers on lax stems so one missed the thrill of looking into an intense blue funnel. There were two or three species with more modest cream or white spotted flowers and a roseroot (*Rhodiola* species) added a warm red glow. A procession of colourful characters heading for the pass made up for the lack of colour in the flowers. Two mule trains had gone by before we left camp in the morning, bearing everything from sacks of rice to

A venerable *Rhododendron sinogrande.*

Smilacina species (*now* Maianthemum, *possibly* M. oleraceum) *in the Pula valley, near Gongshan.*

mini-cookers.[16] The walkers were equally varied: there was a group of ladies in full party regalia with umbrellas and unsuitable shoes; numerous porters grunted by with baskets on their backs supported by brow bands and cordlike muscles in their necks; a soldier was towing a baby monkey which protested as it was hauled over the stones; and even a photographer flashed a press card and a toothy smile as he took our picture.

It was exhilarating up on the ridge in fine weather as we explored along the alpine slopes. Across the valley ahead of us we could see the blue ridges of the Burmese alps and the border was only a few miles to our left. The east-facing slopes were capped by a tangle of rhododendrons, mainly *R. campylocarpum* subsp. *caloxanthum* but with *R. saluenense* and *R. cephalanthum* mixed in. It formed a table only 90cm/3ft high, but if you looked under the

tight canopy the individual plants were 1.8–3.6m/6–12ft across on ancient gnarled stems. It looked as though you could walk on the surface but certainly not through it.

In the year 2000, however, it was 3 June when we left the same camp to head for the pass. It had been a reasonably easy trek up there from Gongshan by the Pula river, passing the taiwanias which again made us stand and gape with our necks cricked, and along the jumbled stones of the causeway. It was a beautiful day and our spirits rose when we came almost immediately on flowering rhododendrons in the scrub above

16. Brian counted 120 jerry cans strapped to mules, the winter's supply of kerosene for the isolated villages of the Dulong valley.

Near the top of the pass were numerous bushes of Rhododendron campylocarpum *subsp.* caloxanthum.

Rhododendron citriniiflorum *var. horaeum was plentiful in spring 2000 on the Nam Wa pass, mostly in shades of orange.*

the camp. They were making a good show, with R. *rubiginosum* and what looked like R. *dichroanthum* the commonest constituents, the latter in rich shades of burnt orange. We were told later that it was actually R. *citriniiflorum* var. *horaeum*.[17] R. *stewartianum* was another species with wide altitudinal range and I revised my rather negative opinion of it formed from poor clones in cultivation. Often the corollas were cream but sometimes a pale yellow fringed with pink or red. However, the R. *arizelum* (CCHH 8140) received low marks. Instead of a tall elegant shrub or small tree, the snow and exposure had squashed it down to a rambling thicket and the flowers were variable, although we did see one or two sporting domes of decent pink.

The hillside above was patched with snow and the previous year's vegetation was plastered against the slopes. Out of this grey mat emerged some brilliant colours: *Omphalogramma souliei*, a relative of the primulas, held trumpets of rich purple on upright stems; *Diapensia purpurea* encrusted rocks and stumps with its tight foliage from which sprouted bright pink flowers; and, the choicest plant of all, Forrest's own rhododendron, R. *forrestii*, had bells of glistening red lying on prostrate mats of foliage.

It was a convivial gathering on the Nam Wa pass with our Chinese colleagues on a bright sunny day with stunning views in every direction and sheets of snow in the gullies. Then we dropped down on the far side, rock-hopping on the remarkable

Sprawling Rhododendron arizelum *survived full exposure where the conifers on the upper east flank of the Nam Wa pass had all been felled some years ago, the flower colour varying from a good pink to creamy-white.*

Omphalogramma souliei *was common just above the deciduous forest on the east side of the Nam Wa pass.*

A *fine form of* Rhododendron tephropeplum *on the west side of the Nam Wa pass.*

Rhododendron lateriflorum *(BASE 9651), a species new to us all.*

Rhododendron cinnabarinum *subsp.* tamaense *in the Dulong valley.*

path, worn and tumbled by water, weather and ponies' feet. It looked ancient enough but we understood that Chairman Mao had commanded it to be made in 1960. The vegetation on the west side was disappointing at the beginning with little coming through the snow-beaten pasture, but among the scrub *Rhododendron mekongense* was in flower, a good yellow but ungainly as usual.

A bit lower were skeletons of dead firs among bamboo thicket. They had obviously been burnt, which we suspected was not an accident but deliberately done to establish views from the ruined guard post that we passed at 3,500m/11,500ft. Lower again the shrubbery became more interesting and there were hoots of delight from Peter as we found *Rhododendron tephropeplum* in fine colour and very showy, then a rather mysterious member of the Triflora subsection with relatively large funnel-shaped flowers of a pinky-white, an elegant thing which has now been named *R. lateriflorum* (BASE 9651).[18] Finally a variety of *R. cinnabarinum* with violet-rose flowers

made up a rare and refined trio. Found only once before, it was Kingdon Ward's subsp. *tamaense*, which he found in the Triangle area of North Burma in 1953.

As the path got steeper and in worse repair, knees complained as we plunged into evergreen forest of *Lithocarpus* and hemlock. By the time we finally spotted the plume of smoke from the camp rising among the trees, we were exhausted and dehydrated, but it had been a good day with an array of interesting and unfamiliar plants, some like *Rhododendron citriniiflorum* occurring on both sides of the pass but most restricted to one side or the other.

The next day we decided to lift the camp back up the hill where there was better grazing, but as we left the mist was rolling

17. Peter and I took this rhododendron to be *R. dichroanthum* subsp. *scyphocalyx* but David insisted it was *R. citriniflorum*. From their descriptions they are hard to tell apart.

18. Related to *R. zaleucum*, so wrongly placed in subsection Cinnabarina.

Mr Wang looking for capsules on Rhododendron hylaeum in the Dulong valley. This rare member of subsection Thomsonia had smooth slate-grey trunks.

up behind us and promising a wet day ahead. We had been too weary the evening before to do more than marvel at the huge smooth trunks of *Rhododendron hylaeum* (BASE 9659) above the camp, an almost indescribable colour of smoky purple-grey, but Bob persuaded the nimble Mr Wang to climb out on a limb and collect a little seed of this rarity. We had passed cushions of a delightful primula on the way down, studded with bright pink flowers. It is still unidentified but another, *P. agleniana*, was immediately recognised. This is a most refined plant with pendant flowers on slender stems, the corollas shaded from a delicate pink to creamy yellow and fragrant to perfection. The serrated leaves have a greenish-white farina below.

The rain came on us as we were pressing specimens of the less well-known rhododendrons and we added *R. xanthostephanum* to our list of no less than twenty-nine species which Peter claimed we had seen on this trek, ranging in size from giant *R. sinogrande* to *R. saluenense* huddled on the ridge.[19] We were wet by the time we straggled into the camp below the pass, an area with little flat ground and strewn with boulders, but I managed to get my tent pitched on one of them where it looked distinctly odd, a bright red mushroom on a whiskery rock. Dinner was rather miserable: under a plastic canopy the

A cushion Primula *species on the open hillside on the west flank of the Nam Wa pass in full exposure.*

The beautiful but hard to cultivate Primula agleniana *on the west side of the Nam Wa pass.*

The Nam Wa pass from the east.

The BASE team on our last days of botanising. Mr Cheng, Steve Hootman, Bob Zimmerman, Maurice Foster, David Chamblerlain, Tom Hudson, Garratt Richardson, Peter Catt, Peter, Hugh Angus and myself.

pots were bubbling on wet firewood so one had to choose between getting choked in the smoke or soaked in the storm outside. One of the ponies had been bitten by a snake and Garratt (a doctor of people not ponies) was called to help, but there was little he could do. He gingerly pressed the swelling on the neck with a wary eye on the hoof area and pronounced that the beast would probably survive, which indeed it did.

The next day Peter decided that with the weather deteriorating we should do a double march down to the forestry huts, missing out the intermediate camp. The 500m/1,600ft rise through the snowfields was easier than expected but the walk down from the pass took nine hours; it was the fourth time I had covered Mao's cobbles and they did not improve with

familiarity. The trouble with extended marches is they tend to be at the expense of examining the flora, but I managed to get some *Iris bulleyana* seed and the pure white *Smilacina* (*Maianthemum*) species which I had noticed lighting the dark woods on the way up. Unfortunately, we had forgotten the message about the other inhabitants of the forestry huts and we were scratching for several days afterwards. The final stage down the Pula river, now swollen with the rain, was easy and it should be put on record that after six days on the march the hot bath and cold beer at the Gongshan Hotel were as good as they come.

19. One more species has been added to this list, a brand new one as yet unnamed, another member of subsection Monantha, this time with white flowers.

Chapter 16

RETURN TO THE SUBANSIRI:

India 2002

Peter Cox

Arunachal Pradesh has long been considered one of the least known parts of India, especially from a plant-hunting point of view (see India 1965, p. 36). Despite determined efforts to return there, all efforts had failed and, by the turn of the century, we had given up hope. My son Kenneth had built up a friendship with the American explorer Ken Storm since their chance meeting in Tibet in 1996 and the two had worked together on the new edition of Frank Kingdon Ward's *Riddle of the Tsangpo Gorges*. Ken (Storm), having completed six trips to the gorge region, had developed contacts in Arunachal to further his explorations of the Himalaya. Rumours of Arunachal beginning to open up started circulating and in 2001, Kenneth, Ken and David Burlinson (previously of Exodus Travels) managed to get access to a remote part of north-east Arunachal.

Kenneth and Ken started to plan another trip to Arunachal in 2002 to reach another part unexplored (by Westerners) and we two Peters were given a chance to join them, together with some other plant enthusiasts.[1] Both of us were not far short of seventy years old and perhaps we would find the trek too tough? Preliminary research informed us that the proposed path was regularly used by the Indian Army and, as most of their personnel come from southern India, the terrain would surely be relatively easy. In any case, neither of us could resist giving it a go. We had been the first to attempt to explore Arunachal in recent years (1965), so in a way considered it 'our' territory.

The area selected was east of the Subansiri river, crossing to the Siyom river, a tributary of the Siang, the Indian name for the Tibetan Yarlung Tsangpo, which eventually becomes the great Brahmaputra in the Assam plain. This area is in the Siang Division of Arunachal, which is inhabited by several tribes including the notorious Abors, or Adis as they like to be called now. We say notorious because they caused the British Raj some serious trouble in the early part of the last century – but more of that later.

From New Delhi, we arrived at Gauhati on 14 September 2002 and then flew by helicopter to Itanagar, the chief town in Arunachal, from where we set off by road towards the Apa Tani valley. Thirty-seven years had elapsed since we were last there and we were very eager to see what changes had taken place. Three things were instantly noticeable: there were far more buildings and people, almost no traditional costumes and surprisingly, rather more trees, mostly Bhutanese pine, around

1. In addition to Kenneth and Ken, we had in our party Gwen Romanes from Canada, Franz Besch, Philip Evans, John Roy and Anne Chambers, the last four being Tibetan veterans from the 1990s (see Tibet chapters 12 and 13). Our trip was organised by Oken Tayeng of Abor Travels and Expeditions and his staff were Katu, Kali and Sanje. Oken did not join the trek but saw us start and met us at the finish.

Above left. Dendrobium fimbriatum near the Apa Tani valley.

Above. A view across the Apa Tani valley towards the ridge we had climbed in 1965.

Right. Itanagar, the administrative capital of Arunachal Pradesh.

Our team (left to right): Ken Storm, Peter, Gwen Romanes, Philip Evans, Oken, Franz Besch, Katu, Kenneth Cox, John Roy, Anne Chambers and Sanje (I was taking the photo).

Tree fern near the Apa Tani valley.

A decorated float at Daporijo. The Indians love decorating their vehicles.

A house in Siyum village from where we started our trek. Peter spent a night here on his return.

the valley sides.[2] In 1965 it had taken us a month to reach the valley from home (see India 1965) and in 2002 it took us only three days. As in 1965, we stayed in a circuit house (government guesthouse) but we were unsure whether it was the same building on the same mound.

In the afternoon we explored the forest which led into the valley, on a little pass at around 1,750m/5,600ft. To our great surprise, we found an evergreen azalea, which we later found out had been newly discovered and named *Rhododendron arunachalense*. Just approaching the pass were small plants of *R. coxianum*. Other plants of interest included two species of ginger, *Hedychium*, a tree fern, an *Agapetes* species with crimson flowers and a cherry in full flower. In spring 1965 we had seen a similar deep pink cherry in full flower and were thoroughly puzzled. It

turned out there are two different varieties of the Carmine Cherry, *Prunus cerasoides*, one spring and the other autumn-flowering.

Setting off once more, we came to another little pass and a north-facing bank. Here we were delighted to find our old friends *Rhododendron nuttallii* and *R. walongense* aff. (HECC 10004),[3] plus more *R. coxianum*. That night was spent at the surprisingly large town of Daporijo, with a nice view of the Subansiri river and then we drove on to the village of Siyum where we were to start our trek.

2. In 2004, my wife Patricia and I had a visit at Glendoick from Mr Sastry, one of the two botanists with us in 1965. He had been back to the valley a few years before and remembered observing the forest deteriorating, contrary to our observations.

3. HECC stands for Hutchison, Evans, Cox and Cox, meaning we all four collected the same plants using these numbers.

Dancing Tagin girls, Siyum.

The Subansiri river looking north.

The Subansiri

The Subansiri river drains a large area of central Arunachal and into south Tibet and yet it does not seem to be much bigger than our river Tay above Perth in Scotland. The villagers of Siyum greeted us warmly but trouble soon emerged when the Tagin people from the rival village of Rai along our trek route also wanted to carry our kit. Tempers rose but eventually it was amicably settled and Rai won the day and each of us was given a personal porter who not only carried all our kit but also helped us over difficult parts of the trail. Our seven-day trek started at the road some 600m/2,000ft above sea level. The lush green subtropical forest rises steeply on both banks and it was one of these banks that we had to descend to cross the river. We had a choice of two paths to the river, one gentle, the other steep; stupidly we chose the latter. By the time we slithered down the greasy path, made treacherous by the night's rain, all knees were wobbling, having dropped 300m/1,000ft in as direct a manner as could possibly be imagined other than jumping.

We had been warned of numerous hazards ahead and, being a bit of a coward over such things as flimsy swaying bridges and cliff edges, I had to steel myself to be brave. The bridge over the Subansiri was made almost entirely of scattered rotten bits of wood, strung together with some rusty wire, with a sag in the middle almost touching the water. Bouncing up and down and swaying from side to side in a most alarming manner, I decided that crossing it without hesitation was the best approach. Clutching the wire on either side, hand over hand, was the only way to get across with some degree of safety. The path started gently through a forest of pandanus, tree ferns and wild banana, with huge strap-like frayed leaves and hung with bunches of inviting-looking fruit. The taste was excellent but there was virtually no flesh, only rock-hard seeds that might easily break one's teeth.

The next hazard took us along the side of a cliff with only flimsy pieces of bamboo and strips of wood to walk on, just preventing certain death. The path coursed up and down, crossing streams, once with a make-shift bridge that our porters hastily assembled with lengths of wood cut with their razor-sharp *daos*, lethal-looking weapons made of a straight steel blade. Another bridge lay ahead with a nasty lean to one side directly above a chasm with a plunging 15m/50ft waterfall directly below us, its roar adding to the fear. I nearly panicked half way across and have rarely been so terrified in my life. Climbing the steep,

muddy bank after the bridge presented even worse dangers; slipping and sliding like mad, we were lucky enough to grab hold of the odd climbing plant to save us plunging into the river. Later I used one to abseil down a particularly steep slope. Furthermore, it was unbearably hot and humid; it was dry, however, so leeches were less likely to attach themselves to us.

All day we made almost no altitudinal gains and, frustratingly, there were no plants of any interest. We were all concentrating much too much on where to place our feet and keep our balance to bother about the flora or photography. Due to the extreme terrain, our party became scattered, with Peter, Gwen and Philip left well behind. Eventually, to everyone's relief, the stragglers arrived at Eru, where we were to camp, Peter and Gwen looking particularly exhausted. Luckily there was a hut available to keep off the worst of what was to be an extremely wet night. We awoke to a beautiful clear morning with fine views of where we were heading: a long knife-edge ridge with one peak above the rest, presumably the 4,000m/13,000ft one marked Vorjing on some maps, for which we had applied prior to 1965 (see Introduction, p.12). We all took stock, it now being crunch time. We had all suffered physically and mentally on that first day and

Balancing act on a Subansiri bridge which the Tagins had tried to repair with twigs.

A modern suspension bridge over the Subansiri, with a sag in the middle.

even Ken Storm was admitting that it had been as tough a day as any he had experienced in the Yarlung Tsangpo gorge. Very reluctantly, Peter and Gwen decided to return to Siyum after Ken, studying his fancy map, hinted that the going looked like getting even worse.[4] The indomitable Anne said, 'What the hell,' and decided to carry on. Having overcome the challenge of that gruelling first day, Philip and I made up our minds to brave all future hazards.

The second day did not prove to be quite so hard as our first and we received a tremendous welcome as we approached Rai, the last village before the Teacock pass and the Siyom valley.

Women and girls were all dressed up, singing and dancing. We celebrated with a huge meal of chicken and rice.

Being at the extreme east of India means that dawn and dusk are very early; in other words it gets light in September before 5.00 a.m. and dark soon after 5 p.m. We might have been better on Chinese time which would have meant getting up and going to bed later but I suppose that really the day is the same length whatever. With no facilities under cover other than our tents, this meant very long nights, which seemed especially so if one was uncomfortable and having little sleep. Another wet night indicated a leak in the top of my tent so I cut open two large poly-bags (which I could ill spare) to patch it.

The third day of the trek was another hard one, with still not enough of an altitudinal gain for rhododendrons, even though we camped at over 2,400m/8,000ft. We had a very muddy start in an enclosed area with a few mithun (cattle), which were so tame they licked our hands. Ken, who showed little interest in plants, decided to study birds. There were plenty of strange calls in the dense forest but the birds were impossible to see.[5]

4. Gwen was really not fit enough but Peter had never given in on previous treks. Both he and I now think he could have made it. His diary notes: 'It was a bitter decision but there could be no turning back. We had been told there would be worse to come and at all costs did not want to hold the party back. . . . We were given a couple of porters and Kali who had a great sense of humour and was marvellous at coaxing Gwen over the obstacles. "You OK marm," he would say, "just put right foot here." Of all the items on the assault course, the least favourite was a cliff where a couple of logs had been strung across the face and one had to edge along, nose pressed against the wet rock, trying to blot out the roar of the river directly below.'

5. Once my porter killed a little bird for Ken with his catapult and wounded another which recovered.

Our head porter with a young mithun.

The cliff-side walk where one false step could have led to instant death.

Building a make-shift bridge.

Rai, the last village before the pass and the Siyom valley.

A new species of Rhododendron *of subsection Falconera.*

Rhus species (HECC 10027).

Ilex nothofagifolia, *discovered by Reginald Farrer and my father in 1919 and introduced by us in 1965.*

The ridge at last

On the fourth day we at last arrived among rhododendrons. It began with hair-raising drops straight into the river away below, a descent to the river, a bridge, and up, up what looked like a cliff from the other side, but it proved to be easier than expected. Suddenly there they were: first *R. arboreum* similar to the ones we found in 1965 with narrow leaves, then the wide-leaved *R. griffithianum*, *R. walongense* (HECC 10006) and the first *R. boothii* (HECC 10007, 10031) any of us had ever seen. One big-leaved species (HECC 10010) looked like a totally new species but then we found a much smaller leaved species in flower and we knew it could only be Kingdon Ward's autumn-flowering *R. kasoense* (HECC 10009, 10024), larger-growing with more flowers than the closely related *R. monanthum* (see p. 354). Soon there were

also *R. maddenii*, *R. edgeworthii* (HECC 10025) and *R. lindleyi* (HECC 10023). Our old friend *Ilex nothofagifolia* (HECC 10038) was also plentiful, one tree covered with its tiny bright red berries. With all this excitement, we immediately lost all sense of fatigue.

That evening, we arrived at our camp at over 3,400m/11,000ft, which we called our jungle camp, the last before the ridge, to find our tents up and tea made.[6] Our porters were proving to be some

6. Somehow Katu and the porters managed to get a good fire going every night, often under very damp conditions, but we had only one kettle which meant that boiled water was always in short supply. During the day we often had no lunch other than a few snacks that we had brought from home. The evening meal was usually pasta or some other packet food we had also brought with us, plus some sauce. On some occasions there were weird mixtures of different ingredients as one packet was not enough for all of us. Our Nepali 'cook' was useless, so the ever-willing Katu did the cooking.

Temperate forest with Ilex nothofagifolia *showing tiered growth.*

Anne Chambers with a fruit head of one of her beloved arisaemas.

My personal porter who was extremely helpful and intelligent.

of the few remaining totally unspoilt people in the world, no doubt due to their having almost no contact with the outside.[7] Highly intelligent and quick to learn, my porter picked up an amazing amount of English, calling me 'Dad'. Despite the near vertical campsite, some of the porters proved expert at making flat platforms out of bamboo stems which made most of our beds springy and comfortable, but Anne was full of complaints about hers.

We were warned of a long day ahead but the plants proved to be so exciting that the over nine-hour trek made us tired but very happy. There were a number of the very widespread *Clethra delavayi*, several vacciniums, gaultherias, *Enkianthus* and the arching *Leucothoe griffithiana* (HECC 10034), a genus usually associated with eastern North America. Further rhododendrons were *R. grande* aff. or perhaps *R. sidereum* (HECC 10014) or

perhaps a new species with tiny growth buds[8] and *R. faucium* that higher up gave way to a large-leaved form of *R. hookeri* (HECC 10035), which may be the same as Kingdon Ward's pinkish-purple-flowered form. *R. arizelum* (HECC 10044, 10068) was the highest of the three big-leaved species and it was omnipresent, possibly the commonest and most widespread of all big-leaved species. Other species were *R. keysii*, rather scrappy here, *R. glischrum* subsp. *rude* (HECC 10040, 10067), *R. exasperatum* (HECC 10039), *R. neriiflorum* subsp. *phaedropum* to 6m/20ft, *R. leptocarpum* (HECC 10029), *R. charitopes* subsp. *tsangpoense* and a few *R. cinnabarinum* and *R. campylocarpum*. A plant that was quite dwarf with almost sessile leaves which were very pale green underneath caused a great deal of controversy and has been variously called *R. stewartianum*, *R. eclecteum*, *R. lopsangianum*

Jungle camp.

Abies densa on the ridge. We saw very few young trees.

aff. and *R. succothii* (HECC 10016, 10043, 10054). And there were some plants that appeared to be closer to *R. sherriffii* (HECC 10042). As is usual in a little disturbed habitat, there were very few natural hybrids, two recorded here being *R. grande* aff. x *R. arizelum* and *R. exasperatum* x *R. hookeri*. Subsequently, at Glendoick, to our disgust, over half the seedlings of *R. exasperatum* have turned out to be the latter hybrid.

Up and up we went and then a seemingly endless traipse around a ridge. Philip and I were told we had nearly reached camp when it turned out we had at least another 5km/3 miles to go. *Ilex nothofagifolia* was still with us right to the top of the ridge where it became dwarfer, to perhaps equal *I. intricata*.

What had appeared to be a meadow above the tree line from our first camp turned out to be bamboo, a tall species with silvery stems that turn black in their second year.[9] Higher up

7. Ken said that even in the still remote Yarlung Tsangpo gorge, the local people are not what they were when he first explored it.

8. Four-year-old seedlings are looking more and more like *Rhododendron sidereum*.

9. This bamboo is so vigorous and domineering that it is threatening to choke out all other plants. Rhododendrons are about the only plant able to exist under its canopy as they can tolerate some shade. But for some distance on the climb up to the ridge the bamboo held sway with often nothing else in sight. To keep a way through, it has to be constantly cut and this creates the hazard of cut spikes which can nearly go through a boot. The cut stems are also easy to slip on.

Rhododendron trilectorum, discovered by Ludlow and Sherriff and introduced by us in 2002.

Rhododendron ludlowii, *first introduced by Ludlow and Sherriff from the Lo La to the north-east of here on the Tibet frontier.*

was a dull, dwarfer species of bamboo and along the ridge were mature trees of *Abies densa*, their gaunt shapes like huge pincushions leering out of the mist. All appeared to be the same age with a few miserable seedlings that seemed unable to compete with the bamboo. Does the bamboo have to flower and die to allow the trees to regenerate?

The most interesting plant of the day was again something totally new to us. This grew in the open along the ridge. It appeared to be closest to *Rhododendron aperantum*, but later we came to the conclusion that it must be *R. trilectorum* (HECC 10019, 10041) and herbarium specimens from London later confirmed this. It was a new species discovered by Ludlow and Sherriff but not introduced, found to the north-east of us on the Lo La. It has very neat leaves in whorls and the plants Ludlow and Sherriff saw had pale yellow flowers tinged pink. Seedlings are doing well at Glendoick but are very slow-growing.

There was one small boggy area with two species of *Primula*, one the ubiquitous *P. dickieana*, the other much more exciting, *P. elizabethae*, named after Ludlow's mother. This is closely related to the daffodil primula, *P. falcifolia* which I had seen on the south side of the Doshong La in 1996 (see p. 303). There were very few perennials but one of interest was *Ophiopogon intermedius* (HECC 10037) with blue and green fruit.

I had to take paracetamol to get to sleep that night and had to be woken in the morning for my tea. Apart from rotten colds and Katu hurting his foot, we all kept remarkably healthy and by the time we had reached the ridge were all acclimatised to the altitude and the hard going. From this camp to the pass was not far and there were more excitements rhododendron-wise. Another Ludlow and Sherriff find on the Lo La which has always been rare and difficult to grow, and invariably a miserable little thing in cultivation is *R. ludlowii* (HECC 10017), a plant that I had never dreamed of finding myself in the wild. Here in contrast, we found masses of superb healthy specimens up to 30cm/1ft high,[10] often accompanied by the equally dwarf *R. pumilum*.

Kenneth was the first to reach the pass at a little over 3,700m/12,000ft, which had a small cairn and a few capsules of *Lilium nanum* but little else. Although it was hazy, we could see the higher peak along the tops to the south, too far for us to reach in the time available. A change in topography on the east side with large slabs of rock meant there was less vegetation, though this change of aspect invariably leads to different plants and, sure enough, we soon found something that had eluded Kenneth in Tibet in the Tsari valley: *Rhododendron tsariense*. I first stumbled on one in the middle of the path, looked at the indumentum and at once pronounced it to be this. There were only a few more on the top of a little cliff but none had any signs

Kenneth Cox and Rhododendron tsariense, *a species that has not been relocated on recent visits to the Tsari valley.*

Porters with tree fern capes.

of capsules or flower buds. Nestled amongst the rock slabs was bergenia with crimson-purple autumn leaves and another puzzling rhododendron, obviously of subsection Neriiflora. David Chamberlain was helpful in tracking this down later. Our specimen matched perfectly a herbarium specimen from London of *R. haematodes* subsp. *chaetomallum* var. *chamaephytum* (HECC 10018), another plant found by Ludlow and Sherriff, yet not introduced. This has very little indumentum compared with *R. chaetomallum*. Alas, the seedlings may all be hybrids. A species found on this side in addition to the other was *R. cerasinum* (HECC 10064), most likely the crimson form named 'Coals of Fire' by Kingdon Ward.

The path then dropped down, down, down towards the valley, with few of the hazards on the other side apart from slippery rocks. Two members of the party dropped their cameras, luckily without disastrous results. There was nothing else new and some of the *Rhododendron* species found on the other side were absent here, most likely because it would be drier. The path was down a ridge, sometimes very narrow before broadening out into a little valley joining the main one, a drop in all of some 1,500m/5,000ft. A *Crawfurdia* species was the plant of the day, a climbing plant of the gentian family with deep blue flowers. A very relieved Oken met us in Mechuka, delighted to find us all safe and well as he had been told that one of the party had been killed. He informed us that the opposite side of the valley was out of bounds, no doubt due to the proximity to the Tibetan frontier. The lower slopes looked uninteresting anyway, having long been denuded of all forest.

10. *R. ludlowii* has been a plant of great significance in my life; I first saw it at the Sherriffs' garden, Ascreavie, and was so taken with the comparatively large bowl-shaped flowers on the tiny plant that I immediately started using it for hybridising, producing such well-known dwarf hybrids as *R.* 'Chikor', *R.* 'Curlew' and *R.* 'Wren'. I had hoped that this introduction would prove to be easier to grow than that of Ludlow & Sherriff, but, alas, this is so far not proving to be the case.

Crawfurdia *species, a climbing plant of the gentian family.*

The view north towards the Tibetan frontier and Ludlow and Sherriff plant hunting territory.

Mechuka and the Siyom valley

Peter and Gwen also met us in Mechuka and had recovered from their ordeal over the 'assault course' to and from Eru. After a night in a Tagin hut in Siyum and a couple of nights in various grotty doss houses, they were in good form. Peter noted in his diary: 'The long houses are built on bamboo stilts and thatched with palm and banana leaves, with pigs and chickens rootling beneath. Bits of the extended family each have a hearth stretching into the darkness and it was warm and welcoming inside.' After supper with a dozen of the family round the fire and

The gompa at Sumdingyamcha.

a tot of the Balvenie (treated with suspicion by the locals), Peter was offered a massage. He eagerly accepted: 'After all it is not every day that one has a pretty Tagin girl in a sari walking up and down one's spine. As sleep drifted in,' he continued, 'I thought of our colleagues up on the wet hillside and the fierce reputation of the Tagins. It was less than fifty years since their last massacre when a troop of the Assam Rifles came up the valley without properly explaining themselves and many were killed. Looking round at the firelit faces it seemed unlikely. But then perhaps not.'

Oken had driven Peter and Gwen up the Siyom river to where the broad Mechuka valley gave a gloriously level walk of about six hours to the base. Peter climbed the hill to some fine hemlock forest where he collected *Rhododendron boothii* and a *Maddenia* with broad leaves and stubby capsules. Then with their two 'guides' of around twelve years old, he played Pooh Sticks in an irrigation channel until it was time to return and greet the rest of us.

Reunited in Mechuka, duck for dinner was very welcome for all, especially for those of us who had had no breakfast or lunch. Three nights here gave us time to do a little exploring. John and Gwen went to investigate the health of the local people. When the locals found out John was a dentist, they queued up for much needed treatment. Seven people had teeth extracted, the last two without any anaesthetic. Franz, Ken and Anne went to search for religious inscriptions on stones, while the rest of us looked over our seed and herbarium specimens.

The Siyom river, said to contain huge trout.

Anne found some cultivated cardiocrinums; the bulbs are mashed up and eaten locally. We visited a local dignitary in the Sumdingyamcha *gompa*,[11] which entailed drinking quantities of *chang*, the local brew made out of millet, luckily not containing much alcohol. We had six girls and two men for an evening's entertainment of dancing and singing, which we joined in. Ken and Uken remarked on my good dancing, somewhat of a joke as I am renowned for my lack of expertise in this quarter.

The Siyom river was a superb trout stream with fish weighing up to 9k/20lb, or so the locals told us. The Chinese invaded this valley in 1962 and we were informed that there had been quite a battle. The Indians are in the process of building a road up to the frontier, making it easier to defend. The finished road had not reached this part of the valley so it was a long walk out to meet the vehicles, partly along the half-made road and partly via short cuts between corners, often exceedingly rough. By a bridge, we suddenly came across an amazing collection of ten *Rhododendron* species,[12] and I wished we had had more time to study them. Later Peter found a

branch of a very small-leaved *Maddenia* (HECC 10075) which may be another new species. A few trees of the *R. arboreum* included one huge specimen of about 15m/50ft, proved to be the last rhododendrons we saw. There were several fine-looking *Schefflera* species. One interesting tree, a conifer, probably *Cephalotaxus griffithii* (HECC 10091), had not been introduced before but is likely to be very tender as our altitude

11. A *gompa* is a small monastery. The Sumdingyamcha *gompa* was not very old, the original having been destroyed in the 1950 earthquake, the same that Kingdon Ward and his wife got caught in, in the not far distant Lohit valley and described in *My Hill so Strong* by Jean Kingdon Ward, Jonathan Cape, 1952.

12. They were *Rhododendron boothii*, *R. kendrickii*, *R. tanastylum*, *R. grande* (typical), *R. walongense*, *R. kasoense*, *R. edgeworthii*, *R. neriiflorum*, *R. griffithianum* and *R. arboreum* var. *peramoenum*.

Monks with ceremonial scarves at the Sumdingyamcha gompa.

In the Siyom valley (left to right): a local person, Philip Evans, Katu and Ken Storm.

Old houses in the Siyom valley.

was only 1,900m/6,300ft. It had bright red oval pendant fruit 20mm/¾in long.

The road down to Along, where we spent the night, went through a gorge with a drop of around 900m/3,000ft into the river, mostly through fine forest, and we passed a magnificent waterfall. Somebody had commandeered one of our vehicles, which meant eleven of us had to squeeze into one with all our gear. Two of our staff hung on the outside. Philip discovered his luggage had been raided by his porter (not the one he had for his trek); a camera and sleeping bag were missing. That night in Along we were almost back to civilisation in a circuit house with loos that flushed and a basic hot water system.

We were very slow to get away as Oken was interrogated by the local police for hours on what we had been doing, including how many teeth John had pulled. We stopped at the confluence of the Siyom and Siang rivers, the former clear running into the latter grey-brown. Then another stop to see the Komsing bridge near to where Noel Williamson, the British Political Officer in Sadiya, and his party were murdered by the Abors in 1909.[13]

Driving through the Himalayan foothills, we had a fine view of the Assam plain with the Siang snaking its way to meet the Lohit coming in from the east. At Pasighat, the headquarters of the Adi tribe, we were met by the Deoris' daughter, loaded with presents for everyone. The Deoris had been very generous and kind to us in the Apa Tani valley in 1965 (see p. 45) when their daughter was just a month old. Now this formidable lady was Assistant District Commissioner and she gave us an excellent meal. While in Pasighat we visited a bookshop where I read that in the wildlife reserves in

13 The British treatment for such uprisings was to mount a punitive expedition. A strong army force with two heavy guns and a large party of Nagas, sworn enemies of the Abors, were sent in. The guns were man-handled up the gorge, but despite the Abors being prepared for the assault with stone slides at the ready, they were attacked from both sides by a pincer movement from above and were routed. We only found out later the Tagin tribe that were so good on our trek had been responsible for another massacre, of a column of Assam Rifles, as recently as 1953. The Indians in turn avoided a heavy-handed revenge and the culprits were sentenced to varying terms of imprisonment.

Schefflera species in flower.

Looking back at the ridge we had climbed over, now with a light sprinkling of snow.

The clear water of the Siyom river joining the huge murky Siang.

The Siang river near where the British Army defeated the Adis.

Part of the vast Brahamaputra flood plain.

Assam, of which there are several, tigers and elephants were holding their own, but rhinos had been poached out, apart from in the famous Kasiranga Reserve.

We were to travel on the ferry down river to Dibrugarh where we were to stay in a very posh tea estate in luxurious comfort. Half way to the ferry Kenneth suddenly panicked; he had left his passport under his pillow. Katu went all the way back for it and found it thrown out with the rubbish. On arriving at the ferry we were told that everyone was on strike including the ferry crew. So

back we went to Passighat where we waited for a helicopter, this time a small one unable to hold all our luggage, which had to catch up with us later. The view of the Brahmaputra from the helicopter was unbelievable, with a vast sea of channels and sandbanks like an old man's hands stretching as far as the eye could see, no doubt making navigation a nightmare.

It had been a week trekking that none of us would ever forget and the toughest week of my life; the journey gave me a great sense of achievement and the rhododendrons were amazingly exciting.

Opposite A waterfall on the drive to Pasighat.

The Nam Wa pass from the east.

EPILOGUE

Peter Hutchison

Peter and I are often asked: 'Is there anything left to be explored and are there any new plants to be discovered?' The answer really lies in this book but to stand on the Nam Wa pass (Chapter 15) looking across to the ripple of blue and white mountains of the Burmese alps, untouched since Kingdon Ward's day, reminds us of unfinished business.

We have to be careful, of course, with words like 'untouched' and 'unexplored' when applied to territory where people are living. The plants are perfectly well known to the local inhabitants, but not by Latin names and usually as food or medicine. Below the alpine region, in order to explore one is totally dependent on their paths, however crude, and an untouched bamboo thicket can reduce progress to yards per hour. In the warm wet forests of the Eastern Himalaya, perspiring foreigners in large boots slither and crunch through the tangled vegetation while the local people slip through with the same adept agility as the other indigenous mammals. In those parts there is plenty that is new in our terms, perhaps not deserving a new Latin tag but able to add value to our gardens and to our knowledge of plants.

Over the period of this book there has been a huge change in the way plant hunters set about collecting. In our early trips we ventured forth with canvas tents on a frame of wooden poles that required a porter each to carry them. On our first India trip a considerable quantity of tinned food was shipped out from Britain and carried up the Himalaya. Latterly the tents have been flimsy domes of nylon supported by wands of fibreglass and we depend largely on local supplies of food, taking only a few items to enliven the routine of rice and noodles.

Attitudes to plant collecting have changed too. Forty years ago much of the Himalaya and the whole of China was closed territory and venturing there was seen as a continuation of the heroic era of the great plant collectors. As China started to open bit by bit, we always tried to be the first in, but now tourists, many of them Chinese, are beginning to flood the scenic areas. Questions are being asked about the ethics of removing plant material, even scraps of seed, from foreign countries. But even in the heady early days we always worked with the authorities, using seed wherever possible and, if it was unavailable, taking live material in the minimum amount necessary to establish a new plant in cultivation.

Of course there are still plants out there that will add value to our gardens, but there is more to it than that. Collecting them, handling them in the wild and then growing them from seed to maturity, with perhaps a visit to the herbarium to investigate the dried remains of their classmates, gives you an intimate knowledge of a plant that comes in no other way. It is almost an accumulating friendship that may be rewarded, sometimes years later, with a flower that will remind you of that first meeting on a distant hillside.

PLACE NAMES

Peter Cox

For many years I have been researching place names in China and a few elsewhere in the various books I have relevant to the areas that Peter and I have explored. I have been astonished by the different names that have been used for the same place. Collectors such as George Forrest, Frank Kingdon Ward, Joseph Rock, Handel Mazzetti mostly used different in many cases and then Chinese Pinyin has led to yet another version, sometimes completely unlike the earlier names, the champion is probably the small town of Deqen for which I found no less than eight other spellings. Even atlases and maps tend to have widely differing variants. The first name is that used in the text and is generally the current usage but some are those likely to be best known by readers. It is all very confusing.

Arunachal Pradesh (North East Frontier Agency, Balapara Frontier Tract) N.E. Indian state

Barkam (Barkham, Ma-erh-k'ang) town N. Sichuan
Baoshan (Pao-shan, Yungchang, Yung-ch'ang) town, W. Yunnan
Baoxing (Pao-hsing, Mupin, Moupin) district, C.W. Sichuan
Batang (Baanfu, Pa-tand, Pa-t'ang, Pa-an) town, E. Tibet/W. Sichuan
Bayi (Paichen, Bayizhen) town, S.E. Tibet
Bei-ma Shan (Pei-ma-shan, Pai-ma-shan, Baima Shan, Bema-schan) mountain, W. Yunnan
Biluo Xue Shan (Nu Shan, Fu-chuan Range, Salween-Mekong Divide) mountains, W. Yunnan
Bomi (Bowo, Pome, Po-mi, Pomi, Po Yul, Pome Tramog) village or prefecture, S.E. Tibet
Bumthang (Byakar, Bumthang, Bumtang, Jakar) town, Bhutan
Burma (Myanmar)

Cangshan (Diancang Shan, Tali Range, Dsang-schan) mountains, C.W. Yunnan
Caojian (Tsao-chien) village W. Yunnan
Champutong (Chamutung, Tsang-pu-tong, Tsam-pu-tong, Tramputang, Tschamutong, Dschondchou) village, N.W. Yunnan
Chendebje (Chendebi) Chortens, Bhutan
Chengdu (Chengtu, Ch'eng-tu, Dschondchou) capital, Sichuan
Chomolhari (Chomolarhi) mountain, S. Tibet
Chongqing (Ch'ung-ch-ing, Chungking,) city, Sichuan
Choxiong (Ch'u-hsiung, Tsuyung, Tsuhiung, Tschuhsiong) town, C. Yunnan
Chusum (Qusum) village, S. Tibet

Dadu (Takin chwan, Dajun, Dajin, Ta-kin-kiang or Great River, Ta tu Ho, Tung Ho, Yang) river, Sichuan
Daguan (Ta-kuan) town, N.E. Yunnan
Dali (Tali, Ta-li-fu, T'ai-ho) town, C.W. Yunnan
Daozhen (Yuxi) town, N.W. Guizhou
Dengchuan (Dongchuan, Teng-ch'uan, Xincun, Tung-ch'uan, Tangdan) town, C.W. Yunnan
Diqin (Deqen, Dechen, Atuntze, Atentse, A-tun-tzu, Adunzi, Te-ch'in, Tehtsin) town, N.W. Yunnan
Dochu La (Dokyong La) pass, Bhutan
Dokar La (Showa La) pass, S.E. Tibet
Doker La (Dokar-La) pass, Yunnan-Tibet
Doshong La (Dozhong La, Dochu La) pass, S.E. Tibet
Dujiangyan (Guankou, Guan Xian, Huan-hsien, Kwanhsien) town, C.N. Sichuan
Dulong Jiang (Taron) river, N.W. Yunnan

Ebian (O-pien, Sha-p'ing) town, C. Sichuan
Emei Shan (Omei Shan, O-mi, Ngomei-schan) mountain, C.W. Sichuan
Er Hai (Erhai, Erh Hai, Orl-hai) lake, C.W. Yunnan
Erlang Shan (Erhlang Shan) mountain, pass, C.W. Sichuan

Fan-jing-shan (Fan-ching Shan) mountain, N.E. Guizhou
Fugong (Fukung) town on Salween

Gansu (Kansu) province
Gaoligong Shan (Kao-li-kung Shan, Jan tzow shan, Jang tzow-shan) mountains, Shweli-Salween divide
Gauhati (Gawahati) town, Assam, India
Guankou, see Dujiangyan
Gongga Shan (Minya Konka, Minyak Gongkar, Kung-ka Shan, Mt Koonka, Kunka) mountain, C.W. Sichuan
Gongshan (Kung-shan, Ma-k'a-chih, Suki, Nuzu Zizhixian, Gongshan Drungzu) town on Salween
Guangzhou (Canton) city S. China
Guiyang (Kwei-yang, Kuei-yang, Kueyang) capital, Guizhou
Guizhou (Kweichow, Kuei-chou, Kwei chau, Guidschou) province
Gyala Pelri (Gyala Peri, Jiala Peri) mountain, S.E. Tibet
Gyamda Chu (Nyang Chu) river, S.E. Tibet

Hailuogou (Hai-loko-ho) valley and glacier, C.W. Sichuan
Hengduan Shan (Heng Tuan) mountains, N.W. Yunnan
Hongyuan (Hurama, Ha-la-ma) county and town, N. Sichuan
Huanglongsi (Huanglong, Huanglong Xue) national park, N. Sichuan

Jakar, see Bumthang

Jele La (Bela La) pass, Bhutan

Jiang (Chiang, Kiang, Chwan, Chang, Chuan, Ho) river

Jinfo Shan (Jinfu Shan, Chinfo Shan) mountain, S.E. Sichuan

Jingdong (Ching-tung) town, S.C. Yunnan

Jiuzhaigou (Zitsa Degu) resort, N.W. Sichuan

Judian (Chu-tien) town, N.W. Yunnan

Kagurpu (Karkapo, Mt Kawa Karpo, Kawakarpo, Kakerpo, Khargurpu, Ka-kar-po, Ka-gur-pu, Kaakerpu,Kakerbo, Kagur-bu,) highest mountain in Mei Li range, Yunnan-Tibet border

Kolkata (Calcutta) city, India

Kanchenjunga (Kanchendjonga) mountain, Nepal

Kangding (K'ang-ting, Lucheng, Tatsienlu, Tatzienlu, Ta-chien-lu, Ta-chien-hi, Dadjienlou, Dartsemdo, Dartsedo, Dhartge Dhe, Dardo) town, C.W. Sichuan

Kenichunpo (Kenichunpu, Kenyichunpo, Ken-ni-chun-po) mountain, N.W. Yunnan

Kongbo (Kongpo) district, Tibet

Kunming (Kun-ming, Yunnan Fu) capital, Yunnan

Lanzhou (Lanchow) capital, Gansu

Leibo (Lei-po, Lu-po) town, S.C. Sichuan

Leshan (Leishan, Le-shan, Lo-shan, Kiatingfu, Chai-ting) town, C.W. Sichuan

Lhasa (Lhassa) capital of Tibet

Lijiang (Lijiang Naxizu Zizhixian, Lichiang, Li-chiang, Likiang, Li-kian, Dayan, Lidjiang) town, N.W. Yunnan

Litang (Gaocheng) town, N.W. Sichuan

Liuba (Liu-pa, Lugba) village, C.W. Sichuan

Liuku (Lusiuji, Lu-shui, Lu-kou, Luzhangjie, Lu-chang-chieh, Luchang) town on Salween, C.W. Yunnan

Li xian (Li-hsien, Li-fan-ting, Li-Fan-Fu, Zagunao) town, N.W. Sichuan

Luding (Lu-ting, Luqiao) town on Dadu river, C.W. Sichuan

Londre, see Yongzhi

Lushui (Luzhangjie) village on Salween, W. Yunnan

Mabian (Ma-pien) town, S.W. Sichuan

Mainkung (Zayu, Menkong, Menkung, Mekung, Mengong) village, S.E. Tibet

Maowen (Mao-hsien, Mao Chou, Mao Xian, Mu-chu, Fengyizhen) town, N. Sichuan

Meigu (Mei-ku) town, C.W. Sichuan

Mei Li (Mei-li, Mt Kawa Karpo, Kawakarpo, Kakerpo, Khargurpu, Ka-kar-po, Ka-gur-pu, Kaakerpu, Kakerbo, Ka-gur-bu) mountain, N.W. Yunnan-Tibet border

Mechuka (Metuchka, Machuka) village, Siang Division, Arunachal Pradesh, India

Mekong (Lancang Jiang, Lan-ts'ang, Za-chu [Tibet], Dza Chu, Di Chu) river, Yunnan

Mengzi (Mengtzi, Meng-tzu, Mongtse) town S. Yunnan

Miling (Milung, Mamlung) village S.E. Tibet

Min Jiang (Min Kiang, Sung-pan-ho [higher up river]) river, Sichuan

Moxi (Moximian, Mo-si-mien) village, C.W. Sichuan

Muli (Bowa) town, S.W. Sichuan

Namcha Barwa (Namche Barwa, Namchak Barwa, Namjagbarwa Feng) mountain, S.E. Tibet

Nanchuan (Longua) town, S.E. Sichuan

Nyingchi (Lin-chih, Ningshi) town, S.E. Tibet

Pa La (Mangshung La Chinese name) pass in Tibet

Panzhihua (Dukou, Tu-k'ou, Jen-ho-chieh) town, S.W. Sichuan

Parlung Zangbo (Po Tsangpo, Po-Chu) river, Tibet

Pe (Pei) village S.E. Tibet

Phokphey (Pokpe) camp, Bhutan

Pianma (Hpimaw) pass and village, W. Yunnan near Burma

Potrang La (Pode La, Gama La) pass, Tibet

Putao (Fort Hertz) village, N.E. Burma

Putrang La (Potrang La, Podo La, Gama La) pass, S. Tibet

Qamdo (Chomdo, Chamdo, Chumdo, Ch'ing-to, Ch'ang-tu) town, E. Tibet

Qiaojia (Ch'iao-chia) village, N.E. Yunnan

Qi Qu (O-I Ho, Nu Chu) river, S.E. Tibet

Rawok (Daba, Yatsa) village, S.E. Tibet

Rudong La (Rudung La, Rudo La) pass, Bhutan

Salween (Nu Jiang, Salwin, Lu-kiang, Lw-Chjang, Gyalmo Ngulcbum [Tibet], Lu-djiang, Ur-chu, Tsarong) river, Yunnan etc.

Sengor (Sangar) village, Bhutan

Shigu (Shih-ku-chilh, Shih-kou, Shihku, Shiku, Shikou, Schigu) town, N.W. Yunnan

Showa (Cha-mu, Zhamo, Zhowa) village, S.E. Tibet

Shweli (Lung chuan chiang, Longchuan jiang) river, W. Yunnan

Shukden Gonpa (Hsiu-teng, Shugden Gompa) S.E. Tibet

Sichuan (Szechwan, Szechuan, Setschwan, Se-chuan, Szechuen) province

Si Gu Niang (Sigunian, Mt 4 Girls) mountain, N. Sichuan

Simao (Szemao) town, S. Yunnan

Siyom (Siyum) village and river, Yunnan

Songpan (Sungqu, Sungpan, Sung-p'an) town, N. Sichuan

Suiyang (Yangchuan) town, N.W. Guizhou

Takpa Shelri (Takpa Siri) mountain, Tibet/India frontier

Tengchong (Teng-yueh, T'eng-yuen, Teng-ch'ung, T'engch'ung) town, W. Yunnan

Thimphu (Thimpu, Timphu, Thimbu) capital, Bhutan

Tongsa (Trongsa) town, Bhutan

Trulung (Pilung) village, S.E. Tibet

Tsangpo (Zangbo) big river in Tibet

Tsarong (Tsa-rung) district of S.E. Tibet bordering Yunnan, not used now

Weixi (Weihsihsien, Weihsi, Weisi, Wei-shi) town, N.W. Yunnan

Wenchuan (Weizhou) town on Min river, N. Sichuan

Wolong (Woolong) Panda Reserve, N.C. Sichuan

Wumeng Shan (Jiaozi-Shan, Wulong Shan) mountain, N.E. Yunnan

Xiaguan (Hsia-Kuan, Siakwan) town, C.W. Yunnan

Xiaojin (Zainlha) village, N.W. Sichuan

Xichang (Hsi-ch'ang) town, C.S.W. Sichuan

Xizang (Tibet)

Yajiang (Hekou) town, N.W. Sichuan

Yalung Jiang (Yalong Jiang, Ya-lung) river, Sichuan

Ya'an (Yachowfu, Ya-chou-fu, Yadschou, Ya-chau) town, C.W. Sichuan

Yangbi (Yangpi) town, C.W. Yunnan

Yangtze (Jinsha Jiang, Kin-sha-kiang, Kinscha-djiang, Yangdse-djiang, Yangzi Jiang, Chang, Chin-sha, Jangtze, river Yunnan etc.

Yarlung Tsangpo (Zangbo) (Tsangpo, Ya-lu-tsang-pu Chiang) river, Tibet, becomes the Siang or Dihang in India, then the Brahamaputra on the Assam plain

Yichang (Ichang) town, Hubei

Y'ong (Yi'ong, Yi'ang, Yigrong, Yong Tsangpo) river, E. Tibet

Yongping (Yung-shan) town, N.E. Yunnan

Yongzhi (Londre, Lungdri, Londjre) village, N.W. Yunnan

Yulong Shan (Yulongxue Shan, Yul ung schan, Lichiang Range) mountain range, N.W. Yunnan

Yutong La (Yuto La) pass, Bhutan

Zhaotong (Chao-tong, Chao-t'ung, Chau-tung, Dschaotung) town, N.E. Yunnan

Zayu (Zayul, Gyigang, Rima, Hsia-ch'ayu, Ch'a-yu) town, S.E. Tibet

Zayul (Dzayul) district, Tibet

Zayul (Zayul Ngu Chu, Rong to Chu, Zayu qu, Ch'a-yu-li Ho) river, S.E. Tibet

Zhongdian (Chungtien, Chungtienting, Dschungdien, Gyalthang, Xiang gelila meaning Shangrila) town, N.W. Yunnan

Zhi Bei Shan (Ziben Shan) mountain, W. Yunnan

Zhi-dzom-La (Chunsien La, Chun tsung La, Shenzu La) pass N.W. Yunnan

GLOSSARY

aff., affinity closely related

baku a hide tent in Tibet

chongpen or **jongpen** village chief
chorten a Buddhist shrine
chu a valley in Tibet such as the Rong Chu
circuit house guest house mainly for government officials
corolla the tube and lobes (petals) of a flower

dao a large knife in India used for chopping
dzo a cross between ordinary cattle and yak
dzong fort, administrative building, monastery

elepidote parts of a rhododendron without scales

goh Bhutanese garment
gompa a small Buddhist worshiping place

hai a lake in China

indumentum woolly or hairy covering on rhododendron leaves
inflorescence a number of flowers closely grouped together as a truss in rhododendrons

karst limestone region, in this case referring to conical peaks

la a pass in China or Tibet
lepidote tiny plates (scales) on parts of lepidote rhododendrons

mani wall Buddhist shrine in the form of a wall
mithun semi-wild cattle in Arunachal Pradesh, N.E. India

pedicel flower stalk of a single flower
petiole leaf stalk
piju beer in China
Pinyin a system of romanised spelling for transliterating Chinese
pokhari a lake in Nepal

rachis the axis or main stalk of an inflorescence or truss
Regius Keeper director of the Royal Botanic Garden, Edinburgh

scale tiny plates on parts of rhododendrons
scape flower stalk of a primula
sessile attached without a stalk
shieling a mountain hut
shan a mountain in China but sometimes also a town (e.g. Gongshan and Wenshan)
sherpa people from a part of Nepal often involved in mountaineering
sirdar in this case a head porter or guide in India or Nepal
speciation the process of forming a new species, say from a hybrid swarm
stupa a Buddhist shrine, round and usually domed

taxon, taxa single or plural entity as recognized by taxonomists of a plant species, etc.
taxonomy the science of the classification of living (in this case) organisms
tsangpo a river in Tibet such as the Yarlung Tsangpo

xue snow in China referring to a snow mountain

yurt a hide tent

zangbo Chinese for a river in Tibet

BIBLIOGRAPHY

Argent, George; *Rhododendrons of Subgenus Vireya* Royal
   Botanic Garden, Edinburgh 2006

Argent, G., Bond, J., Chamberlain, D.F., Cox, P.A., Hardy,
   A.; *The Rhododendron Handbook, Rhododendron Species in
   Cultivation* The Royal Horticultural Society 1998

Bailey, F.M.; *No Passport to Tibet* The Travel Book Club,
   London 1957

Bishop, George; *Travels in Imperial China* Cassell Publishers
   Ltd, London 1990; The Explorations of Pere David

Chamberlain, D.F.; *A Revision of Rhododendron 2 Subgenus
   Hymenanthes, Notes from the Royal Botanic Garden,
   Edinburgh* Her Majesty's Stationery Office, Edinburgh 1982

Chamberlain, D.F. & Rae, S.J.; *A Revision of Rhododendron 4
   Subgenus Tsutsusi, Edinburgh Journal of Botany* Her Majesty's
   Stationery Office, Edinburgh 1990

Coats, Alice M.; *The Quest for Plants* Studio Vista Ltd,
   London 1969

Cox, E.H.M.; *Plant Hunting in China* William Collins Sons &
   Co Ltd, London, 1945

Cox, Peter A. & Kenneth N.E.; *The Encylopedia of
   Rhododendron Species* Glendoick Publishing 1997

Cullen, J.; *A Revision of Rhododendron 1 Subgenus
   Rhododendron, sections Rhododendron & Pogonanthum Notes
   from the Royal Botanic Garden, Edinburgh* Her Majesty's
   Stationery Office, Edinburgh 1980

Feng, Guomei (editor); *Rhododendrons of China Vol. 1* Science
   Press, New York, Beijing 1988

Feng, Guomei (editor); *Rhododendrons of China Vol 2* Science
   Press, New York, Beijing 1992

Feng, Guomei (editor); *Rhododendrons of China Vol 3* Science
   Press, New York, Beijing 1999

Fletcher, Harold R.; *A Quest of Flowers* Edinburgh University
   Press, Edinburgh, 1975; The travels of Frank Ludlow &
   George Sherriff

Grierson, A.J.C. & Long, D.G., Noltie, H.J., Pearce, N.R. &
   Cribb, P.J.; *Flora of Bhutan 9 Vol* Royal Botanic Garden,
   Edinburgh 1983-2002

Handel-Mazzetti; *A Botanical Pioneer in South West China*
   translated & published by David Winstanley 1996

Hillier & Sons; *The Hillier Manual of Trees & Shrubs* David &
   Charles 1972-2002

Kingdon Ward, Frank; *A Plant Hunter in Tibet* Jonathan Cape,
   London 1934

Kingdon Ward, Frank; *Assam Adventure* Jonathan Cape,
   London 1941

Kingdon Ward, Frank; *From China to Hkamti Long* Edward
   Arnold & Co, London 1924

Kingdon Ward, Frank; *Plant Hunter's Paradise* Jonathan Cape,
   London 1937

Kingdon Ward, Frank; *The Mystery Rivers of Tibet* Seeley
   Service & Co Ltd, London 1923

Kingdon Ward, Frank; *The Riddle of the Tsangpo Gorges*
   Edward Arnold & Co 1926

Kingdon Ward, Frank, edited Kenneth Cox: *The Riddle of the
   Tsangpo Gorges* Antique Collectors' Club Ltd, Woodbridge,
   Suffolk 2001

Kingdon Ward, Frank; *The Romance of Plant Hunting* Edward
   Arnold & Co, London 1924

Kingdon Ward, Jean; *My Hill so Strong* Jonathan Cape,
   London 1952

Lancaster, Roy; *Travels in China* Antique Collectors' Club,
   Ltd, Woodbridge, Suffolk 1989

Lancaster, Roy; *A Plantsman in Nepal* Antique Collectors'
   Club Ltd (Croom Helm Ltd 1981) 1995

McAllister, Hugh; *The Genus Sorbus, Mountain Ash & other
   Rowans* The Royal Botanic Gardens, Kew 2005

McLean, Brenda; *A Pioneering Plantsman* The Stationery
   Office, London 1997 The Life of A.K. Bulley

McLean, Brenda; *George Forrest Plant Hunter* Antique
   Collectors' Club Woodbridge, Suffolk 2004

Polunin & Stainton; *Flowers of the Himalaya* Oxford
   University Press, India 1984-8

Pratt, A.E.; *The Snows of Tibet through China* Longmans,
   Green & Co London 1892

Richards, John; *Primula* B.T. Batsford Ltd, London, New
   Edition 2002

Rushforth, Keith; *Conifers* Christopher Helm, London 1987

Stevenson, J.B. (edited by); *The Species of Rhododendron* The
   Rhododendron Society 1930

Shephard, Sue; *Seeds of Fortune, A Gardening Dynasty*
   Bloomsbury Publishing PLC, London 2003 The Veitch
   Family

Synge, Patrick M.; *Lilies (with Cardiocrinum & Nomocharis)*
   B.T. Batsford Ltd, London 1980

Sichuan Rhododendron of China ed. Fang Wengpei, Science
   Press, Beijing, China 1986

PLANT INDEX

Page numbers in **bold** refer to illustrations

GENERAL INDEX

Page numbers in **bold** refer to illustrations